MW01010262

Advance Praise for *Total F*cking Godhead*

"*Total F*cking Godhead* brings Chris Cornell, the voice of a generation, alive on the page. Impressively researched and compulsively readable, *Godhead* pulls no punches in recounting Cornell's remarkable life and prolific career. It's an inspired chronicle of an impassioned soul. Read it!"

—GREG RENOFF, author of *Van Halen Rising*

"For those of us still trying to sort out the tragedy of Chris Cornell's death comes this loving look back at the man's life and music. I wrote my own book about grunge, and I still learned a lot from this excellent biography."

—MARK YARM, author of *Everybody Loves Our Town: An Oral History of Grunge*

"From his days as a struggling Seattle musician at the forefront of the grunge scene to becoming a global icon, *Total F*cking Godhead* thoroughly chronicles the life story and prolific output of one of the greatest and most influential singers of all time. You will discover the man and his music all over again."

—DAVID DE SOLA, author of *Alice in Chains: The Untold Story*

TOTAL F*CKING GODHEAD

THE BIOGRAPHY OF CHRIS CORNELL

CORBIN REIFF

Post Hill
PRESS

A POST HILL PRESS BOOK
ISBN: 978-1-64293-215-7
ISBN (eBook): 978-1-64293-216-4

Total F*cking Godhead:
The Biography of Chris Cornell
© 2020 by Corbin Reiff
All Rights Reserved

Cover photo by Chris Cuffaro
Cover art by Donna McCleer. / Tunnel Vizion Media LLC
Author photo by Jenna Reiff

This is a work of nonfiction. All people, locations, events, and situations are portrayed to the best of the author's memory.

Post Hill Press
New York • Nashville
posthillpress.com

Published in the United States of America

For Paul Fowler
For Adam King
For Tyler Yeoman
For Grant Smith

TABLE OF CONTENTS

INTRODUCTION

'll never forget that terrible morning on May 18, 2017. I woke up just before seven o'clock and reached for my phone. The number of push notifications that greeted my tired eyes tipped me off that something unusual had happened. I quickly typed in the passcode and was rendered speechless by the terrible news.

Chris Cornell was dead.

For several minutes I sat there shocked and numb. Then eerily cold. I was the senior music writer for Uproxx at the time, and my editor quickly tapped me to gather tributes from other artists expressing their own mix of overwhelming grief and disbelief. I did my job in a fog before logging off in the late afternoon. After that, I went for a walk around my neighborhood, with "Like A Stone" blasting in my headphones. I suddenly started tearing up as a version of Chris from sixteen years earlier lamented his own "cobweb afternoon."

Growing up, I was a massive fan of pretty much all Seattle rock music from the nineties, and Soundgarden specifically. The "Black Hole Sun" video left an especially terrifying, but exhilarating, impression on my developing mind. Later on, I moved to the Pacific Northwest and became even more enamored with that city's music history as I caught shows at places like the Paramount, the Moore, and the Showbox.

I'd seen Chris Cornell perform onstage as both a member of Soundgarden and as a solo artist on multiple occasions around Seattle and had always come away with a deeper appreciation of his artistry. The Mad Season performance I caught at Benaroya Hall in 2015 when he reunited Temple Of The Dog and crooned and screamed his way through

"Call Me A Dog," is something I won't forget. They had the audacity to play "Reach Down" right after that, which was equally mindblowing.

One of the greatest nights of my life, however, took place at the Ace Hotel in LA when Chris and Led Zeppelin mastermind Jimmy Page chatted onstage together for two hours about the legendary guitarist's life and music. Just two of my musical heroes chopping it up like the two thousand strong in the audience weren't even there, hanging onto their every word. If only they had formed a band.

Chris's passing affected me in a profound way that other celebrity deaths never had before. It felt like part of my own past had just been ripped away. In the weeks that followed I wrote about other topics, but I couldn't shake Chris Cornell. I remember feeling pissed off that there was a myriad of books about grunge, Kurt Cobain, Nirvana, Pearl Jam, and Alice In Chains, but none about Chris, and only *one* about Soundgarden, a woefully out-of-date biography. It seemed like a miscarriage of musical justice, but at that point I didn't expect it would be me who would set out to right that particular wrong.

I had just recently finished writing my first book, *Lighters in the Sky*, and was talking to my editor about Chris when he asked, "How do you feel about writing a book about him?" The question took me by surprise. I told him all the reasons why I shouldn't, and we left it at that.

A few weeks later I flew out to Los Angeles and visited Chris's final resting place at Hollywood Forever Cemetery to finally pay my respects. As I stood there gazing at the black granite fixed in the perfectly manicured grass, I felt an overwhelming wave of emotion. It suddenly felt real. Chris Cornell was truly gone.

I drove out to Joshua Tree the next day, listening to *Superunknown* and *Audioslave* the whole way, and got pissed off all over again thinking that a songwriter of his magnitude and a singer with his supernatural abilities had seemingly been taken for granted by so many over the last several decades. I called my editor shortly after flying home and told him that I thought I wanted to do it. I wanted to write a biography of Chris Cornell. Looking back now, I was blissfully naïve to the amount of time, effort, frustration, and catharsis I was signing up for.

Over the next three years, I did hardly anything besides think about Chris Cornell, listen to Chris Cornell, read about Chris Cornell, and speak to people who knew and loved Chris Cornell. I flew to New York. I flew to Los Angeles. I flew to Seattle multiple times from my home in Chicago, and eventually moved back to the area altogether.

I pored over hundreds of different interviews that Chris had given over the course of thirty years from every phase of his life. I read thousands more from his friends, bandmates, and loved ones to try to understand both the man himself and the challenges he faced during his time on this planet. I watched hundreds of hours of grainy concert footage and listened to practically every note of music he ever recorded several times over. The Seattle Public Library became a home away from home as I dug through the archives to find any scrap of paper that contained the words "Chris," "Cornell," or "Soundgarden." The Museum of Popular Culture on 5th Avenue—the Frank Gehry-designed building with the bronze statue of Chris out front—and their oral history collection was also a tremendous resource.

I also spoke with as many people who had known Chris as I could. I accumulated dozens of on-the-record interviews with collaborators and friends and had many off-the-record talks with those who knew him best. But, as legal issues surrounding Chris and his estate arose, I could feel people's eagerness to speak about him at length tighten up. Interviews that had been months in planning were re-scheduled, then cancelled altogether. People who had been eager to share their memories and provide additional sources stopped returning my texts, phone calls, and emails.

It was frustrating and disappointing, but as a onetime paralegal in the US Army, I understood that nothing quiets people faster than the threat of impending litigation. There was little reason to believe that the issues at the heart of these conflicts would sort themselves out any time soon, but I remained hopeful. I don't begrudge anyone for their silence; and to those who shared their stories with me, I offer my eternal gratitude.

I suppose I could have thrown my hands up at that point and decided the entire project was more of a headache than it was worth, and that without the direct support of the members of Soundgarden, or Audioslave, or

Temple Of The Dog, or Chris's estate, there might not be enough *there* to tell Chris's story properly. But as I revisited Chris's interviews, I created an enormous outline of his life using his own words and memories alone. As I pieced a quote from a Howard Stern interview here with an excerpt from an old *Rocket* interview from the late '80s there, the story started to take shape. Chris would never get to write an autobiography, but with enough effort, I thought I could weave together the story as he lived it. I had to keep going.

*Total F*cking Godhead* is neither the official, authorized biography of Chris Cornell nor the Soundgarden story. What mattered most to Chris Cornell, outside of family, was the music. I can pretty much say the same about myself, and that's where my focus largely remained.

This is the story of one of the most supremely gifted singers and songwriters to ever emerge from the gloomiest corner of the Pacific Northwest, who helped shape the sound and aesthetic of an entire generation. This is the story about how, where, and why he created so many of those songs and albums that defined his era. This is the story of a man who battled addiction and depression for years and came out on the other side clean, only for it all to end so tragically.

"There's a lot of things about Chris that people don't know," Soundgarden's guitarist Kim Thayil once told me. "He didn't bring a lot of baggage. Meaning, he didn't carry a lot of things or materials or relationships within his life. He was a little bit independent of that. He traveled lightly."[1]

This is the story of Chris Cornell, written as honestly, accurately, and empathetically as I could tell it.

CHAPTER I

SHOW ME HOW TO LIVE

He wasn't stealing the records. He was *rescuing* them. Chris Cornell's friend and neighbor, a kid named John Zimmer, had an older brother who'd run afoul of his parents' rules and gotten himself kicked out of the house. The Zimmers boxed up all of their son's belongings, including his vinyl albums, and stored them down in their dank basement. This proved a hazardous decision in the rainy confines of Seattle, Washington.

The inevitable occurred. Water from a rainstorm poured into the basement and soaked the exiled brother's extensive album collection. Among the stacks was a nearly comprehensive collection of Beatles albums and compilations just sitting there gathering mold, waiting for the day when someone would haul them out and trash them. The Zimmers' precocious eight-year-old neighbor had to do something to prevent this cataclysmic miscarriage of cosmic injustice, so...he swiped them.

Chris took the pile of vinyl home, threw out the damp cardboard sleeves, cleaned off the discs and put paper towels between each of them so that they would dry. Then he listened. Hours passed. Then days. Then weeks. He couldn't get enough. "For over a year, I listened to nothing but the Beatles," he said. "It was my music school."[1]

Sitting alone in a room with his little portable record player, the Beatles were a sonic revelation to Chris. Locked in the tight, rain-stained grooves was a universe of sounds, feelings, and emotions he'd never experienced or imagined. Songs about love, longing, whimsy, friendship, octopi, and a yellow submarine. Every day, all he wanted to do was turn off his mind, relax, and float downstream.

"I was like a normal kid," he remembered. "I ran around outside with my friends, but I also spent a lot time alone in a room just listening to these records, just one after the other, one side of an album at a time."[2] The more Chris listened to John, Paul, George, and Ringo, the deeper he fell under their spell. He started to wonder: *How did they do this? How did they write the words, the melodies? How did they record the noise on the shiny black disc in his hands? Why did it sound and feel so damn good?* And then he started to think about the four Liverpudlians themselves.

Everyone has their favorite Beatle, and for Chris it was the cutting, intellectual John Lennon. The bespectacled songwriter became his hero. His own father, Ed, was a distant presence. After he and his mom divorced years later, he became even more distant, until he eventually disappeared from Chris's life altogether. In the absence of an involved paternal figure, Chris looked to others for a sense of how to navigate the world. There was something about John Lennon, the way he alternated between goofy, intense, and introspective that he identified with.

And yet, of all the world-shaking compositions that the Fab Four recorded, it was Paul McCartney's "Hey Jude" that struck the deepest chord. Each time he listened to the song he felt a strange sense of "Na-Na-Na-Na" induced euphoria that made him want to run it right back and play it again. Like most people stumbling upon something new and thrilling, Chris was eager to share his discovery with friends and classmates. A show-and-tell at school seemed like the ideal opportunity.

Chris proudly clutched his 45 RPM single of "Hey Jude," ready to hand it over to the teacher so that he could open up his classmates' ears to these magic sounds. But after the teacher read the label on the small piece of vinyl, she refused to play it. It was a cruel blow, and he couldn't wrap his head around the reason for the rejection. Maybe it was the length of the song, stretching out past seven minutes. Maybe it was the caustic way Paul screamed "Jude, Jude, jude-y, jude-y!" Maybe it was because it strayed too far from the typical "Wheels on the Bus" fare the teacher usually played in the classroom. Whatever the reason, the rejection stung.

His teacher's harsh rebuff may have only served to strengthen his attachment to the Beatles. They set the template in his mind of what a rock band was supposed to look like, how they were supposed to act, and what they could achieve together. They taught him that you could sing about anything: holding hands, revolution, taxes, blackbirds, LSD, paperback novels, even doing it in the road. They taught him that it wasn't just okay to change your sound and style with each new record, but that the quest for sonic evolution was itself the point.

Along the way, in his self-enrolled year in the school of Beatles, Chris discovered a central truth about himself that would remain constant throughout the entirety of his fifty-two years. "Music for me is a lot more immediate than anything else," he explained. "Other stuff seems to be hidden behind a wall of fog."[3]

* * *

Christopher John Boyle came screaming into the world on July 20, 1964 in Seattle, Washington. Coincidentally, the Beatles played his hometown for the very first time just one month after his arrival. His father Edward Boyle was a pharmacist, while his mother Karen Boyle stayed at home and watched the kids until a variety of professional callings drew her attention elsewhere when Chris was about six years old. She took up numerology around 1975 and subsequently became a professional psychic.

"I grew up with a very stoic family in an Irish Catholic neighborhood filled with quiet, not-so-happy adults," he said. "Many of us ended up with the same struggles: You have every desire to communicate with your friends, family, with anyone, and no skills with which to do it."[4]

Chris was the fourth child and youngest boy in a large Catholic family that included two brothers, Peter and Patrick, and three sisters, Katy, Maggie, and Suzy. He sometimes joked about being the Bobby Brady of the Bunch. Having already raised a few kids before he had arrived, Chris's parents didn't keep too close an eye on his activities and, like many children of the era, he was given free rein to do whatever he wanted around his neighborhood in Greenwood. He took full advantage of that freedom.

Chris sometimes described his earliest childhood years in Huck Finn-like terms. "I could do pretty much whatever I wanted as long as police didn't bring me home," he said.[5] His adolescent fiefdom was a far cry from the antebellum Southern world conjured up by Mark Twain, however. Seattle in the 1960s was a city on the move.

Just two years before he was born, the town famously hosted the World's Fair, necessitating the construction of two of the metropolis's defining architectural features, the monorail and the Space Needle. Much of the growth was fueled by Boeing, the largest employer in the area, who accounted for around eighty thousand jobs at its peak. As money filtered down into the pockets of the aircraft manufacturer's employees and their families, the suburbs ringing the downtown area swelled as new couples purchased their first homes and started families.

Chris's corner of the city in Greenwood was filled with young boys and girls of all ages who shared tastes in comic books, cartoons like *Popeye* and *Speed Racer*, and music. It was a predominantly white neighborhood. Not quite the suburbs, but not quite downtown either. Chris had many friends, but he also had an affinity for solitude. Oftentimes he would take off into the forest, spending long afternoons cutting paths through the wilds of Carkeek Park near his home. He relished in the isolation, finding calm and peace amid the damp brush and towering evergreens. If music was his first love, nature was a close second.

Chris was an introvert by nature who rarely shared his true feelings—not that his father had much interest in hearing from him. Edward Boyle was an alcoholic, prone to acts of violence. The routine in the Boyle house was simple. Edward would come home from work, pour himself a large glass of bourbon and sit in his favorite chair for hours. "He wouldn't speak to anyone, and if he did speak, that meant your ass," Chris recalled. "If you heard a word come from him, you were in mid-air running because you did something to piss him off."[6]

"My father was a tyrannical alcoholic and physically abusive man—he beat the shit out of me and my brothers," Chris's brother Peter wrote.[7]

"He wasn't kind. He didn't show love. He didn't compliment or praise or give the occasional 'atta boy.' Impact, punishment, and ridicule guided us along the path and molded us into the troubled beings that we would carry into the world and the future."[8] The hard feelings between Chris and his father calcified so deeply that when his parents finally separated, he abandoned his birthname, "Boyle," and assumed his mother's maiden name "Cornell" instead. His siblings did as well.

Chris's childhood wasn't a non-stop parade of disillusionment, isolation, and hard feelings. There were happy times, too. He always treasured the memories of a pair of trips down south to Disneyland in Los Angeles when he was nine and then again when he was eleven. The land of sunshine and swimming pools was about as far from the gloom of Seattle as his young mind could comprehend, and he relished the rides and upbeat vibes. "I remember having more fun when I was nine, because I hadn't started becoming depressed yet," he said. "At eleven, you wake up one day and start feeling bad about everything."[9]

Chris began his education when his parents enrolled him into Christ the King, a kindergarten-through-eighth-grade Catholic school located directly across the street from his house. Chris could throw a rock from his front porch and hit the side of the building. From the outset, Chris hated school. Having to wake up early was bad enough, but more than anything, it was the conformity—the constant judgement and severe structure of the Catholic education environment that rubbed him the wrong way. "They judge [you] by the same criteria, make [you] do the same stuff," he complained. "You had to wear the same clothes. Everything was the same."[10]

While he wasn't enamored with subjects like math, English, and history, music continued to fascinate him. Karen Boyle eventually noticed her son's affinity for sound and, when he was about eight years old, she purchased a brushed-black painted piano and placed it in their basement. Chris was fascinated by the instrument. He didn't know any of the rules and couldn't tell a C major from an E minor, but he instantly began plunking out melodies along the white and black keys. His first attempts at songwriting were made on this humble instrument, two- and three-note chords strung together: esoteric, atonal, and shaded with darkness.

Chris's earliest forays into songwriting caught the attention of one of his teachers. She took him to an educators' conference at the University of Washington to show off one of his creations as an example of a child being capable of composing without the benefit of a formal music education. To that point, he'd been a largely unremarkable kid with middling grades, despite his elevated intelligence. Now, people started paying attention.

"I think that's when the switch was thrown," he told *Rolling Stone*.[11] "The first time I had a music teacher play a scale on piano and ask me to sing it, 'cause she just wanted to see if I had an ear or not. I remember singing the scale and she almost jumped off the stool and looked at me. I remember it because that's the first time that had happened. No one had ever looked at me like that."

Christ the King was the first place that Chris experienced the thrill of singing in front of an audience. In the sixth grade, he signed up to participate in the school's talent show, singing a song called "One Tin Soldier." A classmate accompanied him on piano. The song, written in the 1960s and recorded initially by Canadian pop group The Original Caste, was a modest hit up in the Great White North. It was the 1971 cover version, however, recorded by the rock group Coven and included in the film *Billy Jack* that found popularity in the US. Chris's rendition went over well, the performance was a success, and some of his teachers were moved to tears.

Karen eventually signed Chris up to take piano lessons, but he quickly grew bored and abandoned them. It didn't help that his teacher was a white-haired older lady with little personality and even less patience for Chris's attempts at humor. As opposed to the free-form style of creation that drew him to the instrument in the first place, the structure of lessons felt like school outside of school. Practice didn't feel like creation. It felt like homework. And once puberty started wreaking havoc with his piercing, high-pitched choir-boy voice, he stopped singing too.

Chris always regretted his decision to abandon piano lessons, especially three years later when he walked by a classroom and witnessed a girl who'd started playing around the same time he had ripping into an intricate Queen song. He tried to pick up formal music reading again in his thirties, but it didn't stick. "It was harder than I ever remembered," he said. "Not that I can't understand it conceptually, it's just that I've learned now to create music without a language and I work well that way and I work quickly that way."[12]

Despite a lack of a formal musical education, he found himself drawn to a myriad of instruments throughout his life. Early on he picked up his brother Peter's guitar and started messing around with it, eventually figuring out how to play "Sunshine on My Shoulders" by John Denver. It's likely no coincidence that the song is about the irresistible desire to enjoy nature's beauty.

He didn't find his true path into music, however, until he sat down behind a drum kit. It certainly wasn't easy to convince his mom to allow him to bring one into the house. The mere thought of the unsynchronized clatter of tom-toms and cymbals invading the Cornell household was enough to give her fits, but after a sustained campaign of pleading, she caved and bought him a single snare to whack on. After he saved up another fifty dollars, he bought the rest of the kit secondhand from a guy he knew, and started trying to bash out Phil Rudd's parts while listening to AC/DC records.

The act of playing drums was immediately gratifying. No chords, scales, or keys were required to create an intense cacophony. The simple, satisfying act of smacking a wooden stick on a stretched-out polythene skin opened new doors in Chris's mind. "Almost overnight, I found my place," he said.[13] "I felt like, 'This is what I do. This is who I am.'" It was the most crucial step yet on his path to becoming a musician.

By the dawn of the seventies, as Chris was entering adolescence, Seattle's post-war boom period was on the precipice of a devastating free fall. Boeing slashed nearly fifty thousand jobs between 1970 and 1971 after the cancellation of their supersonic transport program. Unemployment surged to 12 percent, and many people departed the area to pursue opportunities elsewhere. The Ironworkers District Council of the Pacific Northwest summed up the ennui of the era by paying for a billboard near the SeaTac Airport that cheekily asked, "Will the last person leaving Seattle—turn out the lights." Communities suffered and seedy elements arose. Drugs were easy to come by, even for a middle schooler, and Chris was not immune to their charms.

Between the ages of eleven and fourteen, Chris experimented with a variety of illicit substances nearly every day. Weed, pills, alcohol—whatever was available that could alter his state of mind. In Chris's suburban, North Seattle universe, the myriad of substances being passed around was either ignored or accepted. Nobody gave a thought to the implications of what they were doing.

"I remember walking by the basement window one time, and this one dude who had like huge, poofy Lynyrd Skynyrd hair and a goatee and a mustache was shooting something at me from a syringe out the window," he told podcaster Marc Maron. "I don't even know what it was, but it was shooting fifteen feet, and I'm walking by, trying to dodge this thing. Those were the kind of people who lived near me."[14]

Marijuana was plentiful, and hallucinogens were fairly easy to come by too. Everyone, it seemed, had a big brother or two who operated a low-key pharmacy out of their backyard. Enlightenment was never the goal. The appeal was escapism from the mundane.

Despite his early extralegal explorations, Chris largely managed to stay out of trouble. "I've always had this amazing ability to run right before the time that all my friends got arrested," he said. "I've never been arrested or in the back of a police car, but I have been across the street while my friends got arrested."[15]

He also had a secret weapon that shielded him from the unwanted attention of authority figures: his baby face. With his wavy dark hair, shimmering cobalt blue eyes, bulbous cheeks, and sheepish smile, most teachers simply refused to believe that little Christopher Boyle would show up to class blasted out of his mind. He later wrote the Soundgarden song "Never Named" about this beneficial asset, even though he didn't appreciate it at the time. "I always looked really young for my age, but I never wanted to," he explained. "I could get away with ridiculous shit like going to school fucking high out of my brain and no one would ever figure it out, because I didn't look like somebody who would do that."[16]

It was around this time that Chris's parents finally split up. Their divorce was finalized on January 8, 1979, when he was fifteen years old. Shortly thereafter, Chris began living with his grandparents who had even less control over him than his mom and dad had. "My parents divorced, and we went from upper middle class to barely middle class," he said. "For me, self-sufficiency was easy. I liked the idea of independence."[17]

With hardly anyone to reign him in, Chris continued to experiment with drugs. Sometimes he'd even swipe his grandparents' prescription Benadryl to trade it for harder stuff at school. Ultimately, it was a traumatic experience with PCP that convinced him to go sober, but the fallout from that terrifying experience lasted for a couple of years and left a deep scar on his psyche. Chris often cited this as the lowest period of his life. "I got panic disorder, and of course, I wasn't telling anyone the truth," he said. "It's not like you go to your dad or your doctor and say, 'Yeah, I smoked PCP and I'm having a bad time.'"[18]

Almost overnight, his lifestyle changed. He stopped going outside. He distanced himself from the bad influences that might tempt him back into their world and became more insular than ever before. "There was about two years where I was more or less agoraphobic and didn't deal with anybody," he remembered. "Didn't talk to anybody, didn't have any friends at all. All the friends that I had were still fucked up with drugs and were people that I didn't really have anything in common with."[19]

School proved even more challenging. He dropped out midway through eighth grade. Whatever it was that the teacher was droning on about in front of the blackboard took a backseat to the vivid daydreams running through his mind. He struggled to concentrate and apply himself to his studies. "My dad used to give me shit because I'd always score in the top of my class on tests, but I could never do homework," he said. "I was on the verge of failing my whole childhood in school because I just couldn't sit down and deal with it. I used to get very angry about it."[20]

He tried to get back on solid footing with his education, but it didn't stick. He enrolled at an alternative high school, P.S. 1, but grew disenchanted by the learn-at-your-own-pace structure. The school was a way station for wayward youth who had run out of options in the public school system. Eventually, he decided to get his GED and bid a not-so-fond farewell to formal education.

During the hours when he should've been attending class, he was working on an unaccredited doctorate in rock and roll. Chris listened to a near-constant rotation of popular music, mostly classic rock—Alice Cooper's *Billion Dollar Babies*, Pink Floyd's *Dark Side of the Moon*, *Led Zeppelin IV*, Black Sabbath, Van Halen, Uriah Heep, Iron Butterfly, ELP, Jimi Hendrix—everything he could get his hands and ears around.

One of his favorite bands was Canadian prog-rockers Rush. Oftentimes, he'd lean a pair of big speakers together, cover them with a blanket, smoke weed, and slide underneath while blasting side one of *2112* or *Caress of Steel*. When *Signals* dropped in 1982, Chris was parked outside of Tower Records with his friends at midnight so he could pick up the record the moment it was released. With his long frame and athletic build, Chris played a little bit of organized basketball, but the charms of a pull-up three pointer paled in comparison to the polyrhythmic drum patterns and clever wordplay created by Neil Peart.

Occasionally, he ventured out of his garage to experience music live and in person. His first concert was David Bowie at the Seattle Center Coliseum on February 3, 1976. The spectacle of the former Ziggy Stardust, presently in the throes of his bleached blonde Thin White Duke period and singing songs off his most recent album *Station to Station*, left an immense impression on his eleven-year-old mind. "Seeing him like this made me think, 'Oh, you can be whoever you want. You can live a hundred lives. You can create you and you can recreate you, and it's viable.' He was the one that proved that that works."[21]

His desire to see more of the bands he grew to love over the radio was stymied by Seattle's lack of all-ages venues and its extreme distance from another major market. It didn't make economic sense for many of the big musical acts of the time to trek up to the remote Pacific Northwest. Undeterred, he'd often sit outside of clubs straining to hear the sounds from within while peering through the windows. He was the moth, and rock and roll was the flame.

As much as Chris reveled in all of these seemingly omnipresent classic rock records perched like trophies of taste in his neighbor's homes, the mystical talent and unfathomable dexterity of rock gods like Eddie Van Halen, John Bonham, and Jimi Hendrix was in and of it itself alienating. The idea he could even come close to measuring up to the raw talent of these otherworldly musical dynamos never even occurred to him. When he flipped through the pages of *Rolling Stone, Creem,* or *Circus,* he simply didn't see people like him within the pages. Technical virtuosos and mystical geniuses decked out in eccentric outfits abounded. He felt like neither.

It wasn't until he discovered blue-collar punk groups like Wire, the Ramones, the Sex Pistols, and the Stooges that the light bulb went off in his head. Anyone could be in a band. *He* could be in a band. "By the time punk rock hit, and I heard it and understood it, the timing couldn't have been better, because it was like, 'Thank god! This is awesome!'"[22]

The records he wanted, like Bauhaus's *Press the Eject and Give Me the Tape,* were harder to come by than Van Halen's *1984,* and it took time and effort to track them down. Fallout Records on Capitol Hill was a favored spot where he managed to score some of the more obscure selections he sought. So was the Tower Records near Seattle Center. One pale, pierced, seedy-looking clerk who ran the imports section was especially helpful in tipping him off to cool, underground records. The English, post-punk group Killing Joke was its own special revelation that re-invigorated his love of rock at a time when the omnipresent commercial sectors of the genre were becoming increasingly teased up and Lycra'd out.

Beyond the volume, there was another aspect of this music that appealed directly to Chris. It was dark. It was angry. It was sometimes even depressing. It spoke to an entirely different side of the human condition that he didn't get from his treasured Beatles records. "I've tried to explain that for years—like, why does it make you feel good to sit in a dark room listening to Bauhaus? Why is that?" he asked. "Maybe it's because it makes you feel like you're not alone with these feelings and dark thoughts."[23]

The discovery couldn't have come at a better time. Chris was back at home at his mother's house and had recently inherited his older brother's room, formerly the family's garage, which had been modified into something like a soundproof rehearsal space fitted out with a monster three-hundred-watt stereo. It quickly turned into his musical laboratory; a sonic sanctuary where he could listen, play, and practice for hours on end.

As it turned out, the garage wasn't *totally* soundproof, because one day while he was practicing drums, one of his neighbors heard the sounds pounding from behind the large door and decided to investigate. He knocked on Chris's door and introduced himself. "He said, 'My name's Mark, I play bass, let's start a band,'" Chris recalled. "He knew people in the neighborhood, and next thing you know, we had two amazing guitar players."[24] After jamming together a few times, they decided to name themselves after the street they all lived on. The Jones Street Band was born.

Their repertoire hewed largely toward contemporary rock: a lot of AC/DC, Rush, and Led Zeppelin. They threw in some punk tracks too, playing Ramones and Sex Pistols songs, while also attempting to imitate local groups like the Fartz, a favorite in punk circles around town. The Fartz, who counted future Guns N' Roses bassist Duff McKagan as their drummer, were a big influence and helped introduce Chris to the idea that music didn't need to be long to be impactful. One of his favorite songs by them ran a mere eighteen seconds long but "had the most energy I ever heard in something you might dare call music," he said. "We would listen to it over and over and over."[25]

Despite the talent of the two guitarists in the Jones Street Band—the fifteen-year-old was a Hendrix acolyte, while the seventeen-year-old was enamored with Jimmy Page and could play note-perfect solos of live, bootlegged versions of "Dazed And Confused"—Chris's musical interests were in a constant state of evolution. He soon dropped out of the group and took up a more nomadic musical existence, hopping from one band to the next.

While he was still getting his footing behind the drum kit—"He made me think of Neil Peart, though he wasn't that flashy," future Soundgarden producer Jack Endino remembered of Chris's percussive prowess, "He could play odd meters, no problem"—Chris took on a variety of different day jobs, either bussing tables, washing dishes, or breaking concrete. He eventually caught on at a fish wholesaler, and the hours he spent away from his room were usually filled cutting the cheeks out of halibut and scrubbing up gelatinous, ocean-bred ooze off the floors.

Chris eventually moved out of his mom's house and into a place with a couple of friends, Kevin Tissot and Eric Garcia, who he had met at P.S. 1. When Garcia moved to West Seattle, Chris and Tissot found a space together on Lake City Way. (Both men would remain friends with Chris for decades, with Garcia maintaining a closer relationship to Chris than almost anyone else. Years later, in the nineties when Chris got married, Garcia stood in as his best man. Shortly after that, when his job on an oil tanker fell through, he became something of an assistant, helping Chris with a wide variety of musical and non-musical tasks. Kevin Tissot (or his mother) was immortalized by Chris in "Full On Kevin's Mom" on *Louder Than Love*.

After months of cleaning fish guts and slicing cod filets at R&R Fish wholesaler, Chris landed a job at Ray's Boathouse through a connect from the restaurant's head chef Wayne Ludvigsen. R&R had recently gone out of business and Ludvigsen initially brought Chris in as a dishwasher. Ray's was one of the premiere culinary destinations in the city, renowned for being one of the first restaurants in Seattle to serve Copper River salmon. While the food was good, it was the captivating views of Shilshole Bay and the Olympic Mountains that drew a steady stream of Seattle's affluent citizens into the dining room.

Around Ray's Chris was known as "Frisbee." His brother Peter also worked at Ray's and everyone on the staff referred to him as Peter B, short for Peter Boyle. When Chris was hired, they started calling him Chris B, but after one of the older staffers misheard the nickname as "Frisbee" the name just stuck.

Out of view of the restaurant's cloth-napkin clientele, Chris was given the most menial tasks to start, spraying down half-eaten salmon filets off sauce-speckled plates. It was dirty, unforgiving work, but he was content as long as he could play music. "I was never unhappy, because while I was at work, whether it was as a cook or washing dishes, I was thinking about my band and music and arranging songs," he said.[26] Eventually, he worked his way up the ranks to lead line cook.

The strong sense of camaraderie among the staff helped the hours fly by. Eleven o'clock pickup basketball games just before the lunch rush were common. So were the pranks they played on one another or on Ludvigsen. One of Chris's favorite pastimes was tricking the head chef into smelling some sunbaked fish leftovers or asking him to taste a sauce that had gone bad. One of Chris's more extreme exhibitions of mischief came over a two-month period where he simply refused to speak. It was a stunt that nearly got him fired.

"With that same group of restaurant people, I sort of kept working even through the first few Soundgarden tours," Chris recalled. "We weren't making any money. We'd sort of go out around the country and come back and then I would still have a job."[27]

As an aspiring musician, one of the biggest benefits to restaurant work was the abundance of free food. Food cost money, and Chris didn't have much. Even if he barely had enough to cover rent and gas for his car, he knew he could rely on Ray's for at least one meal a day. The restaurant also afforded him access to a mountain of unused furniture which he pilfered to furnish his home. "I stole things that were just sort of not used anymore that they would store in a warehouse next to the restaurant that basically rats and cats would pee on," he said. "I would go and take the old restaurant tables and chairs, and that would be my table and chairs. They had doors stacked up, so I would take a door, and that would be my front door."[28]

While most at Ray's were aware of Chris's musical dalliances, they got a true taste of his chops one evening during a staff holiday party. One of the managers' husbands hired a two-man band for the event. While the beer flowed like the Snoqualmie River and everyone loosened up, Chris worked up the nerve to approach the group to ask if he might sing one with them. They launched into a ripping take on the Beatles' "Twist and Shout" that raised more than a few eyebrows. "We're all looking at him, going 'Uh, what are you doing, dude?!'" his co-worker Dean Swanson told the *Seattle Times*. "I mean, his voice was so powerful and wonderful."[29]

Not many can pinpoint the exact moment when their future suddenly became clear, but for Chris the memory remained seared inside his mind. He was driving home one night after a shift at Ray's in his beat-up green 1969 Ford Galaxie 500, thinking about the trajectory of his life. "It was like an epiphany," he told *Rolling Stone* years later. "It occurred to me that there was no guarantee that as a musician I would ever have any kind of financial success, but I was fine with that. And on this drive, I remember making a promise to myself that no matter what happened in terms of success, I was going to be one of those guys playing music until he drops dead."[30]

Chris's father was not thrilled with the idea of his son becoming an itinerant musician and showed his displeasure by waving one of his pay stubs in Chris's face while making the case for him enrolling in college. It was a futile effort. Chris was determined to spend the rest of his life playing music and there wasn't anything anyone could say to change his mind.

In his off hours, Chris regularly perused the back pages of the *Rocket*, Seattle's monthly alternative newspaper, looking for new gigs. Oftentimes he'd audition for a band, nail the gig, play for about a week, grow tired of either the people or the repertoire and start the process over again. It was a never-ending game of musical chairs throughout the fledgling Seattle music scene, with Chris just hoping to find a couple of like-minded souls with the right amount of talent and aspiration.

For about two years from the time he was seventeen, the results were disappointing. "I was in about ten bands around Seattle and they were all really awful and all the songs were awful," he said. "It was usually based around a guy who wrote the songs who was the singer and they were bad songs, and it was bad singing." Genre wasn't the primary concern. All that mattered was the opportunity to bash out a lot of noise in front of a crowd of people willing to forfeit a few dollars for the pleasure. At one point he was briefly a part of a reggae/ska group even though he wasn't that big of a fan of either genre.

Though he struggled to find a stable musical partnership, one thing was becoming clear, as evidenced by the reaction of some of the teen girls that saw him onstage during his occasional gigs. Chris was good looking. By now, he was standing 6'2" and the only baby fat left on his body was in his cheeks. Others around him started to take notice. "The first time I was onstage in a band, the opinion of girls toward me changed in seconds," he said.[31]

"He was just like this beautiful kid. We were all kids, but he was just that little bit more," says photographer Charles Peterson. "We quickly realized when Chris was present, girls were unattainable. Even if we didn't want to attain them, they were unattainable."

Around 1983, Chris was again between gigs. He'd just left a band called Face to Face. He almost joined a group called Scream, that featured a young Mike McCready on guitar, but it didn't pan out. Chris went to pick up a copy of Scream's demo tape from one of the members out in Bellevue. He decided the vibe didn't feel right. Later on, the guy asked Chris to drive back across Lake Washington to return the cassette back, which affirmed for him that his instinct to pass was dead on.

Chris was back to scanning the classifieds in the *Rocket* when a small ad caught his eye. A rockabilly band was looking for a singer. He hadn't been in one of those yet. He called the listed number and arranged a time to meet. Upon meeting the man who'd posted the listing, however, he was surprised to learn that the real musical direction couldn't have been further from the stated genre. "It's this crazy guy from Chicago," he told Matt Pinfield. "Great guitar player. Doesn't know anything about rockabilly. Doesn't even know one rockabilly song or one artist at all. He just kinda wanted to do this cover band because he was this close to being homeless and he needed money, but I liked him. He was a funny guy."[32]

That guy's name was Matt Dentino, and he desperately needed a singer so that he could make some cash playing cover songs at any number of venues around town. He called his band the Shemps as a sort of homage to Shemp Howard of the Three Stooges. Chris auditioned and Dentino was stunned by his talent. "The first song I did with Chris was

'White Wedding' by Billy Idol," Dentino told author Mark Yarm. "I was like, 'Man! You know, dude, you're hired.'"[33]

The Shemps were a bar band. Their regular set included a smattering of Jimi Hendrix tunes, a little bit of the Allman Brothers Band, along with tracks by the Doors and other classic rock staples. They had one original song called "Marilyn Monroe."

Chris later called the Shemps "awful," and just "one of the many horrible bands I was in."[34] The reason that they are important to his story and the story of the burgeoning Seattle music scene in the eighties and nineties is the role the band played as the conduit between Chris and the other two erstwhile members of the Shemps, a pair of transplants from Chicago's south suburbs named Hiro Yamamoto and Kim Thayil.

Hiro Yamamoto was practically a genius. As Soundgarden's on-the-road sound guy and engineer Stuart Hallerman remembered while they were growing up together in Park Forest, Illinois, "His nickname was 'Bean,' actually because of his brain. Smart kid, really good at math." Years later, after putting the music world behind him, Yamamoto went back to college and earned his master's degree in physics from Western Washington University. But that was a long time coming.

Growing up, Yamamoto's tastes gravitated far from the sludgy, doom-laden rhythms that would lay the foundation for much of Soundgarden's sonic aesthetic. Though much of his songwriting ended up sharing sonic DNA with Black Sabbath, as an adolescent he gravitated more to classical and gypsy jazz music. Early on, he was an avid viola and mandolin player. It was only after discovering Neil Young's *Everybody Knows This Is Nowhere* that his affinity for rock began. He traded in his viola for a four-stringed electric bass guitar.

Park Forest in the sixties and seventies was a quiet, run of the mill, post-Vietnam War, middle-class suburbia set about thirty miles south of downtown Chicago, filled with lots of single-story bungalows, ranches, and worker's cottages. Driving down US 30 on the way to Joliet, Illinois from Indiana, you can blink and miss the village entirely.

In his teen years, Yamamoto attended Rich Township High School, which is where he met an aspiring punk guitarist named Kim Thayil.

Thayil was born in Seattle on September 4, 1960, but didn't stay in the Pacific Northwest long. His family moved to Park Forest when he was around five years old. His parents were immigrants from India. Music ran in their blood. Thayil's mother was a classically trained pianist and graduated from the Royal Academy of London when she was just eighteen. She met his dad when they were in the church choir together.

Thayil visited his parent's homeland for the first time when he was eight years old. In a stunning bit of kismet, it was during this trip that he first heard the Beatles, when someone introduced him to *Sgt. Pepper's Lonely Hearts Club Band*. He often spent long, lazy afternoons listening to songs like "Day Tripper" and "Lucy In The Sky with Diamonds" while pining for the comforts of America such as Saturday morning cartoons and Major League Baseball. He was a precocious kid, a voracious reader, and from the first time he picked up a copy of KISS's *Alive* album, a die-hard rock and roll fan. The bombastic, over-the-top music of KISS guided him toward even more savage sounds made by proto-punk bands like the Stooges, the Velvet Underground, and, especially, the MC5.

But it was KISS that had inspired him to pick up a guitar. Images of Ace Frehley producing volcanic solos on his cherry burst Les Paul while smoke poured out of it were utterly intoxicating. He couldn't afford a Les Paul, so for his first guitar, Thayil picked up a cheap Stratocaster copy manufactured by a company called Encore and began the laborious process of learning the fundamental chords and scales.

Around 1977, while still in high school, Thayil formed his first rock band, an outrageously named outfit called Bozo and His Vast Army of Pinheads. They played cover songs, but also dabbled in original material. The first song he wrote was called "Plastic Love," and roughly centered on trying to make it with a mannequin: "Her hair is made of Dacron, her mind is made of cellulose / She's someone I could lay on, who's semi-comatose."

Thayil's first live gig took place at the year-end talent show at his high school in front of five hundred people, including his parents. Their setlist included the Ramones' "Pinhead," a pair of tracks by the Sex Pistols ("God Save The Queen" and "Submission") and a Devo cut called "Mongoloid."

They also threw in a bevy of originals, songs with names like "TV Clones," "Bureaucracy In The US," "Plastic Love," and "If I Were A Bomb, I'd Explode In Your Face." As he remembered, "The audience response was 'You guys are pretty good for that kind of music, punk rock and all.'"[35]

Thayil and Yamamoto hit it off after meeting at Rich Township. Like Yamamoto, Thayil was vastly intelligent and enjoyed pontificating at length on ideas big and small. The guitarist had already technically graduated when their paths crossed in an after-school program called ALPS, an acronym for Alternative Learning Process School, but the two of them regularly hung out with a mutual friend of theirs named Bruce Pavitt.

Yamamoto graduated from Rich Township and decided he wanted to break out of the Midwest and move to Olympia, Washington. His buddy Stuart Hallerman planned on enrolling at the extremely liberal arts institution the Evergreen State College, where Pavitt was already a student, so the two decided they'd go together. Yamamoto hung out around Washington for about three months, but after failing to find a job and falling head over heels for a girl back home during Christmas vacation, he decided to return to Chicago.

Meanwhile, after tendering his resignation as one of the Vast Army of Pinheads, Thayil joined another punk band called Identity Crisis with Pavitt's younger brother and entered a studio for the first time to record a seven-inch EP titled *Pretty Feet* that debuted in 1980. The record didn't do much, and by 1981, Thayil was ready for a change. So too was Yamamoto.

Both men were nursing recent breakups and didn't have much to tie them to the Chicago area. They decided to give Washington state another shot. The pair scrounged together all the money they had, loaded their gear and clothes into Yamamoto's Datsun B210, and took off again for the West Coast.

Shortly after reaching Washington, they both enrolled into the University of Washington where Thayil pursued a degree in philosophy. "He always showed up maybe ten minutes late and would almost invariably bogart the discussion," classmate and future Mudhoney frontman Mark Arm said through laughter. "He really liked to play devil's advocate and try to look at everything from all different angles and sometimes set

the class on all different tangents that I think the professor didn't necessarily appreciate."

By 1982, Thayil was thriving in his new environment. He had his own
apartment, a girlfriend, and a weekly DJ gig at the local college radio station KCMU. He was also playing around town in a variety of short-lived
musical ventures, while making connections within the tight-knit scene.
One of those people was Matt Dentino. The future Shemps guitarist was
another Chicago-area transplant looking for somewhere to live while trying to start a band of his own. Thayil offered to let him crash at his place.

Despite Chris's negative estimation of the Shemps, Dentino was by
all accounts a skilled guitar player. His major problem, familiar to almost
every aspiring musician, was maintaining a reliable group of people willing to jam and book shows. At the moment, he was in search of someone
to play bass, and though Yama`moto didn't play the instrument himself
yet, Thayil offered to show him how for Dentino's sake.

Upon meeting Chris Cornell, Thayil was wary. Chris's hair was short,
and his slick style left something to be desired for the relatively seasoned
punk rock guitarist. "My first impression was that he was some guy who
just got out of the Navy or something,"[36] Thayil said. It didn't take long for
Chris to disabuse Thayil of that notion.

The Shemps' first gig took place at a small, concrete-constructed
restaurant in the University District called the Morning Star Café on 11th
Avenue Northeast. It was a spartan space, but the crowd that night wasn't
exactly fighting for elbow room. Among their number that night was
a drummer named Matt Cameron who came away impressed with the
Shemps' singer. Mark Arm concurred. "If it was like a Creedence song,
he sounded like John Fogerty. If it was a Zeppelin song, he sounded like
Robert Plant. If it was a Doors song, he sounded like Jim Morrison. That
was Chris Cornell," he said. "He seemed like a really young kid at the
time, but he was only like two or three years younger than me. It was
kinda astounding."

The Shemps plugged along for several months, though they didn't
get as many gigs as they would've liked; only eight to ten during the
entire life of the group. Chris and Dentino remained the constants in the

band. Yamamoto quit out of boredom. His musical tastes didn't mesh with Dentino's, and he was moonlighting in another band called Altered whose repertoire hued more toward jangly, new wave songs that he found more interesting.

With nowhere else to turn and a slate of gigs on the calendar, Dentino returned to Thayil and begged him to fill in on bass. Thayil wasn't enthralled by the proposition of exchanging six strings for four, but after consistently applied pressure, he relented. Fortunately for the fledgling bassist, the Shemps' run of dates evaporated shortly after he came aboard, and the band folded sometime around early 1984. Dentino by this point was strung out on drugs, exhausted, and broke. He eventually found Jesus, became a born-again Christian, and left his ambitions of rock stardom behind.

CHAPTER II

MOOD FOR TROUBLE

The distance between the drum kit and the space at the lip of the stage is only several yards, but the psychological chasm might as well be a million miles. Obscured by his kit, a drummer executes a song's rhythmic backbone in relative anonymity. The audience can feel the percussive patterns rattling their ribcages, but the author of that sound is seldom seen with any clarity.

The lead singer, however, is always on display. Every twist, spasm, groan, moan, and wail is eaten up and cheered on by the boisterous crowd. Conversely, every wrong note, flubbed lyric, and misplaced foot is noticed too. The limelight is an unforgiving space to exist, and only a select few have the mental and physical fortitude to impress under its unforgiving glare. In 1985, Chris Cornell decided to give it a shot.

Combined with a pull toward the microphone, Chris was simultaneously reconciling the realization that his drumming wasn't on a level that could carry him beyond his current situation. He was good, sure, but could he ever be great? The amount of time and effort it would take to find out was nearly impossible to fathom. As he was contemplating his options, he witnessed something that resolved any doubt and led him to step out from behind the kit and out to the center of the stage for good.

The epiphany happened one night while Matt Cameron was tearing it up onstage with his band Feedback. Chris wasn't even in the club. He was just looking in from outside as Cameron put on a veritable clinic, showing off the kind of intrinsic talent that would make anyone question their choice to so much as look at a set of drums. "I'm watching what he's doing and I'm hearing what it sounds like and I couldn't really make the connection," Chris recalled. "I thought, 'Oh, that's what a good drummer is supposed to play like. Maybe my talent lies elsewhere.'"[1]

"He was a really good drummer," Soungarden's guitarist Kim Thayil protested to me. "He's not like Matt but he wrote great as a drummer. I think so much so that Hiro and I entertained the idea of getting another singer so that Chris continued to write with us on drums. But Chris really wanted to get up from behind the drum kit."

An introvert by nature, the role of lead singer seemingly ran counter to nearly every instinct Chris had, but still he felt compelled. The biggest challenge, as he would come to learn, wasn't hitting the notes, it was commanding the attention of a crowd demanding to be entertained. For that you needed energy. You needed style. You needed charisma.

Chris's role as "the singer" was an almost therapeutic guise that allowed him to skirt some of his more detrimental tendencies. "If it wasn't for what I'd chosen to do with my life, I'd probably be, more or less, a shut-in," he once said.[2] The inner struggle between the real human being inclined to hide from the world and the person screaming and flailing around on stage was part of what made him such an indelible front man. He'd do whatever it took to keep that dark room filled with strangers entertained. Roll around in glass. Pick fights. Swing from the rafters. Smash guitars. Anything.

Donald Fagen, the lead singer of Steely Dan, a band about as far, from an aesthetic perspective, as it gets from Soundgarden, wrote about the self-destructive impulse of performance in his memoir *Eminent Hipsters*. "Every night in front of an audience, no matter how exhilarating, is a bit of a ritual slaying. You use every last bit of your marrow, every last atom of your energy in an attempt to satisfy the hungry crowd. On some level, you're trying to extinguish yourself…That's what you are, and they need it."[3]

That's what made Chris chug a half gallon of milk and spit it out on the crowd at a concert in Wisconsin in 1990. That's what made him perform whole shows while wearing a pair of shorts he'd made for himself out of duct tape. That's what made him throw his microphone cord over a lighting beam, scream into it while hanging upside-down from the ceiling before diving headlong into the audience time and time again. Perhaps his octave-shattering voice was enough to get his band noticed, but at least early on in his career, he wasn't about to wait around to find out.

"I always thought he was like a shaman figure onstage," Tad guitarist Kurt Danielson said. "He had this mystical energy on one level, and on another, he was more like a real rock frontman. He combined those things in a seamless way that I had never seen before."

"A lot of time he would come across like he was in a complete trance up there. Just screaming and flailing around," Seattle music journalist Dawn Anderson recalled. "There was always a small group of girls sitting up front drooling over him, but he never seemed to notice. I always got the feeling that once Chris figured out that people thought he was sexy, and that people might be trying to capitalize on that, it embarrassed him a little. There was a point where he stopped flailing. He acted a lot more sober onstage. He seemed conscious of it."

Like Iggy Pop before him, Chris had a propensity for performing shirtless. "Going the full Cornell," is how Nirvana bassist Krist Novoselic described it from the stage of the Central Tavern in 2017, the site of many sweaty Soundgarden gigs. "I can't recall him ever playing with a shirt on," said Soundgarden's early road manager Eric Johnson. "On a trip to San Francisco, a bunch of us found these silk pajama tops that we cut the sleeves off and wore almost like vests. He might've started a show in one of those things, and then it came off."

Female admirers certainly enjoyed the view, but some of the more skeptical local scenemakers couldn't relate. Oftentimes they rolled their eyes at the brazen exhibitionism. It didn't matter to Chris, who seemed to relish in bucking convention. "I used to have about fifty ribbons in my hair, which didn't exactly please the jocks in the audience," he said. "They were probably worried because they found me a little too attractive."[4]

In a punk rock-inspired ecosystem that prized the concept of *authenticity* above all else, some felt what he was doing was contrived. "He was a sexy man with a good body, and he wasn't afraid to use it," Mark Arm said. "I remember one show where basically halfway through the set, he just grabbed the middle of the shirt and tore it off him. That'd been like, obviously distressed or something. That was like a planned thing, which is a little bit different than accidentally vomiting and then rolling around in it, which was sort of more my approach to things." Nevertheless, Arm noted, "The ladies loved it! Some of the dudes too."

Hiro Yamamoto wasn't a fan of Chris's bare-chested antics, and often let him know. Chris would just walk away, undeterred. "The punk culture that grunge grew out of put a high premium on flaws because flaws gave music character, and it also made it easier for young amateurs to be appreciated," says Bruce Pavitt. "Chris stood out, sometimes awkwardly, because of his seemingly flawless nature."

"I remember one girlfriend of mine when I was going to see Soundgarden once said, 'How many times can you watch Chris Cornell jack off in your face?'" journalist Dawn Anderson recalled. "I said something smart-ass like, 'Oh, I don't know, what time is it?' He wasn't doing anything like jacking off though."

The persona that Chris presented onstage, the ripped Adonis screaming his head off before leaping into the waiting arms of the churning pit beneath him, was as far from the quiet, introspective loner as it gets. "I was a nerdy shut-in who listened to prog-rock—and then I got on stage," he said. The universe didn't make him a rock star. He willed himself to become one. "Most frontmen are not born hams like David Lee Roth. We're more like Joey Ramone: awkward geeks who somehow find our place in the world on the stage. Nobody ever said a positive thing to me, ever, in my life, until they heard me play music."[5]

* * *

While he was still trying to give the Shemps a go, Chris Cornell was in the middle of an untenable living situation. His roommate was experiencing something like a nervous breakdown over the course of two days and it was driving him up the wall. He had to get the hell out of there, and fast.

Around the same time, Chris called Hiro Yamamoto to settle a debt. While they were chatting, Yamamoto mentioned that his own room-mate had gotten mad at him recently and was on his way out. He wanted to know if Chris knew anybody who might be looking for a place. The following day, Chris was at Yamamoto's with nearly all his worldly possessions in hand.

Almost from the minute that Chris moved in, he and Yamamoto started jamming together. Upstairs in the house was an empty A-frame space that they transformed into a rehearsal area where they bashed out different rhythms for hours at a time. It didn't take long before the duo became a tight little rhythm section, but they knew that if they were ever going to do anything, they needed a guitar player. It was Yamamoto's idea to give Thayil a call to see if he'd be interested in jamming with them.

Once Thayil came over and plugged his guitar into an amp, it was abundantly clear that there was an exhilarating chemistry between the three of them. During that first jam session they hammered out two songs, one right after the other. There was something about the way that Thayil ripped into his guitar with a furious, frenzied abandon that resonated with Chris. He'd never heard anyone play like that before, and it triggered an instant, life-altering, and deeply emotional response.

"There was a really vital expressive amazing music scene happening during a time when commercial music was awful. I felt like we could live in that world immediately," Chris said. "It wasn't something we had to develop. It was literally day one."[6]

The music that the trio wove together didn't sound anything like what casual listeners might recognize as Soundgarden. They were creating the kinds of songs that they wanted to hear elsewhere but couldn't find on the radio or in the imports bin at Tower Records; weird, twisted, and wholly uncommercial compositions that demanded to be blasted at painful amounts of volume. Fortunately, Yamamoto's house was located around 80th Street and Roosevelt Way, just a short walk from I-5 and Green Lake. It was a busy and noisy thoroughfare, so no one ever hassled them over the cacophony blasting through their walls. Oftentimes, the three would play until two or three o'clock in the morning, working up melodies, honing riffs, and polishing basslines, relishing their sonic experiments and discoveries.

By the second day of jamming, they had racked up another three songs; jangly, evil-sounding tracks with foreboding names like "Blood," and "Bury My Head in the Sand." While they connected well on a musical level, there was a social gap between that felt pronounced at times. Chris was only nineteen, a local high school dropout, while Thayil and Yamamoto were college students. Their trajectories couldn't have seemed more dissimilar.

There was also a small clash in personalities. Thayil and Yamamoto were more gregarious and outgoing than their singing drummer. The two old friends would often hang out, drink beer, and watch David Letterman while Chris disappeared into his room. There was also a racial divide, not just between Chris and Thayil and Yamamoto, but between Soundgarden and many of the rest of the bands that made up the Seattle scene at the time. By the 1980s, the rock and punk landscape across America was predominantly white. Now, here was a band with a white singer/drummer, a Japanese bassist, and an Indian guitarist. Even as late as 2020, groups that diverse are scarce. Back in the 1985 it was unheard of—especially in Seattle.

And yet, despite their differences, they bonded over shared influences, similar tastes, goofy senses of humor, and music. The only stumbling block that prevented them from pushing their chips all the way in and trying to make a go at it together was Thayil's schedule. From the outset, Yamamoto warned Chris that their would-be guitar player was being pulled in several directions—romantically, academically, and financially by his day job—and might not be available to commit to what they hoped to do. That didn't stop Yamamoto from hounding Thayil.

The guitarist simply kept putting him off, citing his homework, his job, and his weekly DJ gig. There were a million excuses to put off swinging by Chris and Yamamoto's place, but the bassist wasn't about to take no for an answer. Eventually the incessant pestering paid off. Thayil caved, but it came at a cost when the guitar player lost his day job because he spread himself a little too thin.

The three of them had chops, novel ideas, unique perspectives, and, most importantly, a distinct sensibility that set them apart from other would-be post-punk indie bands scratching and clawing their way up the ranks of the tiny Seattle music scene. All they needed was a name. The Stone Age Alliance was an early contender courtesy of Yamamoto, but they feared it would link them too closely to the synth-drenched new wave movement taking radio by storm.

After running through several more ideas, Thayil came up with the winner. He took their new moniker from a local art installation called A Sound Garden, located within the National Oceanic and Atmospheric Administration near Magnuson Park. It was an impressive and pleasant sculpture. A dozen twenty-one-foot-high steel towers that moved with the wind, producing a pleasant soundtrack to the pristine view of nearby Lake Washington. It had only been constructed a couple of years prior to the band's formation but was already a prime make-out spot for UW students who regularly made the short fifteen-minute drive from campus. Thayil and his then-girlfriend were regular visitors.

Even if it wasn't obvious, the Soundgarden name—for the first year or so they were sometimes billed as "Sound Garden"—proved to have an unexpected benefit. "We would open up for a band that was kind of heavy, like, say we played a show with Hüsker Dü one time, if you didn't know who Soundgarden was, you would think we were sort of a Green On Red, neo-psychedelic, alternative R.E.M.-ey kind of thing," Chris said. "Then you would show up and we would open and come out and be Soundgarden and they would go, 'Holy fuck!'" [7] Crusty scene veterans who were prepared to snark at what they assumed were a bunch of flower children came away impressed by the new group's intense, dark, and abrasive sound. Though, the name also opened the door to some of their early detractors to call them "Noise Cabbage."

Soundgarden continued jamming and writing songs over the next few months. Chris was inspired enough that he bought his first guitar, a Gibson ES-347, just so he could create new material. All at once, songs started pouring out of him. The only downside was that the Gibson was too nice to play in the kinds of frenetic, sweaty clubs that the band hoped to book. He was anxious that it might get damaged or stolen and ended up trading it away for a cheap, Mexican-made Fender Stratocaster and a Twin Reverb amplifier.

Along the way, he also invested in a variety of guitar pedals, some of which, like an Ibanez Tubescreamer, he ended up giving to Kim Thayil. "Chris has been my pedal supplier over the years, starting with the very first chorus," the guitarist told *Music Radar*. "That's been one of the histories of the band—Chris buys some pedal and I end up using it, really liking it and then it becomes mine!"[8]

It sounds antithetical, but early on Chris's scant understanding of the complexities of the fretboard actually helped define Soundgarden's unique, off-kilter style. "I had no idea how to play guitar, so I was just kind of making it up," he said. "I was doing things that were unusual, because I didn't know if it was or wasn't okay."[9]

It's to the band's credit, and their general lack of ego, that they didn't put down Chris's novice noodling at this formative stage. In fact, they encouraged him to keep going, keep learning, and keep innovating. Whereas other guitarists might have become territorial over their role within the band, Thayil had little reservations about hearing what the drummer had to bring to the table and helping him out wherever he could. "I would show him a lot of, you know, little guitar lick tricks here," Thayil said. "Here's a triplet, here's a series of majors, here's a ninth. I would show him various chord positions and patterns; he was really eager."[10]

The songs mattered more than anything else. "Some of the early stuff he wrote was very goth and it was also influenced by a band called Chrome," Endino said, referencing the cult seventies post-punk group out of San Francisco. "Sort of this noisy, semi-industrial, spooky vibe to some of the really old songs that he wrote. 'The Storm' is one of those actually that he demoed by himself. The demo is very weird-sounding."

As the threesome honed their growing repertoire, Chris also became more adept behind the boards. "I remember they used to rehearse at a house north of the U-District in Ravenna. Like up in the attic space had a rehearsal, recording zone," Stuart Hallerman remembers. "Chris was a do-it-yourself audio student on his own and was really quite good at it. He had the whole song in his head before he even touched a tape."

The band's recording setup was rudimentary. A microphone on the bass amp, another on the guitar amp, one for drums and another for the vocals. No overdubs. Everything was played live, at once. Mistakes were common—an out-of-time cymbal crash here, a bum guitar note there—but not necessarily unwelcome. A sonic mistake that seemed to add a little extra something to the song was referred to by the band as a "Meat Puppets fuckup," after the Arizona-based punk rock band the Meat Puppets. That group's second full-length record, *Meat Puppets II*, dropped just months before Soundgarden's genesis and had a tremendous impact on everyone in the band. If a take had a "Meat Puppets fuckup," the trio was loath to try and record over it out of fear of not being able to replicate the rough-hewn, interesting vibe of the song as a whole.

Soundgarden racked up fifteen songs, which were immortalized on four-track and compiled onto a single cassette tape. "We called it *The First 15*," Thayil said. "In terms of audio quality, that's all four-track stuff that we did in our basement. It'd be like bootleg-quality type stuff."[11] Some of the songs were re-recorded for different projects down the line, most notably the dark and spiraling "Incessant Mace," which at this early stage was referred to as "No Warning." They ultimately changed the name of that track because Thayil misunderstood what Chris was singing.

"I was singing, 'Domestic something,' and Kim thought, 'That's cool, 'Incessant Mace.' And I'm erasing it going, 'It sure is cool, thank you very much! Anything else you heard that I said?'"[12]

Even while Thayil's misunderstanding imbued "Incessent Mace" with a cooler vibe, it obscured some of the song's central meaning. The whole thing was inspired by the worst tendencies that Chris saw in his dad—tendencies he hoped to avoid in his own life. "It's about a young man hoping to grow up to not be anything like his father," he told a crowd in Fort Myers, Florida in 2017. "That was my sentiment when I was a younger man. For the most part it worked out. Though, there are aspects of his dickheadedness that I have inside of me that I can't help."[13]

While they continued to jam and make demos, they still hadn't managed to book any shows. That all changed when a band named Vexed bowed out of their opening slot for a group out of New York called 3 Teens Kill 4 at a venue called Top of the Court. "Vex[ed] could not do the gig and they recommended these friends of theirs who only played in their attic and that was Hiro, Chris and I," Kim Thayil remembered.[14] They hadn't even named themselves yet, but they took the gig anyway, and on December 21, 1984, the trio made their live debut.

Top of the Court was located just off Elliott Avenue in an industrial part of town by the Magnolia Bridge and Pier 91. On the first floor was another one of Seattle's poorly lit watering holes called the Back Court Tavern. The live performance space took over the second floor and gave local bands and small out-of-town acts an outlet to rage the nights away. These types of short-lived venues were the bread and butter of the Seattle music scene in the eighties. Spaces with names like Golden Crown, Danceland, Rosco Louie, Washington Hall, Bahamas Underground, Wrex, the Meatlocker, the Funhole, the Mountaineers, Rainbow Tavern, Grey Door, Graven Image, Metropolis, and the Ditto. Venues would pop up, thrive for a few months, maybe even a year or two, then vanish.

Skin Yard's bassist Daniel House was no fan of the Shemps but decided to check out Soundgarden anyway, along with forty or so other people. He was immediately struck by the fact that they were a three-piece without a traditional frontman. Despite that shortcoming, he was impressed by how much better they sounded than when they were playing covers with Dentino. "Soundgarden was nothing like the Shemps, like at all," he observed. "They played an incendiary set of songs that while still rough, was imbued with an exciting angst and an undeniable ferocity."[15]

It took another two months before Soundgarden landed their next gig, but the wait was more than worth it when they locked up an opportunity to open for a savage band from Aberdeen called the Melvins along with Hüsker Dü. The Minnesota post-hardcore group was fresh off finishing their era-defining masterpiece *New Day Rising* when they scheduled a gig in Seattle on February 24, 1985, at an all-ages venue called Gorilla Gardens, located in Chinatown.

Covered in hideous red velvet, the converted movie theater was a critical incubator for local and national underground rock bands. Gorilla Gardens is actually a misnomer. It was one of two venues sharing the same building along with a common lobby under the larger guise of the Rock Theater. On one side was The Omni room, which showcased mostly metal bands from the city's East Side, groups like Queensryche, Sanctuary, and Fifth Angel. Gorilla Gardens was on the other side and was mostly left to the punks and hardcore kids. Guns N' Roses played there during one of their earliest tours of the Pacific Northwest, as did Sonic Youth, Butthole Surfers, and the Ramones.

The Circle Jerks put Gorilla Gardens on the map for all the wrong reasons later that same year after the cops shut down their set just a few songs in on orders from the fire marshal who objected to the amount of people in the venue. Pissed off punks who'd waited outside for hours during an extremely rare snowstorm were enraged at being told to go home before they could blow off their worked-up head of steam. A riot ensued and spilled out into the streets. Bottles flew through the air. Police busted heads. Dumpsters were set on fire. Cars were tipped over. Kids were taken away in handcuffs. When all was said and done, the uproar caused the bigwigs in Seattle to pass a scene-suffocating Teen Dance Ordinance, which essentially killed the all-ages entertainment scene in the city and carried significant negative ramifications for Soundgarden and their contemporaries going forward.

Soundgarden was still able to play the various bars up and down "The Ave" in the University district. They also got some gigs around Pioneer Square and up on Capitol Hill. But because of the ordinance, a large chunk of their potential fanbase simply couldn't make it through the front door, which limited their prospects. "We probably had a larger group of fans who were under twenty-one than we had over twenty-one," Chris posited, "Nine out of ten shows we couldn't play for those people because we had to play the Rainbow and the Central and the Ditto."[16]

By most accounts, the band's second gig didn't go as well as the first. Many in attendance didn't get what Soundgarden was all about. The flagrant masculinity seemed at odds with what was happening in the city's post-punk indie scene. "This was a time in Seattle music where there was snobbery like there is everywhere, I guess, there is alternative or underground music, but Soundgarden was very, very rock, and a lot of these new wave people didn't get it," Seattle music journalist Dawn Anderson said. "They couldn't understand. I heard a lot of people looking at each other saying, 'Are these guys joking or are they serious?' And I was thinking, 'Why does it matter? Who the hell cares? They're awesome!' It was this great big wall of noise."

"To me it had a sort of gothic-y, Bauhaus bent to it. It reminded me of a cross between Bauhaus and Cream or something," Mark Arm said of Soundgarden's early sound. "Kim was playing with a lot of flange and stuff."

While Thayil dominated Gorilla Gardens with his punishing volume, much of the attention was directed at the band's drummer and his prowess on the microphone. "Chris had an incredible voice," Pearl Jam bassist Jeff Ament told author Greg Prato. "That was apparent even at that first show."[17] Like House, Ament was thrown off by the drummer being the lead singer. "It just didn't make sense to me," he said. "There weren't too many rules in the hardcore world but having a singer who acted crazy and ran around was probably one of most important things—in terms of getting the energy across. The energy changed a lot when Chris just had a mic."

It was difficult to bash out the intricate rhythms of Soundgarden's songs while also screaming the vocals with as much fury as he could summon. One facet of Chris's performance always seemed to suffer because of the other. He was constantly trying to catch his breath.

As fate would have it, there was another figure in the crowd that fateful night at Gorilla Gardens, a maintenance worker from Ray's Boathouse named Scott Sundquist. Like Chris, Sundquist was a drummer and recognized right away the limitations placed on the singer. When Chris later approached him with the proposition to join the band, he leapt at the chance.

Sundquist was by no means the obvious choice to join a band like Soundgarden. While the age gap between the Thayil and Yamamoto was pronounced, Sundquist was nearly thirty. He also had a wife and a child, which set him further apart from the other guys in the band, who were still living the footloose and fancy-free life of twenty-somethings playing rock and roll. And yet the man they called the "Sun King"—a nickname bequeathed to him by Mother Love Bone singer Andrew Wood—had the chops that Soundgarden needed to get Chris out front.

"Scott Sundquist is a Ginger Baker style of drummer," Jack Endino said. "He had a swing kind of background. In other words, his drums had a rolling characteristic and his tempo was more elastic in a good way. He was very dynamic."

Even if the decision to bring a full-time drummer into the band seemed obvious in retrospect, everyone in Soundgarden was wary of messing with their hard-earned chemistry. And yet, there was another impetus to bring someone onboard—to relieve Thayil of background vocal duties, as he wasn't comfortable behind a microphone. "Kim didn't want to do backups anymore as it wasn't guitar hero style," Chris recalled. "I mean, you could hardly imagine Jimmy Page singing backing vocals."[18]

Soundgarden's first live show with Sundquist settled all of their concerns, even while Chris wasn't at his best. He was sick as a dog with a temperature reaching 103 degrees. He couldn't remember a single thing that happened from the time he stepped onstage to the time he stepped off, but afterwards was told it went well by his friends. "The first show answered the questions, I think, for everyone in the band as to whether it would be such a good idea or not," he said.[19]

Even with Sundquist in the fold, Chris didn't totally abandon the drums. Not yet, at least. "I remember there was a song called 'Circle of Power' that they wrote together, and Chris played drums on that," Jack Endino said. "For the longest time, even when they played shows a little later, he would sit down at the drums and play that song because it was in 5/4 and Hiro the bass player would sing it."

Freed from the drum stool, Chris was able to explore the full range of his voice, even if that meant pushing it past its natural limit. "The earliest club shows, I had a big problem of walking out onstage, going insane, and losing my voice within the first two songs," he said. "Sometimes within the first part of the first song."[20] He had the power, the dexterity, the charisma and the energy, all that was left to learn was how to control and harness it for maximum impact. One of the most helpful elements, though it didn't feel that way at the time, was the massive volume Thayil produced during rehearsals. Chris had no choice but to sing harder and louder to hear himself over the guitarist's roaring chords and solos. The effort that feat took stretched his voice to what he thought was its limit and then beyond.

"He knew what he could do, we all did," Kim Thayil said. "There was a point when people started saying, 'He's a great singer, perhaps the greatest singer in rock,' and that's when he began to *really* focus on being as good a singer as he could be, so he could be even better."[21]

Even at this early stage, long before they had a single to hawk, the band was worried about burning out their growing audience by playing too many shows around town. They started getting picky about where and when to perform, feeling it was smarter to draw two hundred people once a month than fifty people four times a month.

Not every show was a triumph. During a gig on April 5, 1985, at the Langston Hughes Cultural Arts Center near Garfield High School, Soundgarden was booed off the stage for not sounding or looking hardcore enough. "People in the punk community hated them at the time," Bruce Pavitt noted. "It was definitely a kind of punk/metal crossover."[22] Then there was a show the following year opening for Faith No More at a bar up north in Vancouver where someone shattered a glass ashtray over Matt Cameron's kick drum while derisively calling them "Fucking Led Zeppelin crap!"

Another concert opening for the Beat Pagodas at North Seattle Community College went even worse after Chris kneed himself in the face causing a river of blood to burst out of his nose sending the young coeds streaming from the dance floor to the back of the room. "Here were all these college students who came there with their dates to dance, and here was Soundgarden with this singer who was bleeding profusely," Chris told *Guitar World*. "I threw my mic stand like a spear, and when it hit the floor it slid all the way across the empty dance floor. As it approached the people who were standing against the wall they just separated and let it hit the wall. They had no emotion. Everyone just sat there until we were done."[23]

Soundgarden was already drawing comparisons to Led Zeppelin. Chris was regularly compared to leonine lead singer Robert Plant, and it's not difficult to understand why. Both singers screamed and shrieked with orgasmic fury. Both wrote ethereal lyrics emphasizing emotion and mood over coherent narratives. And both flaunted a sex-god persona. The comparison was a double-edged sword, however.

"It was not okay to the fans of indie music, for example, then, and that was kind of an unapologetic maleness, incorporating heavy riff rock that reminded people of bands that at the time were considered to be completely uncool," Cornell told podcaster Marc Maron. "If, for example, someone said, 'That last song you played reminded me a little bit of Led Zeppelin,' for most bands that was the kiss of death. But for Soundgarden, people kind of started to look at it differently. That was the first time I heard of 'Zeppelin in a good way.'" [24]

In the mid-eighties, hundreds of mainstream MTV rock bands incorporated elements of Zeppelin into their aesthetic, while completely missing the point of what made the British foursome so exhilarating. Power ballad purveyors Whitesnake were a prime example of the aqua velvet and cheese that turned many rock and punk purists off the Zeppelin blueprint. Soundgarden, as intense, loud, raw, and menacing as they were, couldn't have been more diametrically opposed to the prevailing aesthetic on MTV. It would simply take time for the culture to catch up to them.

While they were still getting their footing onstage, Soundgarden continued to write and demo new songs. On April 24, 1985, Cornell, Yamamoto, and Thayil cut seven tracks for a tape they dubbed 6 Songs for Bruce. Six, because the seventh song, a cut titled "The Storm," was a solo Cornell composition. It was one of his earliest attempts at songwriting.

"There was no real guitar part but there was a cool bass line," Thayil recalled of "The Storm." The guitarist eventually overlayed some seventh and ninth chords, to give the song shape and body, and it quickly became a mainstay of their live set. "Scott Sundquist, interpreted the drums as, like, rolling thunder," Thayil added. "Locally, we played that song live all the time. It was a favorite." [25]

All the tracks were recorded on the cassette's A-side. The B-side was left silent, but, as a joke, they titled it *Zen Deity Speaks*. The "Bruce" in the title of the demo referred to Thayil's old pal Bruce Pavitt, who had become a tastemaker in the scene thanks to his popular Sub Pop column in the *Rocket*. He was someone the band relied on to give an honest assessment of their music; an unofficial A&R guy who didn't pull punches when he thought something sounded shitty or underrealized.

Not counting "The Storm," the six Soundgarden songs that made it onto the tape included, "I Think I'm Sinking," "Bury My Head In Sand," "Tears To Forget," "Incessant Mace," "In Vention," and "Out Of My Skin." All of these songs in their nascent forms have remain locked in the vaults. The tape itself was briefly on display as part of an exhibit at Seattle's Museum of Pop Culture—but the band eventually revisited and re-recorded a couple of them in ensuing years. The doom-laden "Incessant Mace" made it out into the world initially on an extremely local compilation tape called *Pyrrhic Victory* put out by C/Z Records in 1986, while "Tears To Forget," a track originally sung by Yamamoto on the demo, comprised one-third of Soundgarden's contributions to that same label's infamous *Deep Six* album, a project that sought to showcase the best the Seattle underground had to offer.

"Seattle is a real city, but in terms of the artistic community at the time, though it was very vibrant, it was very small," Chris told *Indiewire*. "There was just this little family. And because of that, we all knew each other and all be in the audience for everyone else's band. And if the Melvins played, then Soundgarden was there, and when Green River was there, and sometimes nobody else. And sometimes when Soundgarden would play—before Matt Cameron was in Soundgarden, we were playing shows with his band Skin Yard and we were in the audience for them and they were in the audience for us. I saw Pearl Jam's first show, Mother Love Bone's first show, Green River's first show, Skin Yard's first show and they were all there for us."[26]

Deep Six was the brainchild of a Boston-by-way-of-Pennsylvania transplant named Chris Hanzsek. When Hanzsek arrived in Seattle, he immersed himself in a scene burgeoning with undiscovered talent.

Fortunately for him, the Puget Sound region was almost totally devoid of record label interest. "Nobody was putting out records in Seattle," he said. "Everybody thought it'd be kind of a waste of money."

Expectations for success among the bands that comprised Seattle's music scene throughout the eighties were abysmally low. Practically no one had designs on superstardom. Most were in it for the sheer love and thrill of playing music. At least to Chris's mind, it was those low expectations that fostered so much creativity and camaraderie between the various groups that shared stages around town. "There was no outside attention, no carrots dangled in front of the musicians in the scene we were in," he told *Vulture*. "You were lucky if you could release something independently and then, if you did, it would reach a pretty small audience. That was really the height of what we felt we could ever achieve, so the focus was on the artistry and creativity. We were all sort of resigned to a small audience and touring in a van if we were lucky enough to pull that off."[27]

Hanzsek was enthralled enough by some of the groups he encountered in the clubs and bars to record them. Members of the bands he selected pointed him in the direction of other bands worth adding to the project. "All of the bands on the compilation came together through discussions between myself and Tina and two of the instigators behind the whole compilation idea, Jeff Ament and Mark Arm, both of the guys in Green River," Hanzsek said. "They were friends with everybody."

"We introduced him to our friends who were playing locally around town," Arm confirmed. "He went to shows and stuff to see what was cool too, but we were like, 'Hey, you need to check out the Melvins.' Or, 'Hey, Malfunkshun's cool.' 'Don't forget the U-Men!'"

Soundgarden was one of the first bands that came up in conversation. For Hanzsek, the deal was sealed once he listened to the band's demo. "Hearing Soundgarden on tape, it just pushed us over the edge," Hanzsek said. "Like, 'Yeah, okay, let's round up all the money we have. This is definitely gonna be worth it.'" Hanzsek's partner Tina Casale fronted $2,500 out of her own bank account.

It wasn't as simple as making a phone call and scheduling a recording session, however. "They were cautious," Hanzsek recalled of Soundgarden. "They wanted to meet us, ask some questions, then huddle together and come back and give us their verdict." After a while, the producer got the answer he'd been waiting on: Soundgarden was in.

By the time August 1985 rolled around and Hanzsek actually began recording *Deep Six*, Soundgarden was more than ready to go. "That band just prepared and prepared and prepared," the producer said. "There was nothing they did that was not prepared. And I don't mean prepared in the sense that everything was cut and dried and robotic, I mean they knew what they wanted to do and when given the chance, they were quite able to do their thing."

The countless hours of practice in the attic space had paid off. They were a solid unit together, while their singer was constantly pushing himself to get better. Some of his nearby neighbors couldn't help but overhear Chris practicing his screams while standing in front of his kitchen window.

Soundgarden ultimately cut three songs during their quick session with Hanzsek at Ironwood Studios. Among the tracks that made the final cut were "Heretic," the aforementioned "Tears To Forget," and "All Your Lies." "Heretic" shows up first in the track list, giving it the distinction of being the first officially released Soundgarden song. Beginning with a faint "one, two, three, one, two, three" count-in, "Heretic" is propelled by a reverb-drenched riff written by Thayil. Chris adds his own stamp on the song thanks to some truly abrasive screeching, before sliding into a more thoughtful, double-tracked vocal on the verses. It's a song filled with images of witches burning at stakes, blood consumption, and spell-casting. The menacing lyrics were written in service to a more pointed allegory about scientists being persecuted throughout history only to be vindicated much later.

In addition to its distinction as the first Soundgarden song, "Heretic" also played an important part in Chris's development as a singer, or, to put it more precisely, a screamer. Yamamoto, who wrote the lyrics, was a limited vocalist and opted to scream the words when demonstrating it to the rest of the band. It was the blueprint that Chris was familiar with, so he pushed himself in rehearsals to capture the bass player's abrasive fury. That's when he made a shocking discovery.

One day as he was singing "Heretic" up to what he thought was his highest limit, his voice pierced through and all of a sudden, he discovered he had a whole new palette of glass-shattering highs to play with. His dynamic range stretched far beyond what he previously thought possible: four entire octaves. It took months of trial and error before he learned how to access them at will, but once he did, Chris's gave Soundgarden's sound a whole new dimension.

"Tears to Forget" came next in the *Deep Six* track listing. It's a rage-fueled track in which Chris busts out his most grating, hardcore screamo voice over a frenzy of guitars that sound more pissed off than a gasoline-soaked wasps' nest set on fire. Thayil used one of the leftover recording tracks to mix in an additional layer of feedback, giving the song an extra dose of abrasive aggression.

Finally, there's "All Your Lies," Soundgarden's strongest contribution to *Deep Six*. Chris sounds particularly in command, shouting out the song's title in the opening chorus before shifting into a funky, syncopated singing pattern through the verses. Yamamoto was responsible for creating the chorus part as a counter to the main riff, while Chris introduced the lyrics during rehearsals.

The band didn't have a lot of time in the studio to mess around during their lone *Deep Six* session, and they were all business once they got there. "Chris was, number one, very quiet. He didn't get very chatty in the studio. Just very purposeful," Hanzsek recalled. "It was almost as if it was just another day at work. The other thing I remember was that he was very switchable. In other words, you could see him be very calm sitting on an easy chair, and then when it was time to get up in front of the mic, he'd simply turn it on and give into that spirit or the mindset and deliver it, then come back and have a listen. There wasn't a lot of futzing around with, 'Oh wait a minute, I'm not ready,' or, 'I don't feel like it.' He was very in control of what he was doing as a singer."

After recording was completed on *Deep Six*, Hanzsek allowed some of the members from each band to help mix their respective tracks during a quick, four-hour window. It was his attempt to give the various bands a say in how their music would sound. But that old adage about too many cooks in the kitchen making bad soup proved true. "Tears to Forget" suffers the most from what Thayil ascribes to a fight that broke out between Hanzsek and Casale that sidetracked the session and affected the final mix, burdening the songs with a noticeable muddiness. It wouldn't be the last suite of Soungarden songs to be impacted by a fraught mixing process.

Just prior to the release of *Deep Six*, Soundgarden played a Halloween show at an artist studio in Belltown. In attendance that night was a young woman familiar to Chris. Her name was Susan Silver.

Silver was dressed up for the evening in an over-the-top drag outfit that included a kimono, a blonde wig and about a pound of makeup. "I told Susan for half a year from when I first saw this band that you gotta see this band," Sub Pop cofounder Jonathan Poneman said. The Halloween show provided the perfect setting to see what all the fuss was about.

Soundgarden raced through their repertoire and, when they were done, Chris stepped off stage and sought out Susan. Though not a musician, Silver was a prominent member of the local music scene. She had briefly taken over management duties for the chaotic U-Men around 1983, while also booking shows at a short-lived all-ages club called Metropolis. She was vastly intelligent—she had studied Mandarin at the University of Washington, figuring that either the Chinese or the internet would take over the global economy at some point—with a keen business savvy that set her apart from other promoters, bands, and labels hoping to pull one over on her.

Silver learned the ins and outs of the music industry from the ground up. "After Metropolis was forced to close, I was putting shows on wherever I could find a venue, not working in a particular club," she wrote in *Rip* magazine. "And then on bigger shows I was doing production work, whether it was running or catering, working in the production office, different aspects of working for the biggest promoters in town."[28]

Chris had made attempts to capture Susan's attention well ahead of the Halloween gig. He'd frequently gone into a local vintage clothing store called Tootsie's where she worked, in order to strike up casual conversations—as one of the only stores in Seattle that stocked Doc Marten boots, a staple of the underground rocker uniform, it was a vital outlet for musicians' clothes. But Silver, who had recently ended a relationship with Red Masque singer Gordon Doucette, either wasn't picking up on his subtle advances or wasn't in a position to reciprocate.

That all changed on Halloween. Chris mentioned that Soundgarden had been trying to land some gigs up around Vancouver in Canada but wasn't having any luck. He wanted to know if she could help them by reaching out to some of her contacts in the area. It just so happened that Susan was planning a trip up north the following week and offered to bring a tape of their music with her to show to some promoters she knew.

Chris and Susan ran into each other a week later at a show at a punk rock club called the Vogue. Afterwards, they went to an all-night diner and talked for hours. "He seemed like a true and good human being, which turned out to be right."[29] After that they tried to head back to Susan's place, but she had misplaced her keys. With nowhere else to go, they made out for a while, before he gave her a lift to her mother's house in West Seattle.

Chris didn't have a great deal of experience with women. He had his first real relationship around the time he was sixteen. It was a tumultuous affair that ended in a bizarre act of violence. One night while hanging out, his girlfriend attacked him with a knife. Chris put his hand up to deflect her and the blade went right through the front and out the back. Blood poured down his arm. Chris ran out the front door, hopped over a wall, and jetted down the dark street. It was one o' clock in the morning, and he was walking down the freeway, heading home while staring at his wounded, bleeding hand, when she appeared behind him with her dog, off its leash.

His next girlfriend was even more dramatic. She attempted suicide while they were together and also tried to kill her own mother. "When you're at that age, you kind of think, 'Oh, this is what relationships are,'" he said. "This is the first thing that's happening to me, so I'm assuming there's more like this, and then that was true." [30]

The emotions that Susan evoked inside of Chris were intoxicating, but also confusing. "I was so fiercely independent that falling in love was a really terrifying experience," he said. The feelings were so intense that he actually went through an entire two-month period where he didn't physically open his mouth and speak to anyone but Susan. For Chris, this fledgling relationship was "the first time I was in love to the degree that I realized this person has suddenly become so important to me that I can't imagine life without her."[31]

As Susan took up more of his time and attention, Chris's duties with Soundgarden increased as well. *Deep Six* was finally released in March 1986 with an initial pressing of just two thousand copies. It took three years to sell them all off. Largely cut off from the rest of the country and the larger rock world, it was beyond challenging to get people to give a shit about anything that was happening in Seattle at that time. Local legend Jimi Hendrix had to join the Army, move to New York, and then to London before anyone took notice of what he was capable of. Heart had to relocate to Canada before anyone took them seriously. To the music industry, Seattle wasn't even an afterthought.

Despite *Deep Six's* miniscule sales, for all the bands involved, the seemingly impossible act of putting their songs on an actual record felt like a major accomplishment. "Just having the finalized thing in your hands, that was the fulfillment of a small dream," Mark Arm said. "It's crazy. Like, 'This almost makes us a real band!'"

To herald the release of the new compilation, C/Z Records mailed out two hundred or so promo copies to radio stations around the world and booked a two-night record release show at UCT Hall on March 21 and 22 respectively. Soundgarden played the first night, just after the Melvins and before Green River. The U-Men headlined the second evening, with Malfunkshun and Skin Yard opening up. By all accounts, both gigs were highly charged, extremely loud showcases of all six groups on the record. Kim Thayil wore a denim jacket and played a Guild S-100 guitar. He'd yet to grow out the long, dark beard that would soon become his signature. Chris went shirtless, wore ripped-up jeans, and had a giant sticker on his right arm.

The reaction to *Deep Six* among the local critical community was largely positive. In her review of the compilation for the *Rocket*, Dawn Anderson wrote, "The fact that none of these bands could open for Metallica or the Exploited without suffering abuse merely proves how thoroughly the underground's absorbed certain influences, resulting in music that isn't punk-metal but a third sound distinct from either."[32] Talking to me later, she said, "I loved all of them, but I thought Soundgarden had the most potential to be popular outside of Seattle, because their songwriting was so much stronger."

For his column in the *Rocket*, "Sub Pop," Bruce Pavitt was even more effusive. "Green River, Sound Garden, The Melvins, Malfunkshun, and even Skin Yard prove that you don't have to live in the suburbs and have a low I.Q. to do some *serious* headbanging," he wrote. "This record rocks."[33] In a later piece about Soundgarden, he distilled the band's essence down to a powerful all-encompassing phrase that the band adopted as their unofficial tagline:

"Total Fucking Godhead."

CHAPTER III

SUB POP ROCK CITY

t was an unseasonably chilly evening in Seattle on July 30, 1985. Having just finished band practice, Jonathan Poneman was driving his buddy Mark home when he decided to swing through the University District to settle up with the promoter of a small venue named the (Fabulous) Rainbow Tavern.

Poneman had recently moved from Toledo, Ohio, and enrolled at the University of Washington where he landed a role as one of the DJs for the college's Audioasis hour on KCMU. To help raise funds for the station, he started booking and promoting a weekly showcase of local bands at the Rainbow. It was a good look for the station, building a tangible link between themselves and the musicians within the local music scene. It was also a good look for the Rainbow who figured that whatever young band might play that typically sleepy weekday evening would bring in at least a few dozen of their friends eager to spend their money on drinks.

Through the large window at the front of the venue, Poneman could see the opening band Skin Yard was onstage. He liked what he heard, and was especially taken by their drummer, a kid named Matt Cameron who was playing out of his mind. "I thought, 'This is a guy who's a cut above everyone else,'" Poneman said. "The guitar player was good, the bass player was good, but the drummer was really great." Skin Yard's singer Ben McMillan, also a KCMU DJ, had lobbied Poneman hard for this Tuesday night slot and was glad to get it, but he also had an added request. "He said, 'Would you entertain putting on a show with my band and K-Clone's band?'"

K-Clone was another on-air talent at KCMU: the alter-ego of Kim Thayil. His band had only been together for about seven months and didn't even have a single out yet. "I didn't know Kim, I just knew him as his air name," Poneman said. "I remember Ben mentioning Hiro from the Altered was in this band, and I used to like the Altered." McMillan's co-sign, along with his affinity for Hiro Yamamoto's other group, was enough for Poneman to add Soundgarden to the bill, despite their hippie-dippy name.

Soundgarden hit the stage after Skin Yard, and Poneman hung around for a bit to hear K-Clone and Yamamoto for himself. A few dozen people seated in chairs dotting the floor watched the four-piece group as they launched into their rage-fueled set. They opened with "No Wrong No Right," and Poneman's eyes widened. Brimming with menace and stacked frenetic guitar runs, this was about as far from shoe-gazing hippie jams as it got.

Yamamoto and Thayil concocted an impressive cacophony, but Poneman couldn't take his eyes off the young lead singer. Chris Cornell was unlike anything he'd ever seen before. He was a total rock star in the making, with more raw, untapped talent and charisma than any of his local peers could ever hope to have. "Chris was bare-chested, as he was apt to be," Poneman recalled. "He was buff and had one of those teenager mustaches. He kinda reminded me of a high school football player on a PCP bender. He didn't look like he belonged there, but his voice was incredible. His stage presence was unbelievable."

Poneman ended up staying for the entire set. When it was over, he raced to say hello to the band. "I walked up to the front of the stage after and introduced myself to Chris, and I said, 'My name is Jonathan, I'm the host of Audioasis and I do the booking down here, and I gotta tell you, that was one of the best shows I've seen in my whole life.'" Chris listened thoughtfully as Poneman gushed over his singing, his music, and his band. "I remember him sitting there, nodding his head and smiling, saying 'That's great!'"

Soundgarden hadn't even played ten shows together, and even this small bit of encouragement from someone like Poneman meant a lot. "He was the first person to me that planted that seed that, 'You guys will be the future of rock music,'" Chris remembered. "You guys will be playing huge places. You guys will be the ones on commercial rock radio stations that kids listen to in their Camaros."[1]

That show at the Tavern that brusque summer night began as just another gig for Soundgarden. Chris had no way of knowing that the guy who booked them, sight unseen, would start up a record label of his own called Sub Pop. He had no way of knowing that Poneman would ultimately use Soundgarden as a critical springboard to showcase the best rock and roll the Pacific Northwest had to offer the world. To borrow a phrase from Bruce Springsteen's legendary manager Jon Landau, Poneman glimpsed the future of rock and roll that night at the Rainbow, and its name was Soundgarden.

"When I went into that Rainbow show, I was a struggling musician," he said. "When I walked out of that Rainbow show, I was a struggling someday-to-be record-label head. When you confront that sort of brilliance, you just go, 'Wow!'"

* * *

Soundgarden didn't allow the lack of enthusiasm for *Deep Six* to deter them from pushing forward. Just a little over a month after the record release show at UCT Hall, they made their television debut on the Seattle public access channel. KCMU was hosting a benefit concert at the Rainbow Tavern on June 7, 1986, and Soundgarden was one of the bands chosen to appear on the bill that was being broadcast across the region. The footage survives to this day, and it's remarkable. Chris is nearly twenty-two years old but looks more like seventeen with his clean-shaven baby face. He wails away in a white tank top that barely covers his midriff while Yamamoto, Thayil, and Sundquist create a searing maelstrom of noise behind him.

Chris had moved out of Yamamoto's place by now and was living with his brother Peter at a little blue house at 625 Melrose Avenue on Capitol Hill overlooking I-5. It was a typical Seattle hillside home, with winding cement stairs that led to a wooden porch and then the front door. One of the nicer amenities was the large picture window from which one could see clear to the Space Needle and Puget Sound just beyond while still sitting on the couch. It's gone now, replaced by condos: the classic Seattle story.

Peter was on his way out, and Chris was in search of a roommate to help cover the $350 monthly rent. He would've preferred to live by himself, but it was almost impossible to make it work on a line cook's salary. He decided to call up his friend Stone Gossard, the guitarist for Green River, to see if he'd be interested in taking over Peter's room. Gossard was still living at home with his parents and preferred that set-up to sharing a space with another musician and paying for the luxury. Before hopping off the call, however, Gossard mentioned that their mutual buddy Andrew Wood had just gotten out of rehab and was looking for a place to live.

Chris knew Andy as the charismatic, blonde, and boisterous lead singer of a local group called Malfunkshun. "I thought, 'Well that would be interesting. He seems like an interesting guy,'" Chris said. "I called Andy up, and he's like, 'Sure, I'm coming over.'"[2] Given the choice between moving back to Bainbridge Island and living with his parents or staying around Seattle and sharing a space with a notably sober Chris Cornell, it wasn't much of a choice at all. After settling up with Chris's brother Peter over two months of rent he had already laid down, Wood moved into the house and officially became Chris's roommate.

"He seemed like a quiet guy. Very soft-spoken," Andrew's brother Kevin Wood said about Chris. Kevin was the guitar player in Malfunkshun and spent a lot of time jamming and rehearsing at their house. "You walk in and it's a small living room to the left with a fireplace and a mantle. There was a picture of Susan Silver on the mantle. To the right, there was a dining area. They didn't have it set up so much. There was a little round table. And then a kitchen toward the back of the house. The place we played was off to the left through a little door through the side of the living room."

Shortly after Wood moved in, the singer's girlfriend Xana La Fuente became a fixture. "At that time, Chris was working part time at this clothing store, Retro Viva, this really cool vintage store," she recalled. The store was run by Scott Sundquist's ex-wife Cindy, so it was a natural fit to make some quick cash. "He always wore shirts that were ripped all down the sides. He'd cut t-shirts off and he'd use the arms to make little bracelets."

The house gained one more occupant after Chris came home one day and caught a burglar going out the window with some of their stuff. As a remedial home security measure, he went out and got a black Labrador named Bill, who became a near-constant companion. "From that time on it was just music, Bill, and hanging out with Susan," La Fuente remembered.

Bill quickly became a key member of Chris's crew. If he and his group of friends were heading out at night to one of the parks around the University of Washington to drink beers, jump off bridges, and skinny dip, Bill was right there along for the ride. He didn't like other dogs or small children but was as loyal to Chris as they come. One of Chris's favorite pastimes was to crack open a few Fosters with his friends and let Bill run loose. Together, the group would scramble to try and corral and catch him. They hardly ever succeeded.

In almost every conceivable way outside of their love of music, Chris Cornell and Andrew Wood were near-diametric opposites of one another. The former was quiet, with dark curly hair and sharp features; intense and magnetizing, but with a goofy personality that undercut his more intense, stoic side. The latter was almost cherubic in appearance, gregarious, outgoing: the life of every party. "He was always on," Chris observed. "Always pretty comical and wild and funny and great, but when he put on the makeup, he'd really go somewhere else."[3]

The makeup was a critical component of Wood's onstage alter-ego, L'Andrew the Love God, a character he created years earlier after watching an episode of *Star Trek*. L'Andrew would show up to Malfunkshun gigs with teased-up hair, decked out in whiteface, regaling the crowd in front of him with zany stories about his home Olympus. It was odd, but incredibly entertaining. One time when he and Chris were walking down the street with their friends, a limousine full of kids heading to prom blew past, and Wood, in full L'Andrew regalia, gave chase, screaming that they had forgotten him.

Wood wasn't the only one in the house given to performing under an alter-ego. Around the same time the pair had become roommates, while he was still trying to get Soundgarden off the ground, Chris became a nominal member of a parody western swing band called the Center for Disease Control Boys. He went by the name "Jake" and performed drums while standing up and wearing overalls. No shirt underneath, of course. Jonathan Poneman and Ben McMillan were members as well and played bass and cowbell respectively.

The Center for Disease Control Boys performed eight or nine shows throughout 1986, mostly at the Ditto Tavern, where they played country classics by the likes of Bob Wills and Woody Guthrie while surrounded by stuffed roosters, rubber trout, and bales of hay. They printed their own "country currency," which they tossed out into the crowd as a swipe at the Federal Reserve and the concept of the dollar itself. The group released a single called "We're the Center for Disease Control Boys." In it, Chris sings his small part in an exaggerated, hiccup-filled country style. The B-side, titled "Who We Hatin' Now, Mr. Reagan?" is something like the Flying Burrito Brothers meets the Replacements meets Weird Al Yankovic.

Chris and Andrew Wood were distinct in the way they created music. "He seemed to really have no editing voice in his head at all," Chris recalled. The future Mother Love Bone singer was open in his writing process, only worrying later if it was worthy of making it onto his band's next record. "I had an editorial staff in my head arguing about what I'm doing. I took that definitely from him as a lesson to just chill out and be creative."[4]

From Chris, Wood learned more about the nuts and bolts of composition. "Andrew was in awe of Chris," Kevin Wood said. "I remember him playing demos Chris was making and just really being in awe of his ability to write." Though Wood was slightly more prolific, Chris had a more sophisticated sense of music. "He knew a lot more chords than Andy, I guess. [Andy] did feel like he was jealous in a way."

Despite their many differences, Chris and Andy got along well and pushed each other creatively. "There was a period of time when he would sit in his bedroom across the hall from mine and we would kind of have these dueling four-track demos and songs," Chris recalled. "He wasn't doing it for Malfunkshun and me doing it for Soundgarden; it had nothing to do with that. It was us just having fun."[5]

When it came time to hunker down, there was a special place in the house where Chris liked to retreat with his tape machine. "The boiler room was always where he hid out and recorded music," La Fuente said. "That's where he did the original version of 'Wooden Jesus,' which sounded totally different. He used all these weird instruments, like clanging and stuff."

There was something about austere spaces that sparked Chris's creativity. "Susan had once rented a house up in the Sand Point area, a small house with no view and rental-house carpet and nothing really to look at," he recalled. "It wasn't an inspiring atmosphere at all. But I had an incredible amount of luck writing in that house."[6]

As the months flew by, the bond between Chris and Andy deepened. "It felt like him and I together, in the same town, or in the same world, doing these things at the same time...in a sense it was like we were in a band," Chris said. "We were a team."[7]

Though much of the work they created together, collected onto simple cassette tapes they passed around to friends or hoarded for themselves, remains lost to history, one song, "Island Of Summer," made it out into the world decades after the fact with the release of a documentary about Wood titled *Malfunkshun: The Andrew Wood Story*. Chris wrote the song, a hazy acoustic piece in which the two men sing over the top of each other about redemption, love, and the passage of time. It's an extremely loose composition, more the germ of an idea than an actual song. Nevertheless, it illustrates the contrast in the ways each approached singing, with Cornell intermittently shooting off into higher pitches while adding a "woo" here and there and Wood maintaining a perfect mid-tempo delivery throughout.

The lo-fi musical experiments and his dalliance with irreverent country music were fun and productive distractions, but Chris's focus remained fixed on Soundgarden. Before the band could plot their next serious steps, however, there was a looming situation they had to contend with involving their drummer. The age gap between Sundquist and the rest of Soundgarden was becoming an issue. As the band plotted their musical future, they understood that it included a heavy amount of touring. Unfortunately, the prospect was a non-starter for Sundquist, who had his family to consider.

Sundquist's son was seven years old, and he and his wife were in a nebulous on-again/off-again status, which meant that he was often a single parent. Long weeks tearing up America's interstate system simply weren't feasible. Sundquist had to leave. It was an agonizing realization for Chris especially, who had formed a strong bond with the drummer going back to their time together at Ray's.

As Soundgarden thought about who they could possibly get to replace Scott Sundquist, one name loomed above all others. "I remember Chris, Kim, and Hiro coming by the Fabulous Rainbow after letting Scott go, and they weren't psyched because Scott was a good friend of theirs," Jonanathan Poneman recalled. "They came by and said they had done it and were gonna start playing with Matt, and I was like, 'Yes!'"

Born on November 28, 1962, Matt Cameron was only about a year-and-a-half older than Chris. He had started playing drums when he was nine years old and, just like Kim Thayil, his rock and roll interests were ignited by the colorful bombast of KISS. In fact, the first time he ever performed in front of an audience was during an eighth-grade talent show as part of a KISS cover band, fully decked out in Peter Criss makeup and a spray-painted gray wig.

Incredibly, Cameron's childhood band received a cease and desist letter from KISS's management to stop performing their repertoire. The band's big sin was calling themselves "kiss" in lowercase, instead of some cheesy cover band name like Black Diamond or Gene Simmons's Tongue. Later, as a teen, he got to meet Paul Stanley. "We gave him a photo album of all of these photos of us playing their stuff," he recalled. "He just looked at it and went 'Yeah, whatever, kid.' And then he was off to soundcheck. We were like 'Whoa!'"[8]

Long before Dave Grohl made Foo Fighters a household name, Cameron notched his recording debut in 1978 under the pseudonym "Foo Cameron" while singing a song called "Puberty Love" in the film *Attack of the Killer Tomatoes*. The nickname derived from Cameron's older brother Pete's inability to pronounce the word "Matthew," instead saying "Ma Foo."

The drummer moved north to gloomy Seattle around 1983 after receiving an invitation to visit from his friend and former bandmate Glenn Slater. The sandy-haired San Diegan made quite an impression early on, first with a group called Bam Bam and then with Daniel House in a band called Feedback. That's where he first impressed Chris and disabused the singer of his own notions of remaining behind a kit. "His drumming abilities match Chris's singing abilities," Stuart Hallerman observed. "Matt wouldn't admit to that, but it's true."

After Feedback folded, Cameron and House linked up with Jack Endino and a singer named Ben McMillan to form Skin Yard. Their first show took place on June 7, 1985, at Oddfellows Hall when they opened for one of Seattle's wildest groups, the U-Men. Over the next year and a half, Cameron was the reliable engine that drove Skin Yard to become one of the more buzzed-about bands in the Seattle underground.

"Everyone in the audience would be watching the drummer," Jack Endino said with mock indignation. "We were okay, but everyone knew we had a world-class drummer in our band, and he sorta upstaged everybody without even trying because he was just so good. He's able to do anything."

After a while, however, Cameron grew weary of playing in Skin Yard and told his band mates he wanted out. He said he wanted to try jazz but was open to playing rock if the right opportunity came along. Just like that, it did. Cameron was already a fan when he heard Soundgarden was looking for a new drummer. He called Kim Thayil to see if they were interested in adding him to the lineup. "I always tried to make their shows whenever they played," he said. "I was always impressed with Chris' natural charisma, and Hiro, the bass player, was fantastic."[9]

Before they brought Cameron on board around September 1986, Soundgarden tried out Scott McCollum from the band 64 Spiders. McCollum's audition went well enough that they almost offered him the job, but when the opportunity with Cameron popped up, Cornell had to make the call to his buddy that he was out. McCollum eventually took Cameron's place in Skin Yard around 1987.

Soundgarden got together with Cameron in Chris's living room at his place in Capitol Hill. It wasn't quite a formal audition *per se*, but they showed him how to play most of their repertoire. Cameron sat down behind Chris's rudimentary, rusted Tama kit and kicked into a song called "Ocean Fronts." The drummer kept pace with the song's extended intro, and then Chris began to wail. Cameron was floored by the volume that came out of Chris's mouth and tried to match it on the kit. "When the song was over Chris turned to me with a big smile on his face and said, 'You played it perfectly, we have a gig at the Central in one week, want to do it?'"[10]

Though Cameron already knew how to play some songs like "Heretic," and "Incessent Mace," the show was a trial by fire. Scott Sundquist stood in the front row, offering on-the-fly advice about the volume of his kick drum or chiding him when he began to play a little too fast. But Cameron had passed the "test" with flying colors. As Jack Endino observed, "As soon as I heard Soundgarden with Matt on the drums, I thought, 'That's it, these guys are gonna do pretty well.'"

Instantly, Cameron proved to be a steadying force in Soundgarden. "I think Matt's kind of easygoing and perhaps a little better adjusted socially in terms of temperament," Thayil said. "He's a good balance to the volatility to the other personalities in the band."[11] Cameron also brought a keen ability to translate the off-kilter time signatures that the other three guys in the group cooked up in their own songwriting into digestible, listener-friendly patterns that disguised some of their inherent complexity. That gift above all others made him the perfect musician to man the drums in Soundgarden.

Cameron's superior musicianship gave Chris the confidence that Soundgarden was a force to be reckoned with as they entered the many seedy clubs and bars that comprised the underground circuit around Washington State. "The first tours we did with Matt, you know, we're going to clubs in towns where you're just sort of intimidated," he said on SiriusXM Radio. "You go into these dirty, dingy clubs that are dark. And they stink like rotten alcohol, you know, and there's guys with neck tattoos wandering around, mopping up, and everyone seems to hate you." When Cameron started pounding his toms, smacking his snare, and annihilating his kick drum, the tattooed set loosened up. "He was the only one in the band, at that time, that had that power, so it made me go, 'Oh, we can hold our head up!' It was very important."[12]

Soundgarden had all the pieces they needed to move forward. They had the dynamic frontman. They had the abrasive and inventive guitarist. They had the cerebral bassist with a punk rock edge. And now they had the drummer who could handle anything thrown at him. All they really needed was someone to come along and help them make a record. That's about the time that Jonathan Poneman entered the picture.

After seeing Soundgarden play at the Rainbow, Poneman made it his mission to help them put out an album. It didn't matter that he didn't have an iota of experience running a label or any clue how to promote and distribute an album, he *needed* to be in the Soundgarden business. Originally, they brought him onboard as their manager, though he considered himself more akin to a booster, or a mascot. "I performed exactly one managerial act, which was [that] I called the Railway Club in Vancouver, which is a music venue and a great punk rock shit hole, and I cancelled their show, because they said they don't wanna go up and play there," Poneman remembered.

When it became obvious that Poneman might be better suited to the label side of things, he relinquished his role as manager and began plotting out ways to help them record and release their debut. Poneman had the resources and conviction to help make their dream a reality What he didn't have were the connections, clout, and insight to the larger industry. Fortunately, he knew someone who did.

Bruce Pavitt had been close friends with Kim Thayil for years. He had dated one of the guitarist's two sisters and was already heavily into Soundgarden, as evidenced by his rosy write-ups in his Sub Pop column in the *Rocket*. "To walk into a Soundgarden show and there's only nine other people in the room, it exaggerated the sense of community there and the sense of drama," Pavitt told author Michael Azerrad. "It made everything that came out of the speakers sound like the voice of God."[13]

Pavitt had spent the last couple years before 1986 writing, DJ-ing, and releasing a variety of cassette compilations which allowed him to scrape by a living. In July 1986, he became a record label of one after putting out his first formal LP, a collection of underground rock music dubbed *Sub Pop 100*. With contributions from bands like Sonic Youth, Naked Raygun, Scratch Acid, and Skinny Puppy, *Sub Pop 100* made some noise on the underground circuit and sold out all five thousand copies pretty quickly.

The wheels of Poneman and Pavitt's eventual partnership were set into motion one evening when the former walked into the Oxford Tavern and caught sight of his favorite band meeting with the latter. Poneman's heart sank. "I got real territorial, because Bruce had a record label. Nevermind that he had no money," he said. "After I confronted Kim and was like 'How dare you?' That's when he said, 'You guys should think about working together.'"

After a whirlwind of back-and-forth phone calls with Thayil acting as go-between, the two men decided to give it a shot. The opportunity to work with Soundgarden along with other local bands like Green River, Fluid, Swallow, and Blood Circus was too enticing to pass up. Poneman had about $15,000 from a savings bond that he'd saved from the time that he was a kid, which he decided to cash in and invest in the label. "I was coming in as an investor, but Bruce and I hit it off so well that we decided to make a go at doing the Sub Pop you know now. Going out of business since 1988," he said. "But it started off as Bruce and I getting together over Soundgarden."

The negotiations between Soundgarden and their would-be label bosses went smoothly. The contract was written out in longhand on four sheets of loose-leaf paper with the label agreeing to "loan Soundgarden three thousand dollars for the production and manufacture of phono-graph records." They also agreed to "provide $1,000.00 for promotion of aforementioned Soundgarden record." And, on the back end, "After man-ufacturing costs are deducted, Sup-Pop [sic] will pay Soundgarden 20% of the remaining net profits. This will be determined on a wholesale cost of $4 per unit."

Thanks in part to an assist from Stuart Hallerman, Soundgarden had more than enough songs to make a true, full-length album. "A few months after they did their *Deep Six* contributions, they're like, 'Hey, we wanna record some stuff,'" Hallerman recalled. "I got invited up to Seattle to record them. And then Chris, instead of me bringing my four-track, he said his brother already had one, so it was already in the house. It was over by Green Lake."

Despite their desire to make a capital-*A* Album, Pavitt convinced the band to cull everything down into a six-track EP instead. His reason-ing, according to Thayil, was that there was an ocean's worth of unknown indie bands vying for the attentions of a small pond of potential fans. Why charge nine dollars for ten or twelve songs, when you could make it easier for them to take a chance by only asking for six bucks? The band agreed.

Soundgarden tapped their friend Jack Endino to produce, and in July 1986, the five men entered a dark, triangular-shaped former antique store that had been refurbished into a studio, fitted with a rudimentary Otari MX5050 MkIII eight-track console. It was called Reciprocal Recordings. The band worked quickly and efficiently, taking only three or four days to record the rhythm tracks, which were all done live. Chris added his vocals later. Under better circumstances, they would've preferred to take more time to work on the songs in the studio, but the demand from their day jobs, especially for Cameron, who was working at the Kinko's copy shop in the University District alongside a portly singer named Tad Doyle, made it impossible.

"They were paying for it themselves, so they would come in pretty regularly, and we would record a couple more songs and try to finish them," Endino said. "They were steady customers. They'd come in every week or two and do a little more work." At $15 an hour or about $150 for a day's work, Reciprocal's rates put it within financial reach for a hand-to-mouth band like Soundgarden to slowly piece together their debut one or two songs at a time. When the final receipts were tallied up, the entire EP cost them around $3,000.

The band decided to title the project *Screaming Life*, and while they spent many of the late months of 1986 into the early months of 1987 working on it, the vast sum of the songs were all written in about a two-week span. Of the six tracks that made it onto the EP's final cut, only two songs, "Tears to Forget" and "Entering," were staples of the band's live show at that point. Other songs they worked on, like "Toy Box" and "The Telephantasm," remained tucked away, only to be revisited on subsequent releases decades later.

Screaming Life is a collection of some of the rawest, most visceral recordings that Soundgarden ever made. Most of the music was put together by Yamamoto and Thayil, with Chris contributing lyrics. Nuance was sacrificed at the altar of aggression. The haunting "Nothing To Say" was an especially revelatory moment in the band's artistic development. It was the first song where Thayil experimented with drop D tuning, which gave the song a foreboding low-end heft.

Thayil had learned the tuning from Buzz Osborne, leader of the furious Melvins, after they saw the Los Angeles-based doom metal band Saint Vitus in concert together. When the show ended, the pair went back to Mark Arm's place to hang out and got into a conversation about how KISS tuned down their guitars to E-flat to make their songs sound heavier. Arm and Thayil were both planning on trying that out themselves, when Osbourne suggested they just tune the lowest E string down to D instead. It was a light-bulb moment for Thayil who had largely been playing in the standard EADGBE tuning familiar to most players.

The technique paid immediate dividends. Thayil was always one to try and find new ways to make his guitar sound as menacing as he could make it. "I asked Kim, 'What do you want your guitar to sound like?' 'I want to sound like Godzilla, knocking over buildings!'" Hallerman said.

"Nothing To Say," is a dynamic showcase of Chris's growth as a singer between the fall of '85 when he worked on *Deep Six* and the spring of

1986 when they entered the studio for *Screaming Life*. Whether it was the series of low, ominous *ooooh*s he crooned over Thayil's brontosaurus-sized riff through the intro or the way he soared to the top of his register while screaming the title of the song repeatedly in the chorus, the level of control he managed to exert over his voice is remarkable.

"I would say meticulous is a good way of putting it," Endino noted of Chris's vocal work in the studio. "He was very focused on the music and he was very hard on himself as far as trying to get a great vocal take. He wasn't crazy. He wouldn't do a million takes, but he wanted to make sure we got the great take. Sometimes if his voice wasn't working on a particular day, he'd be happy to move on to guitar or something else instead."

"Hand Of God," served as an early indicator of how adventurous and open to off-kilter ideas Soundgarden could be. The wild and wooly song opens with a passionate speech by an earnest preacher decrying the sin of vanity. The sermon was snipped from a set of old tapes that Endino came across at a yard sale. "These tapes were from the fifties, and I don't know who they were or where they were," he said. "Anyway, I pulled them out and said, you've gotta listen to these, and someone said, 'Oh, we've gotta put this on the song!' The cadence of the preacher's voice actually matched the music, and this was before digital recording, so I copied it onto eight-track at the beginning of the song and it was amazing how well it lined up."

For their debut single, Soundgarden decided to go with the EP opener "Hunted Down," a hostile, riff-driven wrecking ball of a song. The original version as written by Thayil was played a lot slower, but once they started working on it together, it sped up. Through that process it picked up an enticing, chaotic bent, hallmarked by the scratchy, discordant anti-solos that the guitarist layered in from time to time. Even at this early stage, Matt Cameron showed the rest of the band how his musical abilities surpassed his talent for keeping time, by coming up with the ingenious staccato ending that slowly fades out into oblivion. And in what would become something of a lyrical hallmark throughout the entirety of his career, Chris was already singing about dogs, in this case, a starving pack of them racing after their bleeding prey.

Soundgarden sat in on the mixing sessions with Endino as he manip-
ulated the board and tried to fine-tune the tracks. "They were very
focused on everything—levels and tones—they'd ask about the technical
aspect of what I was doing. They very much enjoyed being in the studio
and took it very seriously," the producer said.

Pavitt tapped local photographer Charles Peterson to come up with
something compelling for the cover. Peterson had been college roommates with Mark Arm and was a close buddy to Kim Thayil. He was into
the vision for the cover as outlined by Pavitt. "Bruce was really aware of
music history like Blue Note and Motown and Stax and Sun and all that,
and how that label identity thing worked," Peterson said. "He wanted to
create that. It was really kind of stumbling in the dark creating a brand,
doing what we wanted to do."

Pavitt invited Peterson to shoot Soundgarden at one of Sub Pop's regular Sunday night showcases at the Vogue Tavern, just down the road
from their offices in the Terminal Sales Building. "We all kind of loved the
almost feminine quality of Chris in that shot," he said of the photo that
made the cover. "He's got his shirt off and in 1987, that wasn't very big on
the indie scene, lemme tell ya. Still isn't. But that photo really drew in a lot
of people into the scene at the time."

Chris was ambivalent about the photo. "Their rationale for using it
was, 'Well, it's mostly Chris, but what the heck, he's sexy, the people are
gonna love it!'" he said. "I don't necessarily disagree with that, but from a
label like Sub Pop it was kinda surprising."[14]

Peterson captured the image of Chris, mouth agape with a blur of
Kim Thayil just behind him, without even looking into his viewfinder.
"Several people have commented on that photo like, 'Dude, it looks like
you're standing on a ladder,'" he said. "I did not drag a short ladder to
shows with me…I'm holding the camera over my head. You get really
comfortable with your lens and the angles and if you overdo it, you blow
off all their heads, but I got that one just right." The image was the start
of a long relationship between Peterson and Sub Pop. Many of his black-
and-white action shots of Nirvana, Pearl Jam, Mudhoney, and others are
held up as the defining images of grunge.

"At the time, there was sensuality and sexuality in music, but you had like the vapid clowns, the LA glam rock scene, you have the sterile, antiseptic new romantic and British pop at the time, and you had American hardcore, which was by and large much faster, much more didactic and full of rules," Poneman said. "This was very natural. It was rock music. There was something celebratory about that whole thing. And the confidence to present Jack Endino, Charles Peterson, Sub Pop, Soundgarden, all in this package, it was a strong introduction to what would become seen as the Seattle aesthetic."

Soundgarden's first single "Hunted Down" with the B-Side, "Nothing To Say," was released on June 1, 1987. The original run was limited to five hundred copies, all pressed on blue vinyl: number SP12a. In a canny bit of guerrilla marketing, Sub Pop used the song as their hold music for anyone calling in to the office.

Four months after the single dropped, *Screaming Life* was released. The band celebrated the milestone with a show at the Central Tavern on November 21, 1987, supported by the pride of Ellensburg, Washington, another underground group named Screaming Trees. Like "Hunted Down," *Screaming Life's* initial run was limited to five hundred special-edition copies but pressed on orange vinyl instead of blue. For the print advertisements, Sub Pop isolated the picture of Chris on the cover, and tagged it with the line: "Six Songs, Twelve Inches, Five Bucks." The "media blitz" wasn't limited to trade publications, zines and alt-weeklies. Sub Pop also sprung for a thirty-second television spot that aired locally, featuring live footage and informing those who had heard of Soundgarden or seen them live that they could "now own a little piece of them," too.

While *Screaming Life's* commercial impact was minimal, "Nothing To Say" attracted the attention of several major labels thanks to a compilation tape titled *Bands That Will Make Money* put together by KCMU's musical director, Faith Henschel. Rather than try to make the case for Seattle over the phone to A&R representatives, she figured it'd be better to let them hear for themselves what was going on around town and stacked the collection with some of the best that Seattle had to offer, including Vexed, Green River, Skin Yard, H-Hour, and Soundgarden.

Simultaneously, Soundgarden landed on the radar of SST, the most prolific and venerated label in indie rock throughout the eighties. Founded by Black Flag leader Greg Ginn in 1978, SST was a safe harbor for purveyors of post-punk and hardcore music, of which Chris Cornell was an acolyte. The opportunity to work with the same company that released albums by Meat Puppets, Saint Vitus, the Minutemen, and Hüsker Dü was the sum total of everything Soundgarden wanted. "That was our goal before Sub Pop was even a label," Chris said. "We started a band in 1984 and probably by 1986 you can say that like sixty or seventy percent of the most vital post-punk indie bands out there were either SST artists or had at least released one album on it."[15]

With interest coming their way, a growing list of shows, and obligations to Sub Pop, it became apparent to Soundgarden that they were in need of a manger to help them navigate the murky waters of the music industry. Record contracts, shady promotors, the press—it was a lot to handle all by themselves. Jonathan Poneman had been their first choice, but given his role as the head of their current label, they had to look elsewhere. When push came to shove, they collectively decided to go with someone who had both experience managing bands before and the trust of Chris in particular to look after his best interests. They chose Chris's girlfriend Susan Silver.

"She had her own resources and was a much savvier businessperson in a conventional sense than Bruce or myself," Poneman said. "I advocated for Susan being their manager because there was understandably, all of us being kind of new to this, and Chris being a natural leader of the band, there was some trepidation about the love interest coming in, but she obviously remains to this day a great manager."

From the outset, Chris was a bit wary about the proposition of comingling his romantic and musical lives. Susan wasn't into the idea when she first heard about it either. She realized, however, that no one else was coming over the hill to help Soundgarden and agreed to take on the role.

Financial practicality ultimately outweighed many of the concerns that the other members of Soundgarden might've had about Susan managing them. Frankly put, she was the perfect person for the job. "Susan

Silver was the genius," Stuart Hallerman said. "The hardest working human I knew. If she could work twenty-four/seven, she would. On the phone. In the air. Writing, fine-tooth combing, microscopically looking at contracts, arguing, defending, putting up with wrangling with all different bands too, from all different sides. She really did right by those guys."

"She's so protective as a manager that I don't think anyone's felt they weren't being taken care of," Chris told *Rolling Stone* in 1994. "There have been situations where I get caught in the middle because Susan will be angry with the band, and I come out championing the band and getting angry with her. And there's been situations where it's the complete turn-around."[16] Though their shared interest in Soundgarden and the music industry would bind them together, they made their relationship work by siloing a large portion of that part of their lives while they were at home together. It was often assumed that Chris was clued into every facet of Soundgarden's business dealings, but that wasn't always the case.

Before they could make a move to SST or a major label, Soundgarden had unfinished business with Sub Pop. *Fopp*, Soundgarden's four-song follow-up to *Screaming Life* wasn't an entirely serious endeavor. Anchored by the song "Fopp" that had originally been written and recorded by the Ohio Players for their 1975 album *Honey*, the EP is more like a twelve-inch maxi single than a legitimate entry in their official canon. In the early days, "Fopp" was just a fun toss-off that Soundgarden threw into their set to keep things interesting. A lot of their fans didn't have the slightest clue that it was a funk deep cut, mistaking it instead for one of the band's latest up-tempo rockers.

Soundgarden worked with Steve Fisk, the keyboardist in the SST-signed instrumental band Pell Mell and producer of Screaming Trees' debut *Other Worlds*. They rented out the Moore Theatre and over a single-day session laid down three separate tracks that they felt good enough to release. It was an odd choice of location. To get the recording right, Fisk utilized the Dogfish Mobile Recording Unit owned by Drew Canulette, who served as his assistant. The band played live, onstage to the empty chairs, sort of like a low-rent version of Pink Floyd playing at the Roman amphitheater in Pompeii in 1971.

Chris had actually broken into the Moore several years earlier with some friends when he was nineteen. "We ended up drunk in the alley and saw that the door was this much open, so we rattled it and there was a little bar there and we pushed it through, opened it and went inside, only, purely for the spirt of adventure," he told a crowd at the theater decades later. Once inside, Chris lit a paper bag on fire to illuminate his way through the dark, cavernous underbelly of the Moore until it burned down to his hand and he dropped it, igniting a tiny fire on the carpet. He and his buddies furiously stomped out the flames before they engulfed the entire building. Then they pressed on through the inky blackness, feeling their way forward by touching the walls on either side of them until they reached the stage. "It was all lit up in here," Chris remembered. "It was kind of a magical moment... We still didn't even really know where we were. We were just like, 'Wow!' We thought that somehow a mystical being had created it just for our momentary experience and when we left it would be gone."

During the recording, Soundgarden ran through "Fopp," as planned, and then busted out another couple of tracks to go along with it, including a cover of "Swallow My Pride," taken from local contemporaries Green River's debut, 1985 EP *Come on Down*, and a new composition written by Chris titled "Kingdom Of Come." The former track is the highlight of what became *Fopp*. Soundgarden's take on the song sears, while the Green River cover sneers. The way Chris's voice hits new crescendos while screaming "If you swallow my pride / Make me feel alriiiiiiiiiight!" through the chorus is exhilarating. The latter track is an upbeat, seventies style rocker with a title that's a pun about ejaculate. It's not exactly the most sterling entry into Soundgarden's canon, but Cameron's drumming redeems it in the end.

After recording the three tracks, Fisk got down to the business of creating a fourth. "Fopp (Fucked Up Heavy Dub Mix)" pretty much says all you need to know about the EP's second track. It's a far more adventurous, expansive, and delightfully weird take on the Ohio Players song, filled out with weird keyboard melodies and voice modulators, echo effects, and even a spoken-word section. The eighties cheese might not be to everyone's taste but showed once again Soundgarden's inclination to take odd detours.

Fopp hit shelves on August 1, 1988. It was a vinyl-only release initially, limited to three thousand copies that were packaged in black die-cut sleeves. It was never intended to be a commercial juggernaut; more of a madcap lark than anything else. To this day, it serves as an important early demonstration of the band's willingness to try off-the-wall ideas. It was that critical characteristic that would serve the band exceedingly well in the years to come.

Around this time, the band was divvying up their share of the profits from gigging and the advance from Sub Pop between them four ways to $600 a month. "Then we got sassy and switched to eight hundred dollars a month," Chris recalled. "I remember the first time I had two thousand dollars in the bank. That's when I could afford to buy a decent car that ran."[17]

Soundgarden didn't dwell on *Fopp*. Greater opportunities were looming, and their attention was centered on creating and releasing their first proper, full-length album. Meanwhile, Sub Pop was plotting a follow-up to Pavitt's relatively successful singles compilation *Sub Pop 100* with a new collection titled *Sub Pop 200*. The 20-track collection featured some of the earliest contributions from bands like Nirvana, Mudhoney, and Tad to name just a few.

"We had all these great bands and were always thinking of ways in which to feed the beast and give people more of what we thought they wanted," Poneman said. "We didn't wanna do a double album, we wanted to do a triple-EP box set. It seemed like the most extravagant, overstated thing. We figured out a way to do it and we did it. Kim Thayil himself helped shrink-wrap a bunch of those records."

For their contribution to *Sub Pop 200*, Soundgarden cooked up a song called "Sub Pop Rock City," a loose rave-up that Thayil wrote while thinking of KISS's seventies anthem "Detroit Rock City." "I thought we'd make it a little butt rock," the guitarist told *Guitar School*. "It's the only time you'll hear a boogie riff in a Soundgarden song. We threw it in mostly for humor."[18]

Even though it was created as a tongue-planted-firmly-in-cheek joke, "Sub Pop Rock City" is one of the best tracks that Soundgarden cooked up under the Sub Pop umbrella. It's not often in his life that Chris Cornell sang about things like "Sex dogs in my Chevy," for instance. He used the throwaway track to vent about some of the different aspects of the scene around town that bothered him. The same plastic people trying their best to act cool and be seen at the different venues up the Ave, over on Capitol Hill, or down around Pioneer Square. "Everyone I hate is at the party tonight!" he screams. The inclusion of both Poneman and Pavitt's voices, clipped out of messages they'd left for the band on their answering machine, remains an inspired touch.

Sub Pop 200 dropped in December 1988. While it's gone down in history as a seminal touchstone of grunge, critics were initially divided over it. Simon Reynolds, writing for *NME*, chided, "Those old and foolish enough to hanker for the next 'revolution' are wasting their time if they're looking here." Yet, he had kind words for Soundgarden: "'Sub Pop Rock City' is a crazed, pervy, twisted blowout like some dream fusion of The Pixies and Dinosaur Jr. and Screaming Trees vandalize Hendrix's 'Love Or Confusion,' with results as solar as the original."[19]

CHAPTER IV

ABSOLUTELY, UNBELIEVABLY NOT BAD

Nearly every summer in Olympia, Washington throughout the eighties, Slim Moon hosted a punk rock showcase dubbed the Capitol Lake Jam. The future Kill Rock Stars label founder was working for the state of Washington at the time and found an unlikely set of co-sponsors for his event in the form of the DARE police unit and the local parks department. In 1988 however, the show was in jeopardy. A Japanese cultural festival was set to take place the same day that he planned to host his event. Even though they'd be about half a mile apart from one another, the volume posed a problem.

Moon had booked four bands. The undercard featured a group called Swallow, another called My Name, and a trio from Aberdeen named Nirvana. Infamous Menagerie were tapped to headline. Given the conflict from the competing festival, however, Moon's only option was to move his show up two weeks to August 20. The unfortunate side effect was that Infamous Menagerie had to drop out. Moon's friend Stuart Hallerman offered a solution.

"I was like, 'I know these guys in Seattle, Soundgarden,'" Hallerman said. Moon couldn't have been more excited at the proposition of including the Sub Pop rockers on the bill. "He's like 'What?! You know

Soundgarden? Can we get their number? That'd be amazing!'" Despite their varied connections to the state capitol, and the many friends they had who attended the Evergreen State College, Soundgarden had yet to perform in Olympia. When asked by Hallerman if they'd be interested in making the sixty-mile drive south to play, they readily agreed.

Nirvana showed up early to the gig on that warm summer evening underneath the imposing, white Capitol dome, but then quickly took off to get some lunch. By the time they made it back, KFC in hand, they were running way behind. They quickly loaded their gear onto the flat-bed truck, which doubled as a stage, and performed their entire set with a bag of the Colonel's finger-licking finest perched on drummer Chad Channing's rack of toms. The Capitol Lake Jam was a big enough show for the band that Kurt Cobain recorded a commercial advertising the event where he changed his voice to portray a variety of oddball characters that he made up on the spot. Even Krist Novoselic's mom showed up to watch them play.

As the headliners, Soundgarden went on just as the sun began to set. Novoselic provided them with a rudimentary light show by pulling Nirvana's van up onto the grass and shining its headlights at them as they played. Soundgarden ran through their regular set, including "Nothing To Say" and "Fopp," which was less than three weeks old at this point. "Chris actually instructed me before the show, 'Hey, we're gonna do the remix extended version, so just do whatever you want with the effects,'" Hallerman remembered.

Their intensity made a positive impression on the young Olympia punk rock kids. Even the local DARE officer was getting into it. "It's the last song they're gonna play, the sun is gone, and they were great!" the sound guy said.

The policeman goes, "Ya know, I didn't know what to expect from this Seattle band. I thought there'd be some craziness, but this is actually really good!"

That's when Chris decided to not-so-subtley modify the lyrics to "Fopp."

"Chris starts screaming from the top of his lungs, 'Fopp and rock, suck my cock! Suck my cock! Suck my cock!'" Hallerman said. Looking back to the cop, "We shrugged at each other and I went back to the mixing board."

Much is made of the intertwined history between Soundgarden and Pearl Jam, for good reason. Soundgarden and Chris's ties to Kurt Cobain, however, were more nebulous. They shared many musical influences and knew many of the same people. They weren't friends but were friendly when they ran into each other at the Central Saloon or the Vogue.

Cobain was an admirer of Soundgarden and a big fan of *Ultramega OK*. In fact, in the spring of 1988, when Cobain posted an ad in the *Rocket* looking for a new drummer for Nirvana, he had a specific ideal in mind. "Hard, heavy, to hell with your 'looks and hair a must,'" he wrote. And for influences: "Soundgarden, Zep, Scratch Acid. Kurdt 352–0992." Chris was enamored with Nirvana's Sub Pop debut, *Bleach*, when it dropped a few years later. He later called it his favorite of all the albums released by Seattle bands in the halcyon years, before the scene blew up.

As they were plotting the next steps in their career, Nirvana looked to Soundgarden's camp for guidance. When Sub Pop approached Nirvana with a contract offer in 1990, Cobain reached out to Susan Silver for guidance, who advised him to get a lawyer. Novoselic later thanked her for "introducing us to the music industry properly" during his Rock & Roll Hall of Fame induction speech.

In 1992, Cobain was asked by *Flipside* to give his opinion about Soundgarden, which he did in his typical, piss-talking manner, albeit layered with a level of affection he didn't always include for other peers. "They used to be great, they were even better in like eighty-five when Chris Cornell had a Flock of Seagulls haircut! They were just like the Butthole Surfers, they were amazing," he said. "I really like them a lot."[1]

While it wasn't readily apparent given their different personas— Cobain, the blonde, sardonic singer who wore baggy t-shirts and flannel and Cornell the 6'2" dark-haired, shirtless rock god—they shared many of the same traits. "Over the years I've had many conversations about Chris and Kurt," Jonathan Poneman said. "The qualities where I bonded with both of them was their sense of humor and they're both not known for their sense of humor."

Speaking years later to Howard Stern, Chris reflected on Cobain's suicide. "It's a shame," he said. "It's a shame for his daughter for one. It's a shame for the fans. But really, it's a personal thing and it was a drag and I wish it didn't happen. I also think that if he had just kind of hung on for six months, who knows? Six months later he would've been a completely different guy."[2]

* * *

While Soundgarden was in talks with SST through the early months of 1988 to record their first full-length album, they also found themselves in the enviable position of being courted by several major labels. Faith Henschel's *Bands That Will Make Money* compilation tape had turned the heads of more than a few A&R reps in Los Angeles who reached out to Susan Silver to find out more about this rock group with the frenzied lead singer. No one was more surprised by this development than Chris.

It wasn't just Henschel sounding the Soundgarden alarm. Geffen Records, home to Neil Young, Guns N' Roses, Sonic Youth, and many of the biggest names in music, caught wind of Soundgarden thanks to a tip from Faith No More's drummer Mike Bordin. Chris gave Bordin a copy of one of Soundgarden's early four-track demos, which he passed along to the higher-ups at the company. Geffen was interested in what they heard, but they had a litany of competitors like Capitol, Epic, and Warner Bros. all vying for the band's attention.

It was A&M Records, however, the artist-friendly label founded by Herb Alpert and Jerry Moss in 1962, that pursued them with a border-line desperate fervor. From the minute he heard Henschel's tape, Aaron Jacoves, A&M's West Coast director of A&R, knew there was something special about Soundgarden and wanted to sign them.

"Nothing To Say" was the only song of Soungarden's included on *Bands That Will Make Money,* but Jacoves loved it and wanted to hear more. It didn't matter that they weren't officially on the roster yet or signed to Sub Pop. He fronted the band a relatively paltry sum, around

$600, to keep making music. "I offered them a little budget to just keep doing what they were doing, and we continued to go back and forth with songs," Jacoves said. "There was a song called 'Uncovered' and I think we played it a hundred times."

Jacoves was impressed by the tapes Chris sent him, but he needed to see and hear what Soundgarden was like in the flesh before he committed to bringing them into A&M. Along with his assistant Bryan Huttenhower, he flew up to Seattle to watch the band perform. "Susan Silver picked us up and we drove to Vancouver to a club called Graceland," he remembered. "We saw the band for the very first time at this…I wouldn't say empty club, but there were few people there. My recollection, it was like an acid trip without doing acid. There was Chris onstage as a rock god. I don't know any other way of describing it. The guy just had presence. It was the band of course, but Chris was the centerpiece. You just knew it."

Jacoves wasn't the only label rep blown away by Chris's star potential. Shortly after the Vancouver gig, Soundgarden played a show in Seattle, which put a spotlight on the local scene. It went down at the Vogue on First Avenue. Soundgarden shared a bill that night with Feast. "Three different labels came, and all three tried to sign us," Chris remembered. More importantly for Seattle's rock scene however, "All the individuals who represented those big labels started coming back."[3]

Representatives from Los Angeles and New York flocked to the area to raid this vast crop of undiscovered, club-hardened rock bands. It's entirely possible that bands like Nirvana, Mother Love Bone, and Alice In Chains would've been discovered eventually, but Soundgarden was a critical catalyst in drawing attention to their rain-soaked corner of the country.

Despite A&M's eagerness to ink Soundgarden to a contract, despite Jacoves's goodwill gesture of cash to help them make demo tapes, despite the promise of fatter bank accounts and worldwide distribution and promotion, and despite having just two EPs to their name on a floundering regional label, Soundgarden turned down all of the lucrative offers sent their way. They just weren't ready to make the leap. "It was partially because we were afraid to take the step to a major and didn't want to fuck ourselves or be put in a position where somebody was trying to get us to do something we didn't want to do," Chris later explained to *Spin*. "The other reason was necessity, because we were not a commercial band, and there was no commercial audience for us then."[4]

Soundgarden wasn't about to let promises of glitz and glamor derail their career before it even got started. They were wise enough to realize that if they didn't grow an audience organically, their prospects of longevity were out the window. Coupled with the bewildering math of major-label economics—like being asked to sign away your twenties to lock in a budget to make an album a decade down the line when you're in your thirties—it just seemed smarter to keep things simple.

The amount of self-confidence and clear-eyed vision it took to spurn the majors is incredible, especially coming from a band of hungry twenty-somethings still holding down day jobs. Many in Seattle couldn't understand how they could pass up on what seemed like the opportunity of a lifetime. "A lot of people thought we were being arrogant, telling the big labels to go fish, but we knew what we were doing," Chris said. "We wanted to make the record we wanted to make, and we knew the majors would still be there after we made it."[5]

While some companies were put off by the band's standoffishness, Jacoves was willing to play the long game. It helped that Soundgarden was always straight with him about their plans and intentions. "We paid for these demos and I recall that Chris called me once and said, 'There's a little label and we want to release a record'—this was before we actually signed the band—'Would you guys mind if we used some of these recordings?' I said, 'No one here is gonna mind. No one here at the label even knows who you are.' It wasn't a contractual situation at that time, so I said, 'Go ahead. Build up a story. I could use it.'"

The record Soundgarden wanted to make was eventually titled *Ultramega OK*. The name itself was kind of a joke. "Like, absolutely, unbelievably not bad," Chris explained to journalist Everett True.[6] The place they wanted to make it was SST. "It was like if the Rolling Stones made an album with Chess Records," *Our Band Could Be Your Life* author Michael Azerrad said. "SST was the coolest label on Earth at that time, at least for that crowd.... It was coveted to be on SST. It was grounds for congratulations."

Mark Pickerel, the drummer for Screaming Trees, was instrumental in making that dream happen. "We were trying to get SST to pay attention," Susan Silver told *Billboard*. "Even though I dealt with [SST owners] Chuck Dukowski and Greg Ginn as a promoter, they wouldn't talk to me as a manager. Mark Pickerel from Screaming Trees talked to them about Soundgarden and that opened the door for that."[7]

Screaming Trees had just inked with SST the year before to record their second album, *Even If and Especially When*, when Soundgarden rolled through their hometown of Ellensburg, Washington, for a gig. Pickerel was among the crowd when he noticed that his band's sound guy Rob Doak was recording the set through the venue's mixing console. After the show he asked Doak for a copy of the tape, which he passed off to Greg Ginn. Ginn liked what he heard, and after getting a few more personal recommendations from members of Saint Vitus, Das Damen, and *Fopp* producer Steve Fisk, he reached out to Soundgarden.

Before the band could officially make the jump to SST, there was one last bit of business. They had to tell Sub Pop they were leaving. There was a genuine wellspring of loyalty and affection that flowed between both sides. But as the music industry has proven time and time again, loyalty and affection doesn't count for a whole hell of lot when you're trying to build an audience. "Our relationship with Soundgarden was odd in that they were already out the door when we put *Screaming Life* out," Poneman said. "I remember Susan sitting down with me very soon after I'd first heard Nirvana, and she was saying, 'Jonathan, you have to understand the band is going to go on and do other things.' This is beyond SST, which was already a fait accompli."

Throughout the mid-to-late eighties, Sub Pop barely managed to stay afloat financially. Things sometimes got so dicey that many of the label's employees would race to cash their checks as soon as they got them so that they wouldn't bounce. For Soundgarden, the prospects of a future in music under their perennially cash-strapped banner didn't seem realistic. "It seemed like a smart and natural move to me," Poneman said. "We had dreams that they would stay on the label, but we were also pragmatic. We didn't have any money."

More than anything, the Sub Pop guys wanted Soundgarden to become a success, whether that meant releasing records for them, or releasing them for somebody else. "Bruce Pavitt from Sub Pop is the one who told us that SST was interested in putting out one of our records, and he told us we should do it," Chris recalled. "He sort of looked at it like 'Well, they can wait around for us to be able to afford it, or pay for it themselves and here's SST that wants to put out a record.'"[8] After a quick meeting with a lawyer who looked over the contract with the band in Chris's living room, Soundgarden signed a one-album deal with SST and were on their way.

Originally, the thought was to record at Reciprocal again. But then their new label suggested that they work with a producer named Drew Canulette at Dogfish Sound Studios in Newberg, Oregon, instead. Canulette, a graduate of the Evergreen State College and friend of Stuart Hallerman, first met the band back in 1985 when Chris was still playing drums. "They had a cassette they gave me, and it was good, pretty raw rock," Canulette said. "Not a very good recording, but you know, goddamn!"

Soundgarden had previously used Canulette's mobile recording setup for the *Fopp* EP so they were familiar with how it all worked. The chance to record on a sixteen-track console over Reciprocal's eight-track certainly sweetened the pot. They also appreciated the studio's relatively close proximity to Seattle, which allowed them to continue earning steady checks from their day jobs. "Drew Canulette produced based on the fact that SST had used his mobile unit for a live Black Flag record. We figured, 'Okay, he was involved in making this live Black Flag record, so he can't be a complete idiot about recording,'" Chris said.[9]

The distance between Newberg and Seattle is roughly two hundred miles, about a four-hour car ride. Initially, Canulette drove his rolling studio up to Seattle where the band tracked some of Matt Cameron's drums in a loft space overlooking University Avenue. He also tracked some of Chris's vocals in the singer's house on Melrose. "Having a truck like that, you could go anywhere and record," Canulette said. "He wanted to sing in his bedroom so, 'Sure, we can do that!' Run the snake up there, run the headphones, get the mics set up, wait for the planes to quit flying overhead and hit record."

Most of the basic tracks, however, were laid down in Oregon. "The expectation [was] that the band would stay the week initially, and then a weekend at a time while Chris and I finished up the vocals and guitars, respectively," Thayil wrote in the re-issue of *Ultramega OK's* liner notes.[10] With so much work to do in the studio to get the songs sounding how they wanted, that meant quite a few weekends cruising up and down I-5 wired on coffee, jabbering about bands, roadside billboards, and different inside jokes. "Kim and Chris were kind of a pair," Canulette recalled. "Hiro was kind of like, done. He did the basic tracks, laid down his bass tracks, and then he was done. He really didn't come down for mixing or anything."

The setting around Newberg was pastoral, at odds with the dark and heavy music Soungarden was creating. The dynamic was reminiscent to the setup that Led Zeppelin created for themselves while making some of their best records at Headley Grange in the English countryside in the seventies. "We had eight acres," Canulette recalled of his countryside spread. "It was this bucolic, rural setting. You could come out and make a lot of noise and nobody would really care."

"Our time there was broken up with shopping trips to food co-ops; dining at progressive cafes run by a collective; eating dinner prepared by Drew's then-partner Norm; exploring the farm areas that they maintained; and visiting the livestock they kept, cows named Hamburger and Hot Dog,"[11] Thayil wrote. While Chris was busy working on his vocal takes, the guitarist would typically while away the hours shooting down floating, terrestrial bodies on Canulette's Asteroid arcade game set up in the main studio room.

During their downtime one night, Soundgarden marked a special occasion. "Chris celebrated his birthday with us," Canulette remembered. "Norm made a nice dinner, made him a cake; we all had a good time." Despite their youth and the setting, Chris and the gang kept things lowkey. "There might've been a beer or two," Canulette said. "I don't remember pulling out a bottle of bourbon and saying, 'Let's get fucked up!'"

Ultramega OK is the crucial bridge between Soundgarden's past and future. "In a sense, we were going back," Chris said. "*Ultramega OK* was kind of a picture of us at the time combined with a picture of what we had been doing since we started the band."[12] Many of the songs on the record like "Beyond The Wheel" and "Incessant Mace" were originally written around the same time they were putting together *Screaming Life*. Some were even older. They also had a bevy of newly written tracks including "Mood For Trouble," "Nazi Driver," and "He Didn't," that the band had been fine-tuning before the recording process began.

Just like *Screaming Life*, *Ultramega OK* opens with the album's lead single, a trippy track titled "Flower." The song's intro immediately puts the record on an eerie footing thanks to a unique technique cooked up by Thayil where he set his guitar on the ground near his amplifier causing it to feed back. Then he blew across the strings in time with the drums to create a disorienting sitar-like effect. Chris wrote the lyrics and about a girl transforming into a woman, throwing herself into her vanity and ultimately burning out.

The second song is a rehash of one of their contributions to *Deep Six*, "All Your Lies," followed by the perplexing sonic soundscape called "665." It's shorter sibling, "667," comes shortly therafter. Written by Yamamoto, both "665" and "667" were early attempts by Soundgarden to show off their warped sense of humor. They were both designed to parody the many eighties doom metal bands and their obsession with Satan and the sign of the beast: 666.

"665" is a particularly off-putting wall of noise, based around Yamamoto rubbing his bass across an amplifier and manipulating the feedback. In its initial live form, Sundquist pitched calling it "Scraping Pig." When played backwards, Chris can be heard screaming the phrase, "Santa, I love you baby / My Christmas king, Santa, you're my king," over and over again, a tongue-in-cheek sendup of the people who thought they could hear "Here's to my sweet Satan," when they played Zeppelin's "Stairway To Heaven" backwards.

"Nazi Driver" is the most eyebrow-raising entry on the album. When they first demoed the song, it was known as "Fearbiter." The song makes no mention of Nazis, but as Thayil explained in 1989, "The song is about cutting up Nazis and making stew out of them. We used driver because it made a cool name. It sounds better than Nazi Stew, Nazi Soupmaker, Nazi Cup-O-Soup, or indeed Cup-O-Nazi."[13]

At Yamamoto's insistence, the band also covered Howlin' Wolf's 1956 blues wailer "Smokestack Lightning." Chris delivers a perfectly wounded take on Howlin' Wolf, even if he remained perplexed as to how it ended up in the final track listing. "He had amazing vocal talent," Canulette said. "His whole enunciation, the ability to go from this really booming voice to vocal fry and go back and forth and work it was pretty phenomenal."

At the heart of Chris's annoyance at the inclusion of "Smokestack Lightning" was that it bumped what he thought was a better song that Yamamato had written titled "Toy Box" off the album. The decision remained a thorn in his side for years. "I don't know if it was him, or who it was, why we wanted to put this stupid cover on the album and not put this brilliant original song instead," Chris said.[14] Either way, the snippet of Sonic Youth's "Death Valley '69" tacked on near the end of the Howlin' Wolf cut remains an inspired touch.

"Circle Of Power" is another Thayil composition but is distinct in that it marks the only time Yamamoto assumed lead vocals on a Soundgarden album. What the bassist in lacks in power, he compensates for with vocal dexterity, shifting and modulating his voice all over the song, which races across its two-minute runtime at a supersonic clip.

The musical and emotional high point on *Ultramega OK* came from a song that Chris put together called "Beyond The Wheel." Kim Thayil considers the song one of the top three tracks in the Soundgarden canon, describing it as "psychedelic, heavy," with "a little sprinkle of evil." Even more than "Incessant Mace," the disorienting, penultimate track on the record, "Beyond The Wheel" in all its psychedelic glory signaled the sonic direction that the band would pursue in the years to come. In many ways it sounds like a savage, plodding prelude to their multi-platinum break-out *Badmotorfinger*.

"This was a young man's take on our country, our government, and all governments kind of sending men off to war," Chris told a crowd in

Rockville, Florida, in 2017. "We were young men at the time we wrote this song, and at the time we didn't want our lives interrupted so that we could go out and maybe die to make people more money that we didn't know... it was about small groups of people with lots of money who don't give a shit about me, and don't give a shit about you."[15]

"Mood For Trouble" provides another small glimpse into Soundgarden's musical future. Written by Chris, the song opens with the quick strums of an acoustic guitar before kicking into a frenzy of speedily chucked off fuzzed-out chords, then descending into a hazy middle section before chaos reigns again. It's an impressively sophisticated composition that's miles beyond the band's early, straightaway punk rock ragers like "Heretic." Even at this stage of their career, Soundgarden and Chris were both exhibiting a penchant for hyper-quick, musical evolution.

To close out the record, the band slapped together an homage to Chris's hero, John Lennon, titled "One Minute Of Silence." Filled out by more than a minute of ambient feedback layered over a collection of finger snaps and other sonic additions, the piece is a tip of the cap to Lennon and Yoko Ono's track "Two Minutes Silence" from their 1969 album *Unfinished Music No. 2: Life with the Lions*. They even gave Lennon a songwriting credit for the track.

The only thing left to do before sending the tapes to SST was to mix down of the songs. By the time that step was completed, however, the whole thing sounded off to Chris's ears. The singer laid a lot of the blame at the feet of the album's producer Drew Canulette, who he thought managed to make a band as heavy as Soundgarden sound thin and brittle. "Even though I thought the material was the best material we had at the time, I started playing the demos and then started playing the real thing and it was pretty crushing," Chris said.[16]

"When we mixed that thing, we mixed it together," Canulette said. "A couple of times they had me make some adjustments, which I did by myself, but for the most part we did that record together." He added, "They didn't like my mixes or the way that record came out, but I don't know if I really accept that. A record's a record. I think *Ultramega* is a fine record by those guys. It's a perfect statement of who they were at that time."

A partial reason for the poor sound of the mix can be chalked up to the rather staid conditions of Pace Studios, where much of the post-production work was conducted. Pace was primarily utilized for commercial and business productions. They didn't take on many rock clients and weren't exactly well-equipped to accommodate their specific needs. Soundgarden and Canulette couldn't even work on the record during the week and were forced to wait until the weekend when the normal office workers cleared out.

Chris took the final mixes home and decided to compare them to the demos of some of the same songs they had recorded earlier with Jack Endino. To his ears, the songs on the official record paled in comparison to the sonic sketches they'd cooked up with Endino. Chris was crestfallen. "That was the single most exasperating and terrifying moment of my career as it pertains to Soundgarden," he said.[17]

This was a critical moment in the band's history. There was a real buzz in the air about Soundgarden within the music industry, along with the expectation that they could break out into the mainstream sometime soon; potentially even with this record. Soundgarden had turned down surefire deals from several major labels in order to make this record with SST, and now Chris felt like they might have just fucked it all up.

Despite his anxiety, *Ultramega OK* was well-received by rock critics and notched a nice write-up in the *Rocket* after it dropped on Halloween in 1988. Gillian G. Gaar wrote that, "It would be no exaggeration to call this the most highly anticipated local disc of the season," adding that, "Cornell shines and Thayil invokes some of the hottest guitar riffs in the Northwest since Hendrix was going to Franklin High School." A few months after the album dropped, Soundgarden was included among nine bands to watch in *Rolling Stone's* "On Campus" issue in March 1989.

Incredibly, *Ultramega OK* nabbed Soundgarden their first Grammy nomination in the Heavy Metal category in 1990. This was a year after Jethro Tull inexplicably beat out Metallica to receive the prize for their album *Crest Of A Knave*, causing massive amounts of confusion and anger from rock fans around the world. The night of the ceremony, Metallica ended up avenging their loss to Jethro Tull while beating out Soundgarden, Faith No More, Dokken, and another Seattle group, Queensrÿche, on the strength of their ballad, "One."

In their typical, sardonic way, the band feigned disinterest in the honor—in an interview with MTV's Riki Rachtman on *Headbanger's Ball*, Thayil claimed he "went back to sleep" after finding out about the nomination.[18] Behind closed doors however, Chris was tremendously excited about what the honor represented. "It was that first glimpse into feeling like we were being taken seriously by a broader demographic that included a jury of our peers," he said. "It was surprising, and it felt good."[19]

For a short time after it was released, there was talk among the band about revisiting *Ultramega OK*, giving the tapes to Jack Endino, and having him remix the album to achieve the sound they wanted. But, by the fall of 1988, things were moving too fast. They wouldn't get around to it until nearly three decades later.

With the nineties fast approaching, Soundgarden's dance with their major-label suitors ended when they signed with A&M Records. Soundgarden had let things drag on so long that executives were getting concerned that they wouldn't have enough quality material to work with after they finally got the band to sign. All of the music that had excited the label was being used up by SST.

Soundgarden was eager to assuage A&M's concerns with the promise of even better material, so they went back into the studio and cooked up some demos of a couple new songs. The executives were so bowled over by the new tracks that they upped their initial offer to the band. Jacoves went out of his way to set up a meeting between the band and the label's famed founder Herb Alpert, a.k.a. the "A" in A&M. Alpert immediately impressed Soundgarden with his collection of oil paintings, fine wine, and the hint of marijuana smoke that lingered in the air. A&M went a step further and licensed *Ultramega OK*, lending it the full, impressive weight of their extensive distribution and promotional arms.

Soundgarden had the music, talent, and story A&M was looking for, but they also had something else. "The rule, number one, is never have a parent or a girlfriend manage you," Aaron Jacoves said. "But Susan [Silver] just had it." He added, "She was the right person. She obviously proved herself, not just with herself but with Alice In Chains, who she also managed. She just had a great sense of who the band was and what they were trying to achieve and could communicate what they were thinking." As long as Susan Silver was at the helm, there would never be any doubt that Soundgarden was a serious group heading in the right direction.

While they finalized their deal with A&M, Soundgarden played shows throughout 1988, including an important gig on one of the side stages at the annual Bumbershoot Music Festival. "Chris took off his shirt and sang and stuff. It was a great show," Stuart Hallerman remembered. "I drove home to Olympia and my housemates and some of his friends are over, and this one girl is describing some things about Bumbershoot, and she's like 'Oh, Soundgarden was great! In the middle of the show Chris Cornell took off his shirt and all the girls were like, "Ahhhh!"' That was her review of the show. It was a group effort. They all wrote music, and they made an effort for it not to be the 'Chris Cornell Show,' but he was the star."

Soundgarden also started branching out away from Seattle, hitting venues up and down the West Coast. There was their LA debut at Club Lingerie in February and a show at the I-Beam in San Francisco where they performed "Gun" for the first time. They even took part in the annual CMJ showcase in New York City, bringing "grunge" to that bastion of punk rock, CBGB. "I vividly remember that night. I remember almost everything about it, you know, just because it was, it's such a, it's such a mecca for, you know, the New York music scene," Matt Cameron told MoPop's oral historian. "We had a blue seven-inch single out, on Sub… Pop and…the first couple rows of people, like, knew the lyrics to those two songs. So that, that kind of blew our minds."[20]

By the end of the evening, they had managed to impress the club's legendary proprietor Hilly Kristal. He recalled they got, "the biggest response since Guns N' Roses," and predicted, "They'll be playing Madison Square Garden in a year and a half."[21] Turns out, he was only about a year and a half off, but in an ironic twist, they'd do it opening for Guns N' Roses.

Early on, the band chewed up the interstate in Yamamoto's beat-up Dodge Tradesman van. It was a brutal ride. "It had no windows, no air conditioning. And that is what we took in very hot weather down the west coast," Kim Thayil remembered. "We worked in this oven for long stretches of time."[22] Visions of Minutemen guitarist D. Boon and his untimely demise after getting tossed out of the back of a van in a 1985 crash flashed in their minds, so they pooled their money together and plunked down the cash to pick up a new ride, dropping around $6,000 for a red 1986 Chevy Beauville, which they rode from one end of the country to the other over the next two years. "They were living in this thing, and they didn't wanna die on the road," Hallerman said. The industrious Yamamoto outfitted the back of van with a futon frame that they took turns sleeping on during long hauls. Beneath the frame was a storage place for their luggage and gear.

"I would always volunteer to drive, because otherwise I'd get bored," Chris said. That didn't always sit well with the other passengers in the Beauville who regularly admonished their singer for driving way past the posted speed limits. "My mission was to go as fast as I possibly could without getting a ticket. With my natural antenna for speed traps, I never received a moving violation."[23]

Every touring band needs someone to run sound and someone to help set up and tear down gear and collect the evening's take from the local promoter. The choice for their soundguy was obvious: it had to be Stuart Hallerman, their friend and faithful engineer. He quickly agreed. Choosing a road manager was a different matter altogether. Soundgarden ultimately found their guy at a show they played in Ellensburg, Washington—the same show that Mark Pickerel recorded and passed on to Greg Ginn at SST.

Eric Johnson was the station manager for Central Washington University. Every year the station sold ads to fund their operation, and when they ran a surplus, he'd book bands to play shows up in his neck of the woods. "At that time, I'd go home on the weekends to Metropolis, or Graven Image or the Grey Door, all these little punk rock shows in Seattle where Susan Silver was one of the promotors," he said. "She was always nice to all the kids. This total, maternal person for all the little punkers and skater kids. I remember calling her when I thought I was going to do some shows to ask for advice, like, 'Hey, what do I do? How do I get a band to come play here?' The first thing she suggested was, 'Why don't you do Soundgarden and Faith No More? Faith No More, I'm paying them $650, and Soundgarden, you can have them for $200 or $250.'"

Soundgarden pulled up to the gig in Matt Cameron's red Volkswagen bus and proceeded to blow the doors off the place. A few months later, after Johnson graduated and was back in Seattle, he ran into Thayil at a supermarket. By now, Johnson was carving out a little side business for himself making DIY T-shirts at home, drying them off in the broiler in his oven. He offered to make some shirts for the band to sell on tour. "The next thing I know, it's like, 'Why don't you come out and sell some shirts and be our roadie, and be our guy?'" Johnson said. "I didn't think I'd ever do it. It's just something that fell on me."

For the duration of his years on the road with Soundgarden, Johnson went by the somewhat inexplicable name "Gunny Junk." It was bequeathed to him during the band's ride to LA where they were set to play Club Lingerie. "It seemed so Hollywood to us," Johnson said. Along the way, everyone made up outlandish rock star nicknames for themselves, à la the members of Poison or Mötley Crüe. Though the other monikers have been lost to time, Gunny Junk stuck. "It was just one of those things were everyone laughed, and all of a sudden, that's what I was called."

There was a strong and friendly camaraderie between the six guys that contrasted mightily with their image onstage as dark and angry young men. "Within minute one of getting in the van with those guys, heading out of Washington, the first thing I noticed was, 'You guys get along great!'" Hallerman said. The group passed time on the road talking, laughing, and blasting tunes, though Chris wasn't always the most verbose of the bunch. "I could be in the van with him for a month and a half and we'd talk about some show necessities, a little food here and there, some good mornings and not really get into anything in-depth," Hallerman added. "Then one day he'd open up and we'd talk for like eight hours, too."

The conditions were predictably spartan for a post-punk band just starting out. "We all shared a hotel room and 'split the loaf,' as we called it. Tear the mattresses apart and two people sleep on the mattress and two people sleep on the box spring," Johnson said. "We usually had one person sleep in the van to watch the gear. Me and Cornell would usually do late-night shifts in the van. I loved sleeping in the van, so it'd usually be either me and Kim or me and Chris sleeping in there. It was fucking great! We'd stay up, drink beer, smoke cigarettes and laugh all night."

In contrast to some of their wilder contemporaries like the Replacements, for whom debauched mayhem was the point, Soundgarden was never much of a party band. "If Chris wanted to do something, we'd go late somewhere and climb a tree and drink beer," Johnson recalled. "Or go to a lake in Seattle somewhere late at night and run through the woods. Little different than most rock guys."

No matter how big Soundgarden became in the coming years, they remained circumspect about giving in to the cliché, on-the-road rock-star behavior. "We were up in Vancouver playing a show with the Melvins, and when we finished our set, [Skid Row's] Sebastian Bach was waiting for us in our dressing room all by himself, with his fist wrapped around a bottle of Jack Daniel's," Chris told *Spin* writer Jonathan Gold. "He looked at us, and he could kind of see that we were putting on our coats or something, and he was laughing hysterically; we couldn't figure out why. We all filed out. He said mid-laugh, 'I can't believe this. You guys are leaving me alone at your own show.' We all went our separate ways and he was sitting there getting fucked up in our dressing room."[24]

Despite their laid-back manner in the van, once they got on stage, Soundgarden transformed into one of the most intense and unpredictable bands in the country. "I used to call Hiro 'Mister Scary,'" Johnson remembered. "He wore this stocking cap and had the long hair and lurched back. He was fucking cool looking. To hear them play was so different. Kim with his scratch guitar and fucking weirdness. It was pretty magical. Sometimes you'd be in clubs with thirty people, but those thirty people got it."

One of the most dynamic shows the band performed during that early run took place at the Kennel Club in San Francisco on February 3, 1988. Soundgarden was booked to open for Gwar, who made quite the spectacle of themselves in their elaborate horror costumes. "When we came to the show and saw the soundcheck, we couldn't believe it," Johnson recalled. "It was like mind-blowing. We were like kids at Disneyland that we were gonna get to see this show. So, they played extra great for that show."

The real fireworks took place after the gig, however, when Hallerman decided to mess with the headliners. "Stuart said something cheeky to Slymenstra, the woman in the band," Johnson said. "So, she grabbed him by the throat and pinned him against the wall and basically said, 'I will fuck you to death!' I don't think any of us ever got over that."

Before entering the studio to get to work on their first album for A&M, Soundgarden ended their live performance schedule in 1988 with a bang. The band was selected to open for Jane's Addiction at Seattle's preeminent concert venue, the ornate Paramount Theatre, as part of a Rising Star Showcase on November 17. Chris and his band shared the bill with his friend and roommate Andrew Wood, who was now fronting a group called Mother Love Bone that had just inked a deal with PolyGram Records and were on the verge of releasing their debut EP *Shine*.

Both Chris and Andrew seemed primed for a huge jump into the rock and roll mainstream and the proposition alone sent their heads spinning. "We went from being these two roommates in these obscure bands that never thought anyone was gonna hear of. I couldn't get anybody to give us enough money to put out a new record. A few months later, we're both getting all this attention from big labels," Chris recalled. "It was pretty wild, but pretty cool to have that happen to your friend at the same time, so you could just be excited together."[25]

Shortly after Soundgarden hit the stage at 8:00 p.m., Chris used the high-profile platform to rail against critics who thought *Ultramega OK* was only *Ultramega So-So*. "Somebody said, 'Put away your Led Zeppelin records because Soundgarden is here," he told the two thousand rock fans gathered in the golden theater. "Well, put away your Soundgarden records because 'Kingdom Of Come' is here!"

It was a big deal for a local band to play a venue of this magnitude in their hometown, a milestone worth celebrating. Even though they were only the opening act, Soundgarden made the most of their time onstage. Sadly, just a little over a year later, Chris would return to the Paramount under very different, and far more tragic circumstances.

CHAPTER V

LOUD LOVE

T he year is 1988. Soundgarden is tearing down America's highways
in their Chevy Beauville, bringing their *Ultramega* sound to some
of the country's dingiest dives and sleaziest clubs. While the band
is stoked to play many different cities around the country, New Orleans
is one they're particularly looking forward to. Soundgarden was booked
to play a club called Muddy Waters, which seemed like a prime chance to
have some fun and eat some good food. "As soon as we got the itinerary,
we're like, 'That's gonna be a highlight there!'" Stuart Hallerman said.

Before they could make it to the Crescent City, the band had played
their way through East Texas, which stressed out Kim Thayil as he had
just seen the Errol Morris documentary, *The Thin Blue Line*. The film
recounted the story of a drifter named Randall Dale Adams who was sen-
tenced to death for allegedly killing a cop in Dallas. It was an egregious
miscarriage of justice. Adams hadn't committed the crime, and after
the film hit theaters he was exonerated and set free. The assumed real
killer, David Harris, was later executed for an unrelated murder. The picture the film painted of the criminal justice system in Dallas and Vidor,
Texas wasn't pretty.

Hallerman was behind the wheel for most of the journey through the
eastern portion of the Lone Star State, something like nine hours, until
they finally made it into Louisiana, where Thayil let him pull over at a

truck stop to change shifts. Soundgarden gassed up, hit the payphone to let the promoter know they were on the way, grabbed some snacks and soft drinks, and relieved their bladders before returning to the road.

Matt Cameron took over driving and pointed the Beauville east with visions of jambalaya, étouffée, and shrimp po' boys dancing in their heads. They only made it another twenty minutes down the highway, however, when flashing lights forced them over to the side of the road. "These DEA seizure cars come up behind us, which meant at the time it was like a black 280Z and just a really fucked up Camaro," Chris recalled of the plain-clothes officials who pulled them over. "They had guns in their pants, and they had neck beards, not like full-on neck beards, but just, like, neck hair, and they had this little badge which they sorta un-velcroed."

According to the agents, they had pulled the van over for failure to use a right turn signal. In fact, the authorities had caught wind of a bunch of longhairs with Washington State plates rolling through their turf, and thought they hit a drug-running jackpot. The Butthole Surfers sticker stuck to the van that they tried to cover up didn't endear them to the uptight, southern-fried DEA officers. "They made us stand in anthills on the edge of the swamp and told us stories about how they would chase people in the swamp and those people would never come out," Chris remembered of their attempts at intimidation.

Everyone got out of the van, and the DEA agents began to dig in. "They said, here's the deal; we can get a search warrant and you can stand here for as long as it takes, or you guys can sign this consent to search and we'll just do it. We'll bring the dog out, and then you'll be on your way," Eric Johnson recalled. "Me, Stuart, and Matt were probably the only guys who smoked pot," he added. "It was the South so everyone knew, don't do it. We all had an agreement: Nothing goes down there. Nothing, nothing, nothing."

Apparently, nothing didn't mean *nothing*, because after tearing through every inch of the van and coming up empty, they finally found a small bit of bud in Hallerman's tool kit next to all the microphones. Jackpot. "They take Gunny away and go, 'whose is that?'" Hallerman recalled. When told that the miniscule amount of marijuana belonged to their sound guy, the authorities started to dig in. "Well, could anyone else go in that?" The road manager responds in the negative. "No, that's Stuart's, only he goes in there."

Frustrated that they hadn't found a few bricks of cocaine, the agents pressed further. "Well, what if he was sick and someone needed a microphone, could someone else go in there?" Gunny hedged. "Well, I guess you know the answer to that," he responds. "If I needed a microphone, I guess I could go into that." The reply was music to the Louisiana DEA's ears. "That's communal property," he barked. "You're all arrested!"

As law enforcement tore apart the Beauville, they found something even more enticing than a thumbnail's worth of stale weed. Johnson's bag contained a wad of around $1,200 that the band had made from T-shirt and ticket sales, money they were using to cover their travel costs. The authorities informed the six men standing beside the highway that their cash was drug money, and subject to seizure. Johnson protested. "I said, that's not drug money, I've got receipts!" But there was simply no bargaining with the officials, who decided among themselves that the band's hard-earned savings was evidence that needed to be confiscated.

"I watched him count it, and apparently in Lake Charles there are six twenties in $100," Johnson said. With cash in hand and a measly half a gram of weed to show for their bust, the cops decide to finally let Soundgarden go on their less-than merry way. Everyone got a ticket for marijuana possession and the band hit the road again, bound for New Orleans. "They dropped all the charges against everyone but me," Hallerman said. "Then that was some suspended thing plus a fine for the miscounted amount."

The gig in New Orleans was a bust. "It turned out to be our shittiest date," Hallerman said. "It was a cinder block hut in the shittiest part of town. We played for this elderly drunk woman who danced very oddly, the bartender, and like three kids came from South Carolina, but didn't have enough money to buy a ticket, so our T-shirt guy was like, 'Can you pool enough together to buy one ticket and I'll let you all in?' Then at the end of the show, they all bought T-shirts, so they had the fucking money."

Soundgarden didn't even get as much as a bowl of gumbo out of the deal either. Already running behind, they were forced to scarf down pathetic hamburgers whipped up for them at the last minute. Years later, the memory of the injustice burned inside of Chris's stomach. "They're probably all dead from emphysema or heart attacks or something by now," he said of the crooked cops from the stage of New Orleans Voodoo Festival in 2011 while recounting the story. "Fuck them!" he added. "If you could die from stupid, they would've died from that a long time ago."

As a final, subtle *fuck you*, the band made sure to include the Louisiana DEA among those they thanked in the liner notes of their next album *Louder Than Love*.

* * *

Soundgarden were now major-label artists, with major-label sales expectations and an impending major-label push into the mainstream. There was a lot of pressure to make their next album a success. To help live up to the hype, the band decided to work with Terry Date, a well-regarded metal producer who'd forged a solid reputation for himself manning the boards for bands like Metal Church, Fifth Angel, and Dream Theater. In the years to come, he'd help Pantera create some of the biggest and most influential records in the history of the genre like *Vulgar Display of Power* and *Cowboys from Hell*.

Not everyone in the band was fully on board with the idea of working with a predominantly metal producer. Even though Hiro Yamamoto liked Date as a person, the way the bassist saw it, Soundgarden was firmly rooted firmly in punk and hardcore and their alignment with Date seemed to signify a slicker, more commercial-friendly sound. Metal was fine to listen to, but he wasn't interested in being *in* a metal band. "The label wanted to sell us to heavy-metal stations. I thought we were different than that," Yamamoto told author Mark Yarm. "Sure, I'd like to sell a million records and live in a castle and not have to work, but at the same time, I want to be able to say, 'This is me. I'm not just part of a mass-marketing machine.'"[1]

Compounding his disinterest in their shift in sound and the band's impending mass-scale commodification, was a growing dissatisfaction with touring. The shows were rewarding, but the sheer effort it took, the long hauls, the bland food, the shifty promotors, and the miserable sleeping conditions were wearing him down. "He didn't like the food we had to eat," Johnson remembered. "He had this cooler out there, and we mocked him for his garlic and funky cheeses he was eating out of the cooler, which is pretty much how I eat now."

The band had an album to make, but Yamamoto already seemed to have one foot out the door. The task required everyone's focus and attention, but it was proving difficult. According to Chris, Yamamoto "contributed very little to *Louder Than Love* and was so critical of his own musical output that Kim and I had to talk him into doing things that were his idea."[2]

Chris didn't have any qualms about broadening his sonic palette and incorporating more commercially appetizing touches to his songwriting. He was growing and evolving at an astonishing clip, and it showed in the music. Seven of *Louder Than Love*'s twelve tracks were attributed to Chris. Yamamoto logged three credits, while Thayil got two. Chris also wrote the lyrics to all of the tracks except one, a song called "I Awake," which was repurposed from a note that Yamamoto's girlfriend Kate had left for him one day.

For recording purposes, the band decided to stick a little closer to home and holed up inside London Bridge Studio in Shoreline, Washington, just a few exits north of downtown Seattle. Prior to Soundgarden's arrival, the studio hosted a collection of future grunge legends like Alice In Chains— while they were still known as Alice N' Chains—who recorded some of their earliest demos there. With its twenty-four-track recording console, it was the most sophisticated studio Soundgarden had worked in yet, and they were excited to explore its full technological capabilities.

At the same time the band was hunkering down at home, they were garnering their first bit of national press in New York City, when the acclaimed alt-weekly the *Village Voice* ran a feature article about Soundgarden just after Christmas in 1988. In the piece, the writer Laurie E trumpeted Soundarden as "a rock-n-roll, heads-go-glue, ice-water-down-your-spinal-column experience." It was a big deal for the band and a big deal for the local music scene from which they came. The *Seattle*

Times even wrote a story about the piece with the inspired headline: "*Village Voice* Praises Local Rock Band."

The *Louder Than Love* sessions began around December 1988 and were completed a little over a month later. Date quickly discovered that Chris knew when he was feeling confident in his voice, and when they should move onto something else. He frequently deferred to the singer's judgement on the matter. "He was his own worst critic," Date told *Tape Op*. "We'd come in on some days, he'd start singing, and within a half-hour he would say, 'It's not there today,' and we'd go on to something else. He knew what he wanted more than I knew what he wanted." [3] In order to make sure their ideas and their identity wouldn't get lost in translation, the band also pulled Stuart Hallerman into the proceedings to serve as an assistant engineer.

While Yamamoto, and to an extent the other members of Soundgarden, still harbored concerns about slick production techniques and major label commerciality, *Louder Than Love* managed to feature some of the most eyebrow-raising songs that Soundgarden ever created. Chris's penchant for riding the edge of accepted cultural norms with his pen created small controversies once the record finally made its way out into the public.

"Hands All Over," the album's third single, inspired a whole lot of handwringing over the lines about killing your mother, which seem shocking out of context, but in reality, are an allegory for Mother Earth and the damage that we all do in our daily lives. If the nation's DJs weren't inclined to play "Hands All Over" on their airwaves, they literally couldn't play "Big Dumb Sex," in which Soundgarden cosplays as one of the glitzy, coitally-obsessed hair metal bands of the eighties like Mötley Crüe and Poison. They gamely hit all the clichés, with Cornell repeatedly expressing his desire to "fuck, fuck, fuck, fuck you!"

Chris himself considered it "one of the hookiest songs I ever wrote," while allowing that he had to subvert it in order to make himself and the other band members okay with adding it to the final track list. "I don't know whether I would've written a song like that for Soundgarden if it hadn't said 'fuck' thirty-five times in it, because it was making fun of that kind of music, really." [4]

The problem was that the joke sailed way over most people's heads. Even Thayil had to explain what was going on to Yamamoto, who hated it, something that probably should have tipped everyone off that it wouldn't register with their Budweiser-crushing fanbase. "All the guys thought that it was like a sex rock anthem and all the girls thought it was some sort of goofy come-on," Chris said. "The record company thought it was, like, worse than…gangster rap or something just because I said the word fuck, ya know?"[5]

Rounding out *Louder Than Love's* conversation-kickstarting tracks is the song "Gun," a monolithic monster that put Matt's time and tempo abilities to the test. The song isn't literally about gun violence. It's more about spreading ideas and breaking through the staid, conservative, Reagan-era "America First" way of thinking about the world. It's another allegory buoyed by a severe, anarchic swarm of satirical sarcasm, in which Cornell croons about having an idea for "something we can do with a gun," namely, forcing "the empire" to "reap what they've sown." "Gun" is simply a desire to tell all the rich, capitalist, Wall Street broker types to fuck off.

It didn't take long before "Gun" became one of the most energetic and explosive moments of the band's live show. While the official version on *Louder Than Love* is good, the live version, almost any live version, is vastly superior. Even as molasses-slow as the rhythm begins in the studio, Soundgarden always seemed to start it off even slower onstage, before building into a chaotic, breakneck speed created by Cameron that the rest of the band could hardly keep up with.

"Loud Love," was chosen as the album's lead single. For an army of metalheads and alt-rock fans who had never heard of Sub Pop or SST before, "Loud Love" served as their first taste of Soundgarden. If the goal of a single is to grab people's attention from the jump, however, "Loud Love" runs about as far away from that idea as you can imagine. The song opens with a full half-minute's worth of Thayil's wailing feedback that sounds like a chorus of agitated angels, until Cameron breaks the spell, slamming into the arrangement like a piledriver while Chris sings about wanting "something to explode."

For the video, Soundgarden tapped Sonic Youth's regular director Kevin Kerslake who shot the band performing in a run-down, industrial factory. Kerslake's commitment to getting compelling footage was made abundantly clear during one take specifically when Chris broke one end of his microphone stand and accidently shoved it into his knee. "The whole chunk came out, so blood was just squirting out," he said. Kerslake reportedly prevented the medical assistant on the set from attending to Chris and kept the cameras rolling so that he could get the wound on film. "But then they didn't cut it into the video, which I was disappointed with," Chris said.[6]

"Full On Kevin's Mom" is an energetic tip of the cap to the band's punk rock roots, with Cornell giving a tip of the cap to his buddy Kevin Tissot's mother in his irreverent style. There's also a small musical reprise of this track tacked to the end of the album. "Ugly Truth" serves as the album opener and remains one of the more "challenging" musical contributions to the album, filled with discordant guitar chords and an alternating plodding and frenetic pace. "No Wrong No Right," a rager written by Yamamoto, is made memorable by an introductory drum solo that rolls like the giant boulder chasing Indiana Jones at the beginning of *Raiders of the Lost Ark*.

Before they could share their music with the world, Soundgarden had to choose an album title. Everyone threw around ideas. At one point they contemplated calling it *Louder Than Fuck*, but the executives at A&M, along with Susan Silver, worried the name would hamper its commercial prospects. *Louder Than Shit* was another non-starter. In the end they settled for the more anodyne *Louder Than Love*. "It's sort of making fun of heavy metal bravado," Chris explained. "Metal bands would say *Louder Than Thunder* or something. So, *Louder Than Love*. What is *Louder Than Love*?"[7]

For the cover image, Soundgarden again utilized the talents of Charles Peterson. The photographer tagged along with the band for a pair of intense shows in the Bay Area around February 12, 1989. "Mudhoney and Soundgarden played the I-Beam in Berkeley Square two nights in a row," he remembered. "For the West Coast especially, I'd pop down and shoot some shows like that. Unfortunately, I had pneumonia on the way back. I got that from Dan Peters in Mudhoney."

"I think we played with them there and in Berkeley Square that weekend," Mark Arm added. "Here we are playing with our friends in San Francisco and Dan's coughing his lungs out. He was super sick."

Peterson captured the brutal essence of Soundgarden in a way that few were able. The picture on the cover features Chris, shirtless as usual, with his face obscured by his long, curly mane in mid-flip. In his right hand, he holds his microphone, in his left, a long tangle of electric cable. In the bottom right-hand corner of the finished sleeve, there's a Parental Advisory warning. It was one of the first records to ever come affixed with that now-iconic black-and-white sticker.

Critical response to *Louder Than Love* was generally positive after it dropped on September 5, 1989, but there were some negative voices. The self-proclaimed "Dean of American Rock Critics," Robert Christgau gave the record a tepid *C+*, proclaiming that it was "covertly conceptual, arty in spite of itself," then predicting that "metal fans don't bite."

Rolling Stone reviewer J.D. Considine was more bullish in his three-and-a-half-star review, writing "The songs on *Louder Than Love* are mean, lean and fighting fit." While he did take Chris to task over his lyrics—"Much of what the band has to say is clichéd, confused or generally incomprehensible"—he praised him for the compelling way in which he sang them: "Cornell delivers them with such full-throated intensity that they actually *sound* impressive. And if that ain't the mark of a great metal album, then what is?"[8] The most effusive review came from the *Rocket*, where local writer Jeff Gilbert called it, "Easily the best album to have sex to since *Led Zeppelin IV*."

The printed, critical assessments paled in comparison to the massive namecheck the band received from W. Axl Rose, however. In 1989, the Guns N' Roses frontman sat down for an extensive feature interview with *Rolling Stone* that hit the shelves in August, just before *Louder Than Love* was released. Guns N' Roses was the biggest band in the world, and their vast army of fans hung on the singer's every word like gospel. When friend and interviewer Del James asked Axl what he was listening to, he threw out several classic acts like Derek and the Dominos and Patti Smith, before adding Soundgarden to his list. "The singer just buries me," he said about Chris. "The guy sings so great."[9]

"That was one of the big turnarounds at the label," Jacoves recalled of Rose's endorsement. "Like, we might have a bigger band than we think we have. A lot of labels aren't proactive. They're reactive people. Something like Soundgarden didn't fit into a mold for these people." The marketing department salivated over the quote and spread the Guns N' Roses singer's words far and wide.

Though *Louder Than Love* wasn't a platinum-selling smash—it peaked at 108 on Billboard's Top 200 on March 10, 1990—it introduced Soundgarden to a commercial rock audience and marked them as a band worth watching. While driving in Los Angeles one day listening to the radio shortly after the album dropped, Chris was floored when the DJ played "Get On The Snake." The song didn't even have a proper chorus and chugged along at an unconventional 9/4 time signature, and yet, here it was pouring out of the speakers of his car. "I heard it on the radio in between Tom Petty and something else, and I thought *this works!*" Chris remembered. "That was a huge moment."[10]

Louder Than Love's impact extended far beyond the bounds of radio airplay and standard album sales. It also helped inspire one of the greatest metal anthems of all time: "Enter Sandman" by Metallica. That band's guitarist Kirk Hammett was listening to the record around two in the morning when inspiration struck. "I picked up my guitar, and out came that riff," he said. "It doesn't sound like a Soundgarden riff. It doesn't sound like a Soundgarden song; I was inspired by Soundgarden for sure, without a doubt, but I moved on to create something completely different."[11]

Just a month after finishing *Louder Than Love*, Soundgarden was back in the Beauville, tearing their way across America. They stayed on the road through March, playing club-sized venues like Maxwell's in Hoboken, New Jersey, The Rathskeller in Boston, and Wacky's in San Antonio, before gearing up for their first-ever trip to Europe come spring. Sub Pop helped pave the way for Soundgarden's success in England especially, cultivating prominent writers for publications like the *NME* and

Melody Maker and expounding upon them the importance of bands rising out of the "Seattle scene." Indeed, record shops across the UK actually had dedicated Northwest Music sections, where the diehards could find the latest releases by Tad and Nirvana.

Soundgarden played their first show in England at the School of Oriental and African Studies in London on May 12, 1989, opening up for Mudhoney. The two Seattle-based groups were essentially passing one another like ships in the night. Mudhoney were capping what had been a weeks-long run supporting Sonic Youth through mainland Europe, while Soundgarden was on the verge of playing throughout the continent in the weeks to come.

Chris, Kim, Hiro, and Matt ripped through their standard repertoire, playing cuts like "Beyond The Wheel," "All Your Lies," and "Kingdom Of Come" to a rapt English crowd. In a piece about the show that ran in *Melody Maker*, a reviewer named Push wrote, "There's no containing the capricious belligerence of Seattle's Soundgarden." He added that they "hammer an unglamorous and bewitching metal montage," before inexplicably referring to Chris as "part monkey, part Adonis and all of a doo-dah."[12] At the end of their set, Chris deadpanned "We're Black Sabbath. Thank you and goodnight!"

Mudhoney was a more catastrophic affair. During their performance, Mark Arm invited members of the crowd onto the stage, causing the evening to devolve into chaos after the stage collapsed. "We played what we thought was one of our best shows," Thayil said of Soundgarden's first set in England. "Mudhoney came out, made a few statements, lost their microphone, the crowd went crazy. Next day, that's all anybody could speak about, the near riot."[13]

Arm was more charitable looking back. "I remember our set being super chaotic, but we were stoked to be playing a show with our friends," he said. He also remembered thinking, "That's probably the only time Soundgarden will ever open for us. That isn't something that would've happened in Seattle." Coincidentally, Nirvana would make their UK debut at this same venue in just a few months' time on October 27.

Soundgarden played another show in Portsmouth the following night, again opening for Mudhoney, before heading back to London where they taped an appearance at Maida Vale Studios for the John Peel Sessions on the BBC that was broadcast the following month on June 7. They opened with a gloriously psychedelic take on their *Ultramega OK* single "Flower," then segued into a funky and searing cover of Sly & The Family Stone's classic "Thank You (Falettinme Be Mice Elf Agin)" and then closed with the Beatles' *White Album* curio "Everybody's Got Something To Hide Except For Me And My Monkey." The latter recordings eventually were added onto Soundgarden's outtake and B-Side collection *Echo of Miles* decades later.

After their English blitz, Soundgarden crossed the Channel and stormed mainland Europe. Beginning in the Netherlands, they showed the rock-loving Dutch what real volume felt like. "They thrash the barren government-assisted Vera Club into near total submission as stacks of speakers threaten to topple from their towers in deference to the sheer volume alone," Everett True wrote in his review of the gig in *Melody Maker*.[14] They moved into West Germany and then headed south in the direction of the Mediterranean. "Dino Galasso was like our guitar tech, and driver and tour manager over there," Hallerman recalled of their Scottish-by-way-of-Italy road hand. "Got us lost leaving every town and entering every town. Every day."

For whatever reason, the band received their biggest and most boisterous reception in Italy. The language barrier couldn't have mattered less to their ferocious new fans. "It was pretty insane," Johnson recalled. "I remember Rome was in this weird cavernous club in this basement. There was one set of stairs that went down there. It was fucking insane. It was wall-to-wall sweat and people. I had the T-shirt thing set up on the steps, on the way out, and I got flooded. People were ripping shirts off the wall, CDs and everything."

Chris caused something of a stir when he tore down one of the posters with the band's name on it and ripped it into pieces. When local journalists caught wind of that, they probed him to find out the meaning behind his actions and were disappointed to discover he just needed some paper to write down the evening's setlist. Kim Thayil nearly got pulled offstage from the overeager horde who simply wanted a piece of him.

The tour ended with one of the wildest shows Soundgarden ever played. It took place in Pisa, home of the famous Leaning Tower. Unfortunately, the band didn't realize until they were onstage that the show was actually a part of a local Communist rally, and one of the motivating reasons behind the event was to try to legalize drugs in Italy. Not just marijuana, but hard stuff like heroin, too. The promoter hadn't told them what the deal was, so when they arrived, they were greeted by a barrage of police with automatic weapons and members of the press applauding them for supporting the legalization of drugs.

The show in Pisa was significant for another reason as well: it was the last gig that Hiro Yamamoto played with Soundgarden. *Louder Than Love* wasn't even out yet, but the bassist had had enough. Yamamoto had been talking about leaving for so long that Chris decided to call his bluff. "Chris said, 'Fine. You keep voicing your dissatisfaction. I'm tired of hearing it. Just leave,'" Thayil told author Greg Prato. Though the singer wasn't 100 percent serious about his ultimatum, Yamamoto was. "Chris calling him on it forced his hand," Thayil added.

The rest of the tour was cancelled. Susan Silver used her mother's credit card to help cover the losses and get everyone home. "I was unhappy before we left for Europe. And then halfway through Europe, I was like, 'I can't keep doing this,'" Yamamoto explained to Prato. "I guess the reason why I left was the whole deal about metal," he added. "We were a hard rock band, but I don't know if we were ever a metal band. We got bigger than I ever imagined we could have—I wasn't really ready for that at the time."[15]

There was nothing left to say. No amount of cajoling, arguing, or convincing could change his mind. Hiro Yamamoto was out of Soundgarden and onto a different path: an academic tract that initially led him to a master's degree in physics and then a career in the petroleum industry working for Mobil. He'd play music again. In the nineties he hooked up with Mark Pickerel from Screaming Trees along with another guy named Robert Roth to form the group Truly. They put out an album on Sub Pop in 1991 titled *Heart and Lungs* before signing a deal with Capitol Records and releasing *Fast Stories…from Kid Coma*. Another pair of albums followed, but the band never took off in the way that Soundgarden did. These days he's one third of a surf rock trio named Stereo Donkey.

Despite the setback, Chris, Kim, and Matt were determined to keep going. They just needed to find a replacement. Of one thing they were certain—whoever they brought in had to be from the Seattle area. They weren't about to go to Los Angeles and pick up some random, recording session hotshot who didn't have the slightest clue about who they were or what they were trying to accomplish.

Among those those they tapped to audition was Jack Endino. "It was a little awkward because we were friends," he said. "I think they decided who was going to be the bass player, and they let me try out as a courtesy. That was the sense I got at the time. We had one little jam together and it was fun."

Another hopeful was Jim Tillman, from the group Susan Silver once managed, the U-Men. The band gave him an advance copy of *Louder Than Love* so that he could learn the parts, then invited him to Chris's place to jam. They tried out a few altered tunings, with Tillman lowering his deepest bass string note all the way down to B. Unfortunately, shortly after they got going, he hit a subterranean note and blew out his speaker. The session ended, and they all went bowling together.

After trying out and passing on a young kid named Ben Shepherd—at twenty years old, he couldn't even legally drink yet—they eventually settled on Jason Everman to fill in Yamamoto's heavy boots. Born in Alaska in 1967, Everman moved to Poulsbo, Washington, when he was still a kid. He first gained attention in the Seattle rock scene as the second guitarist in Nirvana, a gig he locked down through his friendship with the band's then-drummer Chad Channing. Though he didn't work with Nirvana on their debut album *Bleach*, he was the one who laid down the $606.17 for the recording sessions after the fact and received a credit on the record as a result. The band never paid him back.

Everman toured the country with Nirvana throughout 1989, including playing at Sub Pop's infamous "Lamefest" show at the Moore Theater on June 9. That same month, he made his only two recordings as a member of the band, on a cover of KISS's "Do You Love Me?" and an early version of "Dive," at the Evergreen State College's twenty-four-track recording facility. His last gig with the band took place at the Pyramid Club in New York City on July 18. After that, the band cancelled the remaining dates on the itinerary and drove the fifty hours across the country back home to Washington.

"We had some great shows with Jason," Krist Novoselic told Clay Tarver in the *New York Times*. "But then things went south really fast."[16] At the heart of the band's issues with Everman was his inability to open up and connect with the other guys in the group. On way too many of the long drives from this gig to that, he remained silent and kept to himself, which was pretty frustrating to everyone else in the van. Soundgarden chose to ignore some of those early warning signs. Kim Thayil made the call and invited him to try out.

Everman knew Soundgarden's repertoire and could play the songs well enough that everyone agreed that the personality issues would eventually take care of themselves. Shortly after Everman joined, the band re-entered the studio to fulfill a small contractual obligation. "A&M said, 'We need a B-side!'" Jack Endino said. The label was on the verge of releasing the second single from *Louder Than Love*, a song called "Hands All Over," and they wanted something fresh to tack onto the other side. To mollify their corporate overlords, the band went back to their first producer to engineer the session, where they cooked up a hasty cover of The Beatles' "Come Together."

Endino remembers it being "a really strange session," adding, "Even at the time I thought, 'This is not really going anywhere.' They weren't terribly thrilled about doing it for some reason." Chris had difficulty working up enthusiasm for the song and at one point got so frustrated that he kicked one of the studio's wooden orange stools clear across the room. When the time came to add harmonies, he simply shrugged it off.

"I said, 'Hey, what are you gonna do about the Paul McCartney harmony that's on this song?'" Endino recalled. "Chris goes, 'Oh, you gotta record it! Why don't you sing it? I'm sick of working on this song, I'm going home. Let us hear it when you're done with it.'" He took off, leaving Endino holding the bag to play the part of McCartney. The producer's voice can be heard floating just under the surface.

Everman's first show with Soundgarden took place on September 22, 1989, at the Club With No Name in Los Angeles. *Louder Than Love* had been out for only a couple of weeks, and they were using this time to warm up and get their new bassist up to speed in front of a live audience. They quickly followed that gig with a few performances around Southern California, including an in-store appearance at Rhino Records under harsh fluorescent lighting during which Chris implored the dozens of people lined up in between the racks of tapes and CDs to "buy vinyl" after a feedback-filled rendition of "Gun."

The most memorable of Everman's early shows took place at a venue called the Scream, where "Gunny Junk" surprised the band onstage with an eye-popping dance routine. "It was during 'Beyond The Wheel,'" he remembered. "I had on cutoff jean shorts, put tape over my nipples, and put a pumpkin on my head and went out and did a total homoerotic attack on Chris while he sang. We literally wrestled onstage while he was singing. I did it maybe three times over the course of that tour. I may have had a few beers in me or something."

At another gig, Everman tossed his bass back behind one of the drum risers where it smashed into Sex Pistols guitarist Steve Jones's Gibson Les Paul. It was unintentional, but it left a ding in the guitar. Jones' tech went apopletic and threatened to keep Everman's bass, but it was eventually returned. "You'd think Steve, since he's an original punk rock sorta guy, he'd understand that kind of thing," Chris later joked. "I guess not."[17]

The next three months were a manic barnstorm through America's seedy rock and roll club scene. Beginning with a show at the Moore in Seattle on October 7, 1989, Soundgarden drove from sea to shining sea, bringing their visceral brand of post-punk metal to the American Underground. Two weeks after the tour began, they returned to Kim's old stomping grounds near Park Forest, Illinois to play a wild show in Chicago. "Matt Cameron was already showing signs of being the best drummer in the biz and Thayil stood stock still stage right laying out these seismic riffs," WXRT DJ Richard Milne remembered of the band's gig at Cabaret Metro. "And all of them watching Cornell strut and flail and wail and make every person in the room wish they were in a band, too."[18]

From there they hit venues like Stanches in Columbus, Ohio, where Primus opened up; the Loeb Center at NYU; Club Soda in Montreal; and the venerated 9:30 Club in Washington, DC, which was a mecca of hardcore thanks to bands like Minor Threat, Government Issue, and the Slickee Boys. They also returned to New Orleans and ripped the roof off of Tipitina's. By December, they had closed the circuit and were back in Los Angeles for two gigs at the famous Whisky a Go Go on the Sunset Strip in Hollywood on the seventh and the tenth.

Given the historic aura surrounding the venue and the opportunity the gigs presented for them to show off in front of the LA music industry, the band decided to cancel a planned gig in Tijuana, Mexico, and film both of their performances at the Whisky. The footage was later compiled and released on both VHS and CD, as well as a special twelve-inch blue vinyl record. They called it *Louder Than Live*. Shot entirely in black and white, it is a pivotal document of Soundgarden just before the wave of the success and fame crested. The camera movements are chaotic, and the editing is frenzied, but the overall effect accurately simulates what it felt like to witness the band in this nascent stage. The mosh pit never slackens. Stage divers are frequent. The riffs pouring out of Chris's sunburst Gibson Les Paul are pummeling. His voice is searing.

Appearing onstage in either a vest or shirtless, Chris decided to take the waist-down portion of his outfit to the next level for this particular performance. "I remember he spent an hour backstage entirely duct taping his pants," Eric Johnson said. "That was kinda the inspiration for the label putting duct tape on the *Louder than Live* sampler thing that they put out. He was a total duct tape guy."

Whether it's while whipping around his long locks of black hair during "Gun," stomping his feet in time to the chorus of "Big Dumb Sex," dodging stage-crashers during "I Awake," or leaping headfirst into the crowd while Kim Thayil ripped off another savage solo, Chris turned himself into a spectacle demanding the attention of everyone in the room. "He was the first guy I ever saw lean back into the crowd with his guitar strapped on," Johnson said. "Eddie [Vedder] started doing that a lot after, but Chris was the first guy I ever remember going into the crowd. Then I'd have to go in after him." The film ended in the most awesomely absurd way possible, a medley performance of Spinal Tap's "Big Bottom" into Cheech & Chong's "Earache My Eye," after which Chris bashed his sunburst Les Paul into Matt Cameron's drum before casually tossing it into the air and stalking off.

Soundgarden's momentous 1989 ended five nights later with another performance at the I-Beam in San Francisco. After that they drove home to Seattle to spend Christmas and New Year's with their families and girlfriends. The respite didn't last long. Less than a month later, they were back on the road, this time as part of a package run with French Canadian heavy metal group Voivod and California funk rockers Faith No More.

For this higher-profile outing, A&M decided to spring for a fullfledged tour bus to escort the group from show to show. They also got a new road manager named Mark Sokol. The days of jamming econo in the red Beauville were over, though they didn't junk the old warhorse. Chris would regularly take the van out into the woods on camping trips. Kim Thayil also drove it around town. They ultimately lent it out to bands like Alice In Chains to lug gear. "I believe the Screaming Trees used it and the Pearl Jam guys, [the Mother] Love Bone guys," Kim Thayil said. "There was always a point in time where someone calls and says 'Hey, we need that big long van to, like, move stuff from one rehearsal space to a gig. We just need it tonight because we are going to move stuff to this gig and then back to rehearsal space.'"[19]

With their new bus pointing the way, Soundgarden's latest run began on Voivod's home turf. "We were headlining, and at the time, I really didn't know much about them," the band's singer Denis "Snake" Bélanger said. "When I saw the first show of that tour, I was blown away and I said to myself, 'Oh my God, I gotta play after this guy?!'"

Chris enjoyed his time in Canada and had a genuine fondness for his neighboring country to the North. "I like their money," he wrote years later. "It's colorful and on the backs of the different notes are little picture postcards or travel brochures for the country. One bill has people playing hockey! Why can't we have football? They have the Queen on the twenty, which they may not like, but it could be much worse. She was never a slave owner."[20]

The three bands crossed into US territory on January 13, 1990, playing the Midwest before hitting the Big Apple six days later. It was a jam-packed day that began with a filmed interview between Chris and Kim and MTV host Riki Rachtman for the show *Headbangers Ball* around noon. The two Soundgarden members sat on a sofa together with their legs crossed and their boots pressed against one another's for most of the chat.

Rachtman hit them with questions about the music scene in Seattle—"It's boss," Chris dryly responded—and their recent Grammy nomination for *Ultramega OK*. When Rachtman asked Chris about Axl Rose's praise, the singer drolly responds, "Wow," then waves his hair back and forth. Part of the reason for Chris's on-screen obstinance is the fact that he was battling both an oncoming flu and road fatigue.

After the MTV appearance he took part in a ninety-minute radio interview, then a photo shoot, and finally soundcheck, which was cut short. Just like the Whisky gigs out in LA, however, the show at the Ritz was an important one, with a lot of industry insiders coming to have a look at what they thought might be the next big thing. There were around three hundred people on the guest list alone. MTV's cameras were on hand to capture the action, and footage of their performance of "Flower" made it onto the network's airwaves shortly thereafter. Nevertheless, Chris didn't pander to the VIPs and screamed to the crowd, "This isn't Club MTV! You don't have to feel stupid!"

The band hit the stage in Bay Shore, New York, the following night before motoring north to Boston, then back south to Philadelphia where they joined Faith No More onstage to play Black Sabbath's "War Pigs." Faith No More's singer Mike Patton returned the favor during Soundgarden's set where he sang "I Awake," allowing Chris to introduce his body to the crowd gathered near the lip of the stage. Faith No More departed from the tour the following day.

That's how it went over the next two months. Twelve days on, one or two days off. An endless parade of smelly clubs, dingy green rooms, and the interminable wait for that single hour of tumultuous release. Some of the shows were sold-out, wall-to-wall affairs. Others, farther away from the coasts, were sparsely attended. Cramped space on the bus, which constantly jerked this way and that while on the road and wasn't very conducive to a decent night's sleep. VHS copies of *Robocop* and episodes of *The Simpsons* helped break up some of the monotony, along with Nintendo sessions with the members of Voivod. When they got to the next town, they were treated to a never-ending feast of so-called "promoter's pasta" left simmering in hotel pans in green rooms. Baltimore, Charlotte, Fort Lauderdale, San Antonio, Anaheim, Portland, Salt Lake City, St. Louis, Minneapolis, and on and on.

In Orlando, Soundgarden made a positive impression on the local writer for *The Sentinel*, Parry Gettelman, who noted the band's ascendant popularity. "The crowd thinned considerably after Soundgarden's set and, during the break, several would-be ticket buyers turned away when told that Soundgarden had already finished," she wrote. She also singled out Chris's wild mannerisms. "Cornell tossed a microphone high in the air, looping the cord over a lighting beam suspended from the ceiling and then dived into the roiling crowd for some audience-surfing. Back on stage, he attacked Matt Cameron's drum kit with a mike stand, which got the worse end of the conflict."[21]

From his up-close view of Chris during their time together, Voivod's singer couldn't help but note his unique, personal dichotomy. "As a frontman, he was tearing the place down," Bélanger said. "I remember once, he climbed on the speaker, and there was, like, a beamed ceiling and it was pretty high, but he did, like, monkey bars all across the room, holding himself up with both arms. When he came back to the stage, people couldn't believe it. I couldn't believe it myself!" Once the show ended, the madman dangling from the steel beams was nowhere to be found. Instead Bélanger encountered a rather quiet, thoughtful person who really only ever spoke up when he actually had something to say. "As a person, he was really calm. He was not a blah, blah, blah kind of guy."

It was clear to everyone coming out to the shows, watching the clips on MTV, and listening along on the radio that Soundgarden was primed to make some serious moves. Little did they know that tragedy was about to bring them all back down to Earth.

CHAPTER VI

CALL ME A DOG

T he imposing, dingy white slab of concrete and stucco on 62nd Street wasn't much to look at. The drab, forest green awning hanging over the main entryway to the venue offered the only signal that one had made it to the right place. "Rock Capital of B'klyn," it pronounced in big block letters. On March 17, 1990, Soundgarden made their way to the outer boroughs of New York City to this small club called L'Amour with the purpose of living up to the promise emblazoned high above the narrow street. It was St. Patrick's Day, and everyone was in the mood to cut loose, drink beer, and bang their heads.

Chris Cornell was backstage with the band prepping for their performance. Susan Silver had made the trip for this portion of the tour. Everyone was chatting, tuning, and carrying on, generally stoked that the run was nearly over and that they'd soon be back home. That's when their road manager, Mark Sokol, received the phone call from Xana La Fuente, Andrew Wood's girlfriend. Andy had overdosed on heroin and was in a coma at Harborview Medical Center in Seattle. The prognosis wasn't good.

Sokol shared the news with some of the crew but decided to wait to tell the band until after the performance. He figured there wasn't much to be done now, why mess with their heads before sending them out to entertain a few hundred young and hungry rock fanatics? Soundgarden went onstage and delivered their typical, high-energy, sweat-soaked show. Chris was in prime form, screaming, jumping, and stomping his way through the band's aggressive set. Then he came offstage and received the dreadful news.

"It was heavy," Soundgarden's roadie Eric Johnson said. "It was not a fucking great moment. Chris was crushed, obviously. He was the closest of all of us to Andy." Pretty quickly, bottles of liquor were passed around to dull the shock.

Chris was pretty jet-lagged and at first didn't fully comprehend the magnitude of the news. He and Susan eventually made their way back to the ramshackle apartment-hotel they were renting near the Beacon Theater on the Upper West Side of Manhattan and took calls from back home to try to figure out what the hell was going on. Kelly Curtis, Mother Love Bone's manager, was feeding them updates. While they were putting the pieces together and figuring out what to do next, Wood's condition grew worse. He had suffered a hemorrhage aneurysm and had lost all function in his brain. "It didn't seem like someone that alive, and particularly that young, was actually going to die," Chris told *Rolling Stone*'s Andy Greene. "It was like watching a play where there's going to be a surprise ending and your worst fears aren't going to come true."[1]

Soundgarden played another show at Maxwell's in Hoboken, New Jersey, during which Chris spoke about the effects of drug addiction before dedicating the show to Andy. Those in attendance wouldn't understand the full weight of his words for another few days. Afterwards, Chris hopped on a flight back to Seattle with Susan. They dropped their stuff at home and then sped over to the hospital.

In the meantime, La Fuente demanded that doctors not pull the plug on Andy until after Chris arrived and had the chance to say goodbye. "On the one hand it's like 'That's really cool,'" Chris told the filmmakers behind the Andy Wood documentary *Malfunkshun*. "On the other hand [it] was like, 'Well, that's really creepy. That's really awful.' His family is all sitting there waiting to get this over with. So that made it especially weird. I didn't wanna feel like the guy that was holding up this inevitability."[2]

Wood's family didn't mind the delay. "I didn't really care," Kevin Wood said. "The longer we could keep him alive the better, I thought. There was a slight chance that he might just keep breathing. We were camped out in the hospital for days, so it didn't make any difference."

The Andy that Chris saw when he entered the room at Harborview was a far cry from the larger-than-life figure with whom he had shared so many incredible nights on Capitol Hill. The singer lay on the bed motionless, hooked up to a range of machines that kept his heart pumping and his lungs breathing. Chris was shocked and visibly upset. "His mouth was just half-open and he's just looking at Andy," Kevin Wood recalled. "No words."

The decision was made to pull the plug. A few moments later, the line on the electrocardiogram went flat. Andrew Wood was dead at twenty-four years old.

"I didn't deal well with Andy's death," Chris said.[3] "After he died, numerous times I'd be driving, and I would look out the window and I thought I saw him. It would take me five minutes to update to the moment and realize, 'No, he's actually dead.'"

Though Chris would come to terms with the reality of what had happened, the impact of the loss never faded from his mind. Eventually, he'd channel his emotions into song, helped out by some of Andy's closest friends and collaborators. The act of making music brought a measure of solace, but the utter senselessness of what had occurred was impossible to fully overcome.

* * *

The Paramount Theatre on 9th Avenue in Seattle couldn't have been more diametrically opposite to L'Amour. At nine stories tall, with a capacity to hold nearly three thousand people inside its gilded hall, the nearly hundred-year-old building is perhaps the most regal-looking construction in all of Seattle. A rock capital in its own right, the Paramount has also hosted jazz giants, pop stars, and presidents. It was the perfect location to honor Andrew Wood.

On March 24, 1990, fans, friends, family, and loved ones gathered inside the Paramount to celebrate the memory of a man who never got to explore the limits of his outsized potential. In a show of respect that he would have loved, Andrew Wood's name was emblazoned on the marquee hanging over the building's entryway, along with the years of his birth and death. Inside, the co-owner of the club RKCNDY ran sound and played a heavy rotation of Wood's music. Members of Alice In Chains, Mother Love Bone, and all of Soundgarden showed up to pay their respects.

A guestbook was set up. Chris scrawled on the single-lined yellow paper with a sharpie, "2 THE LOVE MASTER, SAVE MY SEAT IN THE NETHER WORLD. 4 I KNOW ITS A SOLD OUT SHOW!" He affixed his signature, which looked like an explosion of barely legible Cs and Ls.

As the program unfolded. Wood's father got up and spoke about the dangers of substance abuse. At one point, a group of religious figures picked to appear by La Fuente led a candle-lighting ceremony. "It had these new age overtones that didn't fit Andy's life at all," Chris recalled.[4] "There was an amazing film of Andy with [his] Mother Love Bone bandmates. All of Andy's friends and family were there, mixed with a bunch of fans who I didn't like but knew Andy would have loved."

Scott Sundquist showed up for the ceremony and couldn't help but notice how much the heaviness of the occasion was weighing on Chris. Together, the pair gathered a handful of helium-filled balloons, took them outside and let them drift into the spring air. After that, Chris and several others gravitated toward Mother Love Bone manager Kelly Curtis's house for an impromptu wake.

Around thirty people told stories of their departed friend's outlandish exploits through tears. "We were crammed in a smallish living room with people sitting on every available surface," Chris wrote years later on his website. "Couch arms, end tables, the floor. I was leaning on the back of one of the couches that face away from the rest of the room and toward the front door. I remember Andy's girlfriend looking at everyone and saying, 'This is just like La Bamba.'"

From outside, Chris could hear a heavy set of footsteps rushing toward Curtis's front door. "Layne [Staley] flew in, completely breaking down and crying so deeply that he looked truly frightened and lost," Chris remembered. The Alice In Chains frontman was in desperate need of solace. "I had this sudden urge to run over and grab him and give him a big hug and tell him everything was going to be okay. Kelly has always had a way of making everyone feel like everything will turn out great. That the world isn't ending. That's why we were at his place. I wanted to be that person for Layne, maybe just because he needed it so bad."

Chris didn't move. Nobody did. The weight of their own individual grief kept them planted in place as Staley unraveled before them. That memory stuck with Chris. It was made even more poignant a dozen years later when he appeared at Staley's funeral. "I was angry," he said. "I kept hearing the 'Twice as bright, half as long' speech and the 'He was just too special for this world,' nonsense that I had heard at so many other funerals for so many other friends that were so young and talented."[5] After rolling it around in his head, trying to figure out the source of his anger, he concluded that, "I was just mad at myself because he was dead, and one time I had a chance to pick him up, dust him off and let him know that there was a person who cared about how much pain he was in, and I didn't do it."

Despite the trauma Chris had to contend with in the wake of Wood's death, the Soundgarden train continued moving full speed ahead. A new tour of Europe loomed, set to kick off on April 5 in Newcastle, England. It was scheduled to last a full month and take them from the Netherlands to West Germany, Italy, and beyond. It was shitty timing to say the least. "I figured it would be this great thing, because I would be away from home and I wouldn't have to look at places where I saw him or see things that would remind me of him," Chris said. "But it was awful."[6]

Things didn't get off to an auspicious start. After the initial show in Newcastle, they were booked to play a two-hundred-person club called International in Manchester, with Voivod and Faith No More. Both bands cancelled, leaving Soundgarden on the hook for the entire evening's worth of entertainment. Only around seventeen people showed up to watch them. A pair of shows at the Marquee in London went much better, with the Technicolour Twins writing in *Metal Hammer* that, "The bare torsoed Cornell delights the masses with his easy stagecraft like a new age temptress," and that, "It seems that all you need to do to make Soundgarden great is add an audience."[7]

Chris continued to dwell on Andy. Though he was loath to talk about his pain, the dark thoughts and wistful memories turned into lyrics, which he married to melodies. Before he knew it, he'd written two songs about his friend. The first was a melancholic ballad titled "Say Hello 2 Heaven." The second was an expansive rocker he called "Reach Down."

Beyond their roles as exquisite outpourings of grief, both songs marked a new evolution for Chris as a songwriter. Traditionally, he'd written from the perspective of a detached character. Part of it was him, but the other was fictional. These songs broke from that method by specifically addressing his real feelings about a real person. Neither song felt right for Soundgarden, but he continued to flesh them out. They were too authentic and too good to be left lingering on a cassette tape stashed in the bottom of his bag. He figured he'd wait until he got back home to Seattle and figure out what to do with them then.

Following the Marquee shows in London and a performance at the Irish Center in Birmingham, Soundgarden crossed the English Channel and began working their way across Europe again. They began at a venue called Paradiso in Amsterdam then headed East. They were escorted across the continent by a roadie named Dutch Michaels. Unfortunately for the band, Michaels wasn't the greatest chauffeur in the world, and the ride through mountainous switchbacks through the steep Alps was a wild one.

"He was driving the Sprinter van in Austria. We were coming down and he's riding the brakes really hard and we all started to smell something," Eric Johnson said. "We were like, 'Hey dude, you should probably pull over.' Our brakes were literally on fire. Melted. So, we end up having to stay at this little inn for the night somewhere in Austria. It was like this ski chalet or something, but it wasn't winter, so we were literally the only people in this fucking place."

When the band woke the next morning and ambled down for breakfast, they were met with a dismal-looking charcuterie, salami and ham arranged on a tray, covered in a rainbow sheen. Everyone was put off except Matt Cameron, who dug in. "A couple hours later on the road, he's writhing on the floor of the Sprinter," Johnson recalled. "Laying on the floor and grabbing the legs of the chairs, moaning. We're like, 'This guy is dying,' but we didn't fucking know where to go."

Soundgarden's next show was hours away, at the Modern Casino Club in Rimini, Italy. Because of the delay caused by the van's brakes, they were forced to cancel a gig in Naples the night before, which led to a small-scale riot that caused thousands of dollars in damage. Rather than pull over at a hospital and have Cameron looked at and cancelling another gig, they decided to press on and seek medical attention later. "We get to the show and he's still out of it. We don't know how it's gonna happen," Johnson said. "They wanted to cut him open in Italy, thinking he had appendicitis, but he was like, 'No, I'm not gonna let you do that here.' This funky little town in Italy. It was a really nervous day thinking, *How is this gonna come off?*"

Chris considered returning to the drums for the show. "He quickly realized 'There's no way I can sing these parts and play drums,'" Johnson said. "It only took a few minutes onstage to figure that out." In the end, Cameron managed to white-knuckle his way through the band's set. They skipped the encore. Shortly thereafter, Soundgarden was on their way back to Seattle. "We got [Cameron] on a plane the next morning and sent him home," Johnson said. "The word was he farted for about fifteen minutes on the plane and felt much, much better."

Italy had defeated Soundgarden once again. More consequentially, it spelled the end of the line for Jason Everman. "Things never gelled, and rather than let them fester, we fired him,"[8] Chris said.

"He was an unhappy person," Johnson said. "The first guy I ever saw trash gear and throw his bass; tantrums. Then he'd sit in the back of the Sprinter with his headphones on. He wasn't involved in the conversations with other people. He'd be listening to some kind of hardcore rap or something. The rest of those guys weren't happy-go-lucky dudes, but they were funny and charismatic, and Jason didn't seem happy."

Andrew Wood's death caused Chris to re-evaluate the types of people he let into his orbit, which may have played a factor in the decision to fire Jason. "It sort of directed me towards worrying about relationships that I have with people who I feel are important, as opposed to wasting my time with people who don't seem to be, who are just sort of trying to be energy vampires sucking whatever they can out of you," he told *Reflex*. "It helped me define differences between the two, and definitely made me a little more aggressive towards avoiding that kind of person."[9]

Once they got back to Seattle, Soundgarden called a band meeting at Matt Cameron's house. Chris did most of the talking during the brief gathering, telling Everman they were going to go in a different direction. The bassist was devastated, but there was nothing he could do to change their minds.

Jason Everman was a talented musician, who was more than willing to match the intensity of the rest of the band for the ninety minutes they sweated and screamed onstage. It was the other twenty-two-and-a-half hours between shows that created the rift that led to his dismissal. As Soundgarden once again considered who could take over on bass, it was that aspect that guided their search the most. They weren't looking for a technician. They were looking for a kindred spirit.

Eventually, Everman moved to New York, where he found work at Caroline Records's warehouse. He played in a few bands, most notably a San Francisco-based group called Mind Funk, before joining the army in 1994. The military lifestyle suited him. Everman became a member of the elite Army Rangers, and then joined up with the even more elite Special Forces. He was still going through the last phase of his training to finally earn his coveted green beret, when two jumbo jets slammed into the sides of the World Trade Center on September 11, 2001. A deployment to Afghanistan was followed by a deployment to Iraq, then back to Afghanistan, where he became a witness to mayhem in a place where life can be snuffed out in the blink of an eye. After obtaining his honorable discharge in 2006, Everman enrolled in school, earning a bachelor's degree from the Columbia University School of General Studies. He got in with a little help from four-star general Stanley McChrystal, who wrote a letter of recommendation on his behalf.

Soundgarden needed to find their second bassist in less than a year. To Chris's mind, at least, there was only one option. If they were going to get a new bassist, it had to be Ben Shepherd.

Hunter Benedict Shepherd was born on an American military base in Okinawa, Japan on September 20, 1968. Over the next several years, his family bounced around the US before putting down roots in Kingston, Washington, a small logging hamlet hugging Puget Sound, just across the way from Seattle. Shepherd fell in love with music at his father's feet. Before heading out for work, Shepherd's dad would often pick up an acoustic guitar and strum out Johnny Cash and Creedence Clearwater Revival songs while Ben dutifully shined up his boots.

The lengths that Shepherd went to to immerse himself in Seattle's musical underground as a teenager were extraordinary. He never had much money, so if he wanted to catch a show, he had to sneak onto a ferry from Bainbridge Island into town, sneak or talk his way into one of the venues, then sneak back onto the ferry and hitchhike home. The Central Tavern near Pioneer Square—above which Susan Silver rented an office space on the third floor along with Ken Deans and Kelly Curtis—was a favorite spot. As it happened, Shepherd was among the audience watching Soundgarden's second professional gig when they opened for Hüsker Dü at Gorilla Gardens back in 1985.

By the time he was a teenager, Shepherd was already playing in punk bands with names like March of Crimes, Mind Circus, and 600 School. At around 6'4" and thin as a rail, he cut a memorable figure onstage. Then came Nirvana. The connection was made by his old friend Chad Channing, who was still Nirvana's drummer at the time around 1988. Shepherd was out at a party one night in Olympia sitting on a couch by himself when Kurt Cobain ambled over and took up the space on the other end. The kindred loners hit it off and by the end of the night were passing an acoustic guitar back and forth, playing snatches of different songs together. Eventually, Cobain offered Shepherd a spot as a touring guitarist.

It was around that time that Shepherd ran into Kim Thayil at a Pere Ubu concert and learned that Hiro Yamamoto had quit Soundgarden. Thinking that it signaled the end of the band, Shepherd kicked an ashtray and let out a hearty "Goddamn it!" Thayil eased his concerns, explaining that they intended to carry on without Yamamoto and then asking if he might like to try playing bass?

Despite the fact that he was a guitarist, he felt obligated to give it a shot. But the twenty-year old wasn't exactly prepared when the moment came. The short notice didn't give him enough time to properly rehearse the parts from *Louder Than Love*. The audition turned into a loose jam session that lasted for three hours. "I remember Matt jumping up from behind the drums at one point and going '*A* for effort man, that's badass,' because he saw me wiping out on a part and recovering as fast as possible," Shepherd recalled.[10]

The three Soundgaren members were interested enough in the lanky guitarist that they brought him back for a second audition, but ultimately ended up going with the older and more experienced Everman. Shepherd was stung when he heard the news from Stuart Hallerman, but having grown up with Everman he felt that he might be somewhat incompatible with the other three Soundgarden guys from a personality standpoint. Shepherd held out hope that he'd get a second chance with Soundgarden at some point.

In the meantime, Shepherd went on tour with Nirvana under the assumption that he'd be playing lead guitar. That didn't turn out to be the case. Though he rehearsed and learned many of the songs from their next album, *Nevermind*, the band was still mostly playing shows packed with *Bleach* material, content to hone their forthcoming songs, like the soon-to-be omnipresent "Smells Like Teen Spirit," in private. Shepherd only ended up playing with Nirvana once, during a soundcheck on the first stop of the tour in Minneapolis. For the rest of the run, he was relegated to selling T-shirts.

Though Shepherd never became a full-fledged member of Nirvana, Kurt Cobain always felt a twinge of guilt about how they weren't able to make it happen. As he told Michael Azerrad for the definitive Nirvana biography *Come as You Are*, "I still kind of regret that because I like that guy a lot. He would have added to the band, definitely," he said. "He was kind of crazy sometimes, but that's okay. I'd rather have that than some moody metalhead."[11] The "moody metalhead" he was referring to was Jason Everman.

Shortly after informing Everman that they wanted to go with someone else on bass, Thayil invited Shepherd out for beers to see if he'd be interested in giving Soundgarden another shot. The next day, the entire band converged on Chris's house where the offer to join was presented. Shepherd simply spat on the ground and said, "Fuck yeah!"

It helped Shepherd's case that he'd grown up around Bainbridge Island, the same small outpost that Andrew Wood had come from. Ben knew Andy and had bought his 1972 Jazz Bass, which he nicknamed "Tree," from the Wood brothers. He was the kindred spirit that Soundgarden needed.

The band spent the next few weeks rehearsing with their new bassist, helping him sharpen his understanding of the material from *Louder Than Love* and preparing him for another full-on assault of North America. Meanwhile, for the first time, Chris took a seat in the producer's chair, helping his friends in Screaming Trees record their album *Uncle Anesthesia*. Susan Silver was managing the Trees at that point, and Terry Date nabbed a producer's credit for that record as well. "It was fun having [Chris] around," Screaming Trees guitarist Gary Lee Conner told Leonardo Tissot. "We were friends with Chris and we asked him to be kind of a go-between [between] Terry Date and ourselves. And he was able to, kind of, trying to convey to Terry what we were about."[12]

In addition to producing, Chris also played recorder on the song "Lay Your Head Down," and added backing vocals to "Alice Said," "Before We Arise," and the album's title track. Conner eventually decided to show his appreciation to Chris by giving him a black 1989 Gretsch G6128T Duo Jet guitar. It quickly became his go-to instrument. "I would never let it out of my sight," Chris told *Guitar World*. "It may only be a reissue, but it's a very important guitar to me."[13]

Soundgarden performed live for the first time with Shepherd at Lake City Concert Hall in Seattle on June 15, 1990. It had only been a year since Hiro Yamamoto departed the band. Soundgarden was an unannounced portion of the evening's entertainment, playing for a crowd of around three hundred at the Mormon Church-owned venue, while opening for a local glam band called Witch Dokters. Two weeks later, Shepherd was on a plane with the rest of the guys for a quick summer run through Europe that kicked off at the Roskilde Festival in Denmark.

The tour was an invigorating success. Shepherd held his own and proved beyond any doubt that he was the right choice. The band hardly missed a beat after returning home to the States, almost immediately hopping on a twenty-seven-date tour opening for Danzig, a popular metal band fronted by the former lead singer of the Misfits. The shows were gothic bonanzas with Glenn Danzig flogging songs from their latest album *Danzig II: Lucifuge* and Soundgarden trying to blow them off the stage each night with their own collection of doom-laden riffs and eye-popping onstage histrionics.

By the time they made it to a gig in Pittsburgh in the middle of the run, Shepherd was already proving his worth to the rest of Soundgarden—beyond even his duties as the bedrock of their rhythm section. Out in the crowd, a skinhead decided he didn't like Chris and tried to take a swing at him. Shepherd threw off his bass, dove headlong into the sea of bodies, latched onto the Nazi punk and proceeded to beat the shit out of him. Security stepped in and hauled the guy out. It wouldn't be the last time that Shepherd confronted someone out past the footlights of the stage.

There were several instances, however, when even the brawling bassist wasn't enough to dissuade a certain portion of the audience from invading Soundgarden's domain. "Soundgarden was touring with Danzig, and a big, blond, bearded, Nordic-looking guy jumped up on stage while we were playing. He wrapped his arms around my legs and just wouldn't let go," Chris remembered. Security swept in to try and pull the Viking wannabe away, but he was simply too strong. Instead of freaking out, Chris took it in stride and embraced the insanity of it all. "I decided, 'Well, this would be a good little challenge to see if I can keep singing the song and keep the rock going. Let's just see what happens here,'" he said. "It took like three-quarters of the song to get him off my legs."[14]

Soundgarden's nationwide tour ended on September 1 with a show at UC San Diego, but their year wasn't over quite yet. Two nights after bidding adieu to Danzig, Soundgarden was booked to appear again at Bumbershoot. Unlike the last time they performed at Seattle's longest-running music festival when they were a buzzed-about side-stage act, this time Soundgarden would be headlining, thanks to a last-minute cancellation by the Psychedelic Furs, ripping and roaring in front of twelve thousand people. As popular as they were in their hometown, they were still only a theater-sized draw nationally, which made Bumbershoot the biggest spotlight of their career thus far. They were determined to make the most of it.

Thayil ambled into view first, slamming into the sludgy chords to "Beyond The Wheel." Chris, clad in his typical stage uniform—Doc Martens, black shorts, no shirt—emerged beside him and started crooning in a low, foreboding register: "Faaaaar beyond the wheeeeeel." To his right, Shepherd plucked out the ominous rhythm while Cameron tapped on his cymbals behind them. Amid the twisted din, Chris soared into an impossibly high falsetto before all hell broke loose. The singer leapt and stomped around to the music while a mosh pit whipped up down in the front. By the time they made it to the next song, "Flower," his mic stand was bent at a forty-five-degree angle from smashing it into the floor over and over again. A multitude of fans swarmed up onto the stage and promptly dived headlong back into the mayhem from which they'd just emerged. Chris applauded their enthusiasm.

The show was a triumph, but the encore took it to another level. Rather than perform one of their own songs, Soundgarden busted out a live cover of Spinal Tap's lust-filled ode to juicy double's, "Big Bottom." Spinal Tap had actually performed at Bumbershoot before and had left behind one of their over-the-top set pieces, which Soundgarden borrowed. Out of nowhere, a large skull with glowing eyes and horns descended from the rafters as Chris wailed. To say the crowd lost its mind is an insult to the concept of insanity. They lapped up every second of it. Then, if things weren't already absurd enough, at the end of the song, Chris began singing "Jesus Is Just Alright," by the Art Reynolds Singers, while Thayil's guitar fed back into oblivion.

Chris followed this triumphant milestone with another. Less than three weeks later, on September 22, 1990, after five years of dating, Chris and Susan tied the knot. The small ceremony took place at their home in West Seattle in front of their closest friends and family. Chris's best friend Eric Garcia acted as his best man. Lisa Dutton was Susan's maid of honor. A small reception followed at a space called Woodsilk in Fremont. After that, the newlyweds departed for a honeymoon getaway in Victoria, BC.

Chris didn't get much time to bask in the glow of newly consecrated matrimony. Just a month later, Soundgarden was back on the road performing at Cult singer Ian Astbury's Gathering of the Tribes Festival, where he received an unwanted back rub from folk singer Joan Baez backstage while trying to finish his dinner. The band ended 1990 with a special show at the Central on October 29, where they were billed as Vince Whirlwind and the Nude Dragons—"Nude Dragons" being an anagram for "Soundgarden."

As his band's star rose, and his personal life evolved, Chris kept returning to those two songs he had written in tribute to Andrew Wood. By now, he'd recorded rudimentary demos of "Reach Down" and "Say Hello 2 Heaven" on his own and mixed them onto a cassette tape. The former track was arranged as a sweeping, gospel-tinged composition that he envisioned with a Neil Young-esque extended guitar jam à la "Down By The River" or "Cortez The Killer." He imagined the song as a dialogue between himself and his departed friend in a different reality where Andy had not only lived but made it: playing to crowds as big as the massive, outdoor US Festival. In "Reach Down" at least, Andrew Wood got to live his dream.

"Say Hello 2 Heaven" is more of a straightforward tribute, loaded with allusions to Andy and the people who knew and loved him. Chris cries in anguish over the loss of his friend who "came from an island" but "died from the street." On the demo, the pace of the song is a bit slower than it ultimately became, and the chorus effect on the guitar is a little more pronounced, but the raw emotion is palpable.

Chris had a few ideas about what to do with these new songs, but none of them involved Soundgarden. One day, he swung by his wife's office, which she shared with Kelly Curtis, and dropped off a copy of the tape. He had in mind an idea to record the songs with some of the members of Wood's band for a special single or something but couldn't quite work up the nerve to give them the tape himself. "I thought maybe they would think it was horrible and that I was an asshole," he explained.[15] That's when Susan stepped up. She reached out to Mother Love Bone bassist Jeff Ament and told him about the songs, then gave him the tape.

Both "Reach Down" and "Say Hello 2 Heaven" sounded fully realized to Ament. He called Chris to tell him how much he enjoyed them, which thrilled the singer. Ament's enthusiasm gave Chris the confidence that they should record the songs together. The bassist even proposed adding other songs into the mix, maybe even covering some of Wood's solo songs as part of the project as well.

At the time, Ament and Gossard were promoting the release of their lone full-length Mother Love Bone album, *Apple*, which finally saw the light on July 19, 1990. What Chris didn't know before that call was that Ament was jamming again with Mother Love Bone's guitarist, Stone Gossard, and a young lead guitar player named Mike McCready. Ament had gotten to know McCready from his job working at Piecora's, a pizza place across the street from his apartment. McCready ended up playing with both of them after Gossard caught him wailing away to a Stevie Ray Vaughan record at a party and decided to see what they could do together. Eventually they started writing songs and were contemplating forming a new band.

In the meantime, Ament and Gossard kept coming back to Chris's tape. The pull to honor their departed friend and write and record some music with Soundgarden's dynamic frontman was simply too strong to ignore. Eventually Chris brought Matt Cameron into the project along with McCready on lead guitar. Temple Of The Dog was born.

Their name was drawn from the opening lyrics to "Man of Golden Words," a Mother Love Bone song written by Andrew Wood: "I want to show you something like joy inside my heart / Seems I been living in the Temple Of The Dog." It didn't take long before the fivesome abandoned the idea of re-recording some of Wood's songs. "A few of Andy's friends and family, and his girlfriend, started grumbling, being a little concerned about our motives for doing Andy's music, which is totally fair," Chris told *RIP* magazine. "But it wasn't something that any of us felt like having to explain or worry about, so we decided we would make our own album, let the Andrew thing go, and have fun collaborating as a band, because we were really having a good time working together."[16]

With Wood's material off the table, the group went back to the drawing board and began cooking up enough musical ideas to flesh out an album. Ament and Gossard gave Chris some instrumental tracks for which he wrote lyrics and ultimately became the songs "Times Of Trouble," "Four Walled World," and the propulsive "Pushin' Forward Back." In a curious twist, the pair had included the "Times Of Trouble" instrumental on a five-track demo tape they had made for Red Hot Chili Peppers drummer Jack Irons. Irons in turn passed it on to his friend, a local San Diego petroleum warehouse employee named Eddie Vedder.

Vedder dubbed his own lyrics on the song, creating a new composition that he called "Footsteps." The singer sent the song back through the mail on a white cassette that also included the songs "Alive" and "Once." On the front, in Sharpie, he wrote, "For Stone + Jeff." The pair was impressed with what they heard and decided to invite Vedder up to Seattle to see if he was the right guy to take over on lead vocals for their new band with Mike McCready.

Meanwhile, Chris's pen kept busy. In addition to the music he was given by Ament and Gossard, he also put together the songs "Your Savior" and "All Night Thing." Both were conscious efforts to try and write something in the vein of "Reach Down" and "Say Hello 2 Heaven." Other songs that ended up on the album, like "Hunger Strike" and "Wooden Jesus," had been bouncing around inside of his head for a while, but because they hadn't felt right for Soundgarden he had left them by the wayside.

Not long after Chris got back from his honeymoon in October, he along with Matt Cameron, Stone Gossard, Jeff Ament, and Mike McCready began rehearsing together at his brother Peter's house in Des Moines, Washington, several miles south of Seattle near the SeaTac airport. The home was an eight-hundred-square-foot cottage built on Chris's grandparents' property. Chris and Peter had knocked down some of the cottage's walls and turned it into a makeshift studio where Soundgarden often knocked around song ideas and where Temple Of The Dog was essentially born. After about four different sessions, the five men concluded that they had a real record on their hands and moved operations over to London Bridge Studio in November, where they linked up with producer Rick Parashar and got down to business.

"There wasn't a budget for it really," engineer Dave Hillis said. Indeed, though Soundgarden's label A&M eventually released the album, it wasn't like the band went into the studio with a large stack of cash to throw around. Studio time wasn't cheap, and time was of the essence. In fact, Parashar deployed some pretty interesting techniques just to keep costs low. "It was used tape, so there were old tracks from whoever recorded on it before," Hillis added.

Given the absence of a real budget and label oversight, Temple Of The Dog was free to do whatever they wanted. "The whole situation was just so non-pressure-filled," Gossard said. "Nobody expected this to be anything, so when we just went in and did it the record company wasn't around, we basically paid for it ourselves." [17] All told, the sessions lasted about fourteen days. Most of the work was done on weekends through November and into December to save even more money.

The stickiest song to record was probably "Reach Down." The green Mike McCready simply wasn't nailing the extended guitar solo in the way that Chris had envisioned. To his ears, there simply wasn't enough passion blasting through the amplifiers. Initially, McCready tried to approximate the guitar solo that Chris laid down on the demo tape, but the singer wanted more than that.

Chris could see McCready was holding back and made several attempts to coax the best performance out of him. He even tried leaving the room, but the results remained the same. After that, the guys converged on the guitarist and admonished him for playing too politely. They wanted to hear him go berserk.

Challenged by his bandmates, McCready dug deep. "He went out of his mind," Chris said with awe years later. "You can tell he's trying to remember every trick he's ever learned."[18] Given the proper motivation, McCready unfurled the nastiest, funkiest, most blistering instrumental passage of guitar music that Seattle had seen since the days of Jimi Hendrix. He got so into the song that, midway through, he knocked his headphones off. Undeterred, he kept playing. During that nearly four-minute span that the aural spotlight centered on him, he notched his place as one of rock's next great guitar heroes.

By now, the band had nine songs in the can. "Pushin' Forward Back," the only track that Ament and Gossard were credited as writing together, leaned on drummer Matt Cameron's ability to beat together odd time signatures, in this case an off-kilter 7/4, for one of the more aggressive offerings on the record. The drummer really excelled on Cornell's composition "Wooden Jesus," busting out all sorts of weird percussive elements and rolling fills.

Gossard's other contributions to *Temple Of The Dog*, "Times Of Trouble" and "Four Walled World," sound far more laid back than many of the other entries on the record, but still simmer with palpable intensity thanks to Chris's searing vocals. On both "Times Of Trouble" and "Wooden Jesus," Chris briefly flashed his surprisingly proficient abilities on two different instruments he's not exactly known for playing; wailing away like Little Walter on the harmonica on the former track, while plucking out melodies on a banjo on the latter.

"Call Me a Dog," a melancholic barnburner that the singer wrote about a couple at odds with one another—"You wore me out like an old winter coat"—remains a thrilling highlight of the album and a heavy contender for best vocal performance Chris ever delivered in a recording studio. "Your Savior" is a funky proto-prelude to Soundgarden's "Jesus Christ Pose," while the closer, "All Night Thing," remains the perfect end-of-the-evening reflection on love and difficult choices.

Of all the songs that made it onto *Temple Of The Dog*, "Hunger Strike" is far and away the most recognized, which is ironic given that the song came together largely as an afterthought. Chris generally hated odd numbers, and as the band finished off the record, he realized that they had nine songs total. Rather than remove a track, he felt compelled to make it an even ten.

"Hunger Strike" is one of the only songs Chris ever wrote after smoking weed. Through reddened eyes, he picked up a guitar and started playing the opening arpeggio for a while before landing on the melody. The lyrics came quickly after that, but only one verse. He tried writing a second verse, but it just wasn't working, so he left what he had, and assumed it'd make for a nice, deep album cut. Then Eddie Vedder arrived.

Gossard, Ament, and McCready were fully invested in getting their band Mookie Blaylock off the ground, with their new singer from San Diego. Chris and Eddie met for the first time during a Temple Of The Dog rehearsal. Vedder flew up to Seattle on October 8 to meet and play with his prospective bandmates. In a strange twist of fate, just a few days earlier, he had been down in Irvine, California watching Soundgarden perform at an outdoor amphitheater. Just another fan.

Chris always envisioned singing "Hunger Strike" with a high, soaring register accompanied by a lower harmony to round it out. He figured he'd be able to handle both parts himself. As he was working through the arrangement with the rest of the band though, singing at the highest reaches of his voice, he felt a presence move in behind him. Vedder had been sitting in a corner, affixing strips of duct tape to a drum. He couldn't help noticing that Chris kept having to cut off one part of the vocal to start the other.

There was only one microphone set up in the room, but Eddie signaled to Chris that he had an idea. It was a bold move from the out-of-towner, but Chris made space for him in front of the mic. Suddenly, the two men were singing the chorus together, wrapping their voices around one another. Chris was free to blast off into the stratosphere while Vedder was right there next to him, keeping his feet on the ground.

From that rehearsal, Chris realized that including two singers, especially one as adept as Vedder, could only work to enhance the overall composition. "Hunger Strike" only had one verse really, but if he sang that verse, and then passed the same verse over to Vedder to repeat it, it would sound fresh to the listener's ears. The next time Vedder was in town, Chris invited him to London Bridge Studio so that they could record their parts together.

While Seattle was gripped by a snowstorm that blanketed the city with fourteen inches of ice-covered powder, turning the city's steep streets into a tangle of treacherous tobogganing hills, Chris and Eddie huddled inside of London Bridge, singing back and forth. No other members of Mookie Blaylock or Soundgarden were around. It took around forty minutes to get the final take. For Eddie, the invitation to add his voice to the song was a gesture he never forgot. "It was such a nice way to be ushered onto vinyl for the first time," Vedder told author Greg Prato. "I'm indebted to Chris time eternal for being invited onto that track."[19] In addition to "Hunger Strike," Vedder also contributed background vocals to "Four Walled World," "Pushin' Forward Back," and "Your Savior."

Seattle was an extremely tight-knit musical community. Outsiders weren't always embraced with open arms, but Chris went out of his way to make Vedder feel like a real member of the scene from the jump. "Ed was super, super shy," McCready told Rolling Stone. "Chris took him out for beers and told him stories. He was like, 'Hey, welcome to Seattle. I love Jeff and Stone. I give you my blessing.' From then on, he was more relaxed."[20]

Chris made his support for Vedder even more well known around town by showing up for Mookie Blaylock's first Seattle concert at the Off Ramp on October 22, 1990. He was impressed, not just by the band, but also by the reaction. "All of the people standing around me, by about the third or fourth song, had this mysterial glow in their eyes, like they understood that this was a special moment," Chris recalled.[21]

Chris wanted Temple Of The Dog to feel like a real band. Just a month after Mookie Blaylock's coming out party, he and the rest of the guys booked a show of their own at the Off Ramp on November 13. They worked hard to try and keep the whole thing as low-key as possible, however. They weren't even billed to perform that night—Bathtub Gin and Inspector Luv and the Ride Me Babys were the listed entertainment—but those in the know caught wind of what was about to go down.

The performance was a disaster. Chris often called it "Seattle's Altamont." The three hundred who showed up didn't know any of the songs and most of the tracks were tame compared to the savage and bois-terous music they were used to hearing from both Mother Love Bone and Soundgarden. The mood in the room turned hostile, violence erupted, and Eric Johnson, Soundgarden's trusted roadie, was taken to the hospital after getting hit in the face by a bottle.

Temple Of The Dog performed again a little over a month later on December 22. Alice In Chains was headlining a show at Seattle's 1,400-seat Moore Theatre to celebrate the release of their debut album *Facelift*. It was billed as an "X-Mas Bash" and the promo poster mysteriously prom-ised "Surprise Guests!?" The guest turned out to be Mookie Blaylock, but by the end of their set Chris was onstage screaming out the words to "Say Hello 2 Heaven" in his trusty "90" sweater with a beret covering his curly mane. After that, he dueted with Vedder on "Hunger Strike" before lifting the newcomer on top of his shoulders and parading him around the stage in a victory lap.

Mookie Blaylock wouldn't be Mookie Blaylock much longer. A short while later, they changed their name to Pearl Jam.

With *Temple Of The Dog* mixed and mastered, all that was left to do was film a video. Chris picked "Hunger Strike" to serve as the album's lead single, so that's the one they decided to service to MTV's *120 Minutes*. Susan Silver, remembering the work that a filmmaker named Paul Rachman had done on Alice In Chains' "Man in the Box" video a year earlier, decided to reach out and see if he'd be interested in taking on this new project. As a fan of both Soundgarden and Mother Love Bone, he quickly booked a flight to Seattle to meet with Chris, Susan, and Pearl Jam's manager, Kelly Curtis.

Chris wasn't enthusiastic about appearing in the video. He preferred something more opaque or cinematic, but the Mother Love Bone mem-bers felt strongly about appearing on-screen. Rachmann spent a week in Seattle with the band to try and come up with an idea that everyone liked. One person's opinion carried more weight than the others. "Chris really was the lead creative on this video," Rachman said. "Once he decided he liked an idea, that's what we did."

Chris took the director out to one of his favorite spots, a large recreational space named Discovery Park. It's a gorgeous, open expanse of land with the crystalline blue water of Elliott Bay on one side and a forest of evergreens on the other. The rest of the park is dotted with a collection of abandoned military buildings and a large waste treatment plant set near the West Point Light House. Totally grunge.

Rachman fell for the location. "There was just this diversity of landscapes and looks that was stunningly beautiful," the director recalled. "I said, 'This is great, let's do it here. We'll have some performance, but out in this amazing landscape.' I think Chris really liked that idea, and it really resonated with what the meaning of this album and this song was to them."

With a budget of about $60,000, they didn't have a lot of time to mess around. Unfortunately, the day they chose to film turned out to be a bit of climatological nightmare. Everyone woke to a light coating of snow on the ground, which fortunately dissipated by the time they arrived at the park. They completed some interior shots inside of some of the buildings before moving outside. Rain drizzled from the hazy gray sky, but during the nighttime portion of the shoot, a quick but violent hailstorm dumped two-inch chunks of ice on their heads and dented Matt Cameron's drum kit.

Chris wasn't a stranger to filming music videos and was comfortable miming his parts and playing along with the production. "He was really great to work with," Rachman recalled. "He was probably one of the kindest rock stars I've ever collaborated with on a video. He just got it."

Eddie Vedder was markedly less comfortable than Chris. "Hunger Strike" was his first time appearing in a video and the act of lip-syncing threw him off a bit. "I kind of directed him to pick something out there to look at and just listen and sing," Rachman said. "You can see he has this faraway gaze in there and it helped him, but he didn't like lip-syncing. It felt weird to him. Inauthentic."

Temple Of The Dog was released on April 16, 1991, at the same time Mariah Carey's self-titled debut was reigning over the charts and R.E.M.'s *Out of Time* was dominating the conversation in the world of rock. Upon initial release, sales of the album were modest. It sold around seventy thousand copies during its initial run but didn't crack the Billboard 200.

It's not hard to understand why the record didn't reach a lot of people at the outset. Soundgarden, though gaining prominence, was still looking for their own commercial breakthrough. Asking fans to take a chance on a side project from the lead singer of that band, backed by a group of musicians from another band they hadn't yet heard of, was a tall order. It was going to take the potential audience out there for *Temple Of The Dog* a little while longer to catch up.

CHAPTER VII

LOOKING CALIFORNIA

A perfect, heavy silence reigned in the remote cabin. Off in the distance, the mighty Pacific Ocean roared with a broiling fury as white-capped waves crashed against the hard sand. Inside this tiny outpost on Washington's Olympic Peninsula, there was nothing. The place didn't even have a phone. If Chris Cornell wanted sound, he'd have to make it himself.

Chris sequestered himself inside this humble outpost in Kalaloch, Washington, in 1991 with a single goal in mind: to write songs. The recording sessions for Soundgarden's next album were only a few weeks away, and he needed lyrics. He had a few thematic ideas and melodies in mind for the batch of demo tapes that Thayil, Shepherd, and Cameron had given him, along with some of his own material, but he needed time and space to flesh them out. Feeling pressure to deliver, Chris packed a bag, loaded it into his grandfather's 1966 Chrysler, and set off for the coast of Washington on a self-imposed ten-day withdrawal from society. No distractions. No bandmates. No modern conveniences. Even his wife stayed behind. The only companion he brought was one of their three small Pomeranians.

Kalaloch is a gloomy wonderland, where annual rainfall is measured in feet, bald eagle sightings are commonplace, and mighty gray whales can be glimpsed breaching the surface of the ocean. The nearby

Hoh Rainforest, lush with moss-covered trees, is only a short drive east. Chris didn't care about any of it. "A lot of people wanna go to inspirational places, where the surroundings will cause them to be relaxed or maybe elevate them," he said. "For me, it's the opposite: the less going on, the better for me to write. If I'm looking at a beautiful thing or I'm in a beautiful environment, I start absorbing that and not paying attention to the writing."[1]

The experiment in sensory deprivation proved fruitful. After a few days, the previously blank pages he brought along filled up with ideas. Sketches of verses melded with chorus lines. Intricate bridge parts in a multitude of meters started to coalesce. Ideas flowed out in a torrent of block letters on lined paper, except for a lowercase *i* here and *g* there that he couldn't resist affixing with a tiny dot above or a tight curl below.

The freedom he enjoyed to wander around and explore the untapped corners of his mind was exhilarating. "No matter what I'm writing, I'm writing a soundtrack to a somewhat imaginary world," he once explained. "I have to get lost in what that imaginary world is, and then start listening and work out, 'What am I hearing here?'"[2]

By 1991, Chris's ability to tap into those imaginary worlds and extract something revelatory had grown substantially. The themes he was exploring were deeper than ever: monolithic concepts like religion, control, and commercialism. He was also finding more of himself in his lyrics, even though he disdained navel-gazing. He never wanted to write songs where he was the center of attention, preferring to couch his thoughts and feelings in a more open and relatable manner.

That's not to say he wasn't inspired by the world around him. Snatches of conversations, distant memories, things he'd seen on magazine racks and on television swirled in his mind, waiting to tumble out over the array of chords and off-kilter time patterns emanating from the strings of his guitar. The music always came first. Lyrics were a secondary concern. There had been exceptions, like "Ocean Fronts," written around the time *Screaming Life* came together. For the most part, however, the mood, the minor and major keys, the dangling sevenths and ninths, dictated everything.

Even for someone as comfortable with solitude as Chris Cornell, ten days is a long time to spend inside your own mind. "It started getting pretty wild after the fifth day," he remembered.[3] "The voice in your head becomes really loud, and since all you're doing is thinking, anything memorable that happens that day, happens in your head." After crossing the midway mark of his self-imposed sojourn, paranoia crept in. He admitted to "freaking out" at one point but refused to head home. He needed to finish what he started. Every songwriter approaches the act of songwriting differently. Some wait for inspiration to strike, allowing huge swaths of time to pass between projects in the pursuit of something that feels right to them. This was not how Chris worked. Elbow grease was his MO.

When in writing mode, Chris would spend hours banging his head against the wall until a decent melody or lyric popped out. Once he had the spark of an idea, he'd spend days, weeks, months, sometimes even years refining them until he felt they sounded compelling and inspired enough to share with the rest of the world. It was a brutal method of creation, bordering on self-flagellation, but he didn't know any other way. He willed himself be creative regardless of whether he was in the mood.

By the tenth day, Chris felt he had enough lyrics together to take back to the band. Just as he was getting set to leave, inspiration struck. He reached for his pad and wrote out the voluminous spray of words to accompany one of Matt Cameron's instrumentals, "Drawing Flies." Now, he was ready to go.

With a dog in one hand and a guitar in the other, he climbed back into that old Chrysler, merged onto Highway 101, and pointed the nose of the car back home. He felt good. But when he turned on the radio, the real world rushed back in. "They were announcing that Desert Shield was turning into Desert Storm and I just thought, 'That's it, we're screwed.'"[4]

* * *

1991 was a year of tremendous upheaval. After four decades of tension, the Cold War concluded with the collapse of the Soviet Union. In the Middle East, UN forces led by the United States pushed from the border of Kuwait deep into southern Iraq, signaling the beginning of America's decades-long armed entanglement within that region. Stateside, *Terminator 2: Judgment Day* was breaking records at the box office, Super Nintendo proliferated living rooms, and the number of computers linked to the Internet reached one million.

The music world was experiencing its own upheaval. Freddie Mercury, the iconic lead singer of Queen, passed away after a heartbreaking bout with AIDS. Miles Davis, Johnny Thunders, and Rob Tyner, lead singer of the MC5, died as well. Hip-hop continued its sharp ascendency into larger cultural acceptance following the release of hit records by A Tribe Called Quest, Ice Cube, and Public Enemy. And in the far-flung corner of Washington State, three bands were preparing to unveil albums that would shift the focus of the rock and roll-loving universe away from the hairspray-teased scene in Hollywood to the rain-swept streets of Seattle.

"It was very chaotic in ninety-one," Chris told the German television network VIVA2. "Everyone was fighting for their own identity, trying to deal with the fact that we're coming from a situation where, in the late eighties, people who were considered rock stars were more or less hated by the community that *we* were in, and now all of a sudden people are suggesting that *we* are rock stars."[5]

At the beginning of the year, the members of Soundgarden hadn't yet been forced to reckon with that new reality. Industry insiders had their eyes on Seattle, but the word "grunge" hadn't become a ubiquitous, catch-all phrase within the media. The fashion world was still a long way off from sending supermodels down Paris runways in tattered flannel shirts. Pearl Jam was still Mookie Blaylock and Nirvana was just another underground buzz band hoping their major label debut wouldn't turn into a belly flop.

Soundgarden was hard at work, seeking to capitalize on the six-figure sales success they enjoyed with *Louder Than Love*. They'd been playing, touring, and recording together in a few different configurations over the last six years and their hard work was starting to pay off. Within the band, among the rock press, and inside the walls of A&M, there was a palpable sense that they were poised to make a huge leap in commercial viability and cultural recognition.

Being tagged as The Next Big Thing comes with a tidal wave of pressure that can be hard to fathom, but Chris was uniquely prepared to meet the moment. The singer was in the midst of one of the most inspired writing periods of his life, consumed by the act of making music. He was taking bigger risks and dedicating more of his time to figuring out how to piece together the varied elements that sprung from his brain. Vivid lyrics, earworm-inducing melodies, unexpected chord progressions, and captivating bridge sections were pouring out of him almost as fast as he could commit them to tape.

Before Soundgarden got back in touch with producer Terry Date and began the process of recording their next album in earnest, the band spent several weeks in Stuart Hallerman's recording studio, Avast!, demoing new songs, rehearsing completed compositions, and jamming. For hours and hours at a time, they holed themselves up inside the cement-floored recording room, intertwining their instruments to create a savage cacophony of envelope-pushing, aggressive metal music. When night fell, they rolled their amplifiers against the back wall to make room for whatever clients Hallerman had booked to record that evening, only to push them back into place the following day when work resumed.

Badmotorfinger—the odd name was a tongue-in-cheek play on the song "Bad Motor Scooter" by seventies rockers Montrose—wouldn't suffer from a lack of commitment. Every single day, for months on end, Chris remained obsessed with shaping and honing each element of every single song. *Badmotorfinger* became his life: an all-consuming passion that he poured every bit of himself into, to the point that he began to lose any semblance of objectivity about whether what he was writing, playing, and singing sounded any good. When that happened, even though he wasn't a big drinker at this point, he took home a bottle of Jim Beam and downed the entire thing by himself just to try to gain a change in perspective.

Thanks in large part to Chris's voluminous creativity, Soundgarden's collaborative nature evolved as well. Working on his own with an eight-track recorder, Chris cooked up a vast array of fully realized compositions in which he played all the parts before presenting them to his bandmates. "Rather than coming back with a memory of having learned a riff or a part on guitar, I came home with a cassette of clear, fully recorded eight-track studio recordings of two or three songs that Chris had done and presented to the band, and I didn't know how to play them yet," Thayil remembered.[6]

The other significant change to the band's process was Ben Shepherd. The young bassist added fresh sparks, creatively and emotionally, that had been missing since Hiro Yamamoto's departure. Shepherd took some of the pressure off Chris, while reaffirming his belief that there was a path forward for Soundgarden. "It was when Ben joined the band that I real-ized, 'OK, we're going to have a future with this,'" the singer said. "'We're going to make great records.'"[7]

Shepherd's presence broadened the band's sonic capabilities, perhaps never more so than during the creation of "Jesus Christ Pose." The bassist was sitting on the floor inside Avast! one day when he started digging into a gnarly, detuned riff that he'd recently come up with. Matt Cameron fell right in, bringing a bracing percussive order to the music. It was all Shepherd could do to keep his eyes off the drummer so that he wouldn't fuck up the bassline.

Thayil stood back for a bit on a stage that Hallerman had constructed, trying to make sense of what the duo were doing. Once the chaos jelled in his head, he joined in with gusto, throwing every noisy trick he had at the song. The jam eventually fell apart, but the band had wisely recorded the moment. Chris took the tape home to write lyrics and was inspired enough by what he heard to touch on some thought-provoking themes. That same year, the photographer Chris Cuffaro mailed a promo card to Chris featuring a picture of Perry Farrell laid out on a white bedspread with his arms spread out like the crucified Christ. That particular image, and others like it that adorned the covers of countless magazines through-out that era, got Chris to thinking.

"Christ is pretty much the most famous rock star out, so Christ has an influence on rock stars and fashion models," Chris told *Seconds* magazine. "That's fine, it's just the way they exploit that symbol, as if they're putting themselves into the light of assuming their self-persecution, which is irri-tating, especially when it comes to fashion models. They sold their souls for rock and roll, they sold their souls for really expensive shoes that hurt when they walk but look really good."[8]

"Jesus Christ Pose" became a lacerating take-down of would-be supermarket-rack messiahs. When Chris brought the completed demo in for the band to hear, they were floored by how he had managed to turn a demolition derby of a jam into an honest-to-God song. "Jesus Christ Pose" remains one of the few Soundgarden songs for which all four members received a writing credit.

Soundgarden had always been a band that worked best when everyone contributed. It was Chris's Beatles ideal writ large. Since Yamamoto left, there'd been a void of input from the bass section that Ben Shepherd gladly filled. In addition to "Jesus Christ Pose," he also nabbed writing credits for the songs "Face Pollution," "Somewhere," for which he also wrote the lyrics, and "Slaves & Bulldozers," a swaggering leviathan of a track that he worked on with Chris.

"Slaves & Bulldozers" is a perfect example of how inspiration can come from the most unexpected places. The song, which served as the band's dynamic live show closer for years, coalesced while they worked on an early version of "Fell On Black Days." As they jammed with it in the studio, the music morphed into something else entirely. It wasn't what the world would come to hear as "Fell On Black Days" in the coming years, but an entirely different, captivating thing. And yet it still wasn't complete.

Everything fell into place once Chris came up with a chorus. He was hanging out at Scott Sundquist's house one day, and the two men were creating weird noise collages together when they ran into a problem. "There was this dead spot where I couldn't get from one thing to another and started playing that riff, and the riff is what connected those two things, and I felt like that's gotta be a song," he recalled. "There was a chant over it, which went 'Take dope, feel good, do it, yeah!' And Scott had an overdub where he would go, 'Take a dope-uhhhhh.' And it reminded me of this Jim Jones kind of scary thing, and I just always liked it, and that riff just sort of fit in with Ben's riff."[9]

The phrase "Slaves & Bulldozers" never shows up in the lyrics. The provocative title actually came courtesy of a small child named Tristan who was enrolled in the head start program at the United Indians of All Tribes Foundation based in Seattle. One of Thayil's best friends worked at the Foundation and noticed the young boy playing a game one day where he was making truck noises while moving in a straight line and pushing past the children that obstructed his path. When Thayil's buddy Brad asked Tristan what he was doing, he cheerily responded, "We're playing slaves and bulldozers!" Thayil told the story to the band, and the name just seemed to fit the heaviness of the song they were working on.

The guitarist received a separate lightning strike of inspiration for another song called "Room a Thousand Years Wide" after chatting with *Fopp* producer Steve Fisk one day. While talking, the subject turned to a 1922 Swedish documentary-style horror film titled *Häxan* and a line chanted by witch during a spell: "Tomorrow begat tomorrow." Thayil enjoyed the metaphor about how time just keeps on moving forward into infinity and thought the concept would make for a cool song.

Among the collection of demos that Matt Cameron shared with the band was a disconcerting instrumental with a heavy chug that Thayil thought provided the perfect aural bedrock to write around. The sound reminded him of a similarly foreboding song called "C.S.C.L.D.F." by the Swiss industrial rock band the Young Gods. He listened to Cameron's tape repeatedly before thoughtfully wrapping some words around the piledriving guitars. He presented "Room a Thousand Years Wide" to Chris by humming the melodies so that the singer could get a feel for what he was going for before trying to sing it himself. The chaotic Iggy Pop and the Stooges-reminiscent sax solo from Thayil's friend Scott Granlund remains an inspired touch.

"Room a Thousand Years Wide" was the first new song the public got to hear from Soundgarden in the wake of *Louder Than Love*. The band decided to hand over an early, less-polished version to their old buddies at Sub Pop, who released it as part of their popular Singles Club program. "Room a Thousand Years Wide" went out on September 1, 1990, along with a B-side rager called "HIV Baby" that Chris wrote after watching Shepherd tease Thayil on tour about the guitarist's mild germaphobia. Thayil wasn't keen on sharing silverware or straws.

While his bandmates continued to present inspired material, much of the way *Badmotorfinger* ultimately sounded stemmed from Chris's experiments on guitar. He was far from a novice by now but was still in the process of figuring out the different things he could do on the fretboard. He became enamored with altered tunings and tried to create music that didn't sound like anything anyone had heard before. What he may have lacked in Eddie Van Halen-style dexterity he made up for in inventiveness. The song "Mind Riot" sprang to life after he tuned all six strings on his guitar to E notes—EEEEEE—and played around with different droning progressions. One of the reasons the band hardly ever played "Mind Riot" live was because of how difficult it was to keep the guitar in tune.

His biggest revelation was the discovery of drop B tuning, the process of dropping the entire guitar down by a minor third and then lowering the heavy bass string down an additional whole note. This new configuration helped him create melodies that were guaranteed to shred stereo subwoofers from coast to coast. Album opener "Rusty Cage" was created in drop B, as were "Searching With My Good Eye Closed" and "Holy Water." Interestingly, *Badmotorfinger* remains the only album where Chris really played around with drop B tunings in a substantial way. Over time, it became harder and harder for him to find unique methods to work within that particular structure without making things that sounded like something he'd already done before.

"Searching With My Good Eye Closed" is a triumph of psychedelic ferocity. Its most distinctive attribute is the demonic-sounding intro, interpolated from a children's toy, that just like Soundgarden's earlier efforts like "665" or "667," playfully takes the piss out of some of heavy metal's oftentimes embarrassing preoccupation with Satan. The effect was serendipitous. One day, Chris and a friend were messing around with a See 'n Say, pulling the string and listening to a variety of animals like pigs and cows mutter their signature oinks and moos. Then after one pull, the toy malfunctioned and made a disconcerting, dirge-like sound. Instinctively, he joked out loud, "And the devil says!" In that moment, he found the intro to "Searching with My Good Eye Closed." When he showed it to the rest of the band, they fell out in stitches.

The frenetic "Rusty Cage" remains the most highly regarded of his many experiments with drop B, however. He came up with the signature riff one day messing around on an electric guitar while lounging on the couch in his living room. Before it had a name, he called the composition "Hillybilly Sabbath," a tip of the cap to the English proto-metal icons. The words came while Chris was riding on a bus during one of Soundgarden's tours through Europe. As he gazed out the window, watching the pastoral landscape slide past, he started feeling trapped. He wanted to break and run free. The lyrics swirled inside his head, but he didn't put them to paper. He let them sit for weeks, before eventually making it back to the US where he tried to create music that could illustrate his inner frustration.

"Rusty Cage" is the kind of song that constantly keeps you on your toes. The time signature shifts throughout, from 4/4 in the first half, to a 3/4 waltz-like vibe, then moving up to 5/4. The complex nature of "Rusty Cage," combined with its volcanic expression of full-throated fury, is what made it so shocking when Johnny Cash, under the guidance of Rick Rubin, decided to strip it down to create his own version four years later.

Originally, Rubin approached Chris with the idea to write a new song for "The Man in Black." As a longtime fan of Cash's work going back to the days when his brother would play the singer's 1969 album *Live at San Quentin* around the house, Chris was more than happy to take on the assignment. The song he wrote and submitted was called "Cleaning My Gun," but after hearing the finished results, Rubin and Cash passed on it. Rather than becoming deflated, the rejection turned into something of an "a-ha!" moment for Chris. "There was too much range in the vocal arrangement," he remembered being told. "His point was that he likes to do songs that anybody can sing, and that went into the back of my mind—my first thought was, 'Oh fuck, I've been doing this wrong my whole career! I've been doing the opposite: I'm writing songs that I can barely sing, let alone somebody else.'"[10]

Once they abandoned "Cleaning My Gun," Rubin came back and asked Chris to try and re-arrange "Rusty Cage" in a manner that would be conducive to Cash's delivery. He tried, but after spending a few hours tinkering with his original composition, he couldn't see a way for it to work. Chris told Rubin as much, so the producer approached someone else to create a chug-a-lugging, Americana-ized instrumental for the Soundgarden singer's lyrics, and the rest, as they say, is history.

Cash was nominated for Best Male Country Performance at the Grammys in 1998 for his take on "Rusty Cage." The album that carried the song, *Unchained*, won for Best Country Album. For the rest of his life, Chris remained touched that one of his heroes thought enough of his work to offer his own interpretation on it. It also validated a facet of his artistry that he felt had been long overlooked. "When Johnny Cash covered 'Rusty Cage,' it was the first time I received compliments from my lyrics."[11]

Once Soundgarden felt like they had a handle on the songs they'd stitched together at Avast!, the four men and Terry Date took off down south to Sausalito, California, just across the bay from San Francisco, to Studio D and began tracking Matt's drums and working out some of Chris's vocals. Studio D was a prime location for Soundgarden. Their buddies Faith No More had used the facility to record their albums *Introduce Yourself* and *The Real Thing* previously, and the building was situated right next to an off-leash dog park.

Studio D was essentially a single-room studio with a couple of isolation booths. While there, Chris's voice was so loud when he tried to sing along during a take it would actually bleed into the drum mics. In order to keep the tracks isolated, Date suggested that he sing and play in the control room with him while the rest of the band raged in the studio.

After completing an initial round of recording in Sausalito, the band returned north and sequestered themselves inside of Bear Creek Studios in rural Woodinville, Washington. There they went about the meticulous business of making the record proper. It was nice to be closer to home in a bucolic setting making music, but at the time, Chris was preoccupied by the Gulf War. He worried enough about the underlying motivation of control over the vast sea of oil pooled under Iraq as a root cause that he actually gave up driving his car for a bit and sometimes rode his mountain bike the thirty miles to and from the studio each day. The long rides were murder on his knees.

The band was well prepared, but there were some bumps along the way. The first time Chris attempted to lay down his lead vocals for "Outshined," he sang the verses for about an hour. When he went into the control room to hear the playback, there was an off-putting layer of distortion over the track due to a technical snafu. Pissed that he'd wasted the best of his voice that day, Chris picked up a nearby coffee cup and hurled it into the wall, shattering it into a cloud of ceramic dust.

If Chris was frustrated, it was probably because he knew he had something really special with "Outshined." This was the era prior to the proliferation of cell phones, when rock groups could debut new songs to live crowds and not worry that shaky videos of their latest compositions might end up on the internet for the entire world to critique. Soundgarden regularly played unheard tracks live before recording them, and just the year before, right around Halloween, they debuted a nascent version of "Outshined" to a crowd at the Central Tavern who went absolutely apeshit for it.

As any English majors reading this would be quick to note, "Outshined" is a malapropism. It seems like a real word but isn't. This was intentional. The title predated the song itself and was inspired by Andrew Wood, who enjoyed coming up with titles and lyrics that sounded like correct English but weren't. The unintended consequence of this stylistic choice were the legions of people who approached Chris over the next several decades to point out that it should've been "Outshone." "I didn't give a shit then," he said while strumming an acoustic guitar onstage in Israel in 2016. "And I don't give a shit now."[12]

"Outshined" was one of the first songs where Chris cracked open a window into his mind and allowed the rest of the world a glimpse of what was going on inside. "It felt unusual and rock and it meant something at the time to me in that sort of confessional, when you're not feeling necessarily confident, but at the same time, you don't view the outside world as being better," Chris said.[13]

Like "Rusty Cage," the central line of the song came to him while he was out on tour. One day, when he wasn't feeling great, he looked into the mirror and caught sight of himself. He was wearing some baggy tennis shorts and a red T-shirt. Even though he didn't feel very good, as he scanned himself up and down, he couldn't help but notice that he looked like a carefree beach bum from somewhere like Venice Beach or Santa Monica. That's when it came to him: 'I'm looking California / And feeling Minnesota."

Those two outlooks smashed together precisely captured not just his own inner turmoil, but also crystallized the disjointed ennui of his audience. "I don't know how everyone else feels, but I definitely go through periods of extreme self-confidence, feeling like I can do anything," Chris told *RIP* magazine in 1992. "But then someone will say something, however insignificant, or I'll get something in my head and, all of a sudden, I'm plummeting in the opposite direction, I'm a piece of shit, and I really can't do anything about it. That's where 'Outshined' comes from, and why I'll never consider myself a hero."[14]

The line was so evocative that the filmmakers behind a 1996 dramatic comedy starring Keanu Reeves and Cameron Diaz decided to snatch it for the title of their film: *Feeling Minnesota*. Chris himself had nothing to do with the movie, however. "My lawyer told me we could sue them, but I just didn't want to be a part of that," he said. "I was kind of embarrassed about it at the time."[15]

With a dozen songs completed and a handful more like "Cold Bitch" and "She's a Politician" set aside for another day, *Badmotorfinger* was pretty much finished by the end of spring. Shortly afterwards, the band flew to Can-Am Studios in Tarzana, California, where they worked hand-in-hand with engineer Ron St. Germain to mix the record. After seemingly fumbling this part of the process on most of their previous releases, they were determined to get the sound right this time and spent two weeks living out of apartments in the San Fernando Valley while tweaking every track to perfection.

A&M started gearing up to release *Badmotorfinger* around the end of summer. The label had originally pegged September 24, 1991, for the release date, the same day Nirvana planned on releasing their second album, *Nevermind*, but production problems caused it to be pushed back a couple of weeks to October 8. The only thing left to do was design a cover.

Everyone in the band agreed that they wanted to go with something more abstract than another shirtless shot of Chris. Kim Thayil and Matt Cameron ultimately approached an artist named Mark Dancey, who was the guitarist in a Detroit-based group named Big Chief. Dancey's band had opened for Soundgarden at St. Andrew's Hall in 1989, where he gave the headliners a collection of his designs. Two years later, the guitarist and drummer recalled his work and thought he'd be right for the job.

"I had more of an idea of a 'Bad Motor Scooter,' motorcycle kind of thing originally, but they said, 'No, we don't want that,'" Dancy said. The artist went back and forth with Thayil with a variety of sketches until hitting on the concept of something more flippant. "Their thing was a middle finger, and finally I managed to do it in this electrical, jaggedy way. The design, all it is, is twelve songs, twelve little flip-off hands going around in a circle." The motor vibe remained in the final design through the inclusion a small spark plug placed in the middle of a dozen visual *fuck yous*.

While Soundgarden was busy creating *Badmotorfinger*, another project was already underway in Seattle that brought together several members of the most prominent bands in the city. Film director and one-time *Rolling Stone* scribe Cameron Crowe had moved up to the Pacific Northwest after marrying Heart guitarist Nancy Wilson in the late eighties. He quickly fell in love with the area and the music pouring out of it and ingratiated himself to the many characters who made the scene what it was.

After working on one movie set in the Seattle area, 1989's *Say Anything*, he decided to follow it up with another, this time incorporating his particular, personal relationship with the city and its music. He envisioned a romantic comedy that captured the travails of a group of thirty-year-olds as they searched for love and a sense of identity. He called it *Singles*. One of the central characters of the film was a self-important young musician named Cliff Poncier who fronted the fictional group Citizen Dick. As Crowe initially considered who might play the part, the same name kept running through his mind: Chris Cornell.

Soundgarden was already one of Crowe's favorite bands, and he'd become friendly with Cornell since moving to the area. He was there the day Andy died and recalled how Chris consoled Jeff Ament by offering to ride mountain bikes and get away from it all. Chris was someone who had the looks and charisma to pop off the screen. He'd also bring with him an unquestionable authenticity as a musician.

Ultimately, Chris wasn't keen on abandoning his day job to chase a Hollywood dream that was never his to begin with. "We worked with him, and he's good! But it just felt like there was going to be months and months of rehearsals and commitments," Crowe told his former publication.[16] Matt Dillion was eventually cast instead, but that didn't mean Chris was out of the picture entirely.

Instead of portraying Dillon's character Cliff Poncier—an artist that the fake newspaper reviewer in the film lambasted as "talentless," while decrying the band's lead single "Touch Me I'm Dick," as "local Seattle humor which isn't really funny"—Chris portrayed himself. He shows up for the first time in the film as a member of Soundgarden, climbing the ceiling rafters and diving into a frothing crowd while screaming the words to the band's latest throat lacerator, "Birth Ritual."

"Birth Ritual" is one of the most savage songs in Soundgarden's entire canon. It began as a riff put together by Matt Cameron for the *Badmotorfinger* sessions, but Chris took it to the next level by adding some of the most piercingly high vocals of his career, wailing away about death, snakes, and cigarettes. For the film, Crowe wanted the band to play the song live so that the scene would look as authentic as possible.

The night before Soundgarden shot their big scene, the band rehearsed the song multiple times to make sure they had it down. Chris was going balls to the wall and Crowe was worried that the singer might blow out his voice and not have anything left once the cameras started rolling the next day at the Central Tavern. Cornell confidently brushed him off. The following day, however, he struggled to match the intensity he'd had the night before. As vivid and menacing as Soundgarden appears in the film, Chris was disappointed that he hadn't saved the best of himself for cameras.

Chris shows up again later in the film as one of Cliff's bemused neighbors, nodding along to the over-the-top sound system Cliff has installed in actress Bridget Fonda's car before the windows burst and the moment ends in embarrassing disappointment. It remains his one significant dalliance with acting outside of music videos. His only previous experience in the world of film was the time he and his brother Peter accidently drove through the set of the 1987 comedy *Harry and the Hendersons* high up in the Cascades on their way to Mount Index. They ruined the shot, but the director liked the look of Peter's purple Fiat Spyder so much he had them drive through the scene again on purpose. Sadly, the Cornell brothers' cameo was left on the cutting room floor.

Though several acting opportunities came Chris's way in the years following the release of *Singles*—including an offer to play a character in the 1995 heist film *The Usual Suspects*—he largely turned them down. Chris preferred to limit his involvement in the film world to soundtrack offerings. More than conjuring up visions of sinking his hands into the wet cement in front of Grauman's Chinese Theater, *Singles* sparked the idea in his mind that he might be able to function in some capacity as a solo artist.

Up to this point, Chris had always written and recorded songs with an ear for how they might fit into the context of a band. Cameron Crowe's project offered him an opportunity to step outside of that framework and put his own name on a piece of music. He answered the bell by writing one of the most exquisite pieces of music of his entire life.

Chris first recorded "Seasons" alone in a small closet with just an eight-track tape recorder and microphone. It's a dark, ethereal, acoustic guitar-based song that shares sonic DNA with some of the most pastoral and evocative contributions to *Led Zeppelin III*. Like many of Chris's early compositions, the lyrics are largely esoteric. He croons in a smoky register about the passage of time and how, no matter how hard one wishes to keep the calendar page from flipping, fall inevitably turns into winter.

The song initially came together as part of an elaborate inside joke. Near the end of the film, after his band abandons him in favor of the promise of steady work from the Boeing plant, Cliff Poncier repurposes himself as a one-man troubadour, busking on the street while trying to sell homemade cassette tapes. To complete the portrait, Jeff Ament, who was doing some art design on the film—Cliff's clothes were pilfered from Ament's closet—designed a prop cassette for the character featuring the silhouetted image of Poncier's arms outstretched, in the Jesus Christ pose, on the front, along with several fake song names on the back. Chris found out about the tape and decided to turn the five made-up titles into real songs.

The five tracks were called "Seasons," "Flutter Girl," "Missing," "Nowhere But You," and "Spoonman." Chris went home, fired up his tape recorder, busted out his acoustic guitar and dashed them off one by one. Incredibly, it only took him a few hours to complete them all. "It was a really fun experience because I learned that writing songs just for the fun of it for no particular destination can create songs that have a life that lives on and on and on."[17]

The most consequential track in the short-term was "Seasons," though "Spoonman" would take on a life of its own in just a few years and "Flutter Girl" would get repurposed on his first solo album *Euphoria Mourning* much later down the line. The inspiration for "Seasons" stemmed from a derivation of an open E tuning that Chris had learned from Ben Shepherd, the same one that the bassist used on the Soundgarden song "Somewhere." After messing around with it, Chris stumbled upon the haunting melody that serves as the revolving bedrock to the song. "I probably tuned the guitar quickly and started playing that little riff arpeggio and the rest happened really quickly."[18]

"Seasons," and the other four songs on the *Poncier Tape*, captured a different side of Chris that couldn't be further from the masculine, chisel-chested screamer in Soundgarden. He liked it that way. "When we were at our most aggressive period in Soundgarden I just wanted to hear something that wasn't guitar feedback," he said. "I started listening to anything that I could find that was super stripped-down. I bought the Nick Drake boxed set, and my favorite album was *Pink Moon*, where it's really just him and a guitar."[19]

When Crowe got a hold of the tape, casually slipped to him by his wife Nancy, he was blown away by Chris's gesture. "Seasons" was its own special revelation. It was the kind of song, powerful and evocative enough, to totally change the perception of the kind of artist Chris Cornell was capable of being. "Songs I obsessed over for weeks nobody ever hears, but the ones I did for fun for *Singles* wound up with millions of fans. The was a lesson," he told the *Hollywood Reporter*. "I have what I call 'brain radio' going on all the time. Most of the time it's not interesting, like a test pattern. Occasionally a song will come from it in a matter of minutes."[20]

Even though the *Singles* soundtrack was put out by rival label, Epic Records, Susan Silver worked out a deal with A&M and eventually both "Birth Ritual" by Soundgarden and "Seasons," credited solely to Chris, appeared on the film's tracklist. It took quite a bit of doing on Silver's part. Executives at A&M weren't thrilled with the idea of one of their bright lights making money for a competitor. Crowe had previously tried to secure some songs from *Louder Than Love* for *Say Anything*, but A&M had blocked their inclusion on similar grounds. Crowe ended up including "Flower" and "Toy Box" from *Ultramega OK* in that film instead.

Chris was joined on the *Singles* soundtrack by many of his Seattle peers like Alice In Chains, who included their own tribute to Andrew Wood, "Would?" The Pearl Jam song "State of Love and Trust," which Eddie Vedder was inspired to write after working on the film, also made the cut, as did "Chloe Dancer/Crown of Thorns" by Mother Love Bone, "Overblown" by Mudhoney, and "Nearly Lost You" by Screaming Trees. Chris also did a little bit of scoring work for *Singles*, and his work in that arena made it out decades later as the tracks "Ferry Boat #3" and "Score Piece #4" on the expanded edition of the soundtrack.

Singles wrapped filming on May 24, 1991, but the movie wouldn't make it into theaters for another year and a half on September 18, 1992. By that point, grunge had fully exploded internationally, and the soundtrack became an omnipresent totem in the households of anyone under the age of thirty. But that was still a long way out. Right now, Chris's main concern was ramping up anticipation for *Badmotorfinger*. What better way to achieve that goal than hitting the road in support of the biggest rock band on the planet?

Soundgarden was hanging out at Avast! one day when Susan Silver strolled in carrying a box of new T-shirt designs. She set the box down and then excitedly presented them with the big news. She'd just scored them the opening slot for the upcoming Guns N' Roses stadium tour. She waited for their reaction, but no one said a word. About half a minute passed, and then finally someone piped up: "What's in the box?"

While the band's reaction may have been blasé, everyone knew the tour was too lucrative an opportunity to turn down, so Soundgarden agreed to go along for what promised to be a wild ride. The run wasn't supposed to kick off for another several months, and there was still a ton of work to be done in the meantime. The band had to prep *Badmotorfinger's* first single, "Jesus Christ Pose," for release, which meant tacking on a couple of B-sides. These were dashed together during a one-day session overseen by Stuart Hallerman.

They ended up choosing to include a straightforward rendition of the Rolling Stones' 1968 cut "Stray Cat Blues," along with an unorthodox take on Black Sabbath's "Into the Void." On the latter, rather than sing Ozzy Osbourne's tale of a rocket man fleeing the ravaged Earth, Chris recited what he thought were the words of the great nineteenth-century Native American leader Chief Seattle, or as he was otherwise known, Sealth. What Chris didn't know was that Sealth had never spoken those words.

The speech, allegedly delivered in 1854, in which the native leader decried the incursion of the White Man onto their lands and his destruction of the environment, was actually penned by a screenwriter named Ted Perry in 1972 for a film titled *Home*. In 1991, a children's book titled *Brother Eagle, Sister Sky: A Message from Chief Seattle* was released with the text of Perry's speech, credited to Sealth. It sold hundreds of thousands of copies and injected the words into the national consciousness, where Chris picked up on them. Despite the murky sourcing of the text, it remains an ingenious and thought-provoking re-interpolation that ultimately netted Soundgarden a Grammy nomination for Best Metal Performance in 1993.

To direct the "Jesus Christ Pose" video, Soundgarden turned to Eric Zimmerman, who'd previously worked with bands like Nine Inch Nails and Megadeth. It was his work on the "Head like a Hole" video in particular that convinced the band that he was their guy. Much of the content in the "Jesus Christ Pose" video stemmed from Zimmerman's own mind, and it created quite a stir once it aired on MTV. Opening with a bold disclaimer that echoed the Bible passage John 3:16—"And God So Loved Soundgarden He Gave Them His Only Song"—the clip interspersed psychedelic multicolored shots of the band roaming around the desert with unsettling religious iconography.

The part that drew the most ire from the public was the depiction of a woman nailed to a cross. That image got the video banned from much of MTV. It wasn't even cleared to appear on the animated show *Beavis and Butthead*, which was a first. The band stood by the video, and it remained one of Chris's favorites. "As a visual, it's powerful and it's also challenging to people, because women basically have been persecuted since before recorded history, and it would almost make more sense than seeing a man on it," he explained in a press release rushed out shortly after the controversy started. "There's upside down crosses and right-side up ones. But there's certainly no blatant direction as far as religious conviction in the video."[21]

Of course, Chris's own feelings about Christianity and organized religion were deeply calcified during his stringent Catholic upbringing. "From the time you're six years old, somebody is telling you that you are inherently a sinner and there's a good chance you might experience eternal suffering and pain," he told *Blender*. "That kind of sticks with you."[22]

Ultimately, the "Jesus Christ Pose" video did what it was supposed to do: it got people talking about Soundgarden. And just in time, too. *Badmotorfinger* hit shelves on October 8, 1991. It wasn't a huge seller straight out of the gate—it topped out at number thirty-nine on the charts a few months after it was released—but as Soundgarden grew in prominence over the next year, the album continued selling several thousand copies each week. As of the printing of this book, it has achieved double-platinum certification for sales over two million units by the RIAA.

To help push sales at the time, A&M went forward with an interesting marketing campaign. The label mailed out 1,500 Walkmen with copies of *Badmotorfinger* epoxyed shut inside to retailers all across the country. The Walkmen came with 1-800 numbers that fans could call to share their favorite song on the album. A select few respondents actually won tickets and airfare to see Soundgarden live and in-person.

Reviews were largely kind. Writing for *Spin*, Lauren Spencer lauded Chris's growth as a lyricist while heaping praise on the band's more aggressive aesthetic. "Tend to this garden of sound," she wrote, "and I guarantee a fruitful crop will rise up and take over the world."[23] Craig Tomashoff in *People* was equally effusive, while also remaining circumspect about its commercial appeal. "Chris Cornell's lead scream, while perfectly suited to this musical style, would probably give Casey Kasem a heart attack,"[24] he wrote, referring to the acclaimed Top 40 DJ. In her B+ review for *Entertainment Weekly*, Gina Arnold singled out the record's deeper themes for special recognition, writing, "Soundgarden sound a hell of a lot smarter than their peers, who seldom get beyond extolling booze, girls, and cars."[25]

A couple of days before *Badmotorfinger* was released, the band celebrated in style during a raucous show at the Hollywood Palladium. It was the RIP Magazine Awards, and Soundgarden was invited to play alongside Pearl Jam, Alice In Chains, and the main attraction, Spinal Tap. It was a boozed-up and extremely loose event made even more memorable when, after Soundgarden finished their eight-song set, the members of Temple Of The Dog gathered onstage and launched into "Hunger Strike." They followed that with a supermassive take on "Reach Down," during which they were joined by Jerry Cantrell. It was a Seattle rock lover's paradise, minus the rain.

Chris linked up with the rest of Alice In Chains once they got back home, and lent his voice to an ephemeral acoustic ballad called "Right Turn" that the band planned on releasing as part of a special EP titled *SAP*. He was joined on the track by Layne Staley, of course, but also Mudhoney frontman Mark Arm. In the liner notes, the single-song supergroup was dubbed Alice Mudgarden.

Rick Parashar, who had produced *Temple Of The Dog*, oversaw the session and decided it'd be funny to try and mess around with Chris while he was in the vocal booth. "He knew that Chris was gonna wanna really belt it out, and he just kept fucking with him, like, 'Let's just try this for a while,'" engineer Dave Hillis recalled. "Rick would be look at me, snickering, and Chris would be like, 'I really feel like I should go for it here.' And Rick would say, 'Just wait a minute, wait a minute,' screwing with his head. Rick had known him since he was a kid, so then when Chris got to let it out, he was in his glory."

Four days after the RIP Magazine Awards, Soundgarden hit the stage for the first MLB-sized baseball stadium show of their career, opening for Metallica at the Day on the Green festival at the Oakland Coliseum. The headliners were riding high on the success of their most recent, self-titled release, otherwise known as the *Black Album*, which debuted at number one on the charts when it came out earlier in the summer and stayed there for a full month. The nightmarish video for "Enter Sandman" was an inescapable presence on MTV and they were widely regarded as the most popular metal band on the planet.

For Soundgarden, the opportunity to play in front of a sea of humanity served as a perfect dry run for what the next year of their lives would feel like. "We were in the metal trenches at that point, just fully paying our dues," Matt Cameron told *Classic Rock* magazine. "We were kind of the opening act for ninety-one/ninety-two."[26]

CHAPTER VIII

SWINGIN' ON
THE FLIPPITY-FLOP

C hris Cornell's long, curly hair cascades over his bare left shoulder. A single, solitary strand falls over his right shoulder while a pair of necklaces dangle around his chest. His face is a torrent of rage with his mouth gaped in a furious scream. His wide eyes are locked onto the camera's lens as his arms stretch out to his sides. His hands are clenched into fists. It seems like any second, he could spring to life, jump off the glossy page, and pummel the viewer into oblivion.

That was the sight that greeted *Spin* magazine subscribers in the fall of 1992. Chris Cornell, in all his livid glory on the cover, relieved in black and white, heralding the onslaught of a new movement. The headline, scrawled in pink, trumpets the news, "The Year of Grunge," followed by tabloid subtitle, "Seattle Spawned It, Madonna Wants It, And Soundgarden's Chris Cornell Has It."

"He was like the Errol Flynn of rock," Jesse Frohman, the man responsible for the photo said. "I don't know how I got that energy out of him. He had that ability to look like he was soaring out into outer space. You see it onstage, too."

The feature began with an open-hearted stroll down memory lane with Sub Pop founder Jonathan Poneman, who wistfully recalled how

Soundgarden changed his life before segueing into a lengthy chat with Chris. The singer was candid with his longtime friend about his history, his new record, the attempts by the media to pit himself and his band against the likes of Mudhoney and Nirvana, and the grim, sausage-making process of becoming a successful rock band in America in the nineties. His most insightful response came when Poneman asks if he ever consciously writes music with the idea of creating a hit, "another American anthem like 'Smells like Teen Spirit,'" he posits.

Chris dismissed the idea. "If you tried, you'd fail," he says. What he knew implicitly was that he didn't need to make an effort to vie for the attentions of America's youth by tailoring his words and melodies to their tastes. His tastes were their tastes. He and Soundgarden created music and toured the world in relative obscurity for years, waiting for a time when pop culture caught up to them. At that moment, it finally had. "The whole idea was that we don't change for the marketplace as it exists, we just continue to exist until the marketplace changes for us," he said. "I think that the marketplace has changed a lot."

Just as *Spin* promised, 1992 was indeed the Year of Grunge. It was the year when preening rock stars in lycra, shrieking about their over-the-top sexual exploits, gave way to a more vital, substantive, self-serious, and seemingly authentic class of musical heroes. This new breed of rock star not only looked like their audience, they cracked the same jokes and watched the same shows. They also bonded over their shared anxieties about societal issues like feminism, environmentalism, and increasing corporate control. Soundgarden, Pearl Jam, Nirvana were all relatable in their own ways. Teens and twenty-somethings could gaze at the covers of magazines like *Spin* and *Kerrang* and see themselves. Or at the very least, an idealized version of themselves.

"I remember with Nirvana they thought two hundred thousand [in album sales] was going to be a huge success," Chris said. "That was their benchmark, two hundred thousand. We all surpassed that so quickly."[1]

Soundgarden spent nearly all of 1992 among this crowd, springboarding from stage to stage, state to state, and country to country, stomping their way through stadiums, arenas, and amphitheaters, bringing their brutal sound to their flannel-adorned worshippers. It was a year of hype and a year of toil. By the end of it, nothing would ever be the same.

* * *

The tour with Guns N' Roses was supposed to start around September but ended up getting pushed back a few months and didn't kick off until December 5, 1991, with a show at the Worcester Centrum, near Boston. It's hard to overstate just how big a deal it was for a band on the come-up to secure this slot. Guns N' Roses was, by nearly every conceivable metric, the biggest rock group on the planet, and it wasn't close. Their most recent albums, *Use Your Illusion I* and *Use Your Illusion II,* were flying off the shelves. For two weeks in a row in October, they had the number-one and number-two bestselling albums in the country.

Soundgarden wasn't awed by the outsized fame of the five guys at the top of the bill. A significant culture clash between the intense and relatively straight-laced Seattleites and the party-hard LA headliners helped keep their feet on the ground. "They were a favorite band of ours and it was cool to have them, but we didn't have a good rapport with them at all," Guns N' Roses guitarist Slash recalled in his memoir. "Coming from their more underground, indie point of view, they thought of us as 'Fat, lazy, and self-indulgent.'"[2] The circumspection was mutual. Backstage, many within the Guns' camp tagged the dour opening band with the nickname "Frowngarden."

Chris's didn't have many issues with the behavior of Guns N' Roses as a whole. It was the man who'd once touted his vocal abilities in the pages of *Rolling Stone* who sometimes got under his skin. "Without saying anything negative about Axl, what I remember the most was Duff and Slash and everyone else being regular, sweet, warm guys in a rock band that just wanted to play rock music," he told *Vulture.* But then, "There was this *Wizard of Oz* character behind the curtain that seemed to complicate what was the most ideal situation they could ever have been in: they were the most successful and famous rock band on the planet. Every single show, hundreds of thousands of fans just wanted to hear songs.

For some reason there seemed to be this obstacle in just going out and participating in that."[3]

Rock stars aren't exactly known for their punctuality, but Axl Rose took tardiness to a legendary level. There were some nights when Guns N' Roses wouldn't hit the stage until well after midnight, hours after the opening act had come off stage. The performance at the Ervin Nutter Center in Dayton, Ohio on January 13, 1992, was an especially egregious late-starter, with the headliners hitting the stage close to one in the morning. The next evening's gig, again in Dayton, went even more disastrously after Rose sliced his hand open on his microphone stand during "It's So Easy," then proceeded to get into a verbal sparring match with Slash before ending the show a few songs early.

The following dates on the itinerary at Auburn Hills, Michigan, were summarily postponed so that Axl could get stitched up and recuperate. As frustrating as episodes like this must've been, it was fortunate for Soundgarden that they managed to escape some of the truly scary moments along the Use Your Illusion Tour, like the riot in St. Louis several months before they hopped on board and the riot in Montreal several months later. Compounding the insanity was a weird set of rules put in place by Guns N' Roses management. Chris wasn't having much of that. "You were not allowed to be in a hallway or anywhere Axl might see you when he was walking between the dressing room and the stage," he recalled of one particularly ridiculous edict.[4]

One day, as Chris was walking down a corridor, he ran into the reclusive frontman and his bodyguard. Rose was decked out in a backwards baseball hat, a pair of red shorts that didn't leave much to the imagination, and a long fur coat that grazed the floor, nearly obscuring his sneakers with his name embroidered on them. Chris steeled himself for a tantrum, but nothing happened. Rose just said, "Hey, bro!" and kept on walking.

"At that point, it's one of those moments where you think about your life as a comic book; this isn't really happening." [5]

Rose's outlandish requests and unprofessional behavior ran counter to everything Chris and Soundgarden were about. The opposed mindsets were best exemplified by the time the headlining singer tried to convince his manager to rent out the Goodyear Blimp for a show. Chris overheard the conversation and jokingly commented that the Fuji blimp was actually much larger than the iconic tire company's marquee airship. Rose either didn't detect the sarcasm in Chris's voice or was so enamored by the idea that he instantly demanded they get the Fuji blimp instead.

Chris was even more flippant about another rule that directly impacted his ability to connect with the crowd during Soundgarden's set. Heading into the tour, he and the rest of the band were informed that under no circumstances would they be allowed to step out onto the trio of long, metal catwalks that extended from the main stage out into the crowd. Those were reserved for the headliners and the headliners only. Chris knew that he and the other members of his band would look like four largely undynamic ants to the crowd if they remained in place on the main stage. That wasn't going to work for him, so instead of abiding by the rule, on that first night in Worcester, Chris walked out and sang from the farthest position of each catwalk. He made his point a little clearer by screaming his lungs out while on top of the teleprompters that Rose used to read the words to his own songs, just to show the powers that be that he wasn't going to be easily controlled.

Over the next two months, Soundgarden gamely played cuts from *Badmotorfinger* to an alternating sea of rock fans in arenas and stadiums up and down the east coast, including a three-night stand at Madison Square Garden where Billy Joel roamed the backstage area in search of a bottle of Johnnie Walker Black. Joey Ramone was another visitor who showed up along with his girlfriend who was decked out in a tiger-striped bikini. "Joey and Chris started talking," Soundgarden's sometime saxophonist Scott Granlund recalled. "It was kinda noisy back in the Green Room, so those guys crawled under this big table and just hung out under this table and had a long conversation. The two shy vocalists hiding under this table talking about all the weird shit they drink."

Many among the crowds were aware of who Soundgarden were, but most saved up their enthusiasm for the headliners, which was frustrating. They had just forty-five minutes to make a good impression, and they poured everything they had into each sixty-second interval. There was no time for pacing. They craved kinetic energy. It was usually around the end of their set, when they busted out their biggest hit to date, "Outshined," that they got the response they were seeking. The video for that track, which featured the band performing in a spark-filled steel mill that appeared ripped from the set of *Terminator 2*, entered MTV's coveted Buzz Bin around the beginning of the year and was by now well-known to even the most causal rock fan.

Chris had been in Mississippi the first time "Outshined" was played on MTV. He was out at four in the morning when he was recognized by a butcher. It was a surreal moment, but an important one. It was the beginning of his life as a public figure; a persona that bore little resemblance to who he was as a person. It changed him. "That was the beginning of me becoming isolated," he told *Spin* writer Chuck Klosterman years later. "I never liked being recognized to begin with and I was never much of a social person, so this gave me a chance to play the 'I don't want to go out' card. I would just stay in and drink."[6]

The tour slowly lumbered west, hitting Las Vegas and San Diego along the way. Soundgarden finished their stint with Guns N' Roses with a performance at Compton Terrace in Chandler, Arizona on February 1, 1992. To send their dour openers off in style, Slash, Duff McKagan, and drummer Matt Sorum pranked Frowngarden by crashing their set. The trio pulled off most of their clothes—Slash went entirely nude—and proceeded to engage in mock coitus with a harem of inflatable blow-up dolls. "They were mortified," Slash recalled. "I was drunk, and I fell."[7]

Soundgarden picked up with Guns N' Roses again a few months later for another run through Europe beginning in May, but in the meantime, the band headed back onto the smaller theater circuit, opening shows for another long-haired LA metal band, Skid Row, throughout the Midwest in venues like the five-thousand-person Aragon Ballroom in Chicago, the palatial Fox Theatre in Detroit, and Roy Wilkins Auditorium in St. Paul, Minnesota. On several occasions, Sebastian Bach invited Chris out during their encore of the Yardbirds classic "Train Kept a Rollin'" and was blown away by his incredible energy and cutting sense of humor. "He'd look at the stage like a track meet, running in a figure eight and doing somersaults," Bach told *Billboard.* "And he'd be on a trampoline doing jumps behind the drum riser. I could tell he was sending up the sort of heavy-metal performance we were trying to do, always with a twinkle in his eye, laughing."[8]

On May 4, 1992, the band rolled into Toronto, Canada, to play a show with Fishbone at the Concert Hall on bustling Yonge Street. What everyone anticipated to be another night of rock and roll revelry turned near-disastrous when a full-blown riot erupted outside. Just a couple days earlier, a plainclothes Toronto police officer had shot and killed a twenty-two-year-old black man named Raymond Lawrence. This was shortly after the four LAPD officers who had beaten Rodney King in the streets were acquitted, so tensions were already high. What started as a protest turned violent as day turned to night. The hordes almost flipped Soundgarden's bus on its side, and bassist Ben Shepherd was nearly arrested along with some of the members of Fishbone by the edgy Toronto cops. Fortunately, both groups made it out unscathed, and the tour resumed four days later in College Park, Maryland.

Soundgarden's year thus far had been a non-stop stretch of performances, but they were only just getting started. The opening-act runs led directly into to a pair of heavily-anticipated, headlining performances of their own at the Paramount Theatre in Seattle near the beginning of March. They were important gigs, which the band planned to film and release on VHS. Tickets sold out within hours and *Motorvision,* as the concert documentary came to be known, remains the definitive live document of Soundgarden at their fiercest.

The show opened, bizarrely enough, with an introduction by a mainstay of Seattle local television, a clown by the name of J.P. Patches. "They sent me a tape," Patches recalled. "It wasn't really my kind of music, but I said I would do it."[9] The nearly 3,000 alt-rock-loving teens and twenty-somethings decked out in flannel button-downs, Michael Jordan jerseys, and snapback Mariners baseball caps went nuts as soon as the local icon shuffled into view.

"Who did you come to see?" Patches asked them.

"Soundgarden!" they responded.

"You're supposed to say me!" he complained. "Who did you come to see tonight?"

"Soundgarden!!" they roared.

"Would you rather have me here or Soundgarden?" Patches pleaded.

"Soundgarden!!!"

"I can take a hint. And here they are!"

Watching from the wings, Chris was impressed by how his childhood hero held his own in the face of such unbridled fury. "I was blown away by how unruly our audience was, but he seemed totally in his element," he recalled. "He worked them in a way that probably only he could."[10]

After ceding the stage to the four men of the hour, Soundgarden promptly ripped into a ferocious set stacked with *Badmotorfinger* cuts that culminated in an apocalyptic, feedback-drenched version of "Slaves & Bulldozers," during which Chris sang a portion of Howlin Wolf's immortal blues burner "Back Door Man." The scene onstage remained a chaotic montage of somersaulting stage-divers, searing vocals, and the onstage presentation of a gold record for *Badmotorfinger* surpassing 500,000 units sold.

Once again, Soundgarden roped Kevin Kerslake into directing the shows, but unlike *Louder Than Live*, which had been filmed guerilla-style in the tiny Whisky A Go Go, the beauty and breadth of the Paramount demanded a larger production. "We probably had nine or ten cameras, along with a crane," the director said. "You just have to have enough coverage. That's actually pretty frugal compared to some other shows."

Intermixed with scenes of the band performing onstage was a compendium of shots of Soundgarden riding around Seattle in a van piloted by Matt Cameron, scoping out different sites and commenting on their personal journey. "We didn't have the resources to do a full crew, but that would've fucked up the energy anyway," Kerslake recalled. "I was in the back of the van, just me, asking questions, making sure the tape was going and hoping that something was watchable. We went out to the Sound Garden and all that. It was a full day."

Once he had the shows filmed, Kerslake picked out what he thought were the best performances and edited them together. But then he ran into a problem. "Chris wore different clothes," he said. "He wore a black shirt one night and a white shirt one night. So, that was a little difficult to cut around." But then in true Chris Cornell fashion, the singer eliminated the problem entirely. "He ultimately took the shirt off, so at a certain point it wasn't an issue."

As "Slaves & Bulldozers" reached its inevitable, noisy conclusion, Chris ripped off all the strings from his Les Paul and started grinding the guitar against his amplifier, filling the room with cascading walls of gnarly feedback. Then he crawled onto the top of a metal cage at the rear of the stage, raised his arms in triumph, and leapt off the back and out of view. He and Thayil's guitars continued to whine and cry as the exhausted revelers shuffled off into the crisp Seattle evening.

With *Motorvision* in the can, Soundgarden had only six days to themselves at home before they had to depart for the road again, this time for a month-long run through Sweden, Germany, and the UK, followed by another month-long run in the US that started in the middle of April. While the band navigated their grueling slate of shows, the music world was caught in the midst of a dramatic shift. Grunge had finally exploded into the mainstream.

After months of steady sales, in January of 1992, Nirvana's *Nevermind* improbably knocked Michael Jackson's gargantuan *Bad* off the top of the charts. By May 30, 1992, Pearl Jam's debut *Ten* had finally cracked into the top ten on its way to reaching the number two spot. Alice In Chains were on the cusp of releasing their heavily anticipated second record *Dirt*. Then there was the *Singles* soundtrack, which was rushed out three months ahead of the film in order to capitalize on all the hype. It sold like hotcakes, too.

Alternative rock was no longer alternative. Aggressive, angst-riddled post-punk had taken America by storm. The shift flummoxed many of the artists at the center of the maelstrom. "It's a really strange counter-culture," Kim Thayil told *Spin*. "It's the counterculture as referenced by *MTV*. There are no wars, no race riots, no women's liberation or gay liberation—it's a counterculture based on successfully marketed radio songs and snowboarding."[11]

Amid the flannel-fueled fervor for anything Seattle, A&M approached Chris about re-releasing the *Temple Of The Dog* record, which he was open to doing. With Pearl Jam rising in popularity, the project wouldn't be viewed as a Chris Cornell solo project any longer, but instead a collaborative effort between two of the most admired and exciting entities in alt rock. It also presented an opportunity to educate more casual fans about Andrew Wood.

To capitalize on the moment, a new version of the "Hunger Strike" video was cut together, filled with even more wistful shots of Chris and Eddie Vedder crooning into the middle distance. It was thrown into heavy rotation on MTV. *Temple Of The Dog* tore its way up the charts, selling tens of thousands of copies on a weekly basis before topping out at number five around September 1992. It was certified platinum by the RIAA for over a million copies sold that same month, becoming the bestselling release of Chris's career thus far.

It was inevitable that the powers-that-be would try to cash in on grunge, sometimes to ludicrous result. The most absurd attempt by the traditional media to explain what was happening in Seattle occured when a *New York Times* reporter named Rick Marin called up former Sub Pop Records receptionist, and current CEO, Megan Jasper and asked her to help him understand some of the grunge lexicon. She fed him a string of nonsense words and phrases like "cob-nobbler" (a loser), "wack slacks" (an old pair of ripped jeans) and "swingin' on the flippity-flop" (hanging out) as a goof. The fake slang made it into a pullout in the paper of record to their eventual embarrassment. Ironically, the joke ended up being on Seattle in the end when people started using Jasper's fictional phrases for real.

With the mainstream press huffing to catch up with what was going in the Pacific Northwest, the media demands on Soundgarden became overwhelming. The band spent much of 1992 talking to nearly every print publication imaginable, from old warhorses like *Rolling Stone*, *NME*, and *Melody Maker*, to relative newcomers like *Spin*, *Kerrang*, and *RIP*. As the group's resident pot smoker, Matt Cameron even sat down for a revealing interview with *High Times*. Meanwhile, Kim Thayil waxed rhapsodic to nearly every guitar publication under the sun. All of them made frequent appearances on MTV's *Headbangers Ball.*

As the frontman, most of the spotlight naturally fell on Chris. Everyone wanted a piece of him, and it only got more out of hand as the months churned on and his celebrity increased. Soundgarden hardly turned down any request, but it was hard to come up with new things to say to questions like: *What's it like to play arenas with Guns N' Roses? How did you cope with the death of Andrew Wood? Are all the bands in Seattle friends? What did you think about what Kurt Cobain said about [insert any subject here]?*

The more rote lines of questioning were typically dispatched with a biting, sarcastic remark, but during one marathon press event in a hotel banquet hall in Paris promoting *Badmotorfinger,* he and the band reached their breaking point and decided to have some fun with the last interviewer of the day. "We hid behind these partitions and he thought he was alone," Chris recalled. Once the reporter realized he wasn't the only one in the room, an absurd situation played out with the band refusing to step out of their hiding place to the journalist's growing frustration. "He started to take it really seriously, so we steered into it and said, 'Two of us were badly injured in a car accident and we don't want anyone to see our scars.'" Back and forth they went, until, "Finally the record company lady threatened that they would like, drop us from the label if we kept torturing people like that."[12]

There wasn't any time for rest. No time to take stock of the outside world or of their increased fame. The road beckoned. Show, after show, after show, after show. Once their tour of Europe wrapped up, the band enjoyed a brief two-week break back home before hitting venues in major American markets like San Francisco, Dallas, Chicago, New York, Philadelphia, and Boston on a sold-out, headlining tour of their own with Swervedriver and Monster Magnet. Then it was back across the Atlantic Ocean where they linked up again with Guns N' Roses and their old buddies Faith No More for a two-month slog through the biggest stadiums in Europe, beginning with a show at the fifty-thousand-seat Strahov Stadium in Prague, Czechoslovakia on May 20, 1992.

The concerts only got bigger from there. Fifty-eight thousand people showed up at the Hippodrome in Paris, where Guns N' Roses brought out Steven Tyler and Joe Perry from Aerosmith for "Mama Kin" and "Train Kept a Rollin'," and Axl took expletive-filled swipes at the actor Warren Beatty for trying to co-opt the youth movement to make himself appear cooler. That particular gig was filmed and broadcast worldwide as a pay-per-view special. Sixty thousand appeared in Hannover, Germany. Sixty-five thousand in Turin, Italy. Seventy thousand in Budapest, Hungary. And roughly seventy-two thousand people packed Wembley Stadium in London on June 13, where Guns tried to capture some of that fabled Queen magic from years past by inviting Brian May to guest on "Tie Your Mother Down," and "We Will Rock You."

Soundgarden's set earlier in the day was far less triumphant. Someone in the crowd had a heart attack just as the band began to play and had to be resuscitated. "Paramedics were banging on his chest, and one of them hit him good, and he woke up swinging," Chris said. "I remember thinking, 'I don't like this.'"[13]

When he wasn't onstage, Chris usually secluded himself in his hotel room, eager to write new songs. It was a way to stay busy and prep for Soundgarden's next record, but it was also a sanity-saving measure. "If I stay in my room and write songs, it's like I'm home," he told Jeff Gilbert of *Guitar World*. "The only way I can tell that I'm not home is if I look out the window," he remembered thinking.[14]

The gargantuan size of the crowds presented a unique opportunity to get Soungarden's music across to a new audience, but the sheer effort it took to connect with the placid fans waiting to hear Axl, Slash, and company rip into "Sweet Child O' Mine" was draining. "Soundgarden were half-way through their first song before most people noticed there was a band on stage," Kerrang writer Paul Henderson noted in his review of the Wembley show. "In a small club a couple of months ago, Soundgarden were stunning, cracking skulls with pounding, well aimed sonic ice picks. But in the vastness of Wembley Stadium, and with a sound that relied on a lot of imagination in order to identify the songs, the audience was being bit with nothing more effective than a plastic hammer."[15]

In addition to battling apathy among the vast crowds, Soundgarden also had to contend with the unpredictability of their headliners, which oftentimes manifested itself in cancelled gigs. A show in Belgium had to be called off because Duff McKagan got sick. Another show in Rome was cancelled for the same reason. What turned out to be the final gig of the tour on July 2 in Lisbon, Portugal, was marred when Axl took a tumble onstage in the middle of "It's So Easy" and the crowd started setting off fireworks during "Live and Let Die." The next two concerts in Spain were called off, and Soundgarden was finally free to return to Seattle.

Soundgarden had played dozens of concerts across the globe over the previous six months, in venues of all sizes, and in front of crowds that were alternately indifferent and excited. They'd more than earned a break, but their year was far from over. Another major, months-long commitment loomed on the calendar just a little over two weeks after Chris got home, so time away in the mountains to clear his head would be brief.

Lollapalooza was never intended to be an ongoing, live music institution. Conceived by Perry Farrell the year before in 1991, it was originally conceptualized as a travelling farewell concert for the singer's band Jane's Addiction, accompanied by a collection of similarlyminded alternative acts hand-picked by the band members themselves. That first year, Jane's was joined on the road by Nine Inch Nails, Ice-T's Body Count, Butthole Surfers, Siouxsie and the Banshees, Living Colour, Rollins Band, and Violent Femmes, among others.

The tour proved far more financially lucrative and culturally impactful than anyone could have imagined. It was feverishly covered in the media as Gen-X's version of Woodstock on wheels. Five hundred thousand people turned out to the twenty-six shows, spending millions of dollars along the way. By the time it was over, a sequel seemed like a foregone conclusion.

The biggest challenge was putting together a lineup that could top the original. Any whiff in the press that the second iteration was an inferior attempt to cash in on the success of the first would probably have doomed Lollapalooza's long-term prospects. Farrell, along with executives Marc Geiger, Ted Gardner, and Don Muller were under major pressure to deliver. Originally, they'd hoped to nab R.E.M. and the so-called "Godfather of Grunge" Neil Young as the headliners. When those fell through, they booked the Red Hot Chili Peppers, who were selling ungodly numbers of their most recent album *Blood Sugar Sex Magik*.

They rounded out the rest of the bill by filling it with a diverse cross-section of artists from a multitude of genres and backgrounds: groundbreaking acts like Ice Cube, Ministry, and the Jesus and Mary Chain. It was Muller, the booking agent for Pearl Jam and Soundgarden, who advocated adding both of those bands to the lineup. Even though he got some pushback from Geiger and Farrell about including *two* bands from Seattle, Muller won out.

As grueling as their concert calendar had already been, Soundgarden knew that Lollapalooza represented the most receptive audience possible for their music. The opportunity to spend a few months hanging out with their buddies in Pearl Jam didn't hurt either. "I think it was one of my favorite tours of my career, because we shared a lot of camaraderie," Chris said. "It's like your buddies you grew up with that you played in front of ten people with for years, and now you're on tour together playing for twenty-five thousand people."[16]

The second Lollapalooza dwarfed the first in terms of scope and sales. There were more shows, more tickets sold—750,000—more politically and socially conscious booths to visit, and more non-musical activities to consume. There were art displays, a temporary tattooist, interactive sound sculptures, even bungee jumping. Most significantly, the organizers set up a second stage for a variety of rotating bands like Rage Against The Machine, Stone Temple Pilots, Cypress Hill, and Farrell's new band, Porno for Pyros.

To capitalize on the exposure, A&M re-released a limited edition of *Badmotorfinger* that included a new Soundgarden EP titled *Satanoscillatemymetallicsonatas*. The title is a palindrome; another bit of canny, Soundgarden humor. The five-song EP included the band's version of "Into the Void," along with a cover of The Rolling Stones' "Stray Cat Blues," and the Devo song "Girl U Want." It also included a live rendition of "Slaves & Bulldozers" and a previously unreleased cut written by Chris called "She's a Politician." The latter track is a brief, straight-ahead rocker about a woman who knows how to confuse the issue with her "machine gun talk" to get what she wants.

Three weeks after *Satanoscillatemymetallicsonatas* dropped on July 18, Soundgarden arrived at the Shoreline Amphitheater in Mountain View, California, and steeled themselves for the first performance of Lollapalooza '92. "I remember the beginning of that tour," Perry Farrell said. "Just to fuck with them, because Chris seemed a little edgy—he was a shy person—we were all going to get into an elevator, but he hadn't seen me, so I let him get in the elevator then I jumped in the elevator at the last second so that he would think I was a stalker. I stood too close to him and he goes, 'Oh fuck!' Then he looked at me and goes, 'Man, I thought you were one of *those* people.' I always meant to ask him, 'Who are *those* people?'"

Despite the fact that Pearl Jam had the fourth-best-selling album in the country—headliners the Red Hot Chili Peppers were sitting at number five—the order of artists had already been solidified and the newcomers were given the second-to-last spot on the bill, playing in the afternoons just after Lush opened things up. Soundgarden hit the stage a couple of hours later, following the Jesus and Mary Chain, and proceeded to regale the alternative nation with a pummeling, fifty-five-minute set of songs comprised mostly from *Badmotorfinger*, but with some curveballs thrown in, depending on the show. The second day of the tour they covered the Ramones' "I Can't Give You Anything," for instance.

By the time they got back around to their neck of the woods at the Kitsap County Fairgrounds in Bremerton, Washington, on July 22, Soundgarden gave the hometown fans a thrill by inviting Eddie Vedder onstage to sing back-up on "Outshined." Chris returned the favor a couple weeks down the line in Barrie, Ontario when he backed up Pearl Jam during a rendition of "Jeremy."

The friendship between the two Seattle bands was tight, and the opportunities for unexpected collaborations were plentiful. In Reston, Virginia, Chris nearly filled in for Eddie during Pearl Jam's set when the singer missed the bus to the gig, hitchhiked a ride, and got stuck in traffic outside of the venue. "I don't know all the lyrics to any of these songs," Chris warned the crowd from the stage. "Eddie is not here, he can hear this, you gotta sing loud. Eddie will never come up on stage if you guys don't know the words, I guarantee it."

Fortunately, Vedder showed up right before the music started. Chris hoisted him up from the security pit and carried him to the microphone stand, no doubt grateful for not having to ad-lib his way through "Even Flow" and "Once." Near the end of their set, he returned to the stage for an impromptu take on "Hunger Strike."

Those kinds of once-in-a-lifetime opportunities weren't limited to the main stage. "There was a second stage at Lollapalooza, so Eddie and me worked up an acoustic set and got some space on the second stage for the middle of the day," Chris told *Spin*. "We got a golf cart and drove through the crowd to the stage, and it was like the Beatles. There were, like, a hundred people running and screaming and chasing the golf cart."[17]

The biggest draw on the second stage was the Jim Rose Circus sideshow, an eye-popping revue that featured the likes of the Amazing Mister Lifto, who would lift heavy weights from the various piercings on his body, including his scrotum, along with Bebe the Circus Queen who laid down on a bed of nails and allowed people to cut watermelons in half while they rested on her back. Going into Lollapalooza, American music fans weren't familiar with the concept of a second stage, and the crowds were thin. That all changed when, during their set on the main stage, Chris started telling people to check out the Circus. "Starting that day, I had thousands of people and the media started coming," Rose said. "I owe my career to Chris."

Rose's biggest and most nauseating attraction was a guy named Matt "The Tube" Crowley. During every performance, Crowley would gross out gape-mouthed spectators by inserting a seven-foot-long tube into his stomach through his nose and start pumping in a variety of disgusting liquids like beer, chocolate sauce, eggs, and Maalox. Once he hit capacity, he then pumped the contents back out into a glass for people to drink. They called the concoction Bile Beer and one of the first people to step up and swig it was Chris.

"Boredom must have driven him to it," Rose posited. "In the middle of our show, while I was pumping Matt the Tube's stomach, Chris strode out on the stage, took the mike, and said something to the effect of 'I sure am thirsty. Might I try the vile bile?'"[18] Vedder caught wind of Chris's gastronomical antics, and the next night, showed up and downed a glass for the cheering audience. Then Al Jourgensen from Ministry got in on the disgusting act, and before long, many in attendance were clamoring for an opportunity to drink fresh human vomit.

During Lollapalooza, while in the company of his longtime buddies, Chris felt freer to let his proverbial hair down. In between gigs, he and Vedder found themselves in the room of one of their crew members, who bemoaned the state of the current crop of polite and professional rock stars. Eager to show him that he could wild out with the best of them, Chris took a nearby amplifier and hurled it through a glass window, where it smashed into bits on the alley floor stories below. They all laughed for a few minutes until Chris realized he'd written his name on a piece of tape stuck to the amplifier. He raced downstairs to rip it off, but that didn't stop the local cops from coming up to their room to investigate. Vedder spun a yarn about a jealous dude destroying his property after he learned that the singer had slept with his girlfriend. Satisfied by the tale, the officers let them off without so much as a warning.

The tour pressed on through August, hitting most of the big cities on the East Coast. Along the way, Soundgarden's set took on a controversial bent when the band started covering Ice-T's "Cop Killer." The So-Cal rapper had been on the bill during the first Lollapalooza and was recruited to act as a sort of host during this second run. His inflammatory single, in which he threatens to shoot police officers, had brought waves of condemnation from many within the law enforcement community as well as President George H. W. Bush. In the face of mounting pressure on Ice-T's label to pull the song from stores, Chris offered support in the best way he knew how.

First Amendment rights were a cause near and dear to Soundgarden's heart. In Washington State, just a few months before Lollapalooza kicked off, the governor signed an "Erotic Sound Recordings" statute into law that sought to outlaw the sale of music deemed obscene to minors. Any retailers or record store employees caught running afoul of the edict could face up to six months in jail and incur hefty fines.

Soundgarden promptly sued the state's attorney general, Ken Eikenberry, arguing that the rule violated the constitution. More allies jumped on board, including A&M, Tower Records, the RIAA, and fellow artists Nirvana, Alice In Chains, Pearl Jam, Heart, and Sir Mix-A-Lot. The band's lawyers argued that the statute "interferes with their ability to express themselves, manage their businesses, and access ideas; and interferes with society's notion of a free marketplace of ideas and, in general, the evolution of society itself." The Supreme Court of Washington agreed, and two years later declared the statute void.

In Miami, Soundgarden brought out "Cop Killer" composer, Body Count guitarist Ernie C, to back them up on guitar, and Chris launched into a passionate defense of freedom of speech. "I don't wanna kill any cops personally, but I wanna make sure anybody lets me write any song that I wanna write and everybody lets you buy any song you wanna buy, so I'm gonna do this song for all fucking time," he roared.[19] The music started, and the crowd in front of the stage turned into a tumultuous frenzy of bare-chested bodies slamming into one another.

By September, Lollapalooza had reached the end of the line. It was a heady moment for Chris. *Singles* held its premiere on September 10 at the Park Plaza Hotel in LA and was filmed for an MTV special. Though Pearl Jam and Alice In Chains served as the evening's musical entertainment, Chris was on hand to help celebrate the film and reprise his cameo in the film while standing and nodding alongside VJ Riki Rachtman.

The next three nights were consumed by the final dates of Lollapalooza at the Irvine Meadows Amphitheater. One only needed to look at the charts to see that the ceaseless pace of touring, the hundreds of interviews, and the quality of the music Chris produced had had a tremendous impact on American music. *Temple Of The Dog* had reached the top five. The *Singles* soundtrack was sitting pretty just outside of the top twenty, while *Badmotorfinger* was still hanging around in the top one hundred a

full year after its release. By this point, the album had been officially certified gold and was well on its way to platinum.

Backstage at Irvine, Chris busted out a polaroid camera and snapped
shots with everybody he came into contact with before handing the pictures out as souvenirs. During Pearl Jam's set, he emerged one last time,
along with Matt Cameron, to join his friends for "Hunger Strike" and
"Reach Down." Then Soundgarden hit the stage with Al Jourgenson,
treating fans to a memorable rendition of "Cop Killer."

It was the last time fans would see Soundgarden onstage for a full
year. It was time for a change.

CHAPTER IX

ALIVE IN THE SUPERUNKNOWN

Chris Cornell was standing in front of his closet, flipping through his clothes and growing increasingly agitated. Hanger after hanger was weighed down by a lived-in long-sleeve or random T-shirt he'd picked up along the way. It was the same set of clothes he'd seen hundreds of thousands of kids wearing to so many of Soundgarden's gigs over the last couple of years. The same clothes that his contemporaries in Alice In Chains, Pearl Jam, and Nirvana wore in their videos. The same clothes that had been co-opted by the arbiters of cool for commercial purposes. His look had become a uniform.

Everywhere he turned, Chris saw an army of people who wanted to look like him, act like him, crack sarcastic jokes like him, kick around in chunky combat boots like him, and dive into crowds like him. He was growing sick of it. "I had an identity crisis in the early nineties," he told *Revolver*. "I was the first guy sort of running around climbing up into the rafters, like a jungle boy, and smashing guitars and crowd surfing. And then I started seeing it [in other bands] a lot."[1]

Chris was enjoying a month-long block of much-needed downtime when he went wardrobe diving. Susan was preoccupied with one of her other groups, and he had ample time to chill out around the house by himself. He wasn't going out often and didn't speak to many people on the phone, which put him in a weird frame of mind. "If I hadn't been alone so long, I would not have gone as far as I actually went."[2]

Thoughts about what he wore turned into thoughts about his appearance. Chris's nearly two-foot-long mane of curly black hair was his most recognizable feature. He'd worn it that way for years. It was a great look, except for the times he tried to inhale while singing and sucked in a mouthful of his own hair. Now, out of the spotlight, far from the worshiping masses, and away from the people who might talk him out of it, Chris considered shaving it off.

The idea of wiping the slate clean was enticing, but a day passed, and he did nothing. Then another. And then another. The more he thought about it, though, the better the idea seemed, until finally he got over his trepidation, seized a pair of clippers, and sheared his cranium down to the scalp. Staring into the mirror, he felt like a new man, partially free, at least in the moment, from the expectation to look or act a certain way. He gathered up some of the remnants of his long locks, stuffed them inside of an envelope and mailed them to his wife.

Chris Cornell never enjoyed celebrity, especially in the nineties. When he wanted to go album shopping, he'd duck into Easy Street Records after hours, pull the brim of his baseball cap down, and peruse the carefully curated bins in solitude. When Soundgarden was home, he tried to make himself unreachable, usually by taking off into the wilds of western Washington. He was shocked when he opened an issue of *Time* magazine to find an article about his haircut. *How in the hell did they find out? Why in the hell did Time magazine readers give a shit about his head?!* It was enough to drive him crazy.

Outlets like MTV and *Newsweek* also covered his chrome dome, which was irritating, though he managed to find some validation in the coverage. "I didn't want to march to anyone's drummer," he said. "Sometimes when you're accepted, that edge goes away. But other times when you're accepted there's a conflict, and the conflict is, 'Oh, why now?' You didn't like me then, so now my *F yous* are gonna get bigger."[3]

* * *

The red brick recording studio on 4th Avenue has gone by many names. When it originally opened in 1976 as the dream of a Borscht Belt comedian named Danny Kaye and his business partner Lester Smith (part owner of the Seattle Mariners) they called it Kaye-Smith Studios. Thirteen years later, a local radio DJ named Steve Lawson took it over and named it after himself. In more recent years it was called Studio X, but before that and throughout the bulk of nineties when some of the biggest names in music—Johnny Cash, Nirvana, R.E.M.—recorded there, it was known as Bad Animals. Long since displaced to make room for a tower of luxury condos, back in 1993, there was no better place in the city to record.

Bad Animals, named after Heart's 1987 album, was owned by Ann and Nancy Wilson. The sisters took over the building at the beginning of the decade and gave it much-needed sonic and aesthetic upgrades, not only for their own purposes, but so that local bands had a proper, high-tech recording studio in their backyard. For Soundgarden, who had just spent the last year performing in nearly every major metropolis in the western hemisphere, the opportunity to create music in a facility where they could play all day and then go home to sleep in their own beds at night was too enticing to pass up. It was here that they would work on their next album.

Kim Thayil has sometimes compared *Badmotorfinger* to the Beatles' *White Album*, but the description is more apt to capture *Superunknown*'s fragmented genesis. As opposed to their last record where they spent weeks writing together inside Avast!, each member initially worked alone to produce new material. Chris secluded himself in his basement with a few instruments and an eight-track ADAT recording machine and spent hours in self-imposed isolation, conjuring up fresh ideas.

"I went really deep into trying to experiment with how I wrote—trying to shirk some of the fear I think that anyone, when they write songs alone, might have of making mistakes," he told radio host Redbeard. "I wasn't really in touch with the expressive nature of songwriting, the honest aspect of it. I was trying to manipulate it too much and failed. But I also kind of found myself more so as a songwriter than ever before."[4]

Inspiration came from unexpected places and struck in unexpected moments. Sometimes literally, like in the song "Like Suicide." One day, while Chris was working in his basement, he heard a loud thump. He thought it might be a burglar, so he went up to investigate. After searching around a bit, he opened his front door and found a female robin lying on the ground. The small bird had flown into a window and the impact had snapped its neck. The robin was alive, but suffering. Chris grabbed a nearby cinderblock and put the bird out of its misery. As he returned to his basement, the phrase "Like Suicide" popped into his mind, and he decided to write a song about it.

Many have misinterpreted the song's central meaning based on its evocative title, but the opening line alludes to the tragedy in specific terms: "Dazed out in a garden bed with a broken neck lays my broken gift / Just like suicide." Tonally, Chris wanted to capture the vibe of Creedence Clearwater Revival's "Born on the Bayou" and tuned the guitar in such a way—standard D, with the high string dropped to C—to get the song's entrancing spiral of notes to ring out properly.

"4th of July," maybe the best song on the album, was another track easily misinterpreted. It was based on the memory of an insane acid trip he experienced heading out to an Indian reservation around Independence Day. While in the throes of his trip, Chris found himself walking along a path with a chorus of voices trailing ten feet behind him. When he turned around, he spied a figure clad in a black shirt and jeans and another person in a red shirt. The more he tried to focus on either person the more the figures seemed to slip away into the ether. Rather than finding the pair unsettling, however, he found their presence comforting because he didn't feel alone.

The song's central refrain captures the ephemeral, dizzying nature of the experience with supreme poignancy. "I feel it in the wind, I saw it in the sky / I thought it was the end, I thought it was the 4th of July." Beyond the message, it's the way Chris delivers the lyrics, as if trapped in a foggy miasma from which he'll never emerge, that makes "4th of July" so entrancing. If the Four Horsemen of the apocalypse ever wanted for a soundtrack, they could hardly find a better piece of music.

By now, Chris had secured his place as the preeminent screamer in rock, but as he wrote this latest batch of songs, he tried to explore the full dynamic range of his voice. He went deeper, and remained more subdued in spots, which only made the moments when he took off into the stratosphere that much more explosive. Each of the tracks on *Superunknown* has its own vocal flavor. Purposely mid-tempo deliveries give way to avalanches of screaming. Drudgy, syncopated verses are accented with twinkling falsettos. Sometimes he's pressed right up into the front of the speaker, other times he hovers just underneath the music. Everything was by design.

Chris started to think of his voice as a separate entity; a character he could inhabit for the duration of a given track. This technique opened up a unique set of questions, chief among them being, "Who is the person singing?" and "What do they sound like?" Of all the aspects of his songwriting, this was the most difficult to nail down, but it was paramount to his new approach.

It all went back to the formative period when he was sitting alone in his room listening to the Beatles. He thought back to how the four distinct voices of John, Paul, George, and Ringo alternated between tracks, providing a different approach and feeling to each one. He couldn't always tell who sang what, but the variety sounded so damn good. "I thought that's what rock music was, and I thought that's what making an album was," he said. "You sang in the style and with the feel that the song was asking for."[5] Without another singer in the band to help him, he'd simply have to do it himself.

Before Soundgarden got down to the brass tacks of recording their next album, however, they had to select a producer. It was nearly guaranteed that more people than ever before would be interested in what they did next, and Soundgarden wanted a fresh set of ears to help pull the best out of them. Originally, the plan was to work with Rick Rubin, but then they decided to take a meeting with a producer from New York named Michael Beinhorn.

Beinhorn had previously worked with the Red Hot Chili Peppers on some of their earlier efforts like *The Uplift Mofo Party Plan* and *Mother's*

Milk but had branched out into other genres, helping artists like Herbie Hancock, Soul Asylum, and the Violent Femmes. He was also no stranger to the Pacific Northwest. One of his more recent projects was a record titled *Far Gone* by another Seattle alt-rock band named Love Battery.

Beinhorn flew to Seattle and met with the band at Avast! where they spent a couple of hours getting to know one another. It seemed to go well enough, but Soundgarden still wasn't convinced that he was the right man for the job. They took the producer out for a test run and set up a session at Bear Creek Studios to cut a couple of tracks with Beinhorn manning the boards.

Over the course of three or four days, the band recorded "She Likes Surprises" and "No Attention." "It was more like a precursor to recording," Beinhorn said. "It wasn't the kind of thing where I had a lot of time or resources to muck about, so it moved relatively fast. Everyone got their parts done in a reasonable amount of time." Not long after that he got the call. The job was his.

The creation of *Superunknown* began in earnest after the band mailed their new producer a cassette with a couple of fully realized songs like "Fresh Tendrils," along with some riffs like the one that ended up being the basis for "Mailman" and a few instrumental jams. Beinhorn was impressed with some of the selections, but he felt there wasn't enough material yet to justify entering the recording studio. "I think there were about five songs that ended up on the record, and the rest was kind of meandering a little bit," he said.

The band wasn't exactly thrilled to receive such unsparing criticism so early on this process, but as they would come to learn, Beinhorn was adamant about achieving the best results. "This record came at a time when you could really tell who the next big band was gonna be, and at that point in time, it was clearly Soundgarden," Beinhorn said. "The entire music community was aware that *if* their next record had all the right ingredients it was gonna be humongous, and I had to do everything in my power to push it over the edge."

Over the next few months, Soundgarden worked to create demos they hoped sounded good enough to everyone's ears to make it onto the final tracklist. Chris traded the solitude of his basement for a week-long writing session at his best friend Eric Garcia's small, octagon-shaped cabin across the water from Seattle in Port Townsend to get some more writing done. *Superunknown* wouldn't suffer for a lack of preparation.

From the outset, Beinhorn was impressed by Chris's skills as a DIY engineer. "Chris was an absolute first-rate demo-maker," the producer noted. "He was one of those guys who could do everything. Write the music, record all the instruments, play everything himself; he had an enviable set of abilities." Still, he got the sense that the singer was pushing himself too much. "He was kinda going off the rails a little bit," Beinhorn said. "He was sending me a tremendous volume of music, but I noticed they were all cut from the same cloth. There was a sameness to them, and they didn't have much purpose. They didn't demonstrate his skills as a songwriter or a performer."

At one point, Chris sent his producer a tape filled with eleven new songs, none of which made it onto *Superunknown*. "It's so funny, but there was a point where I actually started to dread getting tapes from him in the mail," Beinhorn said. After that episode, the two men had a conversation where Chris explained that he felt pressure to write songs that appealed to Soundgarden fans, a notion that the producer felt was counterproductive. To get him back on track, Beinhorn started talking about his musical roots and his general taste. "I was like, 'What are you listening to? What's inspiring to you?' And he said, 'The Beatles and Cream.' And I said, 'Write a song that's like The Beatles and Cream.' That was basically what precipitated the next tape I got from him, which was a home run."

The new tape was anchored by a song that had come to Chris late one night while driving home. As the lines on the highway glided past, a dark and ephemeral melody popped into his head. It was entrancing. Once he made it back to his house, he raced to a tape recorder and whistled the part into the tiny machine so that he wouldn't forget it.

"The first song on the tape was 'Fell On Black Days,'" Beinhorn said. "The next song was a song called 'Anxious,' which didn't get used, but it had Jerry Cantrell on guitar. It wasn't appropriate for *Superunknown*, but it was great. More of a bluesy type thing. The song after that was called 'Tighter & Tighter,' which we did record, but never finished and they did after [on *Down On The Upside*]. And the last song on the tape was 'Black Hole Sun.'"

The next day after his late-night moment of inspiration, Chris went down to the basement and started to transpose the music he'd whistled into the recorder onto the frets of his guitar. Once he nailed that part, he thought about a phrase he'd misheard recently during a television newscast that sparked his imagination. "I heard 'blah blah blah Black Hole Sun blah blah blah,'" he told *Uncut*. Those three words were an intoxicating bit of imagery. "A black hole is a billion times bigger than a sun, it's a void, a giant circle of nothing, and then you have the sun, the giver of all life," Chris explained. "It was this combination of bright and dark, this sense of hope and an underlying moodiness."[6]

Once Chris had the title, a compelling collage of word-images that fit the dark mood of the music poured out of him, which he eventually honed into verses. Amid the snakes, the invocation of heaven and hell, and an allusion to the stench of summer, there were two lines rooted in recent experience. "Times are gone for honest men," captures his perspective on the outside world, an increasingly cynical place, especially within the music industry. The other, "No one sings like you anymore," was more personal, stemming from a comment a fan had made to him while on tour. Its true meaning and inclusion remain a mystery.

With lyrics married to the melody, Chris started mixing in the unique musical elements that make "Black Hole Sun" the zeitgeist-bending piece of music that it became. The process moved quickly, and the early demo version included on the deluxe edition of *Superunknown* is remarkable for how complete it sounds. Right away, that mystically tuned, arpeggiated guitar intro gives way to the haunting, chorus-painted chord progression through the verses before the quick drum break signals the beginning of a disembodied chorus. Even the psychedelic, wah-wah drenched solo is there. It doesn't sound anywhere near as dynamic in this nascent form— Chris's vocals are far more subdued—but every element is intact, ready for the addition of Cameron's drums, Shepherd's bass and Thayil's frenzied lead guitar to realize its full potential.

"Black Hole Sun" was a breathtaking revelation for Beinhorn. "I played it fifteen times in a row," the producer said. "Once I pulled myself away from it, I called him, and when he picked up, the first thing I said to him was, 'You're a fucking genius!'" Chris was surprised. "He was like, 'Oh, do you like it?' I was like, 'Do I like it? It's one of the best songs I've ever heard!'"

Even his bandmates knew that "Black Hole Sun" was a different animal. Ben Shepherd equated it to Stevie Wonder. Hiro Yamamoto, who had heard an early version one day while stopping by Avast! to say hello, immediately declared the song a hit, before bursting into laughter. The only person who couldn't wrap his head around its whimsically brooding appeal was the guy who wrote it. Chris figured it might make for a decent third or fourth single. The idea that it could become a worldwide smash seemed impossible. "When I think of hit songs, they have to be somewhat anthemic in the world of rock, and I didn't see 'Black Hole Sun' as being that," Chris said.[7]

One of the other songs Chris included on the "home run" tape he sent to Beinhorn was "Fell On Black Days." It had bounced around in different configurations for years, to Chris's increased frustration. He just couldn't seem to crack it. During the recording of *Badmotorfinger*, an early version of the song was re-configured into "Slaves & Bulldozers" while another attempt morphed into a song dubbed "Black Rain," which Soundgarden cooked up during those sessions back in '91 but didn't get finished until years later for the compilation album *Telephantasm*.

"Fell On Black Days" is fueled by fear. The minor-key vibe is decidedly gloomy, but the lyrics are even darker as Chris aimed to capture the sense of feeling shitty for no particular reason. "You're happy with your life, everything's going well, things are exciting when all of a sudden you realize you're unhappy in the extreme, to the point of being really, really scared," Chris explained. "There's no particular event you can pin the feeling down to, it's just that you realize one day that everything in your life is *fucked*."[8]

There is a word for that particular feeling: depression. That unpredictable emotional monster that can crop up at any time and consume your state of mind. Chris knew the feeling well and struggled with it multiple times throughout his life. "For me, I always had one foot in this very dark, lonely, isolated world," he said. "If you're depressed long enough, it's almost a comfort, a state of mind that you've made peace with because you've been in it so long. It's a very selfish world."[9]

"The Day I Tried to Live," a vital expression of battling back against internal forces, is the counterbalance, examining the attempt to come out of hiding and engage with people to understand their points of view. "One more time around," indeed, "Might do it."

"Black Hole Sun" wasn't the only song inspired by a misunderstanding. Chris had a VHS tape filled with a collection of J. P. Patches's notable television moments titled "Vol. 1: Getrude Reveals Superklown," lying around the house. While glancing at the cover one day, he misread Superklown as Superunknown and figured it'd make an outstanding title for a song.

Kim Thayil had created a tape of different riffs that all connected together linearly. It wasn't a song yet, but it certainly had the potential to become one. Chris was bowled over by the wealth of options. "There were a lot of different parts that could've become the verse and were a lot of different parts that could've been a bridge, or an intro or transition, so it took me a long time to make those decisions and figure out what worked best," he told Howard Stern. "I had to try and sing the verse over a whole bunch of different parts and see which one made sense."[10]

Chris and Kim weren't the only ones studiously making tapes. One of the better tracks on the album, "Fresh Tendrils," sprung from the mind of Matt Cameron, who was entering a songwriting prime of his own. The name of that song, which never appears in the lyrics, is a euphemism for a new bag of weed. The phrase was coined by Stuart Hallerman who helped the drummer record a demo version.

Cameron also brought in what became the sludgy and psychedelic "Mailman" and, along with Thayil, cooked up "Limo Wreck," a simmering, heavy metal waltz that concludes with a volcanic eruption of shrieks and frenetic guitar runs. The title stemmed from a trip down the LA freeway where Chris took note of all the broken-down pickup trucks and El Caminos mixed together with Porches and limousines. He thought about how the people riding around in their opulent cars, behind tinted windows, must go through life feeling that they're not susceptible to mortality. They ride around above it all, chiding their drivers anytime they're inconvenienced by a bump in the road. "Under the red under the lights / Lies the wreck of you for the rest of your life."

"Mailman" was a particularly heavy piece of music and Chris came up with a heavy message to match the vibe. "This song isn't really an ode to that person, that postal worker, that mail carrier, that person who snaps a twig and kills innocent people. This is just taking a second to imagine getting inside someone's head who has a sense of powerlessness, because I think at all times, we do," Chris explained to an audience at Webster Hall in 2014. "The difference between you guys and those people, is that you're not fucking disgusting, ridiculous murderers where your last act in life is to take someone else's."[11] Soundgarden actually held rehearsals not far from a post office in the early nineties, and there was a modicum of anxiety that one day they might walk by and catch a stray bullet.

Ben Shepherd rose to the occasion as well. He was responsible for writing both the words and music to two of the weirdest songs on the album. The first, "Head Down," is the more conventional of the two, but still pretty out there with its open C tuning and ping-pong-ball-sounding percussion up top. It's a reflection on bullying as seen alternately from the perspective of the bully and the bullied. The other was called "Half," and it's far more out there.

Chris doesn't even sing on "Half," which was its own special thrill for the frontman. After hearing the tape, he was convinced that Shepherd should be the one behind the microphone. He just couldn't hear how he could enhance what Shepherd had already achieved, but the bassist had his reservations. The idea of someone filling in that role was especially appealing to Chris, who was striving to break norms wherever he could. "My response was, 'That's what I'm talking about,'" Chris said. "This is about the song's best foot forward, and that should always be the most important thing."[12]

With way more than enough songs at their disposal to flesh out a full record, Soundgarden entered Bad Animals in July of 1993 and started building tracks. They had no idea how long and arduous the process would become. They were also blissfully unaware of how much their producer's meticulous approach would fray their nerves. Local engineer Adam Kasper was brought in to man the boards for the project and as he observed, "Everyone in the band is very particular about how things should be. A lot of discussion and analyzation and over-thinking. I don't mean that as a criticism because it's not, but then you add a Beinhorn and that made it worse."

Early on, Kasper got a heavy dose of how demanding Beinhorn could be with even the most mundane tasks. "I recall three or four days of tape aligning, just to see what the optimal way would be to align a tape machine," he said. "And that just went on and on with microphones and other things. At some point, the band just gets fatigued and wants to play. It was just a different approach and eventually it just kinda wore on everyone. Anytime you spend six months in a small room with that many people, it gets tough."

The first song they worked on was one of Thayil's, a ninety-four second punk-rock barnburner titled "Kickstand." Chris wrote the lyrics based on the title that the guitarist had already given it. "I think we did twelve to fifteen passes of that song," Beinhorn recalled. "We went through a whole bunch of passes with [Matt] getting his wiggles out, so to speak, and it was interesting to see it happen. He did a bunch of passes where you could just tell he was sort of marking time almost. He wasn't really present. But then all of a sudden, he starts to come into the song more and more and you can feel his personality until there was one pass where it was like, 'Oh shit, that's really good!'"

"What I saw was Matt realizing pretty early on was that he was going to have to call his own takes, meaning, 'That's a good one, that's a keeper,'" Kasper said. "I think he realized he could've been ground down into dust by Beinhorn. 'Let me change the room mic, play it again fourteen more times!' In the years of working with Matt, he's very much a one, two, three max take kind of guy."

The band largely recorded in batches, tackling three or four songs at a time before putting them aside and cooking up the next three or four. The process usually began with Chris and Matt working together to create the bones of a given song before Shepherd and Thayil joined in and filled the whole thing out. "Most of the big hits happened that way, just hitting with a scratch guitar and laying it down with Matt," Kasper remembered. "Usually they'd nail it in two or three takes. And then we'd have the bed and then everyone would individually spend a day or two on their parts and sounds and ideas."

Figuring out how to add unique sounds and sonic textures was the most time-consuming and frustrating part of the process, especially when it came to the guitars. Throughout the sessions, Chris primarily played a Fender Jazzmaster and either one of his trusty Gretsch Duo or Single Jet guitars plugged into either a Mesa Boogie Dual Rectifier or a JMP 50-Watt Marshall, with a half-stack slant cab. And yet, one of the most vital pieces of equipment almost didn't make it onto the record.

Back when Chris was recording the demo for "Black Hole Sun," he played through a rotating Leslie amp that he rented from a local music shop. The amp was crucial because it lent the song that all-important, eerie ephemeral quality. In the studio, they tried a few different Leslies that just weren't cutting it, so Chris went back to the shop where he picked up the first speaker, but it was gone, sold to a member of another Seattle band, the Walkabouts. With a gnawing sense of urgency to get the song to sound exactly the way he heard it in his head, Chris went to the Walkabouts, who allowed him to borrow it for the sessions. Years later, when the amp went up for sale on Ebay, Chris bought it through an intermediary to avoid creating a bidding war.

After completing the first batch of songs just two weeks or so into the process, the band decided to take a break from recording and join Neil Young on an eight-city tour of outdoor amphitheaters through the Midwest and into the East Coast. In 1993, the mercurial singer-songwriter was in the midst of a renewed critical and cultural appreciation. To many, the flannel-wearing Canadian who created jagged, loud, and gloriously unkempt guitar jams with his band Crazy Horse on albums like *Rust Never Sleeps* and *Ragged Glory*, had pioneered much of the grunge aesthetic. In fact, at the beginning of the decade, *Pulse!*, the in-house magazine for Tower Records, ran an issue with Young on the cover titled "The Godfather of Grunge Rock." Just a couple of weeks after finishing up his run with Soundgarden, Young joined Pearl Jam onstage at the MTV VMAs for a jam on his song "Rockin' in the Free World," sealing his bonafides with the millions of members of the alt-rock nation watching from home.

Young's people had put in requests to bring Soundgarden out on the road with him multiple times before, but prior commitments had always prevented them from taking him up on the offer. At this point, they were concerned that if they turned him down again, he'd stop asking, so they agreed to put everything on hold and debut some of their new songs to Young's audience.

The run began in Rapid City, South Dakota, where the annual biker meet-up Sturgis was in full swing. For many, this was their first look at Chris Cornell with his newly-shorn head, and it caused quite a stir among those expecting to see the long-locked screamer who'd graced the cover of *Spin* just a year before. Even though they were once again in the open-er's slot, the tour with Young, who was backed onstage by R&B legends Booker T. & The M.G.s, was a rewarding experience. The vibe couldn't have been more different than the run with Guns N' Roses, and most of the shows performing before Young went off fine, except for a gig at Jones Beach in New York which was nearly flooded by a massive thunderstorm. From the stage, Chris thanked God for the light show, while Ben Shepherd smashed a beer bottle against his bass in frustration as the sound flickered on and off.

The gig at Exhibition Stadium in Toronto on August 18, on the other hand, was a major highlight, especially after Pearl Jam was added to the lineup. Chris was in good spirits and praised Canadian open-mindedness onstage for refusing to ban the "Jesus Christ Pose" video, unlike the media in their own country. During their forty-five-minute set, they introduced the crowd to three new songs from their next record, "Let Me Drown," "My Wave," and "Mailman."

Most nights, Soundgarden were preceded by Blind Melon, who had supported them on tour a couple of years back during their

Badmotorfinger run. The two groups had grown close, and Chris was especially taken by singer Shannon Hoon. "Myself and Shannon went to lunch with him, and Chris said that Shannon reminded him so much of Andy Wood that he was tripping," Blind Melon's guitarist, Christopher Thorn, said. "They had a similar essence and personality, and Chris was not like that. He was more quiet."

One of Hoon's pastimes was to bend forks into intricate necklaces and give them to friends. Hoon made a twisted design for Chris, who liked it so much that it became a near constant fixture in photos, including on Soundgarden's first *Rolling Stone* cover. "I remember Shannon was so proud that Chris would wear it," Thorn said. "We were intimidated. We hadn't done anything yet and these were guys who made records that we really loved."

Not long after the twenty-eight-year-old Hoon died of a cocaine overdose while on tour in New Orleans on October 21, 1995, Chris decided to put the fork necklace away. It was another depressing reminder of yet another talented friend gone too soon. "The other thing I wore was this ring that belonged to Andy Wood," he said. "It's like, 'I don't wanna wear these fucking things from people who died.'"[13]

By the end of August, Soundgarden was back in Seattle, ready to tackle the remainder of recording. Prior to leaving for the Neil Young tour, Chris typically worked on his vocal parts with Beinhorn and Kasper present in the large recording room. After they got back, he changed things up and, for the rest of the sessions, largely sang in solitude. The producer showed him how to work the console, how to set up the tape machine, and then left him to figure out the most compelling way to approach each vocal. The method to Chris's madness was simple. "Sometimes when you try to communicate with somebody else, they may not understand, so you just give up," he explained. "On my own, I could experiment."[14]

While recording *Superunknown*, Chris destroyed five Neumann U 87 microphones through the sustained power of his voice. He didn't give a shit. The music had to be perfect. Anything less was unacceptable, as even the perfectionist Beinhorn learned while listening to some early vocals Chris had laid down for "Black Hole Sun." As the producer recalled, "I comped the vocal and he came in and listened to it and when I was done playing the finished vocal, he looked at me and said, 'Not good enough.'"

Beinhorn was stunned. Chris had spent hours alternating between glass-shattering screams and doom-laden crooning, but it didn't matter. Scrap it all and let's start over, he commanded. "He critiqued his own vocal, which is something up to that point in my career I'd never seen a vocalist do," he said. "I just thought, 'Jesus Christ, this guy is amazing!'"

To help inspire him, Beinhorn suggested that Chris listen to Frank Sinatra's "I Get Along without You Very Well" and "Only the Lonely" before singing "Black Hole Sun." He wanted Chris to hear how Ol' Blue Eyes could soar over an arrangement, how he *performed* even in a staid studio setting.

One of the more interesting days at Bad Animals was when the band brought in a street musician named Artis The Spoonman. Originally, Soundgarden didn't plan on re-recording Chris's *Poncier* tape cut "Spoonman," but as they worked on new tracks, Matt Cameron kept bringing up the 7/4-timed song as something they should try. The original tape features a breakdown with Chris clanging away on pots and pans. For the Soundgarden version, they had Spoonman add his own flatware-enhanced flair to the song.

Artis knew Ben Shepherd from around town—he'd often run into the bassist at the OK Hotel—but he wasn't aware of how popular Soundgarden was until he was invited to the band's show at the Paramount with the Melvins. "Backstage that night, Susan [Silver] said, 'Chris is writing a song,' I'm not sure if she told me it was titled 'Spoonman,' but when they're finished with the song would I like to record on it? I said, 'Yeah, sure!'" Artis remembered.

"He went down into the big room and laid out a bunch of rugs or blankets and then about several hundred spoons," Kasper said. "We set up some mics and then I think he did three takes. We'd start the song and he'd start from the first beat and just go nonstop until the end of the song. He did that three times in a row then just about passed out." Artis literally sacrificed his body for the sake of music. "There's blood flying everywhere because he was really hitting himself hard," Beinhorn recalled. "He was just a bloody mess. We were aghast. Everyone in the room had their mouth on the floor."

Because Artis played straight through from start to finish instead of solely on the single breakdown they hoped to fill, once they had his parts recorded, Beinhorn and Kapser went about the laborious process of splicing different sections together to create the solo heard on the finished tape. It was quite the ordeal, especially given that the Spoonman didn't give much thought to things like time signatures. It all worked out in the end though, and Artis remained touched by Chris's tribute to him. "What an unbelievable, incomparable honor to be celebrated in such a song," he said. "Especially with all the celebration it had."

Recording on the album continued. Days turned into weeks, weeks into months. After a while, cabin fever set in. "We were going nuts," Kasper recalled. "We were throwing fruit at the speakers. Chris would break a towel rack in the back or kick a stool. It wasn't terrible, but there was a lot of beer and garbage and crap everywhere."

Thayil hit his breaking point while working on "4th of July." Chris's particularity about the sound of the guitars combined with Beinhorn's insistence on trying every possible method of recording drove the guitarist crazy. "I just remember three days of Kim trying to play that guitar part," Kasper said. "Beinhorn is changing microphones and screens so the poor guy was in this little sound booth for three days before he finally snaps and goes, 'Why don't you get fucking Yngwie Malmsteen to play it!' Then he storms out."

"It was definitely a problem," Beinhorn said of his propensity to push the band for additional takes. "I knew that I was veering on occasion to getting my ass canned, but I didn't care because my attitude was that this really had to be something that was gonna stick around and have legs." In a classic show of their signature Seattle-based passive aggression, at certain points throughout the process the band would break out into singing "Kumbaya" whenever their producer would try and communicate with them over the talkback microphone.

It wasn't all a slog though. Moments of levity were numerous, like the time Chris sang a take of "Let Me Drown" in the funkadelic style of

Anthony Kiedis. Then there were the times when Chris teased Beinhorn, who had produced the Herbie Hancock hit "Rockit," by clucking that song's melody like a chicken. To the public, Chris Cornell was the brooding representation of Generation X at their most disaffected and pissed off. Behind closed doors, he was kind of a ham. Case in point: a short while after *Superunknown* dropped, Heart singer Ann Wilson hosted a Halloween party at her home. Everyone had to come dressed as their favorite song. Chris showed up as "Black Hole Sun," decked out in platform boots, black face paint, and a papier-mâché sun around his head. He was the hit of the night.

"There was always an emphasis on me as the angry young man, the hesitant rock star," Chris complained to *Harper's Bazaar*. "When people met me in person, they'd be defeated before they walked in the door, then be pleasantly surprised because I didn't hate them or the human race. Sometimes, they'd end up liking me more than they should."[15]

When the members of Soundgarden weren't working on their parts, there were video games set up in the back where they could play racing games or first-person shooters. At the beginning of the sessions, Thayil insisted on leaving baseball games on television while they were working. "This ended promptly in the midst of a take when he stopped playing and yelled, 'Did you see that?' at the TV screen," Beinhorn remembered.

Sequestered in the studio as long as they were, Soundgarden welcomed a variety of visitors. Some presences were welcome, like members of Pearl Jam and Nirvana who dropped by to see and hear how things were going. Another time Josh Homme, then playing guitar in the stoner rock band Kyuss, rolled through and challenged Kim to a game of ping-pong. The most awe-inducing presence of all was Johnny Cash, who was working down the hall on a song for a Willie Nelson tribute album while the Red-Headed Stranger was trying to get the IRS off his back.

Then there were the unwelcome intruders, like Smashing Pumpkins leader Billy Corgan who swung by and tried to chop it up with Chris about recording equipment. "It was really awkward," Kasper said. "Corgan comes in and he's just talking, holding court. Chris is just kinda on the couch with a dazed look, looking forward. He's like, 'Oh yeah, our gear got held up in Portland because of the snowstorm and, hey, Is that an AGR 150 tape machine?' Blah, blah, blah, blah, blah. Ten minutes this goes on and not a word out of Chris. Then he just gets up and walks out."

The most unexpected visitors swung through near the end of the process. One day the band received a request from the producers of the kids' educational show *Bill Nye the Science Guy* to film them while they worked on a song. It seemed like a good cause, so they agreed. One afternoon while Chris was out doing something else, Thayil, Shepherd, and Cameron gamely plowed through a take of "Kickstand" for the cameras, while Kasper explained the finer points of recording.

By September, almost a full year after they had started, Soundgarden had nearly finished *Superunknown*. They'd begun with a batch of about two dozen songs, but by the time they made it to the end of the sessions, they'd whittled that number down to a comparatively svelte fifteen—sixteen if counting the LP version that included the bonus track "She Likes Surprises." The mammoth collection of tracks tested the upper limits of a CD's storage capacity, clocking in at just under seventy-four minutes, by far the longest studio record that Soundgarden or Chris would ever release.

All that was left to do was the mixing. With memories of how underwhelming *Ultramega OK* had sounded, the band knew that this was a crucial part of the process, and to get it right they tapped producer Brendan O'Brien, who had worked with Pearl Jam on their last two records *Vs.* and *Vitalogy*. "If you listen to the raw tracks, there was so much crazy distorted compression and things, unless its mixed right, it can really sound awful," Kasper said. Immediately, O'Brien started cutting everything back to its most elemental and sonically crystalline level. "Brendan came in and sat down with me and was like, 'So you say you got forty-eight tracks, right?' He would go, 'What's this?' And I'd go, 'That's the super compressed—' Fader down. 'What's this?' 'That's the distorted—' Gone. Just got rid of them. It ended up getting down to the kick, snare, guitar, vocal."

The approach was exactly what the album needed, and when Chris heard the final mixes, he couldn't have been happier. In fact, it was only after O'Brien had finished his part that Chris realized just how great

Superunknown sounded. All the hard work, torment, sweat, and frustration suddenly seemed worth it.

Even while his duties in Soundgarden took up a massive amount of his attention, Chris still managed to find time to work on a couple of outside projects. The first was a semi-reunion of Temple Of The Dog, featuring Mike McCready, Jeff Ament, and Matt Cameron. They called themselves M.A.C.C. for a remake of "Hey Baby (Land of the New Rising Sun)" that was included on a Jimi Hendrix tribute album titled *Stone Free*. The other was a collaboration with Alice Cooper.

Chris had been a fan of Cooper's since he was a teenager. Thanks to the shock rocker's hilarious appearance in *Wayne's World* in 1992, Cooper was enjoying a career resurgence. For *The Last Temptation*, his first album since the release of that film, he went all out. The album is a sort of morality play centered around a boy named Steven with supernatural abilities. To flesh out the backstory, he released a three-part comic book written by Neil Gaiman. To flesh out the music, he drafted Chris Cornell.

The pair connected through a mutual A&R friend named Bob Pfeifer. Chris had already written a couple of the songs for the record by the time that he actually got in touch with Alice. The first, "Stolen Prayer," was an acoustic-painted power ballad, while the second, "Unholy War," was a menacing and brutal rocker. "'Unholy War' really fit into the concept with just a little surgery," Cooper remembered. "'Stolen Prayer,' the other song that he wrote, wasn't quite a song yet, and we sat down for six or seven hours working on it. That song ended up being one of my favorites."[16]

Another outside opportunity presented itself when Ann and Nancy Wilson approached Chris and asked him to add vocals to a cover of Bob Dylan's "Ring Them Bells" that they were working on for their album *Desire Walks On*. Chris figured they meant backing vocals, but when he showed up they asked if he wouldn't mind taking lead on a verse. He had some reservations but agreed. Ultimately, Chris's label blocked his participation on the song, so the Wilson sisters turned to Layne Staley. Chris's take remains in the vault.

On January 7, 1994, Soundgarden played a private show for around fifty people at the Moore Theatre where they unveiled some of the music they'd been working on. Less than two weeks later, they were on their way to Australia for their first run down under as part of the Big Day Out Tour, the Aussie answer to Lollapalooza. Joining them on the bill were one of Chris's favorite bands, the Ramones, as well as Björk, Primus, the Breeders, and Smashing Pumpkins. The run took them from Sydney, the Gold Coast, Melbourne, Adelaide, and Perth to Auckland, New Zealand, where they caused a frenzied stampede during their encore at a show at the Powerhouse after promising to toss out limited edition Soundgarden frisbees and instead pelting the crowd with wilted pieces of bread.

In between shows, the band soaked in the sun on Bondi Beach and feasted on kangaroo steaks, lamb, and blue-eyed cod. They also ran into Billy Corgan again at a hotel lobby in Surfer's Paradise. Chris and Kim Thayil drank beers. Corgan sipped a strawberry margarita. As the Pumpkins leader groused about his band, Chris excused himself, while Thayil read Corgan the riot act after he tried to distill the guitarist's argumentative personality down to his astrological sign, Virgo. "I'll bet he's going to call his therapist in Chicago, wake her up at four in the morning, and tell her about that big, mean bear who made fun of him,"[17] the guitarist cracked to *Spin* writer Jonathan Gold. The next day, the Pumpkins reportedly played their most savage set of the tour.

Shortly after the Australian run ended, Soundgarden hit Japan, where they experienced what it's like to perform in front of a generally stoic Japanese audience. It's a phenomenon that can be a little unsettling to Western bands going back to the Beatles. "Even though I was knocking people in the head, they loved it," Chris observed in Nagoya. "They want to be free and have a good time. It's not the people who are uptight. It's the culture they're surrounded by."[18]

Then it was back to America where the promotional push behind *Superunknown* was already in full swing. On February 15, 1994, "Spoonman" was released by A&M as the album's lead single. Along with the song, they put out a video featuring footage of Artis clanging away in an abandoned warehouse superimposed with staid photographs of the four members of the band. For a group who never really enjoyed the process of filming videos, it was the perfect compromise.

The band's next video was a far more elaborate endeavor. For "Black Hole Sun," Soundgarden brought in an ambitious English director named Howard Greenhalgh who was filled with surreal ideas. "At that time, I loved *Blue Velvet*, and anyone can see a lot of similarities to that film," Greenhalgh said, citing director David Lynch's 1986 neo-noir masterpiece. "I just thought, here's a village of the damned, where everybody is fucking nuts in their own way and things are just not right. I thought about a lot of different images that could happen in this bum-fuck town in the middle of nowhere, where they start sucking humans off the planet."

The images are as compelling as they are disconcerting. The video is a rogues' gallery of mad hatters and housewives, Great Danes, and young children all wearing the widest and most unsettling smiles you've ever seen. And smack in the middle of this disconcerting hellscape is Soundgarden wailing away while the entire world is obliterated around them.

"Our time with the actual band was about six hours," Greenhalgh said. "Chris was so easy to work with. He just listened to what I wanted to do and just did it." That included getting blasted by an industrial fan to achieve the look of chaos driving the video's apocalyptic climax. "It was this petrol-driven jet engine thing," the director noted. "I think he rather enjoyed that!"

"Black Hole Sun" wouldn't hit MTV until June. In the meantime, "Spoonman" was making its mark on FM radio, peaking at number three on the mainstream rock charts, which gave *Superunknown* a welcome head of steam ahead of its official release on March 8, 1994. The album was already one of the most hotly anticipated releases of the year, and when it hit shelves that Spring, the sales numbers dwarfed anything that Soundgarden had enjoyed before. In its first week alone, *Superunknown* sold more than three hundred thousand copies, enough to knock Toni Braxton off the top of the charts and secure their first number one record.

Even more encouraging was the avalanche of positive reviews. In his four-star assessment for *Rolling Stone*, J.D. Considine wrote that the album "demonstrates far greater range than many bands manage in an entire career," and that it "offers a more harrowing depiction of alienation and despair than anything on [Nirvana's] *In Utero*."[19] In a glowing piece that must have brought a smile to Chris's face, *New York Times* critic Jon Pareles compared many of the songs to a variety of latter-era Beatles cuts, while applauding the band for "breaking heavy-metal genre barriers that Soundgarden used to accept."[20] Ann Powers in *Blender* declared the album a "masterpiece."[21]

But it wasn't just members of the music media who went gaga over *Superunknown*. "I remember seeing an interview with Judge Ito, who was the judge on the OJ Simpson case," Chris recalled. "They're asking him all the typical silly questions, and one of them was 'What kind of music do you listen to?' and he said, 'I really like Soundgarden.' That had to have been one of the weirder testimonials I've heard."[22]

After watching other bands like Guns N' Roses, Skid Row, Mötley Crüe, and Poison have their days in the sun throughout the eighties and then seeing how their friends in Pearl Jam and Nirvana dealt with the crush of fame and expectation in the wake of *Ten* and *Nevermind*, Soundgarden had finally wrestled the spotlight away for themselves. They were the new Kings of Rock. The only question that remained was how long their reign at the top would last.

CHAPTER X

BLOW UP THE OUTSIDE WORLD

B y the time the Thirty-Seventh Annual Grammy Awards rolled around in 1995, Soundgarden had done the dance at the glitzy ceremony three times and come away with nothing. In 1990, *Ultramega OK* lost out on Best Metal Performance to Metallica. Two years later, *Badmotorfinger* lost to Metallica again in the same category. In 1994, they had been up for Best Metal Performance for their rendition of Black Sabbath's "Into the Void." That time they lost out to Nine Inch Nails, who claimed the prize for their explosive industrial anthem "Wish." There was hope that this year would be different.

During the ceremony at the Shrine Auditorium in Los Angeles on March 1, 1995, Soundgarden was up for awards in four categories: Best Metal Performance ("Spoonman"), Best Hard Rock Performance and Best Rock Song ("Black Hole Sun"), and Best Rock Album (*Superunknown*). The commercial success and critical plaudits pegged them as a favorite to win at least one. Chris brought along his mom, Karen, who shared a story with MTV about how he used to beat on the drums in their garage when he was a teenager. "I'm really proud of him!" she enthused. Chris cracked a joke about trying to set her up with Tony Bennett, who was lurking nearby.

Whoever was charged with picking the presenters for that year's ceremony had a unique sense of humor, because when it came time to announce the winner for Best Metal Performance, previous award winners like Lemmy or James Hetfield were nowhere to be found. Instead, the task fell to blues icon B.B. King and soul music legend Al Green, both of whom looked immaculate in their expertly tailored suits. The prevailing feeling in the room was that Soundgarden wouldn't win this particular prize. Most were expecting Rollins Band, who had just performed their song "Liar," to take home the trophy. But then King opened up the envelope and read the words within: "Spoonman! Soundgarden!"

The band ambled up from the crowd and appeared onstage dressed uncharacteristically dapper. Chris went with a black suit and black shirt, which he dressed up with a variety of silver necklaces and a large red ribbon to support AIDS awareness. Ben Shepherd appeared in a black suit jacket and white shirt and didn't say a word. Matt Cameron chose a blue jacket and black shirt and took a brief moment to thank his mom. Kim Thayil spoke last, thanked his loved ones, and then chided the Grammys for making Rollins Band perform and then passing them over for the award.

As the frontman, and song's writer, Chris spoke first and spoke the longest. It was more difficult than he had expected, especially given the added shock of receiving the prize from one of his musical heroes. "All of a sudden it's Al Green giving out the award and I go up and I shake his hand and I didn't know what to say," he remembered. "That was one of the few fan moments I've had. It was like, I feel like it's great to get this, but we're all standing there as a band feeling like we gotta look like we don't care."[1]

Chris joked about Soundgarden's classification as a metal band, marveled at the talent of the men who presented him with the award, then thanked his wife and manager Susan Silver, his label A&M for "putting up with us and letting us do whatever we want and letting us not do anything if we want," his former labels Sub Pop and SST, "For being there early on when nobody else cared." He also thanked Cameron Crowe, and his parents.

Soundgarden's night didn't end there. They also bested their buddies Alice In Chains and Pearl Jam to win Best Hard Rock Performance. In the end, however, *Superunknown* failed to take home Best Rock Album. That prize went instead to The Rolling Stones for *Voodoo Lounge.*

For years, Soundgarden had been pushed by a loud contingent of hard rock- and metal-loving fans as the next big thing. Now here they were, receiving the critical recognition long lavished on so many of their peers. It was another winner that night, Bruce Springsteen, who summed up the bizarre phenomenon that are the Grammys while taking home a prize of his own. "If you stick around long enough," he said. "They give these things to you."

Soundgarden had stuck around for far longer than most of their newest fans had realized. They'd done the van tour thing. They'd done the independent record label thing: twice. They'd lost members, gained new ones, changed their sound multiple times, and had played in front of crowds from Osaka to Oslo. And now here they were, reaping the benefits superb artistry and tenacity had sown.

The trophies and sheen of respectability that came along with them were great. So was the commercial and cultural acceptance. The money was nice, too, but at the end of the day, the success was all the sweeter knowing the hard road they had travelled to make it to this moment. They had stayed true to themselves and waited for the world to come to them. Now, it finally had.

"That's one thing I feel really proud of when I think about Soundgarden, that a fifteen- or sixteen-year-old, or even a nineteen- or twenty-year-old buying our music is buying into an honest thing," Chris told *Request* in 1994. "It came from the heart of this band and it became a part of them, and it was honest. We weren't pandering to them. I can go to sleep at night knowing I wasn't trying to steer them in a direction where they'd give me money and I'd walk away laughing all the way to the bank."[2]

* * *

After finishing out their tour of the Pacific Rim, Soundgarden only had about a month to regroup back home before catching a flight to Europe to start their next run with a show at the stately Shepherd's Bush Empire in London on March 12, 1994. It was a quick-hitting performance made memorable by the appearance of Artis the Spoonman. "Chris picked me up onstage once the song was over, about two feet above the floor," Artis recalled. "I said, 'No man, I'm heavier than you think!'" Despite his protestations, Chris had no problem manhandling the muscular Spoonman. "He was a strong, strapping man," Artis noted.

A week later, the band crossed the Channel and formally kicked off their Days We Tried to Live Tour in Dortmund, Germany. In a fitting touch, the first performance took place in a venue called Sound Garden. Before the gig, Chris managed to learn how to speak the phrase "Take off your pants" in German, and during the show, more than a few audience members were eager to oblige, including a group of army officers who crowd-surfed in their boxer shorts.

From there they hit all the familiar markets in Scandinavia, before looping back around to Germany, Switzerland, the Netherlands, and Belgium. A lot had changed since the band first stormed Europe in the late eighties. Grunge-mania had hit the continent hard, and its effects were visible whenever Chris looked out into the crowd. "Five years ago, we'd go to a country where they all dressed completely differently," Chris told MTV in 1994. "Five years later we go to the same country, and everyone dresses like they're from Seattle."[3] Where once they had been the alternative in rock, now they were living, breathing avatars of the mainstream.

On April 8, 1994, Soundgarden rolled into Paris, one of Chris's favorite cities in the world. The four guys were pretty worn down on the drive to the two-century-old Élysée Montmartre. They were even more tired than usual that afternoon after having been awoken at around six in the morning by the sound of jackhammers on the street outside of their hotel. Chris made a top-ten list of reasons why they should just go ahead and cancel the gig, but with Paris being such an important market, no one took his complaints seriously.

Soundgarden played through soundcheck, further annoyed by a local noise ordinance that capped the decibel level, then waited for the gig to begin. Tad served as the supporting act. Soundgarden opened the show proper with "Jesus Christ Pose." During one segue, Chris flashed a bit of his French, telling the crowd, "*Va chiez* Paris." ("Go shit, Paris.") By all accounts it was a solid performance. Soundgarden delighted their French fans with copious cuts from *Superunknown*, ending with "Head Down," before off to the wings, eager to crack open a few beers and gear up for the final push through the UK in the coming days.

On their way backstage, Kim Thayil was intercepted by Kurt Danielson, Tad's guitarist. He had bad news to break. "I wanted to tell them myself because I thought they should hear it from a friend," Danielson said. Everyone gathered together in a room and shut the door behind them. Kurt Cobain was dead.

The Nirvana frontman had been unreachable after escaping from the Exodus Recovery Center in Los Angeles. It had been the latest in many attempts made by Cobain to get sober. Chris had heard through the grapevine that Cobain had been struggling lately. Many had tried to get through to Cobain and offer help, including R.E.M.'s Michael Stipe, who sent him a plane ticket and a driver in a futile attempt to get him out of Seattle and away from his worst influences and impulses. Chris had thought about reaching out himself once he got back stateside, but now it was too late.

After leaving Exodus, Cobain hopped a flight home. He was seated on the plane next to Guns N' Roses bassist Duff McKagan, but once they touched down, Cobain vanished. There were sightings of him around town, but nobody could seem to get in touch with him. His body was eventually discovered in the greenhouse above the garage of his home near Lake Washington by a visiting electrician. Three days earlier, he had injected a lethal amount of heroin before turning a shotgun on himself.

"It's hard to convey what a shock it was," Danielson said. "Chris was moved and saddened by the news and wept openly. We all did. There wasn't a dry eye in the room."

Ben Shepherd had been closer to Kurt than anyone and was devastated. Chris turned to the bassist, apologized, and wrapped him in a big hug. It was Andrew Wood all over again. A great personal trauma, the loss of a respected friend and peer, and here Soundgarden was, once again stranded thousands of miles from home. The next day, the tour rolled into Manchester, England. They were fortunate to have the night off. Some of the band, along with members of Tad and the touring crew, wound up in a nearby pub, before migrating to the hotel bar to wash down their sorrow. Chris stayed in his room.

"Are you guys up for this?" Chris asked the audience roiling before him the following night at the Manchester Academy. They screamed affirmatively and the show turned into a semi-cathartic exhibition of anger, confusion, and melancholy. In the quieter moments between songs, Chris howled like a wolf. Alcohol dulled the pain, as did wanton acts of destruction. Once offstage, the band ripped the steel door to their dressing room off its hinges and pulled a motion detector off the wall. The next night in Glasgow, Scotland, they destroyed a table backstage, ripped off one of its legs, wadded up a piece of white bread, and played a rough-and-tumble game of baseball which caused even more damage. The tour manager phoned Susan Silver to ask what he should do. She essentially told him to leave them alone.

Soundgarden played a final, boozy gig two nights later in London at the Brixton Academy during which Chris invited a sauced fan onstage to sing "God Save the Queen." The drunken Englishman obliged in truly reprehensible fashion to Chris's obvious delight. "You just won a fabulous set of steak knives!" he joked. Shortly after that, another fan fell down in the mosh pit, causing a lengthy delay. To entertain the crowd while medics attended to the person, Chris implored the Brits to chant like Soundgarden was their home football team before kicking half-full cans of beer into the audience. "I'm trying to score!" he yelled. When everyone was safely out of the pit, the gig resumed for another twenty minutes before ending with a performance of "Mailman."

The next day, Soundgarden hopped on a plane back to Seattle. Coverage of Cobain's death was still leading the national news when they landed. Networks carried multiple stories about the departed Nirvana leader and MTV put the band's videos into near-constant rotation.

Over the next several months, the members of Soundgarden were asked repeatedly to give their thoughts on Cobain, his death, the proliferation of heroin in Seattle, the general ennui of Generation X, depression, rock stardom, the so-called "27 Club," and a whole host of other morbid topics. They did their best to satisfy the inquiries, but sometimes there are no good answers. Sometimes a tragedy is just a tragedy.

For Chris, the questions about Cobain never really stopped. Throughout the years, he did the best he could to try and put the tragedy in the context of his own experience. "It's a misconception that all rock stars and movie stars are into drugs and heavy drinking," he told the *Irish Independent*. "When I went to meetings to get myself straightened out, I would literally be the only musician in a room full of fifty people. I'd be there with longshoremen and housewives and sub-contractors. The reason people sometimes walk away with the idea that young starlets and rock stars all have drug problems is that those are the people you talk about. If someone is a construction worker and they crash their car or they OD, nobody writes about it. There are lots more people like that who are struggling with the problem."[4]

He also went out of his way to discourage those from reading too deeply into Cobain's lyrics to try and find clues that could point to his eventual end. "What are you going to do when you read mine?" Chris asked in 1994. "A lot of people have had that sort of pain and didn't necessarily end it that way. Or had that sort of pain, and planned on killing themselves, but were unfortunately hit by a bus on the way to the gun store."[5]

Even as the black cloud of Cobain's suicide hovered over them, the demand for Soundgarden was at its zenith. The singles from *Superunknown* dominated FM radio stations across the country, and everyone, it seemed, wanted a piece of the group. The band only managed to carve out a month and a half of downtime before kicking off the North American leg of their worldwide tour just a few hours up I-5 in Vancouver on May 27 at the PNE Forum. Two nights later they were back in Washington, playing a semi-hometown gig at the Kitsap County

Fairgrounds in Bremerton. During the encore, Chris paid homage to Cobain. "This is for Kurt," he told the crowd before launching into "Head Down," Ben Shepherd's mournful, psychedelic ballad.

The next three months were a whirlwind of non-stop concert dates. The shows were marked by a noticeably elevated production budget and featured more lights, more volume, and bigger stages than ever before. A massive screen displayed colors and video clips behind them, including an ominous one of a child riding a bicycle that opened each performance. The band largely eschewed material from the earliest portions of the career, opting instead to play more familiar tracks from *Badmotorfinger* and *Superunknown*. On rare occasions they treated crowds to old favorites like "Flower," "Ugly Truth," or "Beyond The Wheel."

Despite their newfound status as a big-time rock band, Soundgarden was hell-bent on remaining grounded as human beings. That meant treating their opening acts better than some of the mega-star bands had treated them in years past. "It felt more like a caravan," Eleven guitarist Alain Johannes said. "It wasn't like, 'Oh don't talk to me,' or 'Here's my bodyguard,' or 'Don't go into certain areas.' Thankfully, none of that. We were pretty lucky to have been around that."

Chris enjoyed touring with Eleven so much that years later when they lost their deal with Hollywood Records and didn't have a budget to go out on the road, he dipped into Soundgarden's pocket to make sure they were on the bill. "He calls and says, 'We chipped in fifteen grand so you guys can come on tour with us,'" Johannes recalled. "'You can use our techs, or you can hire a tour manager and a van. Just come with us.' It was a really amazing thing to be invited because the opening band never gets supported like that from the headliners. That never happens."

Two of the most notable performances from this run took place at the Armory in New York, one of the most loathed venues in the city. "It was this huge hangar-like structure, so even Soundgarden felt like a tiny thing in this immense place," Danielson said. "Besides that, it was extremely hot and humid, so everyone was soaking with sweat. There was a micro-atmosphere in that place, so it was like raining in there." It didn't take long before fans started passing out from heat exhaustion. From his position onstage, Chris compared the venue to hell.

The next evening's performance went pretty much the same, albeit with an added cameo on the song "Fresh Tendrils" from Natasha Shneider and Alain Johannes from Eleven. Soundgarden's performance was ultimately overshadowed in many people's minds however, by O.J. Simpson's infamous freeway Ford Bronco chase earlier in the day. Chris cracked a couple of different jokes about the former NFL running back between songs.

Around the same time that the band sweated it out among their fans in the Armory, A&M Records released the "Black Hole Sun" music video to MTV. Soundgarden had high hopes for the song, but they couldn't have anticipated how deeply the single would resonate with people. The surrealistic clip quickly became a fixture on MTV, captivating an entire army of Gen-X kids home from school on summer break.

By July 16, the song hit number one on Billboard's Mainstream Rock Radio chart, where it reigned for seven consecutive weeks. Whether it was the compelling video, the surrealistic lyrics, or the way Chris's voice pierced through the kaleidoscope of psychedelic guitars, there was something about "Black Hole Sun" that captured the imaginations of an entire army of young music lovers, much in the same way that "Smells like Teen Spirit" and "Jeremy" had a few years earlier. It became *the* song of 1994.

In August, Soundgarden crossed the border into Canada where they played a one-off festival show with Nine Inch Nails at Molson Park in Barrie, Ontario. It was a momentous meeting of the musical minds and a rare treat for alternative fans who couldn't get enough of either *Superunknown* or *The Downward Spiral*. Both albums had been released on the same day a few months earlier, and both groups had dominated commercial radio ever since.

A new group named Marilyn Manson opened things up, playing cuts from their just-released debut album *Portrait of an American Family*. Nine Inch Nails played later in the evening and did everything they could to make life difficult for Soundgarden, turning in a bracing set filled with some of their most intense songs like "March of the Pigs," "Sin," and

"Terrible Lie." The headliners responded with energetic renditions of "Jesus Christ Pose," "Rusty Cage," and "My Wave."

Less than a week later, the band trucked a few thousand miles west to Calgary, where they were followed around by Shepherd's brother Henry and the crew for the documentary *Hype!* The filmmakers sought to chronicle the proliferation of the Seattle music scene in the eighties and nineties. One of the film's producers, Lisa Dutton, had served as the maid of honor at Chris and Susan's wedding a few years earlier.

Finally, on August 13, 1994, the band rolled back into Seattle for the final show of the exhausting tour at Memorial Stadium. The timing of the concert seemed curious to some outside observers because many of Soundgarden's peers, including Nine Inch Nails, were on the other side of the country in upstate New York, taking part in the Woodstock '94 music festival. Soundgarden had been offered a slot along with a hefty payout, but they turned it down, viewing it as a cynical nostalgia play. "Woodstock, to me, is really nothing more than a way to do a Lollapalooza this year," Chris told the *New York Times*. "I think we've spent enough time playing in situations like that. It isn't our show. For people that are nostalgic, they can go see some band that's re-formed like the Eagles."[6]

Soundgarden's hometown return wasn't quite the triumph they'd anticipated. The band was worn out from so many months on the road, and Chris was plagued by vocal issues. Yet, out in the crowd, the mish-mash of scene veterans who recalled the band's earliest, fiercest shows at the tiny Central Tavern up the road near Pioneer Square and the younger newcomers who saw Soundgarden as vital spokesmen for their genera-tion were whipped into a chaotic frenzy. They slam-danced with abandon as multiple mosh-pits swirled while the band played their hits. "It was as if the crowd were pocketed by maelstroms of mayhem, each one closer to the stage a more rapidly whirling whirlpool of humans in hyperdrive," *Seattle Times* reviewer Tom Phalen wrote. [7] As soon as the show ended, a frustrated Chris walked straight from the stage and into a waiting car.

Chris's vocal struggles turned out to be worrisome enough that he saw a doctor who diagnosed him with strained vocal cords. In order to prevent permanent damage to his voice, the physician recommended that the singer take some time off to heal. Soundgarden already had plans to return to Europe for another run of standalone shows and festival appearances, including a marquee slot at the venerated Reading Festival, but under doctor's orders, they decided to cancel all of their pending plans.

Soundgarden issued an official statement offering their apologies to fans who had already purchased tickets, with Chris adding, "I always want to give Soundgarden fans and my band the best performance I can. It wouldn't be fair otherwise. I take seriously the fact that our fans pay hard-earned money to buy our records and see our show. They deserve the best show I can give, and I wouldn't want any of them or myself to be disappointed with my performance."

After calling off the tour, Soundgarden largely went off the grid outside of a few sporadic appearances. Chris spent some time out at his cabin on Gamble Bay, on the other side of Puget Sound from Seattle. There was an eighty-foot-tall tree just outside of the small house that he liked to climb with friends. He also had a boat which he moored at Duff McKagan's place. In the summer he regularly took it out with his closest buddies and spent his days wakeboarding and drinking.

One day, while cruising along the water, his foot slipped off and the board hit him square in the face, knocking him unconscious. When he came to, the greenish water around him was mixed with blood pouring from his head. "Somehow, I convinced my buddies that I was fine to drive myself to the ER alone and that they should continue to enjoy their sunny day of boarding," he recalled. "That was a mistake."[8]

Heavily concussed, Chris drove around Seattle aimlessly and couldn't find his way to the hospital. Finally, he noticed a big blue *H* sign and pointed his car in that direction. He ran a red light and tried to park his car but got stopped by a cop who looked past his wet hair and blood-drenched face and threatened to give him a sobriety test. Chris tried to make his way into the hospital, but then "Police Man puts his hand on his gun and starts making intense threats that I don't really remember, but I wasn't able to make it inside." Finally, mercifully, another officer showed up, recognized what was going on, and physically picked him up and carried him to the nurses' station.

When he couldn't hit the waves, Chris took to the mountains to carve up some fresh powder. A couple of years earlier, Eddie Vedder had gifted Chris a full set of snowboarding gear, which he left on the singer's doorstep to open on Christmas morning. Chris had let the equipment gather dust for some time, but eventually hit the slopes and fell hard for the sport. Visits to the nearby Cascades became frequent.

He was writing songs as well, but at least for the moment, Soundgarden wasn't his primary concern. "I'm usually the one who starts calling everyone and saying, 'Let's get together, I have tons of songs to play,'" he said. "I didn't, and I wasn't calling anyone. I don't think they were waiting by their phones."[9]

Chris and Kim Thayil briefly resurfaced at the MTV Video Music Awards ceremony on September 8, 1994, where they presented the Breakthrough Video Award and picked up a prize themselves for Best Metal/Hard Rock Video for "Black Hole Sun." About a month after that, they returned to Bad Animals Studio and filmed a performance of "Fell On Black Days" for their next video. Directed by Jake Scott, the black-and-white clip captures the band in tight close-ups performing a more subdued version of the song than the one on the album. Chris cuts a menacing presence as he stares into the eye of the camera, hardly ever breaking focus while crooning his despondent lyrics.

That off-the-cuff version made its way out into the public a little over a year later on November 21, 1995, as part of a five-track EP titled *Songs from the Superunknown*. The truncated collection gathered together a few scattered tracks from the *Superunknown* sessions, including a haunting, acoustic rendition of "Like a Suicide," that Chris worked up by himself at home, along with a truly odd cut called "Jerry Garcia's Finger" that's less a song, per se, than a sonic churn of backwards echo and tinging cymbals.

By the end of 1994, *Superunknown* had sold four million copies, placing it just behind *The Lion King* soundtrack and Ace of Base's *The Sign* as one of the best-selling records of the year. And yet, for all the commercial success they were enjoying after so many years of being overshadowed by their more well-known peers in Seattle and beyond, the year didn't feel like a triumph. The band had a hard time trying to square their personal success with what they saw as a rough year for their city and the music that came out of it. Speaking with Charles Cross in the *Rocket*, Kim Thayil summed up their collective ennui. "At one point, you had four bands from Seattle entering the charts at number one within half a year and then, all of a sudden, one of these bands is gone forever," he said.[10]

Kurt Cobain was dead. Pearl Jam was in the fight of their lives after taking a Don Quixote-like stand against concert behemoth Ticketmaster, who they argued were gouging their fans with obscene and unnecessary fees and service charges. Layne Staley from Alice In Chains was deep in the grip of heroin addiction, forcing them to abort a tour with Metallica and go underground. Soundgarden's tour openers Tad were dropped by their label. "There were these incredible high points in our career and incredible low points in our personal lives and in the careers of other bands," Thayil added. "It was hard to make sense out of it. Were we supposed to feel good or bad?"

On January 8, 1995, Soundgarden emerged from seclusion and made an appearance on Eddie Vedder's independent radio broadcast that he dubbed Self Pollution Radio. For four-and-a-half hours, Vedder curated a lineup of his favorite Seattle-based friends to come and play for an audience of whoever had a shortwave radio capable of picking up the signal. In many respects, the show was another front in Pearl Jam's ongoing battle against the corporate monopolization of the music industry and the efforts by the powers that be to make them conform to their way of doing things.

Pearl Jam played a few songs, as did Mudhoney, the Fastbacks, and Mike McCready's new "supergroup" Mad Season, which was fronted by Layne Staley. Krist Novoselic submitted a spoken-word piece, while Dave Grohl debuted songs from his upcoming solo project Foo Fighters. During their slot, Soundgarden eschewed their most well-known material and busted out a variety of deep cuts like "Kyle Petty, Son of Richard." They also played an early version of "Fell On Black Days," a methodical wailer leftover from the *Badmotorfinger* sessions called "Blind Dogs," and for the first time, a chaotic new cut they were considering for their next album titled "No Attention."

"Kyle Petty, Son of Richard," is one of the more interesting selections in Soundgarden's vast canon. It was included as the B-side to "Fell On Black Days," then released again two years later on a 1996 charity compilation titled *Home Alive: The Art of Self-Defense*. As Chris told Radio.com, the sendup to the legendary race car driver was, "This little sliver of me being able to be someone else for a second, this asshole." He sounds like a seriously pissed-off version of Trent Reznor, spitting the words into the microphone. "I was imagining this other band and this other guy, which I do sometimes," he added. "A lot of the voices I've created, and how I've created a voice, is to ask, 'What does this singer singing this sound like?' And try to figure out how to do that."[11]

Soundgarden popped into the public eye again in March to pick up their Grammys, then disappeared until August when they kicked off a slew of make-up performances in Europe, beginning with a show at the Sunstroke Festival in Dublin, Ireland, on August 23. The string of gigs was only scheduled to last a little under three weeks, but the timing of the tour could hardly have been worse. Just a few weeks prior to crossing the Atlantic, the band gathered together inside of Stone Gossard's new recording studio, Studio Litho, to begin work on their next album. The work was just getting underway when they had to break for rehearsals and the show their European fans had been patiently waiting a year to see.

A few days after the Ireland gig, Soundgarden supported Neil Young as the second name on the bill at the renowned Reading Festival at Little John's Farm. It was an important performance, not just for the pedigree of the festival itself—one of Britain's oldest and most highly-regarded—but because it was also being filmed for a special on MTV's *120 Minutes*. Soundgarden rose to the occasion and delivered a ferocious eighteen-song set that honored their past while also hinting at where they'd be heading in the future.

Aside from offering a half-hearted apology for missing the previous year's festival—"We got lost on the way," he joked—Chris didn't address the crowd much, preferring to save his voice for the songs. Fan favorites like "Rusty Cage" and "Black Hole Sun" got massive receptions, but they also treated the crowd to a pair of new songs they were working on in the studio. The first, "Ty Cobb," was a short, rage-filled punk track that shared many of the same characteristics as *Superunknown's* shortest cut "Kickstand." The other was called "Kristi," a swaggering monster of a song made memorable by its heavy, detuned guitars and weird echo effects.

Soundgarden decided against including "Kristi" on their next album even though it was one of Matt Cameron's favorites. "Chris would just never allow it out," producer Adam Kasper explained. "We're all like, 'Man, it's so good!' But he was just like, 'Nope. The vocals aren't right.'" The song became a long-lost fan favorite for years, until it finally showed up on the *Echo of Miles* compilation.

For their encore, the band tore into a cataclysmic rendition on the swirling, psychedelic coda from the Beatles' "I Want You (She's So Heavy)," during which Chris interjected "Your football team sucks!" as Thayil coaxed abrasive sounds out of his guitar. Once the Reading gig ended, the band motored on to Scandanavia, Germany, and Switzerland before ending the tour in Reggio Emilia, Italy. Shortly after arriving back in the States, work on their next album began in earnest.

After a dozen years spent in recording studios up and down the West Coast, collaborating with various producers, Soundgarden decided to pilot this project themselves. They did, however, bring Adam Kasper back to man the boards and serve as engineer and co-producer. "I think they wanted to do it themselves, and I feel like they realized that's kind of hard to do," Kasper said. "As a co-producer, you're the guy who's gonna sit with Kim and relay what Chris feels about his part or bass sound. It's hard for band members to sit there and criticize each other."

Studio Litho was formerly a lithography shop, featuring one large room for the band along with a control room where Chris recorded most of his vocals. All told, the band spent about four months writing songs and working on basic tracks, before returning to Bad Animals for two months of overdubbing and mixing. *Down On The Upside* wasn't quite as strenuous a record to make as *Superunknown*, but a myriad of other factors made it perhaps the most challenging recording experience of the band's career.

"It was a little bit of a weird time," Kasper recalled. "I think there was some tension. I don't know what was happening at home, but I could tell people were tired. It was a very tiring process. Fun and great, but there was also a fatigue factor. They were doing so many songs. It was a mammoth undertaking."

By 1995 Soundgarden had spent nearly a decade out on the road and in the studio together, going non-stop from album to tour and right back into the next cycle. The work had paid off, but the journey had exacted a toll. Chris was stretched especially thin and there were moments when the process became so emotionally taxing that he would come home after a long day in the studio to his wife, lie down on the floor and sob inconsolably. Increasingly, Chris managed his mix of exhaustion, pressure, anxiety, and depression by turning to alcohol, which had a profoundly negative impact on his state of mind.

Out on the road, he'd down an entire red solo cup full of ice and vodka before hitting the stage. Though he'd always been able to hold his own, he was drinking more than ever and communication between the band suffered. "They were getting along better independently to some degree," Kasper said. "Matt and Chris cut a bunch of those songs like 'Burden In My Hand,' together. He's just sitting on a stool with a scratch guitar and Matt's just nailing it."

Susan Silver tried multiple times to break the ice between the four guys and get them to talk to one another about how they were feeling and what they were thinking. She went as far as recommending they each read *The Paradox of Success*, a self-help book which she'd heard had helped Aerosmith, but they laughed her out of the room. It didn't help that Chris was withdrawing from Susan as well, refusing to open up to her about the issues that were bothering him and, instead, drowning his anxiety in vodka and beer. It only made matters worse. "I didn't give a shit," he said. "Alcohol is a depressant, so I got depressed."[12]

And yet, Chris still managed to maintain his unique sense of humor. Just before Soundgarden entered Studio Litho to work on *Down On The Upside*, Pearl Jam had used the space to record their fourth album, *No Code*. Among the more curious items Pearl Jam had in their possession during the recording was a life-size dummy called "Safety Man" that they would throw in the passenger seat to take advantage of Washington State's carpool lanes without getting ticketed. After Pearl Jam finished *No Code*, Mike McCready left Safety Man behind on a couch where he sat and silently observed the proceedings. One day, Chris got to the studio before everyone else, stripped Safety Man down, and dressed himself in the dummy's clothes. Then he sat and waited. About twenty minutes passed before engineer Matt Bayles walked in the room to get everything set up for the day's work. As soon as Bayles turned around, Chris jumped up and screamed, scaring the ever-loving shit out of the unsuspecting engineer.

The most tangible impact that Soundgarden's lack of communication had on *Down On The Upside* was a dearth of fresh material offered up by Kim Thayil. Of the sixteen tracks that made it onto the finished album, only one, the supercharged and psychedelic "Never the Machine Forever," was attributed to the band's lead guitarist. While Thayil added his own flavor to nearly every song on the record with his off-kilter, noisy, and vitriolic musical additions, his diminished output left a sore spot. "It does bum me out, but I couldn't see replacing the songs we do have on there," he charitably explained to *Guitar* magazine. "It can be a little bit discouraging if there isn't satisfactory creative input, but on the other hand, I write all the solo bits and don't really have limitations on the parts I come up with for guitar."[13]

It's no coincidence that of all the tracks on *Down On The Upside*, "Never the Machine Forever," sounds the most apiece with Soundgarden's earlier, more abrasive records. "Kim really needs a co-conspirator, such as Chris, to work on songs," Kasper explained. "His motivation was a little subdued, and Matt and Ben had thousands of songs, so they were gung-ho to do all their stuff." Ultimately, "Never the Machine Forever" only made the final cut by the skin of its teeth. The band recorded the song at the last minute, while simultaneously mixing the second-to-last song on the album.

Communication was so poor between the members that they couldn't agree on whether they were actually making an album. "One of Kim's hindsight things was, he wasn't sure if we were actually recording," Kasper said. "It's like, 'Kim, we've been in here for months!'" Before and after returning home from Europe, Chris was working on songs that Thayil assumed were demos; part of the pre-production process for the album that they'd work on together eventually. Soundgarden was on a runaway train of momentum, carrying everyone along with it, regardless of whether they wanted to go. "When we went in to start in July, we got about five songs into it and realized we probably needed more songs," Chris told *Metal Edge*. Then the European tour happened. When they got back, they hit the ground running. "I wrote another four songs, then when we went back into the studio, it was just me and Matt demoing those songs, that was the same time Kim was recording, then we all went into the studio. Then Ben and Matt brought in different stuff; things started to cascade at that point." [14]

Unlike Thayil, Ben Shepherd was enjoying an impressive moment of inspired creativity. When all was said and done, the bassist notched six credits on *Down On The Upside*, including a sonically diverse three-pack of tracks stacked near the front. The triumvirate begins with the somber ballad "Zero Chance," which sounds like it sucked a lot of Stone Gossard's Pearl Jam DNA into it, before segueing into the uncharacteristically upbeat pop song "Dusty" and ending with a bracing, expletive-filled middle finger of a song called "Ty Cobb."

"Ty Cobb" was originally called "Hot Rod Death Toll," but Chris tweaked it to namecheck the famously cantankerous baseball player. "It was basically coming from the frame of mind of some sort of hardcore pissed-off idiot," the singer explained. "I was just thinking of a character who was a combination of a lot of people I've met and didn't like." [15]

Two of the best songs on the album were holdovers from the *Superunknown* sessions. The first was a scream-riddled barnburner called "No Attention," which flips halfway through from a breakneck punk rock flurry of words and sounds to a swaggering seventies-rock-style stomper, tailor-made to induce maximum headbanging. The more compelling song, however, was "Tighter & Tighter," a dreamy, Leslie amp-washed track that shared a similar doomed vibe to "Black Hole Sun."

Chris had written "Tighter & Tighter" around the same time as "No Attention" and had included it on the "home run" demo tape he'd sent to Bienhorn. The reason it didn't make it onto *Superunknown* was simple; they ran out of time. Soundgarden had already laid down the rhythm tracks. All the song needed was Chris's vocals and some extra guitar parts. In its initial form, "Tighter & Tighter" was much slower, but with a brusque kick in the ass and the addition of a wah-wah-slathered solo from Thayil it morphed into a psychedelic elegy.

"Tighter & Tighter" proved to be a surprisingly contentious cut. Kim was strongly against including it on *Down On The Upside*. An outside voice broke the stalemate. "It's Stone Gossard's favorite song," Kasper said. "Stone had mentioned it a few times, so Kim was like 'Alright, whatever.' Everyone in Pearl Jam loved that song."

The mood throughout most of the songs on *Down On The Upside* was decidedly grim, even by Soundgarden standards. The first song on the album, and subsequently the first taste of *Down On The Upside* that the public received, was a track called "Pretty Noose." During his life, Chris used the noose as an allegory. "An attractively packaged bad idea," he said. "Something that seems great at first and then comes back to bite you."[16]

"Pretty Noose" was one of the more difficult songs for Chris to record because he's singing near the top of his register throughout the whole thing. "It was a challenge," Kasper said. "Recording-wise, the guitar part really had to be just right. I remember that one being really hard and personally never feeling entirely satisfied with the end result."

"Burden In My Hand," is another fatalistic entry. It's also the most radio-friendly sounding song on the album; a jaunty acoustic piece written in the same open C tuning Ben Shepherd used on "Head Down." The vibe of the music belies a murderous narrative that evokes memories of Jimi Hendrix's "Hey Joe." "The mental image was this sort of destitute guy, I guess he'd lost his cool, if you want to put it that way," Chris explained. "He's trying to figure out how he would stand up and put one foot in front of the other—or not—and the song never really resolves any of that. It's just that moment of somebody sitting in the dirt."[17]

Incredibly, the vocals to "Burden In My Hand," "Pretty Noose," and another track on *Down On The Upside* titled "Boot Camp" that ended up on the final record were Chris's first attempts at singing them. He literally read the words off a piece of paper as he poured his soul into the microphone. Given his druthers, it was his preferred way to record. "I have better luck if the vocal is the last thing I do," he said. For Chris, the initial spark of inspiration remained the key to getting his voice to sound and feel right on record. "I've beat my head against the wall many times where I did a demo at home, obviously not well recorded, but there's something about it that I just can't replicate no matter what I do or where I'm recording or who is engineering or what mic I am singing into."[18]

And yet, neither of those tracks were as dark as "Blow Up the Outside World" which opens with the line, "Nothing seems to kill me, no matter how hard I try." Chris started writing this song while sitting in the back of the band's tour bus on the way out of Toronto and over several months built it into an eye-widening tapestry of explosive sound and nihilistic fury. The whole thing sounds like a cross between "A Day In The Life" and "Happiness Is A Warm Gun." It builds from a single, disembodied voice over an acoustic guitar and snare drum to an avalanche of power chords and screaming, before receding like the tide into a hazy coda with Chris intoning the name of the song over and over again. Near the end, explosions can be heard faintly, bursting in time with Matt Cameron's martial drumbeat, an effect the band achieved by dropping an old Fender tube amp on the ground and recording the blast.

For Matt Cameron's haunting composition "Applebite," Chris wrote about how nothing really matters in the grand design of space and time. "Grow and decay, grow and decay," he warbles. "It's only forever, it's only forever." On "Boot Camp," he evokes many of the same themes and feelings about the pressure to conform and be accepted by society that Roger Waters explored on Pink Floyd's magnum opus, *The Wall*: "I must obey the rules / I must be tame and cool." And in Ben Shepherd's "Zero Chance," he wonders "Why doesn't anyone believe in loneliness?"

There's a pull to try to read into Chris's lyrics to get a sense of what his headspace was like in a given moment and search for clues to explain why he chose to end his own life. More than any other album he had a hand in creating, *Down On The Upside* lends itself to this kind of macabre line of detective work. And while Chris understood the impulse after seeing the same thing happen to Andy Wood and Kurt Cobain, he consistently downplayed the darkness in his own lyrics as a window into his own inner turmoil.

"If you're writing about a subject that's depressing or melancholy, ultimately, it's going to speak to someone who is in that environment who feels lonely, and they rise up because of it," he told *Alternative Press*. "I would always sit in my bedroom and listen to music by myself. That was my favorite thing to do. I would often listen to really dark music, and if I was in a very dark period of my life, it made me feel happy. If I listened to Ted Nugent at a keg party, I felt horrible."[19]

Chris always prided himself on being one of the self-proclaimed "normal ones" to come out of the Seattle music scene, and, throughout his life, consistently brushed away questions framed in a manner that suggested they were symbols of the author's psyche. Throughout the nineties at least, he didn't feel like he completely understood himself as a person and couldn't imagine anyone thinking they knew who he was based on the songs he wrote.

By February 1996, Soundgarden had largely finished work on their fifth album. All the while, they bandied about titles before finally settling on one of Chris's early suggestions, a song lyric taken from "Dusty," *Down On The Upside*. It had been a tough and taxing process, but the roughest stretch of road lay in front of them.

CHAPTER XI

WAVE GOODBYE

A spark: A tiny burst of energy introduced into the wrong environment at the wrong time has the power to ignite a firestorm with the force and power to alter destinies. It's the kind of blaze that devours the bonds of history and memory, while reshaping the landscape into a wholly unrecognizable and terrifying new terrain. In the face of such unfathomable destruction, one is presented with two options. Rebuild by picking up the pieces and trying again, or start fresh; leave behind the world that once seemed so inviting and comfortable and seek out a new one.

For Soundgarden, the spark that would alter their story forever was a malfunctioning bass rig. It was February 9, 1997, and the band was in Honolulu, Hawaii, preparing for the final gig of their three-week long tour around the far side of the Pacific Ocean. On that warm winter day, smack-dab in the middle of paradise, hours before the horde of eight thousand fans descended upon Blaisdell Arena, the band ran through their soundcheck. The only problem was that Ben Shepherd's bass kept dropping out of the mix.

A tech seemingly fixed whatever was causing the issue, but nobody knew what would happen in just a few hours when they'd start to play. The show in Hawaii was important; a semi-victory lap before a hard-earned vacation. Susan Silver flew in a myriad of friends and family to watch the band cross the finish line, while also soaking up the sunshine, far from overcast Seattle.

After a local band warmed up the thousands of fans huddled together, eagerly awaiting the arrival of their heroes, Soundgarden emerged and kicked off their set with a rousing rendition of "Spoonman." Over the next hour, they poured through selections from *Superunknown*, *Down On The Upside*, and *Badmotorfinger* with an inspired fervor. Chris had hardly ever sounded better.

"But then the bass player was clearly pissed off about something, and he was getting more and more agitated," concertgoer Daniel Peterson recalled. "He started flipping us off. I don't know if he was flipping the crowd off or if he was flipping the sound guy off. The more agitated he got, the more I realized his bass was coming in and out of the sound system like something was wrong."

Backstage, everyone raced toward the dressing rooms. Shepherd was drunk and in no mood to negotiate with his bandmates. He especially didn't want to hear from their manager. When he reached the door of the dressing room, Shepherd wheeled around and met Susan Silver face-to-face. They both stood looking into one another's eyes for a good thirty seconds with Shepherd's fist raised like he wanted to punch something. Silver backed down and walked away.

Thayil cornered Shepherd and pleaded with him to finish the gig. The bassist refused. Thayil continued until Shepherd relented and agreed to follow them back out. But he lied. When Thayil realized he'd been deceived by one of his oldest and closest friends and collaborators, he became so upset that he also bailed on the gig.

"Ten or fifteen minutes went by, and the crowd grew restless," Peterson remembered. "Chris Cornell finally came out by himself and apologized. He had a Telecaster guitar, and he played some songs, just him."

Chris felt the weight of responsibility to make up for his volatile bandmates' unprofessional behavior and, at Susan's urging, played a few cuts to satisfy the fans who paid their hard-earned money to be entertained for the evening. "The one I remember was 'Black Hole Sun,'" Peterson said. "Clearly there's so much emotion in that song anyway, and there was so much emotion in the stadium where we were because of whatever was going on with Ben. It was really powerful. The crowd was just going crazy because he sounded great."

That night in Hawaii, while the majority of Soundgarden sulked in the shadows, Chris Cornell took his first step out into the spotlight by himself. His past was several feet behind him, but his future was wide open.

* * *

Down On The Upside had taken much longer and been far more challenging to record than they had ever expected, but on May 21, 1996, Soundgarden finally released their latest creation. After waiting a little more than two years to hear the follow-up to *Superunknown*, the band's fans rushed out to get their hands on Soundgarden's latest hour-long cacophony of serrated sound and twisted imagery. In its first week, the album sold 175,000 copies in the US. It was an impressive showing, but still came 5,000 albums short of knocking hip-hop group the Fugees' monster-selling record *The Score* off the top of the charts.

Critical response was positive, but generally less effusive than it had been for the band's prior two releases. *Spin* gave the record eight out of ten stars. In his review, writer Ivan Kreilkamp praised Chris for getting "better and better at communicating down-to-earth feelings in grandiose musical settings."[1] *Rolling Stone* reviewer Rob O'Connor enjoyed the album's brashness but knocked it for lacking the eye-widening sonic execution of its predecessor. "From a less ambitious band, *Down On The Upside* would be a grand display of technical prowess, showcasing rhythmic shifts, interlocking guitar lines and firm control of dynamics," he wrote. "But ambition is what has always made Soundgarden stand out." The three stars out of five that he ultimately gave it must've been graded on a curve.[2] Meanwhile veteran rock writer David Browne relished in the record's dark themes and sludge-covered sheen. "It's music as primordial ooze," he wrote for *Entertainment Weekly*. "And no matter the song, Chris Cornell never stops bellowing hysterical bummers."[3]

Despite the personal challenges he experienced while making it, Chris always held a rosy view of *Down On The Upside*. "I think it's the crowning achievement of Soundgarden's life cycle," he told *Revolver* in 2006. "It's my favorite of our records. I wasn't really aware of this at the time, since we produced it—which meant that I had no objectivity—but it was the record where the whole band was involved and the whole band was there for everything. It's not like we were falling apart and couldn't sit in a room. In fact, it was the opposite: we faced our biggest challenge together, which was following up a monster."[4]

In 1996, all four of the big Seattle bands released successful records. Pearl Jam and Nirvana both notched number ones. The former released a studio album called *No Code* while overseers of the latter stitched together a collection of live cuts for an album titled *From the Muddy Banks of the Wishkah*. Alice In Chains put out an *MTV Unplugged* album that sold over a million copies. Meanwhile, *Down On The Upside* hung around in the top twenty on Billboard's album chart for over two months, regularly trading positions with *Evil Empire*, the second record from a rap-rock hybrid named Rage Against The Machine, on its way to eventual platinum certification.

While the numbers suggested grunge still reigned supreme, the cultural sands were shifting beneath the feet of Soundgarden. Emerging musical movements like Britpop, led by bands such as Oasis, Blur, and Pulp; nü metal popularized by Korn, Limp Bizkit, and Deftones; and pop punk trumpeted by Green Day, Blink-182, and the Offspring were stealing the focus among the next generation of fans. At the same time, new mainstream pop/rock acts like Counting Crows, Bush, and Hootie & the Blowfish were notching astronomical sales numbers and dominating commercial radio.

Soundgarden was hardly old news, but they weren't driving youth culture the way they a had a few years earlier. Chris took it in stride. "The media can make you out to be more important than you really are," he told Everett True in 1996.[5] "Cultural shifts don't last very long. Ultimately; does it really matter if we've affected the way people dress for a few years?"

Well before *Down On The Upside* dropped, the band had already lined up their next high-profile live run that would keep them out on the road for most of the summer. In 1996, the organizers behind Lollapalooza tapped

Metallica to headline the fifth iteration of the travelling festival. Metallica, in turn, requested Soundgarden appear with them. Soundgarden wasn't totally enamored with the idea of a Lollapalooza redux, but once they found out about Metallica's headlining status, they agreed to participate. "They more or less said that, 'If we are going to do the tour, then Soundgarden will be doing it with us,'" Kim Thayil remembered.[6]

Though Metallica was one of the biggest live draws on the planet, their selection as the main headliners generated enormous controversy online among alternative rock fans who viewed the metal icons as too far afield from the festival's alt-rock roots. Even Perry Farrell, Lollapalooza's founder, voiced his displeasure with the pick. "I was very angry the first time they played Lollapalooza," he told *Rolling Stone*. "I helped create the genre alternative, and alternative was against hair metal, teased-out hair, spandex, bullshit rock music. Metallica, in my estimation at that time, wasn't my thing."[7]

Not that Metallica cared. "Fuck all those fucking elitists who say, 'Metallica's not alternative' or 'They're too big of a band to play Lollapalooza,'" the band's guitarist Kirk Hammett told *Guitar World*. "They're just being very narrow-minded." Soundgarden largely eschewed being lumped in with criticism of the festival. Ben Shephard jokingly referred to the run as "Larsapalooza" after Metallica's effusive drummer Lars Ulrich.

Before Soundgarden formally agreed to appear on Lollapalooza, however, they had a request. If they were going to sweat it out across the summer playing to a sea of Metallica fans, they in turn wanted the Ramones on the bill as well. The New York punkers had had a tremendous influence on each member of the band. Back in 1991, they even covered one of their songs, "I Can't Give You Anything," for a BBC Sessions recording. Just a year before Lollapalooza, the Ramones announced plans to disband by the end of 1996. If their heroes were going out, it was important to Soundgarden to help give them the biggest stage possible from which to say farewell.

On May 18, 1996, more than a month out from Lollapalooza, Soundgarden broke one of their foundational rules. "We had two things we said we'd never do," Chris said that year. "One was play when the sun was out, which we've now done, and the other was live TV."[8] It was the season finale of the twenty-first season of *Saturday Night Live*, and the band had been specifically requested by host Jim Carrey to appear as musical guests.

Carrey was at the apex of his fame after releasing some of the most commercially successful comedies of all time, screwball masterpieces like *Ace Ventura: Pet Detective, Dumb and Dumber*, and *The Mask*. As reticent as the band was about doing live television, it was too good an opportunity to pass up. The episode ultimately scored the highest rating of the season with millions tuning in to watch Carrey's zany antics. It remains one of the most-watched *SNL* episodes ever aired.

Soundgarden was originally supposed to appear in a skit with Carrey, appearing in a daydream during a job interview where they would say, "Hi, we're Hootie & the Blowfish." But between dress rehearsal and the actual show, the piece was cut for time. Their moment in the spotlight came about a third of the way through the show, just after Norm MacDonald's turn on *Weekend Update*. The band was introduced by Carrey, as well as Chris Kattan and Will Ferrell who were both dressed as their night-life-loving *Night at the Roxbury* characters. The camera zoomed in on Cornell, dressed head-to-toe in black, his black hair standing straight up like he'd just plugged himself into an electrical socket, as he sang the opening words to "Pretty Noose."

On a good day, "Pretty Noose" tested the upper limits of Chris's prodigious vocal abilities. Unfortunately, this wasn't a great day and the performance came off a little sloppier than the band probably intended. The band made up for it though with a superb performance of "Burden In My Hand."

Once the night was over, Soundgarden expressed their appreciation to Carrey by giving him a black Fender Telecaster that they had all autographed. "Dear Jim, please take this as a token of our appreciation (or something)," Chris wrote in silver sharpie on the guitar's pickguard. The comedian held onto the guitar as a treasured possession. They also gifted him an autographed straitjacket.

Shortly after *SNL*, Soundgarden played a few small shows in the Pacific Northwest, including a dismal corporate gig sponsored by the Molson beer company at a small venue called the Town Pump in Vancouver, during which Chris pointedly thanked their rival Labatt's onstage, before kicking off the latest iteration of Lollapalooza in Kansas City, Missouri, on June 17, 1996. It didn't take the band long to realize that this Lollapalooza was far different than the one they enjoyed the first time around four years earlier. "It had become an institution," Chris said. "I think that there was a lot of fans there to see a lot of the other bands, but it seemed like the Metallica fans were hardcore Metallica fans, and they came there just to see them, and everyone else kind of was there to see everybody but them."[9]

Gone was the intense camaraderie that Soundgarden enjoyed with the other groups during their previous trek. This time out, Chris and the band spent much of the day hidden backstage, drinking beer and whisky, waiting for their turn to play. The shows weren't the most fulfilling either. Performing truncated sets to a sea of unruly Metallica fans who relished in chucking bottles, frisbees, food, and beach balls toward the stage was an exceptionally grueling challenge.

Depending on the venue, Soundgarden would come on each night around eight or nine at night, play for about an hour and then cede the stage to Metallica. Given the setting, the band largely avoided their newer material from *Down On The Upside*, relying instead on familiar songs like "Spoonman," which typically opened the show, "Fell On Black Days," and "Rusty Cage." One of the more interesting curveballs regularly thrown into the mix was a cover of the Doors' psychedelic stomper "Waiting for the Sun." Chris's attempts at Jim Morrison cosplay went over especially well when the band played it around dusk at the Gorge in the Columbia River Valley, just three hours east of Seattle. The other attention-grabber was "Black Hole Sun," which Chris played each night by himself on a Fender Telecaster while the other members took a breather backstage.

The lowest moment of the tour came after a performance in Rockingham, North Carolina, on July 20, which also happened to be Chris's thirty-second birthday. After the show, in which Ben Shepherd sang "Happy birthday, Chrissssstopher!" during his response part in "Spoonman," the band retired to their hotel to rest up before catching a lift to the next gig. A group of people who hadn't attended the concert but were part of a drunken wedding party spotted Kim Thayil and company in the lobby and began pestering them for pictures while being generally unpleasant. He confronted them and eventually the cops were called. After the authorities gathered everyone's statement, the guitarist was led away in handcuffs.

Thayil spent a few hours in a cell before being released on a $2,500 bond. "It blew out of proportion," he said. "It wouldn't have been that big a deal had I not been who I am, a guy in a rock band."[10] Despite the arrest, Thayil and Soundgarden still managed to make it to the next evening's rain-drenched show in Knoxville, Tennessee.

Lollapalooza '96 ended with a pair of performances at Irvine Meadows Amphitheater in Southern California at the beginning of August, both of which were broadcast over the internet. Rather than hightailing it back home, however, Chris and Ben Shepherd hung around Los Angeles. A few days later they joined Eddie Vedder, Motörhead's inimitable frontman Lemmy Kilmister, and half of Rancid at a converted nightclub called the Palace to send the Ramones off into retirement with a bang.

During the second encore of the band's final show, Chris strode out in a peach-colored T-shirt and asked, "You wanna hear some more fucking Ramones? This is your last fucking chance, so make some goddamn noise!" The fearsome fivesome emerged with Shepherd and hit the rapturous crowd with an intense rendition of the Heartbreakers song "Chinese Rock." Chris and Johnny Ramone stayed in touch and became increasingly close, right up until the pioneering guitarist's death in 2004.

Soundgarden continued to do their best to promote *Down On The Upside*. In November they released a video for "Blow Up the Outside World." The mind-bending clip found Chris strapped to a massive metal chair à la Alex in Stanley Kubrick's *A Clockwork Orange*, with his arms spread wide in a full-blown Jesus Christ pose while being forced to watch himself and the rest of the band perform the song on a video screen. At the end, both Soundgarden and the set explode, leaving Chris alone, squirming to break free in a debris-strewn room.

According to the film's director, Devo bassist Gerald Casale, the filming, which took place over three days, wasn't exactly a kumbaya experience. "Everybody had their own dressing rooms and only came out for the takes and then disappeared back in their dressing rooms," he told Songfacts. "They were very professional when they would come on the set, they were ready to do what they were supposed to do, but it was all business." [11]

By this point a man named Jim Guerinot, who had worked with Soundgarden going back to their earliest days with A&M, was taking a more hands-on role with the band to try to help mitigate some of their divisive tendencies. Guerinot was intelligent and a canny music executive. He had originally earned the band's trust in the *Louder Than Love* days when he suggested they attach two clip-on lights to their merch area so that they could show off their t-shirts and make a few extra bucks while running around the club circuit.

Guerinot had since left his role with A&M and gone into business shepherding the careers of bands like the Offspring, Social Distortion, and No Doubt as well as skateboarding legend Tony Hawk. He also did some work with Soundgarden and was one of the few people that the band thanked by name when they picked up their Grammy awards the previous year. But while Guerinot was close with everyone in Soundgarden, he was closest to Chris. Oftentimes when Susan needed to ask Chris about a prickly issue that might draw some of his ire, it was easier to call Guerinot to act as go-between. His importance as an advisor and an advocate would only grow in the years to come.

In September 1996, the band departed for Europe, running through a majority of the major markets throughout the continent over the course of five weeks before kicking off the North American leg in Salt Lake City in November. Chris was drinking more and withdrawing from everyone around him, while Ben Shepherd was growing increasingly volatile onstage: smashing equipment and physically confronting fans and security personnel. It was usually left to Matt Cameron to step up and take on more of a leadership role.

In a development that might've horrified the younger, motel-dwelling iteration of Soundgarden, the volatility sometimes erupted offstage, like after a gig at the Roseland Ballroom in New York City. "Chris was sick," the band's producer Adam Kasper recalled. "His voice was just gone." Frustrated that his body had failed him midway through an important gig, Chris took his anger out on his hotel room. "He and Kim were back at the hotel and decided to tear up the bathroom and the bar and the hotel room later," Kasper remembered. "Susan was very pissed off. It was the classic TV-out-of-the-hotel-window thing."

Chris's drinking caused him to make questionable decisions, like the time he got plastered and jumped out of the window of a ten-story apartment building and onto the top of a nearby pine tree. He easily could've been killed. Fortunately, he was adept at scaling evergreens and managed to scamper down the trunk unscathed.

By December, Soundgarden made it back to Seattle. Originally, they planned on ending their year with a pair of shows at Mercer Arena on December 10 and 11, but Chris fell ill, and they pushed them both back by a week so they could go out on a high note. The rest proved worth the delay. By most accounts both shows were among the best Soundgarden had played all tour. They even brought out Artis the Spoonman for old times' sake to rattle his cutlery to the hometown fans' everlasting delight. Chris's solo from the final night, a stripped-down and gut-twisting rendition of "Black Hole Sun," was eventually included on the band's official live record *Live on I-5.*

Two weeks after the Seattle gigs, they flew across the Pacific Ocean and began a nearly month-long slate of performances throughout Australia and New Zealand. The band's decision to keep playing live instead of taking a breather was probably the worst mistake of their career. Ben Shepherd wasn't in the greatest headspace, and there were moments he walked offstage while the band was still playing. Meanwhile, Chris was hardly reachable, preferring to spend most of his time alone in his hotel room.

Then came Hawaii. On February 8, 1997, the band played a normal gig at the Maui Arts & Cultural Center. The next night came the disastrous gig in Honolulu. Shepherd stormed off. Thayil and Matt Cameron gave chase. And at the end, Chris came back out to try and give the fans their money's worth, but it was the last straw. Chris couldn't even bring himself to talk to his wife about how angry, frustrated, and hurt he was. After more than twelve years, his mind was made up. Soundgarden was done.

Two months after the show in Hawaii, Matt Cameron was walking home with his dog when he saw Chris's truck in his driveway. At first the drummer was excited. It had been a long time since his buddy had visited him at his house. Cameron walked through the front door and said hello to his wife who told him that Chris was waiting to talk to him downstairs. Cameron made his way to the basement where Chris, reeking of booze and cigarettes, and looking like he'd been awake for days, greeted him.

Initially, Cameron assumed that he was there to talk about Soundgarden's next album. Cameron even played Chris a few tracks that he'd been working on. After listening politely to his buddy's music, Chris lowered the boom and told him he was leaving the band. Cameron was stunned by the revelation, but over time, shock gave way to relief. The Hawaii experience combined with the recent run of unfullfilling gigs had worn on him as well, and he didn't know how Soundgarden was going to get back on track.

Cameron wasn't the only one to receive a visit from Chris that day. The singer went to Ben Shepherd and Kim Thayil's places to deliver his news in person. Outwardly, the bassist put on a brave face, spitting on the ground after Chris told him his decision, merely saying "All right." Inside, however, he was broken. Shepherd had always been a tremendous Soundgarden fan first and foremost. A world without the band was nearly too much to fully comprehend.

"My most intense feeling was relief," Kim Thayil told *Guitar World*. "There's just a point in time where you just want to get out of high school, you know? You're driving the car you're driving, but it doesn't shine like it used to, and doesn't go as fast as it used to without it making weird sounds on the highway. That's the only reason."[12]

In an effort to shield his wife from any sort of legal ramifications for ending the band, Chris only told Susan about his visits to the other members after he had delivered his decision. He even went as far as to hire a separate lawyer to put her as far away from the fallout as he could. Once it had all been taken care of, he came home and let her know what had happened. Then he grabbed a bottle and got hammered.

On April 8, 1997, just two days shy of the twenty-seventh anniversary of the Beatles' breakup, Soundgarden shared their dismal news with the world. The statement from A&M was matter-of-fact. "After twelve years, the members of Soundgarden have amicably and mutually decided to disband to pursue other interests," the label said. "There is no word at this time on any of the members' future plans."

The announcement sent shockwaves of disbelief and anguish around the globe. Online, fans gathered on message boards to commiserate while sharing unsubstantiated rumors about why Soundgarden was no more. MTV played their videos. Radio stations played their hits. And in the media, there was an outpouring of tributes and appreciation pieces. Writing for *Vox*, Jerry Ewing called it "Possibly the worst thing that's ever happened to metal. Ever."[13]

Chris Cornell had led the charge in Soundgarden since he was twenty years old. In that time, he had evolved from the lanky singing drummer to the chiseled, brooding leader of an entire generation. Soundgarden was all he'd ever known and now, as he approached his mid-thirties, for the first time in his musical life, he found himself alone. The possibilities that lay in front of him were as terrifying as they were exhilarating.

"In Soundgarden there was always a lot of loyalty and camaraderie, the feeling of us against the world," Chris said in 1999. "We supported each other, we could make mistakes, we could do amazing things. The gang mentality, that's what I lost…but what I gained is absolute freedom."[14]

In the immediate aftermath of Soundgarden's demise, Chris kept a low profile. He stayed at home, visited his cabin, played around with his dogs, and considered what he wanted to do next. While he wasn't certain about what his next musical project might sound like, he was absolutely against the idea of jumping into a band, despite several interesting offers.

More than anything, he wanted to take charge of his destiny, revisit old song ideas, and flesh-out demos and discarded tracks with an eye toward making a solo record.

Before he could truly dive into that project, however, an opportunity fell into his lap that piqued his interest. In 1997, Mexican filmmaker Alfonso Cuarón was in the midst of adapting Charles Dickens's 1861 novel *Great Expectations* into a feature film starring Gwyneth Paltrow, Ethan Hawke, and Robert DeNiro. For the soundtrack, the producers reached out to a variety of contemporary artists like Tori Amos, Pulp, and Stone Temple Pilots frontman Scott Weiland, who all contributed pieces of music. Another name they hoped to add to the final tracklist was Chris Cornell.

Chris had enjoyed working on songs like "Seasons" for *Singles* five years back, and the *Great Expectations* project seemed like the perfect chance to dive back into the world of cinema. He wrote a tender ballad called "Sweet Sunshower" that was about as stylistically far-removed from Soundgarden as it gets. Nevertheless, he was having a hard time finishing it, so he called his old friend Alain Johannes for help.

Chris first heard about Johannes back in the eighties when Kim Thayil, who was still working as a DJ for KCMU, brought in a pre-release copy of an album by Johannes' band What Is This to a Soundgarden rehearsal. The group featured Johannes on vocals and future Red Hot Chili Peppers members Jack Irons and Hillel Slovak on drums and guitar respectively. They petered out shortly after 1985, but Chris never forgot the impression it made on him. Then one day in 1991, he heard a voice from the other room that sounded a hell of a lot like What Is This on television. He rushed in just in time to catch Eleven's latest video on MTV. He quickly became a fan.

Eleven eventually hit the road supporting Soundgarden on several tours throughout the nineties, and Chris, Johannes, and Eleven's other musical half, Johannes's partner Natasha Shneider, grew increasingly close. "Chris was calling all the time," Johannes said in that period just after Soundgarden disbanded. "He basically came over and stayed with us at the house just to kind of decompress." Johannes and Shneider's home, an inviting 1932 construction with Frank Lloyd Wright-designed windows, a wealth of skylights, and a large coat of arms that hung over the fireplace, was a welcome sanctuary far from Seattle where he could work on the Great Expectations song in peace.

After tweaking the track for a bit and dropping "Sweet" from its title, "Sunshower" was finally finished and ready for its big-screen debut. *Great Expectations* hit theaters in January 1998, signaling the arrival of Chris Cornell as a solo artist. Meanwhile, his work with Eleven continued.

After finishing "Sunshower," Chris laid down some aching vocals for the duo's rendition of Schubert's immortal 1825 composition "Ave Maria" for the benefit compilation *A Very Special Christmas 3*. They also recorded a song called "Heart of Honey" for the unreleased animated film *Titan A.E.* before moving on to work on a song called "Someone to Die For" that was in contention for the theme song for the next James Bond movie. "It was going to be in the Bond film *Tomorrow Never Dies*," Johannes said. "In the end, there was a fight between the label and [Bond series producers] the Broccolis. Eventually Jimmy Gnecco sang it with Brian May." "Someone to Die For" ended up on the *Spider-Man 2* soundtrack instead.

While the movie themes and compilation songs were a fun distraction, Chris was still trying hard to conceptualize what the first album released under his own name would sound like. He'd abandoned the idea of polishing off unreleased older cuts from his archive and began writing new material. For hours, he sat down in his basement, strumming a Telecaster or one of his acoustic guitars, waiting for inspiration to strike. When cabin fever set in, he rented a place near Elliott Avenue, not far from where Soundgarden played their first show at Top of the Court, and set up a makeshift studio where he recorded a litany of fresh demos.

Originally, his plan was to work with French-Canadian producer Daniel Lanois, who was renowned for his work with U2 on their era-defining masterpiece *The Joshua Tree* as well as their engrossing follow-up *Achtung Baby*. Lanois was also a close collaborator of Bob Dylan's and helped the Nobel Prize-winning singer-songwriter realize one of his most critically beloved albums, *Time Out of Mind*. Lanois ultimately backed out of the project. "I think he realized that with the kind of songs I was writing, he wouldn't be able to influence the record enough," Chris said. "He does atmospheric, spherical kind of treatments, and that means the music has to be really straightforward; three chords, open, unstructured. My songs weren't like that."[15]

Rather than bring another hotshot producer on to the project, Chris decided to keep working with Alain Johannes and Natasha Shneider. "He's sitting at our house like, 'What the fuck am I gonna do now?' And Natasha goes, 'I'll tell you what we're gonna do. We're gonna fucking start recording your record!'" Johannes recalled. Eleven had recently received a $200,000 advance from A&M to work on their fourth album *Avantgardedog*, but instead of pouring it into outside studio fees and gear rentals, they built a world-class recording setup inside their own home. Work on Chris Cornell's debut album began on the Fourth of July, 1998.

Just like his last few releases with Soundgarden, Chris maintained a deliberate pace when it came to recording. "He'd come and go over a period of seven months," Johannes said. Chris typically spent a couple of weeks down in West Hollywood, cooking up new arrangements and laying down vocals. Then he would fly back to Seattle to dream up new ideas. "It was pretty much a big secret," the guitarist added. "It was just like this cool party hang. We'd go out to dinner then work until 2:00 a.m. Then, the next day, we'd say, 'Ah, I don't feel like working,' and go to the movies or we'd go to the beach. It was creatively fulfilling, tense and focused, but also really fun. There wasn't any pressure, or anybody looking over our shoulder."

A key factor that contributed to the lengthy process was Chris's drinking. He simply had a hard time getting himself in the right frame of mind to make music. "I was at my worst during *Euphoria Morning*," he told *Lollipop* magazine. "It was the lowest point. I was doing really badly. It took me six times longer than usual to finish that record. I wasn't writing under the influence—I've never been able to do that—but most of the time it would take me entire days just to get over a hangover or something to be able to work. When I was in the studio for 'Preaching the End of the World,' I literally spent more than half a day just waiting for this terrible headache to go away."[16]

The title of his first solo album *Euphoria Morning* originated with one of the record's central songs; a sparse, acoustic ballad called "Sweet Euphoria." Originally, he wanted to spell it *Euphoria Mourning*, but was talked out of it. The name was always something that irked him. "Someone reviewing the record said that the title sounded like a potpourri scent, and when I read that I was just like 'Fuck! Fuckin' bullshit!'" Chris said. [17] Years later when he re-issued the album, he made sure that *Euphoria Mourning* got its much-missed *u* back.

If there was a single, guiding principle that informed his decisions during this time, it was a desire to push his sound as far away from Soundgarden as he possibly could. *Euphoria Mourning* is quieter and brighter than anything he'd released up to that point, and as he thought about how he wanted the music to feel, he kept returning to unexpected sources of inspiration like Ray Charles and Otis Redding. He wasn't so much interested in recreating the musical style of "Georgia on My Mind," or "Sitting on the Dock of the Bay," but as he wrote new material, he thought a lot about the way those singers used their voices to evoke distinct feelings. He wanted to create more space to show off the complexity of his greatest instrument.

Chris had developed a keen instinct for how and when to deploy that instrument for maximum effect. At one point during a break from recording, the three musicians were dining out when Chris felt an overwhelming urge to lay down vocals to a song called "When I'm Down." They abruptly asked for the check, raced back to the house, and got the vocal locked in after just two takes.

"Usually he'd go into one of the towel rooms and he'd take a cigarette or maybe a glass of red wine or maybe some tea, and he'd just sit there, then he'd sing it all the way through," Johannes said. "Then he'd take a little break, you'd see him thinking and feeling his way through it, and we'd just be sitting in the control room waiting for him to say 'Okay.' It might be five minutes, it might be ten minutes, it might be one minute, before going into another take."

Songs like the glistening "Moonchild," which he wrote for Susan Silver, "Preaching the End of the World," "Disappearing One," and one of the only holdovers from an earlier era, the Poncier tape cut "Flutter Girl," were constructed in such a way that the focus was always Chris's ever-shifting voice. These were largely tender compositions that dealt with his thoughts and feelings on a wide variety of subjects. It was paramount that each had its own vibe. "If you listen closely to each song and the texture of his vocal, each one is its own world," Johannes added. "It wasn't like he was getting into character per se, but he just had this instinct and you could feel him searching to find it. And when he got there, he just did it so effortlessly."

One of the more touching entries on *Euphoria Mourning* is a funky, wah-wah-painted elegy called "Wave Goodbye." Chris wrote the song shortly after Jeff Buckley drowned in the Mississippi River on May 29, 1997. At the request of Buckley's mother, Chris performed "Wave Goodbye" at Buckley's private memorial service in New York. The song, a nakedly despondent account of what it feels like to lose someone too soon, gave Chris pause before he ultimately included it on *Euphoria Mourning*. The feelings were too real, and the topic so close to him that he felt wary about sharing it with the public.

In the several years prior to Buckley's death, the two singers, perhaps the two most naturally gifted vocalists of their generation, bonded over their shared talents, frustrations, successes and travails. "It's pretty rare to be able to call someone up on the phone and explain what you're going through as a songwriter, or a singer, or a bandmate, or what you are going through with the music industry and have somebody totally understand everything you are talking about," Chris told *Guitar One*. "I think that was the main part of our relationship. We were on some sort of common ground."[18] The loss was devastating.

Chris lent a hand to the curation of the posthumous Buckley collection *Sketches For (My Sweetheart the Drunk)*, where he was credited as "*Il Dottore Di Musica*" or "Music Doctor." Buckley's mother was so touched by Chris's involvement with the project that when it was finished, she gave him one of her son's guitars, a twelve-string Rickenbacker 360. She also gifted Chris Buckley's red telephone: an item he treasured for the rest of his life.

While Chris, Johannes, and Shneider were able to handle many of the musical duties themselves, they still needed a drummer. Josh Freese, one of the best session drummers in the world, who logged credits with Nine Inch Nails, Devo, the Replacements, and Guns N' Roses, handled most of the percussive duties on the album. When he wasn't available, Greg Upchurch, Victor Indrizzo, and Bill Rieflin were all brought in to play drums as well, but for one song in particular, "Disappearing One," Chris wasn't getting the right sound he was looking for and he turned to an old friend for help.

In the time since Soundgarden had disbanded, Matt Cameron had become the permanent drummer in Pearl Jam. He just happened to be in Los Angeles with the rest of his new group when he called Chris to see if he wanted to go out to dinner. The singer was down to break bread with Cameron, but first he asked if he wouldn't mind stopping by the studio to see if he might be able to help him finish "Disappearing One." The drummer arrived and, within an hour, managed to listen to the song, get a feel for what it needed, and lay down the finished take on the record.

With twelve completed tracks, Chris felt ready to release *Euphoria Mourning*. But as he was gearing up to share his first solo endeavor, the music industry was in a state of tremendous flux. A new peer-to-peer file-sharing software program called Napster had emerged in June 1999 and was beginning to siphon off CD sales from the big record companies. At the same time, A&M, Chris's home for nearly a decade, was purchased by Interscope Records. Suddenly he found himself at the mercy of a new set of corporate masters, largely unfamiliar to him. A&M had meant so much to him that on the label's final day of existence, he visited their offices one last time to say goodbye to many of the folks who had worked tirelessly behind the scenes to help make Soundgarden a worldwide phenomenon.

The biggest change of all was on the management side. For the first time in Chris Cornell's creative life, Susan Silver wasn't the primary guiding force pushing his latest project. While she remained involved, Jim Guerinot took over running the day-to-day operations of the singer's business affairs. The couple decided for the sake of their relationship that Silver should take a step back as they worked together to start a family. Almost everything surrounding the release of *Euphoria Mourning* would be wildly different from anything Chris had ever experienced before.

The propulsive opening track "Can't Change Me" was the first single released from the record in the early months of 1999. He also recorded a French version of the song for international release. The song did well and peaked at number five on the mainstream rock charts. It also nabbed him a Grammy nomination for Best Male Rock Vocal Performance, though the prize ultimately went to Lenny Kravitz for his take on the Guess Who's "American Woman."

Several months later, on September 21, 1999, the full album hit stores. Despite the heavy anticipation to hear what Chris Cornell sounded like on his own, sales were modest. *Euphoria Mourning* debuted at number eighteen on the Billboard Album Chart and in the ensuing weeks slowly slid down the rankings. "I don't feel that was a record made for mass consumption," Chris said years later. "My chief goal on that record was to make something that didn't sound like anything I'd done before."[19]

The same month *Euphoria Mourning* dropped, Chris launched his first solo tour backed by Johannes and Shneider along with Ric Markmann on bass and Greg Upchurch on drums. The run began with a performance at the Sanders Theater in Cambridge, Massachusetts, on September 13, 1999. It wasn't, technically, the first solo concert of his career. That distinction had come came many years earlier when Soundgarden was still around and he performed an hour-long local gig playing a twelve-string guitar, with Scott Sundquist on percussion and Matt Cameron on backup guitar.

The stakes were much higher now. So were his nerves, especially when he heard a rowdy, hard rock-loving fan wearing a Soundgarden T-shirt causing a ruckus in the front row. Emerging in tight black jeans, black T-shirt, and his hair slicked down and parted across the center of his forehead, Chris dove headlong into much of the material from his new album, peppering the hour-long set with selections from his career like "Seasons" and the Temple Of The Dog deep cut "All Night Thing." He performed only one Soundgarden song that night: "Like Suicide."

"I remember playing my first gig in Boston; I walked out, started playing the first song, and nobody shot me," he told *Rolling Stone*. And the rowdy Soundgarden fan in the front row that caused him so much concern? "He jumped up towards the end of the first song and shouted, 'All right, fuck yeah!' I guess he just decided he liked it and went with it."[20]

After a quick sprint through theaters across America, Chris and his band flew to Europe and barnstormed their way across the continent, beginning in Manchester, England, in October and ending in Copenhagen, Denmark, by November. While the show kept the packed theaters rapt, some of the more memorable moments took place behind the scenes. "I remember him climbing around the outside of a hotel in Paris, going from room to room knocking on the windows," Johannes recalled. "He's hanging outside our window balcony, like 'Hey, how's your minibar? You got any champagne in there?' Then he takes it and goes, 'Alright, I'll see you guys later!' And goes back out the window again. I guess he went to our drummer's room after."

Shortly after the European run, Chris notched his first appearance on *Late Show with David Letterman* on November 15, 1999, performing the song "Can't Change Me." Two months later he played *The Tonight Show* for the first time, busting out *Euphoria Mourning*'s second single "Preaching the End of the World." A new North American leg of the tour kept him on the road until March 3, 2000, and a final, very loose gig at the House of Blues in Las Vegas, at the end of which Chris joked, "We're gonna go out and beat this house and every house in this town, and we're gonna walk home with truckloads of money!" Then, he added, "Actually, don't bet. Don't give these fucking people your money. Fuck 'em."

By now, Chris had something far more important than music taking up much of his attention. During the winter, he announced to the world that his wife Susan was pregnant with their first child. Lillian Jean Cornell was born on June 28, 2000. She was named after Susan's mother, Jean Lillian Silver. After becoming a first-time father, Chris laid low to spend time with his burgeoning family and decompress from the months spent far from home.

"When they start to become a person, these babies, you just can't imagine or remember life without 'em," Chris told *CMJ* in 2003. "I'm doing the typical Dad stuff, pushing the baby in a stroller at Disneyland and having to drive slower cause your baby's in the car." [21] For the speed-loving adrenaline junkie that Chris was, trying to remember to cruise below posted speed limits remained a bit of a challenge.

Just three years after ending Soundgarden, Chris Cornell was again at a crossroads. The sheer number of paths he could walk down in the coming months and years was almost too numerous to contemplate. Another new solo album? More soundtrack work? There was even talk of forming a new group with Johannes, Shneider, and Matt Cameron. Then, a totally surprising opportunity came knocking at his door.

CHAPTER XII

SET IT OFF

S even stories above the pavement, the inky black shadow of Chris Cornell watches a Chevy C/K truck motoring his way. He hardly moves a muscle as a row of floodlights guide the pickup toward the immense scaffolded structure that is his domain. Three men hop out of the vehicle. The first is shirtless, his long dark hair just touching his shoulders. Brad Wilk. The second is also shirtless, an immense black tattoo plastered across his back, his blonde hair twisted into a pair of Pippi Longstocking braids. Timothy Commerford. The third figure is decked out in a green jacket, his head covered by a black-brimmed hat. Tom Morello.

Together, the trio piles into an industrial elevator, smashes a button and begins their journey upward. As the cables pull them towards the heavens, one floor flying past another, a spastic, stuttering guitar electrifies the air. The sound mingles with the low rumble of bass and morphs into a tidal wave of noise. High above them, the silhouette of Chris's blonde-highlighted hair sways in time to the boom-boom-whack of the beat. Volume swells until the elevator clicks into place and the red cage door swings open. The three men rush to their instruments, joining their silent brother who's been patiently awaiting their arrival. Off in the distance is the dark outline of the Sepulveda Dam.

On cue, the simmering cacophony detonates into an atomic guitar riff. Chris leaps high into the air before slamming his boots down onto the swaying platform as an explosion of red fireworks rips the sky open behind him. A colorful, unceasing parabola of flame arcs across the stars as the foursome plow into their savage composition. The inferno rages so close that the spent mortar rounds ping off Wilk's cymbals and leave burn marks on the drummer's back. They call this molten tsunami of music "Cochise," and it sounds as ferocious as anything Chris Cornell has sung since "Jesus Christ Pose."

Not far from the scene of this controlled mayhem rests one of the most densely clogged freeway arteries in the US: the intersection in Los Angeles where Highway 101 meets I-405. Drivers slow to a crawl to gaze at the distant chaos, grinding the already-molasses-thick sea of cars, trucks, and limousines to a standstill. "The local police and news station literally received thousands of calls from people who thought the city was under siege," Morello told *MTV*. "Like someone had decided to attack and [the target] was going to be the San Fernando Valley."[1] Coming just a few weeks after the one-year anniversary of 9/11, the anxiety the spectacle produces among the locals is all too real.

Epic Records didn't spare a cent for this music video. It was critical to give their new act the most explosive coming-out party they could conceive. To the powers that be, these four guys were primed to take over the genre. The $700,000 it cost to shoot them over two nights was a drop in the bucket compared to what they stood to recoup.

It was never a given that Chris Cornell would make it to this moment. In fact, the odds were far greater that he wouldn't. So much had gone down since the first time he'd jammed with this ferocious trio. Jam sessions, recording sessions, break-ups, make-ups, firings, hirings, personal upheaval, and a brush with death. And yet, somehow, here they were, still standing. In Chris's case, standing and screaming with a fevered intensity matched only by the constant shower of fire bellowing at their backs.

If the scene seemed surreal to rubberneckers, it was all the more mind-bending to the man at the heart of it all. "There was that quick moment where I looked back and see Rage Against The Machine," Chris told David Fricke. "It's like, 'Whoa, this is like a weird video game. Like I'm playing *Guitar Hero.*"[2]

A massive detonation brings the song to a close. Even though his "Soul Power" Stratocaster is dangling around Tom Morello's waist, Chris wraps the guitarist up in a bear hug. Wilk and Commerford amble over and join the embrace. They are no longer three-fourths of Rage Against The Machine and the singer from Soundgarden. They are a band; as super a supergroup as it gets in the new millennium.

They call themselves Audioslave.

* * *

The person who deserves the lion's share of the credit for sensing Audioslave's potential was Rick Rubin. The legendarily Zen producer had the foresight to understand that if you matched Tom Morello's riffs and the locked-in rhythm of Brad Wilk and Timothy Commerford, with the pen, face, and voice of Christopher John Cornell, you could make some especially devastating rock music.

The genesis of Audioslave began with the demise of Rage Against The Machine in 2000. After nine years of making some of the most innovative, lacerating, and loud albums of the decade—multi-platinum masterstrokes like *Evil Empire* and *The Battle of Los Angeles*—the politically-conscious rap-metal hybrid imploded amid a litany of personal resentments and a seemingly impossible-to-navigate decision-making process. Frontman Zack de la Rocha had had enough.

A little over a month before their split, Timothy Commerford made headlines by scaling a gigantic setpiece during the MTV *Video Music Awards* after Rage lost the Best Rock Video award to Limp Bizkit. The stunt landed the bassist in jail, but he remained unrepentant. "We were up against Limp Bizkit, one of the dumbest bands in the history of music," he told radio host Dan Le Batard years later.

Commerford couldn't stand the thought of losing to a video directed by that band's leader, Fred Durst, when he felt that their own clip for "Sleep Now in the Fire," directed by esteemed documentarian Michael Moore, was artistically superior. He noticed that MTV's cameras gravitated toward the winners before they were announced, and so he turned to Moore and said, "'Hey man, if that camera doesn't come over here, I'm climbing up that structure, and I'm gonna sit there like a fucking gargoyle and throw a wrench in this show.' And he's like, 'Tim, follow your heart.'"[3]

On October 18, de la Rocha put out a statement announcing his decision to leave Rage Against The Machine. "It is no longer meeting the aspirations of all four of us collectively as a band, and from my perspective, has undermined our artistic and political ideal." The remaining members quickly followed with a statement of their own. "We are committed to continuing with our efforts to effect change in the social and political arena and look forward to creating more ground-breaking music for our fans," they declared. "We'll keep it loud, keep it funky and most definitely rock on."

The united trio was an eclectic group. Brad Wilk and guitarist Tom Morello grew up around Chicago and had known each other a long time. The pair had played together early on when the drummer tried out for Morello's band Lock Up. Morello ended up picking someone else, but when Rage was getting off the ground and in need of a drummer, Morello pulled Wilk into the project.

Born in Harlem, New York, on May 30, 1964, barely two months before Cornell, Tom Morello spent his adolescence in Libertyville, Illinois, about ninety minutes north up I-294 from where Kim Thayil and Hiro Yamamoto attended high school in Park Forest. His mother, Mary Morello, was a schoolteacher with a master's degree from Loyola University, while his father, Ngethe Njoroge, was Kenya's first ambassador to the United Nations.

From a young age, Morello was politically engaged, advocating for a variety of anarchist and progressive causes. After graduating high school, he attended Harvard, where he earned a bachelor's degree in political science in 1986. After that, he moved to Los Angeles and attempted to realize his musical dreams while working a variety of menial jobs, including a brief stint as a male stripper.

Like Thayil, Morello was inspired to start playing guitar after hearing KISS and Black Sabbath, though he also mixed in a lot of Public Enemy and Iron Maiden. One of the first bands he formed was called the Electric Sheep and featured his old friend and high school classmate Adam Jones on bass. Jones later abandoned the bass in favor of the guitar and formed the legendary prog-metal band Tool.

In 1991, Morello met Zack de la Rocha. Shortly thereafter, they formed Rage Against The Machine. Tim Commerford came in to play bass through his connection to his old buddy Zack. Commerford was four years younger than Morello and had grown up around Southern California. He had met de la Rocha in Elementary School. Like Chris, he enjoyed the outdoors and had an affinity for mountain biking. His father was an aerospace engineer who worked on NASA's space shuttle program and on the Apollo missions. Years later, Commerford actually got into it with Buzz Aldrin at a movie premiere where he peppered the second man to land on the moon with questions about the veracity of the mission's existence. He came away from their debate unconvinced.

Over the next decade, Rage Against The Machine burnished their reputation as one of the most passionate and unpredictable bands on the planet. Songs like "Killing In The Name," "Bulls On Parade," and "Guerrilla Radio" became anthems to a generation eagerly seeking an avatar to express their own fury at the gilded hands guiding the ship of capitalism. Their chaotic live shows became legend, sometimes for the wrong reasons, like the quickly scuttled tour with Wu-Tang Clan in 1997, or the riot-marred disaster that was Woodstock '99. Mayhem seemed to follow the band wherever they went.

Following de la Rocha's departure, Morello, Wilk, and Commerford gathered together at Rubin's home to consider who on Earth had the skills and charisma to front them. Rubin had just produced the band's most recent album, a covers project titled *Renegades*, and was invested in figuring out a way forward. The four men ran through dozens of names, singers and rappers alike, quickly dismissing them one by one. Then came Rubin's lightbulb moment.

While they were hashing things out, the producer threw on Soundgarden's monolithic stomper "Slaves & Bulldozers." Chris's signature wail filled the room. "We all looked at each other and unanimously exclaimed, 'That's the fucking guy!'"[4] Morello remembered. When Rage Against The Machine was first starting out, there were two albums used as aesthetic guideposts. The first was Cypress Hill's 1991 self-titled debut. The other was Soundgarden's *Badmotorfinger*. Who better to bring in than the guy who helped influence their sound?

Chris had crossed paths with Rage a few times. They met on the Lollapalooza tour in 1996 and, at one point, Chris and Morello talked about working on some things together. Nothing came of it, but now the guitarist was riding alongside Rick Rubin, driving the hour and a half north from Hollywood to Chris's house in Ojai to make their pitch.

They reached the singer's Spanish-style abode around dusk, walked past several motorcycles parked out front and toward the gilded front door. As they approached, the door seemed to open by itself. Rubin was at once freaked and suggested they bail. But before they could leave, Chris glided into view and cordially invited them inside.

Chris was reluctant upon hearing their idea. He'd been part of a group for a dozen years and was more than familiar with how dysfunctional the inner workings of a band could be. *Euphoria Mourning* hadn't set the charts on fire, but there was something rewarding about releasing music under his own name. And it wasn't like he'd be joining up with any old band here either. Rage Against The Machine were infamous for sparking chaos wherever they went.

This was the band that tried to invade the New York Stock Exchange in January 2000, then sparked a riot outside of the Democratic National Convention just eight months later. This was a band who palled around with honest-to-God guerrilla warriors, the Zapatista Army of National Liberation in Chiapas, Mexico. The prospects of jumping into any regular old band were already fraught. The chances for calamity that came from fronting Rage Against The Machine were incalculable.

Chris was also aware that if he signed up, he'd be the new guy entering a long-established power dynamic. That's not to mention the army of Rage and Soundgarden fans who might immediately be inclined to resent their new musical partnership merely by dint of the fact that it didn't look or sound like the groups they had fallen in love with. Or the fact that rock audiences and critics alike have a long history of expressing disdain for seemingly manufactured supergroups looking to cash in on their collective fame without offering much in the way of musical substance. To go along on this particular ride could be a career-killing decision. Then again, it could also be extremely creatively and commercially fulfilling too. There was much to consider.

What the Rage Against The Machine guys didn't realize as their excitement built over the mere possibility of making music with Chris Cornell was that the singer was in the midst of one of the lowest points of his life, made especially dire by a burgeoning addiction to prescription opioids, specifically, the painkiller Oxycontin. "It was mentally, physically, and spiritually a fucked-up point in my life," Chris told *Spin*. "I was waking up and drinking a glass of vodka just to get a dial tone. My marriage wasn't working at all, and rather than face that, I turned to constant inebriation and then drugs."[5]

With not a whole lot to do after the end of the *Euphoria Mourning* tour, Chris started consuming more and more Oxycontin. He also dabbled with valium, cocaine, and, on at least one occasion, crystal meth. "The thing is, when you pick up the pipe for the first time, you don't know that that's your fate," he said years later. "And then that was it—I didn't want to care anymore."[6]

As the twenty-first century began, Chris was still trying to figure out what to do next. He was writing songs, presumably for another solo album, but the more he thought about working with Morello, Commerford, and Wilk, the more attractive the idea seemed. By April 2001, he decided they should get in a room together to see if there was any chemistry between the four of them.

They met in a space in Hollywood, chatted for a bit, then picked up their instruments and played. "Right off the bat I felt like the missing spark plug was put in and suddenly we were firing on all pistons," Brad Wilk told *Modern Drummer*. "Chris is one of my favorite vocalists, and all of a sudden he was in the room. It was an awesome feeling."[7]

The funky, bombastic riffs cooked up by Morello, paired with the propulsive rhythm produced by Wilk and Commerford, blended perfectly with Chris's sometimes-savage, sometimes-menacing voice. "I think I was actually kind of cocky," Chris recalled of that first jam session. "Not cocky like, 'I'm better than you,' but just very confident in the fact that I could stand in front of a microphone and sing and people in the room were going to think it's good."[8]

Before long, they had the seeds of their first song. It was eventually titled "Light My Way," a hard-hitting, wah-wah-painted piledriver, where Chris alternates between smoldering crooner and maniacal screamer slicing through the sonic torrent that serves as the track's atomic chorus. Over the next nineteen days, the foursome re-assembled multiple times to feel each other out, test their limits, and share ideas. For Chris, the sheer amount of creativity exploding all around him was gob-smacking. "We wrote songs so fast that sometimes we'd have to go back to like a rehearsal tape from a week before to remember what it was."[9]

By the end of their three-week testing period, they had twenty-one songs stitched together. For the former members of Rage Against The Machine, the prolific clip of creation was a welcome breath of fresh air after so many years struggling with their former frontman to scrounge together enough material to fill a single album. "Every day it was really pretty thrilling just to drive down to rehearsal," Morello said. "It was the newest, greatest thing we'd ever done, and it also felt like we'd been playing together for ten years."[10]

"Light My Way" was just the tip of the iceberg. Almost immediately after putting that track together, they cooked up another pair of winners. The first, titled "Exploder," boils over with as much fury as its name suggests, while another, "Bring 'Em Back Alive," chugs along like a forty-thousand-ton freight train barreling straight to hell. It was clear to Chris that, whatever this was, he was excited enough to throw himself into it with everything he had. His plans for a second solo record were dropped as he pushed all his chips in to record with the remaing Rage triumvirate.

He did have some conditions however, before they made their union official. First, he didn't want to write political lyrics. Throughout his career, Chris had largely written intensely self-reflective and sometimes esoteric words for his varied soundscapes. He had no intention of changing that now, especially seeing as how doing so would invite unwelcome comparisons to Zack de la Rocha.

Second, he wanted to leave most, if not all, of the guitar duties to Tom Morello. "I refused to play guitar in Audioslave because that didn't make sense to me," he said. "Singing to somebody else's music would, to me would [sic] make it easier for it to be further away from anything that would sound like Soundgarden."[11]

Finally, he didn't want this new project to be "Chris Cornell fronts Rage Against The Machine." If they were going to be a band, they were going to be an entirely new thing: a complete break from their collective pasts. The other three readily agreed.

Near the beginning of June 2001, the new group met with Rick Rubin at Cello Studios, just off Sunset Boulevard in Hollywood, to begin work on their first album. Over the next two months, the band locked themselves inside the large wood-adorned room in Studio 2 and carefully honed their abrasive collection of material. Among the immortal albums that had been created within those walls are the Beach Boys' *Pet Sounds*, Crosby, Stills & Nash's self-titled debut, the Stooges' *Raw Power*, and Marvin Gaye's *Let's Get It On*. Chris and his new band wanted to leave their own mark.

Rubin wasn't an unrelenting task master, but he did like to explore every possibility before committing to a specific direction. Sometimes they worked through thirty or forty takes of a song, making slight adjustments along the way. No idea was too absurd to attempt, whether that meant playing the verse as a chorus, re-formatting the bridge into a verse, or playing in a different key.

The first piece they tackled was the slow, simmering ballad ultimately called "Getaway Car." The band set up in the large room, while Chris was ensconced in an isolation booth. "All the hairs stood up on the back of my neck when he started to sing," Engineer Dave Schiffman recalled. "He was still tinkering with lyrics at that point, because there were times where it was just him mumbling or rambling and the lyrics weren't quite there yet, but it still sounded great. He'd have the melody nailed. It was just a matter of getting the words to fit."

Chris's house in Ojai was an hour-and-a-half drive from the studio, which meant three hours of his day was spent in Los Angeles traffic. It's no wonder so many of the songs on Audioslave's debut have automotive motifs. "Getaway Car," certainly, but also the apocalyptic barnburner "Gasoline," and most notable of all, "I Am The Highway." Opening with a quick reference to the pearls and swine from Jesus Christ's sermon on the mount from Matthew 7:6, Chris reflects on his decision to move forward by setting fire to his past and getting on by himself. "I am not your carpet ride," he cries. "I am the skyyyyy!" The song is a clarion call for anyone chasing freedom; a breathtaking meditation made all the more poignant by Tom Morello's pristine chords and a twinkling solo that feels like the sonic equivalent of hope.

That song's genesis was indicative of the creative electricity flowing between Morello and Cornell during those early rehearsals. The guitarist already had the progression for "I Am The Highway," but was worried that it sounded too gentle given the heavy territory they were treading. During one rehearsal, he strummed the chords, hoping that somebody would be inspired by them. Chris ambled over to get a better sense of what Morello was playing. The next day, they returned to the studio and fleshed the song out as a band.

"I Am The Highway" was far from the first or last time Chris invoked shades of religious imagery into his music. It wasn't even the most acute example on this project. "Like A Stone" takes the cake on that account. Opening with a simple drum pattern and some delayed single-notes from Morello, Chris slinks his way into the song, sedately singing about cobwebs, freeways, and a "book full of death." There's a creepy vibe to the intro that's shattered the instant he breaks into the chorus, soaring over Morello's crashing chords, then diving headlong into the morass of the instrumental. In the next verse he's on his deathbed, praying to gods and angels, waiting to be taken to heaven. "The sky was bruised," he observes, "The wine was bled, and there you led me on."

"It's a song about concentrating on the afterlife you would hope for, rather than the normal monotheistic approach," he said. "You work really hard all your life to be a good person and a moral person and fair and generous…and then you go to hell anyway."[12] The openness, the inner turmoil and the darkness that lies at its heart, along with the stunning arrangement, featuring one of the more touching, and melodic solos Morello ever conjured out of his Telecaster, made it the most emotionally impactful song on the record.

On the other hand, "Cochise" works a blissfully unnuanced sledge-hammer to the solar plexus. The origins of the song date back to the mid-nineties, to Tom Morello's side project the Weatherman, a duo that he put together with Chicago punk rocker Vic Bondi. You can hear an embryonic version of the distinctive "Cochise" riff throughout the frenetic, lo-fi punk track that the pair cooked up called "Enola Gay." Once Chris and the rest of the Rage guys got their hands on Morello's riff, however, they transformed it into one of the most awe-inspiring rock songs of the decade.

Incredibly, Chris recorded his speaker-shredding vocals on "Cochise," along with most of the songs on this record, while sitting in a chair. He often sang along with the band while they were tracking songs in the studio together, but most of the finished vocal takes were completed later in Seattle with the help of another engineer, the legendary Andrew Scheps. "It was astonishing because the thing about Chris is that it sounds like he's yelling at the top of his lungs all the time, but he's actually a quiet singer," the engineer remembered. "He didn't have to stand up and belt, which is why I think he could sing all day."

Even for someone like Scheps who has worked with some of the most widely heralded vocalists of all-time, including Adele, Beyoncé, Michael Jackson, and Bono, there was something astounding about the way Chris approached singing. "You'd realize he was in a zone," he said. "When he was singing, he'd be inside it. Super inside of it. It wasn't like he'd sing a sad song and then at the end make a joke and go, 'Alright, let's do it again.' He would stay in it."

Chris was also a harsh critic, mostly of himself. "He was always paying attention," Scheps added. "And he would never let anything go that he wasn't into. There was never a moment where you thought, 'Well, maybe that's good enough.' There was no such thing as 'good enough.'"

"Cochise" went by a couple of different names before it received its final moniker. While they were working on it in the studio, it was referred to as "Shifty's Revenge," an inside joke referring to their engineer Dave Schiffman. For a while they considered calling it "Save Yourself," a straightaway grab from the song's chorus. Finally, they decided to name it after the Apache war chief Cochise, who frequently attacked US forces throughout the Southwest in the 1860s. The name matched the song perfectly: Defiant, angry, and unrepentent.

While the atmosphere in the studio remained congenial, especially in those early weeks, the four musicians had yet to coalesce into a real band. "Chris really kind of kept it to himself," Schiffman remembered. "There was a refrigerator filled with Mickey's largemouth beers, and he'd sit in the lounge and have a beer or two. He'd be more quiet some days than others. He'd come in and you could tell he was in a good mood and he was friendly and he'd joke around with everybody. He was present. And then there were days where he wasn't. He was a little off and kind of distant. Everybody kind of gave him his space. Nobody would go, 'Hey, c'mon, Chris. What the fuck?' It was just like, 'Alright, let him do his thing.' There would be some days where he'd be like, 'You know what, I'm just not feeling it today,' and he'd leave. He'd go wherever he went, and we'd just keep working."

The biggest divide that still remained between Chris and the other three guys was the fact that they had different management teams. Chris was still represented by Jim Gueirnot, while the Rage guys were managed by Peter Mensch and Cliff Burnstein at Q Prime. Over the next several months, the arrangement made it increasingly difficult to reach a consensus on seemingly anything and was made all the more complicated by the fact that they were beholden to two different record labels, Epic and Interscope. For the most part though, the four guys didn't let these concerns affect their daily interactions. There was still important work to be done and songs to finish.

Most of the album was filled with scorching rock tracks like "Show Me How to Live," "Light My Way," "What You Are," and "Set It Off," which was inspired by a riot that Chris envisioned in his mind after hearing their ferocious, jittery music for the first time. One of the album's under-rated gems, a song that was surprisingly never released as a single, is the cinematic "Shadow on the Sun." The riff was inspired by the chorus on the Commodore's Motown classic, "Brick House."

"Shadow On The Sun" is the kind of song that demands to be listened to at a decibel level commensurate with a jet taking off and features one of the most blood-curdling screams that Chris ever committed to tape. Somehow, he managed to summon forth a guttural wall of noise that sounds more animal than human. The song was later used to incredible effect in a pivotal scene in Michael Mann's LA noir *Collateral* starring Tom Cruise and Jamie Foxx.

The album wasn't all Marshall stacks and vicious screaming. There was a tender side as well. The aforementioned "Getaway Car" allowed the group to show off their bluesier sensibilities, while the final track on the album, "The Last Remaining Light," stands as a monument of pent-up, slow-boiling fury. It's an intricate arrangement, touched up with jazzy guitar lines and sparse, snare-packed silences, before erupting into an avalanche of buzzing bass notes and emotional screaming. As the song comes to its conclusion, Chris repeatedly cries out the word "Liiiiiiiight," until the album fades out.

Chris didn't always have the clearest sense of what he wanted to sing, but still found ways to fill in the melody, usually by employing stand-in lyrics or nonsensical words. In the meantime, he continued to hone in on each song's central message, constantly scribbling words and lines in a notebook that he carried with him. "He would get ideas together and be like 'Hey, I wanna try this verse out, could you throw me into record?'" Schiffman remembered. "While we're taking a lunch break, he'd be like, 'Hey, I wanna try this verse out.' Then he'd run down the verse a couple times, and I'd be like, 'Oh wow, that's great!' And he's like, 'Eh. I'm not sure about that last line. I gotta work on that last line. He was always batting around ideas, and as we were tracking, he'd try out different approaches."

While they had all the songs they needed to make a mark on the world, one thing they didn't have was a name. No one seemed to be tak-ing the task seriously. At one point they thought about calling themselves

Shitstorm. At another they considered going with Plato's Surprise after Tom Morello drew a picture of the ancient philosopher exposing himself. Then there was the brief moment they thought about calling themselves After School Special or ASS in all-caps, like KISS.

Finally, Morello brought the name Civilian to the table, and everyone agreed it was a winner, until they discovered there was already another group out there by that name, so it was back to the drawing board. It was Chris who came up with Audioslave. He said it popped into his head while poring over lists of names he'd put together. He pitched the moniker to everyone over their two-way beepers and got the thumbs-up. Then they learned that a group in Liverpool, England, was already performing as Audioslave. Rather than try to come up with an alternative, they cut the UK band a check for $30,000 to assume the rights to the name.

Audioslave still hadn't announced their union to the public, but as they finished up in the studio, word of their collaboration became one of the music industry's worst-kept secrets. The group became official on March 20, 2002, when the still-unnamed band was announced as one of the acts on the upcoming Ozzfest. The live run would keep them on the road from the beginning of July through September, joined by the likes of System of a Down, P.O.D., Rob Zombie, and the Prince of Darkness himself, Ozzy Osbourne.

Their record wasn't even out yet, but heavy anticipation to hear what this unexpected alliance would sound like was growing. Then, a few days after the tour announcement, Chris decided he wanted out. At the heart of his frustration was the double-headed managerial set-up. "I had a lot of personal crisis stuff going on," he told *Classic Rock* magazine. "And a lot of what we talked about in terms of this being fun and uncomplicated started to become un-fun and very much complicated by the two separate management camps."[13]

Chris returned to Seattle to collect himself and figure out what to do next. Just a few weeks later, however, Susan Silver received a dreadful phone call that put everything on hold. Silver had stepped back from managing Alice In Chains back in 1998 while she and Chris started a family, but she remained close with the band. On this day she received a call informing her that no one could get in touch with Layne Staley.

Silver called Staley's mother who subsequently phoned the police. The authorities went out to the singer's apartment in the University District to do a welfare check. When no one answered the door, the cops kicked it in and found Staley's decomposing body on the couch. He'd been dead for two weeks, having overdosed on a heroin/cocaine concoction known as a speedball. By some cosmically macabre coincidence, Staley had passed on April 5, eight years to the day Kurt Cobain had taken his own life.

After receiving the devastating news, the remaining members of Alice In Chains, along with Susan and a bleached-blonde Chris, gathered with dozens of friends and fans near the large International Fountain just under the Space Needle to mourn his loss. Someone in attendance left a note scrawled on a paper bag near the fountain, echoing Chris's lyrics. "There is only one thing left to say," the note read. "Say hello to heaven." A more formal service was held for Staley on April 28 on Bainbridge Island. Susan Silver delivered a speech as did Jerry Cantrell. Barrett Martin, Staley's bandmate in Mad Season, delivered the eulogy, while Chris joined Ann and Nancy Wilson in a touching performance of the Rolling Stones' "Wild Horses."

While Chris continued to try to come to terms with Staley's passing, his Audioslave bandmates were doing everything they could to stay in touch and offer support. Finally, about six weeks after he bailed, Chris decided to give the band another shot. The only catch was that he had to fire his manager Jim Guerinot and come to an agreement with the other three guys on who should represent them together going forward. It was hard business and a tough series of phone calls, but Chris went through with the move, parting ways with his longtime friend. When the dust settled, Audioslave signed up with The Firm, headed by Jeff Kwatinetz. The person who would handle their day-to-day affairs was a guy named Daniel Field who had cut his teeth managing Ministry. He had first met Chris on the Lollapalooza tour in 1992.

Field had his work cut out for him. On May 17, the raw files of Audioslave's album leaked on the Internet a full six months before the band was planning to release them. Tom Morello described the material that made it onto file-sharing spaces like Limewire and Kazaa to MTV as "inferior sketches of works in progress which we had sent to a studio up in Seattle for Chris to listen to and work on…someone at that studio helped themselves to a copy, and it then took about eight months to make its way to an Italian website." [14]

It was a disaster. The songs weren't anywhere near up to snuff. Brad Wilk could be heard counting everyone in with his sticks and many of Chris's vocals were unfinished scratch takes. Even the names were wrong. "Cochise," was labeled "Save Yourself," "Like A Stone," was called "I'll Wait," "I Am The Highway" was called "I Am Not," and "Getaway Car" was called "Drive." The leak also included a brash rock track featuring a truly unhinged Morello solo tentatively titled "Turn To Gold," which never made it onto the official album and remains in the vaults. This was hardly the introduction that Chris and the rest of the band had hoped to make.

There was nothing Audioslave could do about the leak other than to keep moving forward. Once their managerial issues were sorted, they had to then figure out a way to align their separate record deals. They worked out an arrangement where the band's first album would be released on Epic, while the second would go to Interscope. After that problem was dispatched, they moved onto the promotional stage. Field lined up a photo shoot with veteran rock photographer Danny Clinch to get some press pictures for the all-out media assault to come.

When the day came for the shoot, the four guys convened at a hotel in downtown Los Angeles. It was clear to everyone that Chris wasn't in great shape. He kept nodding off. "It was so bad that Chris would have his eyes closed and Danny Clinch would go, 'One, two, three!' and he'd open his eyes for a second and Danny would take the photo," Field recalled.

Despite their singer's alarming state, the group managed to grab some pictures in the hotel's old ballroom before moving to rooms on an upper floor to get some more intimate shots. "Chris was so out of it, and then he sat in the window and it looked like he was about to fall out. It was just super scary. I remember Tom Morello praying out loud because he was so worried that Chris was going to fall out the window," said Field. "It was a total visual metaphor for what was going on."

Chris's addiction to Oxycontin had grown more severe over the previous several months. There were days when he didn't eat. His muscular frame grew wiry, and he claimed that his weight plummeted to a meager 145 pounds. Those closest to him grew concerned about his physical and mental state, but he didn't care. "I was doubling and tripling up on depressants," Chris told Howard Stern. "You don't know what's going on. You don't feel anything."[15]

Something needed to be done and fast. "Those three guys have really big hearts and they were concerned about Chris," Field said about the others. "I think beyond anything, they wanted him to be healthy and get better, even at the risk of losing a band they loved and music they'd worked hard on. They're like, 'Let's figure out the right way to do it.'"

The band got in touch with Bob Timmins, a well-respected addiction specialist who had a history of working with other high-profile rock bands like Aerosmith and Mötley Crüe. They decided to stage an intervention. The night before the intervention, however, Chris, who was staying at the Mondrian on Sunset, went missing.

"The reports we were getting were pretty bad," Field said. "Owen Wilson saw him at some bar and texted like, 'Chris is out here and not looking good.'" Fortunately, Chris showed up the next day and met with Morello, Wilk, Commerford, Timmins, and Susan Silver, who convinced him that it would be a good idea to spend some time in a rehabilitation facility. Chris agreed and checked into Passages.

"Realizing how I was affecting people I cared about made a big difference," Chris said to *Spin*. "The other three members of Audioslave didn't know me that well, and when we started making the first record, I was pretty much at my worst...I felt a sense of sadness and fear in them that made me wake up."[16]

Passages had been founded the year before by a father-and-son duo named Chris and Pax Prentiss. The former real estate investors spared little expense constructing their opulent seaside facility in Malibu. Featuring gorgeous vistas of the Pacific Ocean, rich mahogany doors, and a marble-adorned atrium, the environment was designed to be as relaxing and private as possible. "It was me, a thirty-five-year-old Seattle musician, and a bunch of billionaires' kids," he said. "Billionaires are too smart to end up in rehab, but it's full of their kids."[17]

Passages eschewed the traditional twelve-step process of recovery and relied on an intensive program of one-to-one counseling instead. "At first, it was terrifying," Chris said. "It was like being in hundred-degree heat and diving into an ice-cold pool from a great height. I had a lot of fears about being around people I didn't know and talking about personal things in front of people who I wasn't sure if I could trust or not. Getting that all out of the way was a great thing for me…I treated it like someone might treat going to a health camp or a spiritual retreat, because it was that for me."[18]

Shortly after Chris entered Passages, Richard Patrick, frontman for the band Filter, checked in. After spending the first couple of days getting clear and seeking therapy, Patrick, a staunch atheist, decided he'd had enough of the religious undertones that proliferated the program and decided he wanted to bail. Chris convinced him to stick it out. "I was literally getting up to leave, and he goes, 'Listen, stay here. Stay with me.'"

Though he didn't know him on a personal level, Chris talked to Patrick about giving himself up to a higher power. Not God necessarily, but the power of a group of people urging him on to achieve sobriety. "G-o-d," Patrick said. "Group of drunks." Spurred by Chris's pep talk, he stayed in the program. "My sense of ego was being told by an even bigger, stronger, more amazing, real, legitimate rock star that wrote number one songs and played arenas, a real rock star was saying, 'This is the only deal in town that works, I've only got five days and if you leave, it's really gonna bum me out.' I'm supposed to help the guy with four days. I heard him and said, 'I'm here for you?' And he said, 'Yeah,' and I go, 'All right.'" Patrick has remained sober ever since.

Chris remained in rehab for the full thirty-day treatment. When his time was up, he decided to re-up for another thirty. He was determined to stay sober.

Outside the walls of Passages, Audioslave continued moving full steam ahead with hardly anyone the wiser about Chris's addiction troubles. The release date for the album was pushed to November, but there was still a lot of work to be done. Field even temporarily checked Chris out of rehab to film the band's video for "Cochise," and brought him back to the facility when it was over. The singer did press from inside Passages, infamously revealing his whereabouts to a reporter from *Metal Hammer* while chatting on the facility's payphone.

Simultaneously, Chris arrived at a monumental personal decision. After seventeen years of partnership and twelve years of marriage, he no longer wanted to be with Susan Silver. A counselor at the facility convinced him it was necessary to maintaining his sobriety once he returned to the outside world. He let Susan know his decision in late October. The split was wasn't without acrimony, but by March 2004, their divorce was officially signed off on by a judge.

After leaving rehab, Chris stayed at a variety of places around Los Angeles while focusing on his sobriety and the launch of Audioslave's debut. "Most of the time, coming out of rehab, people have a destroyed life, [and] struggle to just work again and get a job," he told the *Mirror*. "I sort of had an identity sitting there waiting to be embraced. I was very lucky I was able to see that and not take it for granted. It helped me climb out of the mire."[19]

The project had ground on for over a year, and he and the rest of the band were more than ready to share the fruits of their labor. "Cochise" was released as a single on October 11 and was immediately embraced by FM rock radio. By the end of the year the song had climbed all the way to number two on Billboard's Mainstream Rock chart.

Before the band could sell their CD, however, they needed a cover photo. For that crucial task, they turned to one of the greatest album designers of all time, an Englishman named Storm Thorgerson who gained fame for his covers of albums like Pink Floyd's *The Dark Side of the Moon*, Led Zeppelin's *Houses of the Holy*, and Paul McCartney and Wings' *Band on the Run*. For *Audioslave*, Thorgerson, with Peter Curzon and Rupert Truman, ventured out to Lanzarote in the distant Canary Islands, just off the coast of Morocco. Once there, they trained their cameras on the desolate, alien-looking landscape of Volcán El Cuervo, or "The Crow's Volcano." A volcano, the artist thought, perfectly represented the menace that streaked across Audioslave's music. In the middle of the finished cover sits a gigantic, metal sculpture of a five-fingered flame with a rounded bottom. The eternal flame. To the left, seemingly for scale, a small figure in a red shirt gazes up at the towering golden statue. In an alternate version, the man was nude.

On November 19, 2002, *Audioslave* was released. Critics largely hated it. In his three-star review for *Rolling Stone*, writer Pat Blashill lambasted the band's efforts. "Do Audioslave rock?" he asked. "Sure. Is that enough? Well, no...Audioslave just seem sorta engorged."[20] A new, upstart online publication called *Pitchfork* was even harsher, assigning the record a score of 1.7 out of 10. They savaged Chris's lyrics, and at one point called him "an embarrassment." Their piece culminated with the line, "Duck, because America's gonna vomit."[21] At least *Pitchfork* didn't simply run a video of a monkey peeing into its own mouth like they did in lieu of a written review of Jet's second album *Shine On*.

Fans disagreed with the critics and signaled their approval with their wallets. In its first week, *Audioslave* sold 162,000 copies and debuted at number seven on the Billboard Top 200. The top three spots that week were taken by Shania Twain's pop-country mega-seller *Up!*, the eleventh entry into the *Now That's What I Call Music* compilation series, and Eminem's *8 Mile* soundtrack. Later, when the Grammys rolled around, Audioslave received a nomination for Best Rock Album, while "Like A Stone" got nominated for Best Hard Rock Performance. The band lost out on both prizes to Foo Fighters and Evanescence respectively.

Despite failing to crack the top five, *Audioslave* had incredible staying power, and as the band rolled out new singles over the next five months, thousands of copies flew off the shelves each week. A CD-ROM version included a downloadable bonus track called "Give," a rare political statement by Chris, castigating the rich, who've "got enough food on your table," to give to those in need. The record was eventually certified as triple platinum for selling over three million copies.

Just ten days after releasing *Audioslave*, Chris and the band flew to New York to make their live debut in front of a televised audience. They were scheduled to appear on the *Late Show with David Letterman*, but as this was their first-ever live performance, they were eager to do something special. Instead of performing inside of the Ed Sullivan Theater like the Beatles, the Rolling Stones and Elvis Presley had, they would play their new songs on top the building's marquee overlooking Broadway, one of Manhattan's busiest streets. For all the decades of music that had been showcased within the theater, Audioslave would be the first band to play atop the marquee.

The large platform overhanging the entryway was never intended to host a rock band. In order to get out onto it, Chris and the band had to crawl through a window, up a ladder, and onto the makeshift stage. Despite the chill in the late-autumn air, when the time came to kick into their set, Chris stripped off his sweater, revealing a white tank top underneath. His formerly blonde hair was back to its natural shade of dark brown and from his ears dangled two matching hoop earrings.

They began with the explosive "Set It Off" and then kicked into "Gasoline." The street below was clogged with police, firefighters, and rock fans. From the windows of the offices ringing the theater, businesspeople set aside their pursuits and gazed in wonder at the display as well. "Like A Stone" followed before the band hit passersby with the only song that made it to air, "Cochise."

"If Soundgarden and Rage Against The Machine got into a fight, who do you think would win?" David Letterman asked his bandleader Paul Schaefer after returning from commercial break during the broadcast.

"Definitely Rage Against The Machine," the keyboardist answered.

The bemused host concurred, then held up a vinyl copy of Audioslave's debut before announcing their performance. Cameras swooped in from all directions to get cinematic shots of the band as they shook the foundations of the nearby skyscrapers with their vicious sound. If there were any lingering doubts about Chris's ability to rise to the occasion after months of personal turmoil, they were erased the second he opened his mouth and screamed out the song's twisted opening. "Still some rage there I think," Letterman quipped afterwards.

Less than two weeks after the Letterman gig, Audioslave was preparing for their next live appearance in Los Angeles, KROQ's Almost Acoustic Christmas show at the Universal Amphitheatre. Before they got there however, they staged a secret gig at the Roxy on Sunset to work out kinks and calm their nerves. Their name wasn't even on the marquee, but people showed up anyway. The only giveaway of the evening's entertainment was the red Rage Against The Machine star painted all over the various equipment cases.

The Roxy gig went off like gangbusters. The band played half a dozen songs from their new album, culminating with "Like A Stone," and seemed poised to rip the proverbial roof off the Universal Amphitheatre the following evening.

The Almost Acoustic lineup was an eclectic mix of artists Chris had known for years, like Billy Corgan's Zwan and Queens of the Stone Age, as well as relative newcomers like Sum 41 and the Used. Opening with "Light My Way," the group ripped through six songs during their half hour onstage. Just after hitting the amped audience with "Gasoline," Chris decided to introduce the band, while making a stunning personal statement.

"This is Tom, this is Brad, this is Tim, I'm Chris," he said. "These three guys saved my life this year." No one outside his inner circle knew how close to the brink Chris Cornell had come, but here he was now, still standing and still screaming in the way that only he could. At the end of the set, just like he did at the culmination of the "Cochise" video, Chris wrapped his bandmates in a gigantic hug.

CHAPTER XIII

OUT OF EXILE

T he cabin of the private jet rocked gently as the rubber tires touched the tarmac. The few dozen people on board—an opulent loaner from the NBA's Miami Heat that for the purposes of this trip was designated Audioslave One—peered out of their windows and gazed out at the foreign landscape as they taxied toward the modest blue terminal. The flight had only taken about an hour and traversed just 228 miles, but the amount of effort and time it had taken to make it possible was herculean. More than a million dollars had been spent to stage this single show. The pressure was on.

No American rock band had ever performed on the isolated island of Cuba. The communist Caribbean country had been largely cut off from the rest of the world for decades thanks to a strictly enforced commercial embargo put in place by the United States shortly after Fidel Castro came to power in 1960. Though Cuba had hosted other American musical acts before, like Billy Joel and Kris Kristofferson in 1979, the kind of performance that Chris Cornell and his band had planned was far beyond the scale, scope, and volume of those intimate musical gatherings. The logistics of securing the necessary equipment and getting it across the Caribbean presented its own degree of difficulty. Getting the green light from two adversarial governments to put on the performance was an entirely different ballgame.

"Before they went over, there was all this bullshit like, weird word that would come to the band like, you're not allowed to bring any recording devices," Audioslave's manager Daniel Field said. "Don't talk in your room because your rooms are gonna be bugged. Don't wander off because you might get hijacked. All this bullshit that wasn't true at all. Once they got there, people couldn't have been nicer."

Audioslave and their entourage, which included their wives, tour managers, publicists, bodyguards, camera crew members, and Tom Morello's mother Mary, debarked the plane just after noon and were greeted by a coterie of Cuban officials, eager to extend the hand of friendship and guide them around the island. The three former members of Rage Against The Machine had long hoped to perform here, but Zack de la Rocha had nixed the idea. Chris had been more receptive.

Shortly after landing, the band was ushered into white vans and whisked around Havana. They visited Plaza de la Revolución where the Cuban National Flag had been hoisted for the first time in 1902. They listened to a local stand-up bass and piano combo at Cuba's National School of Arts and marveled at the centuries-old Havana Cathedral. They snapped pictures of the large, omnipresent murals of Che Guevera that dotted the different buildings. Tim Commerford even busted out his mountain bike and carved up the walls of the Castillo de los Tres Reyes del Morro, the fort guarding the entrance to Havana Bay.

One of Chris's favorite stops was John Lennon Park, which had been dedicated by Fidel Castro just five years earlier to commemorate the twentieth anniversary of Lennon's death. "For an unveiling like that to be done by Castro himself, that was something that made me feel more welcome as I sat next to the statue," he said. "I thought 'Okay, well, a rock band coming here and playing is going to be endorsed and appreciated.'"[1] During soundcheck, Chris busted out a cover of Lennon's Beatles classic "You've Got to Hide Your Love Away," for the one hundred or so people craning their necks to get a better view.

Audioslave was determined to treat their gracious hosts to a spectacle they would never forget. After fixing a bum monitor system that crapped out just after they hit the stage around eight o'clock, the band launched into the longest set of their career, playing twenty-six songs over the course of two and a half hours. They milked almost their entire arsenal of music, pulling out songs from their first record, songs from their upcoming album, *Out Of Exile*, even songs from their previous bands. The Rage guys hit the crowd with an instrumental version of "Bulls on Parade," while Chris regaled them with a solo, acoustic rendition of "Black Hole Sun."

Around seventy thousand people flooded La Tribuna Anti-Imperialista Plaza to watch, listen, and bang their heads. American culture was slow to seep its way across the Atlantic. Residents on the island were largely cut off from the Internet then, and it was difficult for rock fans to keep up with what was cutting edge in the States. Despite the fact that many people who showed up for the free gig were largely unfamiliar with Audioslave, there was a large contingent familiar with Chris and his work in Soundgarden. Out in the crowd, someone held up a gigantic white sign that read, "HELLO SEATTLE, WELCOME AUDIOSLAVE."

Even those who had no idea who Soundgarden, Rage Against The Machine, or Audioslave were lost themselves in the celebratory spirit of the evening. They danced. The sang. They chanted the band's name. ""Ow-dyo-slave! Ow-dyo-slave! Ow-dyo-slave!" Chris couldn't have been happier. "They were not only seeing a rock concert for the first time, they were seeing a *huge* rock concert for the first time," he said. "As I looked at the audience there was a vast appreciation, but of a different kind that could be deeply felt even if it was only from their eyes."[2]

It was a watershed moment for the band. By the time they finished playing "Shadow on the Sun," Chris hoisted the Cuban national flag high over his sweat-soaked hair and boisterously waved it before the sea of screaming faces. The show reaffirmed his belief in the power of music to unite people, while also bringing him closer to his bandmates. "I really didn't think the same after I left," he said. "I really understood what music is and how it's that language that everybody speaks no matter what other audible language you speak."[3]

Not long after the band left the stage, cable news channels ran myriad stories about their groundbreaking performance. It was covered in newspapers, magazines, and an army of online outlets. While the US was still mired in a war in Iraq—a war they were slowly losing—this small piece of news about a rock band crossing hard borders to bridge seemingly impossible political divides and give some people a night of fun resonated.

While Chris never made it back to Cuba, Audioslave had put a crack in the invisible wall that separated the two countries. In the years that followed, Beyonce and Jay-Z both visited the island as tourists, as did Roots drummer Questlove, Kool & the Gang, and EDM duo Major Lazer. And just five days after President Barack Obama normalized relations with Cuba and became the first sitting President to visit the country on March 20, 2016, The Rolling Stones cemented Cuba's bonafides as a rock-loving Mecca by staging their own free show in front of five hundred thousand people at a sports complex in Havana.

Maybe it was all inevitable. Maybe time truly was the medicine that both the US and Cuba needed to heal old wounds. But then, perhaps, the unlikely salve of "Cochise," delivered with as much fury as its creators could conjure, helped speed the process along.

*　*　*

A little over a month after Audioslave rocked the Almost Acoustic Christmas show in Los Angeles, the foursome jetted across the Atlantic to embark on their first tour. The whole thing was planned as a ten-day, quick-hitting promotional campaign with the band playing some of the continent's most important markets like London, Berlin, and Milan. After that, they hopped on another plane for a standalone gig at the Zepp Tokyo in Japan before kicking off an extensive theater run through North America.

The band landed in Paris on January 13, 2003, checked into the Hôtel Plaza Athénée and started preparing for the performance the next evening at L'Olympia, an historic venue opened in 1888 by the co-founders of the Moulin Rouge. One of the pre-show tasks that needed to be handled were the preparations for the party Audioslave planned to throw after the gig. One of the people tasked with making the event happen was a young woman named Vicky Karayiannis.

Karayiannis was of Greek heritage; strikingly beautiful with long brown hair, large almond-shaped eyes, and bronze skin. As she was introduced to Chris, she couldn't help but notice his eyes, those brilliant blue orbs—eyes like a Husky—that pierced right through her. She didn't attend the show the next night, but at the after-party at L'Avenue their paths crossed again.

"Well, where were you, out having a sandwich?" Chris playfully asked. Over the course of that first evening together in the City of Lights, they made a connection. They talked until the sun came up, then agreed to stay in touch to talk some more.

With his commitments in France completed, Chris jetted across the channel to London for another round of interviews, radio gladhanding, and a show at the Astoria Theater. But he just couldn't get the incredible woman he'd met in Paris out of his head. He called her as soon as he was settled in England. A few days later, she jumped the channel herself to join him. In the coming months their bond only grew stronger and deeper. Despite the draining work of getting a new band off the ground and the punishing schedule he was on, Chris always seemed to find a spare chunk of time to book a lengthy flight back to Paris just to be close to Vicky.

In the meantime, Audioslave was taking America by storm. "Like A Stone" was released as a single in January and performed even better than "Cochise" had just a few months earlier. The song was an omnipresent force on commercial rock radio and ultimately hit number one on two different Billboard singles charts, Alternative and Mainstream Rock. One reason for the success of "Like A Stone" was the captivating video directed Meiert Avis, which featured the band miming a performance of the song inside an opulent Spanish-style mansion that had once been owned by Jimi Hendrix. As of the printing of this book, the video has well-over 600 million views on YouTube.

Then there were the concerts, beginning with a full, month-long tour that kicked off in Denver on February 21, 2003, at the Fillmore Auditorium. Midway through, Chris grabbed a bottle of water and grabbed a sip, joking at his own expense that, "This is about all I can drink anymore." An inebriated heckler held his beer aloft in protest, and

Chris quickly replied, "Tell me about it in a few years, tough guy." In a more somber moment, he dedicated his performance of "I Am The Highway," to the victims of a terrible, recent fire in a club in Rhode Island that had broken out during a Great White concert and claimed one hundred lives.

After that, they hit a wide range of intimate venues like First Avenue in Minneapolis, the Hammerstein Ballroom in New York, and the Bronco Bowl in Dallas. Every night, they played almost every single song off their debut album, along with a cover of Funkadelic's *Maggot Brain* deep cut "Super Stupid." What they refused to do was perform anything from the catalogues of their previous bands.

That run ended a month later with a show at the Paramount Theatre in Seattle where the band diversified the setlist a bit, throwing in renditions of Elvis Costello's "(What's So Funny 'Bout) Peace, Love, and Understanding," along with Rush's "Working Man." After that they did a quick swing through Australia and New Zealand before hitting a myriad of different festivals in Europe, like Super Rock in Lisbon, Portugal, Donington in the UK, and Rock am Ring in Germany. These fans were treated to a true rarity when the band busted out a funky track called "Techno Ted," an unfinished outtake from the album. The title was a reference to Detroit rocker Ted Nugent because it sounded a little bit like his song "Great White Buffalo" if played by a techno act.

Audioslave was boisterously received almost everywhere they went, but these preliminary shows were just a prologue to their biggest, and most lucrative, commitment of the summer. Lollapalooza had been on ice for six years before 2003. Perry Farrell's alternative showcase had managed to stage only one more nationwide tour after Chris and Soundgarden's run with Metallica in 1996. As Y2K had loomed, it seemed the enthusiasm and willingness to keep the festival going had simply burned out. Other travelling showcases like Ozzfest and Warped sprung up in Lollapalooza's wake, vying for the dollars in the pockets of America's youth, but Farrell was determined to resuscitate his dormant festival. With help from Microsoft—the tour was presented by Xbox—Lollapalooza was ready to make its comeback.

Jane's Addiction was on board to headline. They added Incubus, Queens of the Stone Age, A Perfect Circle, Jurassic 5, the Distillers, and the Donnas to the lineup. Farrell even brought along DIY stuntman and *Jackass* star Steve-O who fulfilled the Jim Rose Circus sideshow role with his "Don't Try This at Home" showcase. But for the second spot on the poster, the organizers knew they needed a dynamic name that would create a buzz in the alt-rock community. Audioslave was the answer.

The plan going in was to play thirty-three shows from sea to shining sea beginning on July 3. Ultimately, due to sluggish ticket sales, several dates had to either be rescheduled or cancelled, including the first gig on the docket. Lollapalooza instead kicked off on July 5 at the Verizon Wireless Amphitheater in Noblesville, Indiana. It wasn't exactly a banner day at the office. Roughly twelve thousand people showed up to the twenty-four-thousand-seat venue. Even worse, during the middle of the day, a massive downpour turned the farthest lawn area into a mud-soaked slip-and-slide. The second stage was cancelled, while the main stage schedule was pushed back an hour so that the rain could dissipate.

Despite the many environmental and logistical travails and the less-than-enthusiastic response other bands on the bill garnered, Audioslave remained a constant bright spot each day of the tour. Thousands of people screamed along with Chris, clad in a gray tank top and camouflage shorts, not only during the songs, but between them as well. The band fed not only off the energy from the crowd, but also the meteorological events that threw a wrench into so many of Farrell's best-laid plans. "I like the fireworks with all the thunder and lightning and the God shit," Chris said while lightning flashed in the distance. Jane's Addiction, who had to follow Audioslave's maniacal, high-energy set, never stood a chance.

"I just remember how powerful and amazing the shows were," Daniel Field said. "The band was all getting along, and everyone was having fun. It was sort of like an environment Chris was used to because he'd done two Lollapaloozas before that."

In Milwaukee, they got one hell of an introduction from Tom Morello's mother Mary, who declared, "I was a fan of Soundgarden, and

I was a fan of Rage Against The Machine, but the next band on is the most kick-ass band I've ever heard!" They still weren't playing songs from their previous careers, but they added a bombastic cover of The White Stripes' recently released anthem "Seven Nation Army" into the back half of the set, which kept the mosh pit churning. And when they made it back to the Seattle area at the White River Amphitheater, the band invited A Perfect Circle frontman Maynard James Keenan out for an arm-hair-raising take on Elvis Costello's "(What's So Funny 'Bout) Peace, Love, and Understanding."

After plowing through the Midwest, Lollapalooza shifted to the East Coast near the end of July. Vicky flew over from Europe to join Chris on tour while the band was based in New York and threw him a thirty-ninth birthday party at the Deck at Pier59. The celebration was briefly invaded when a Secret Service member strolled over to their table and asked if George W. Bush's twin daughters could say hello to Chris. The singer agreed and gamely engaged in the generic chit-chat, smile-and-take-picture routine he'd done for thousands of other fans over the years before sending them on their way.

Little did the Bush twins know how much the singer disdained their father. "I don't like bombing people in the name of people who pay taxes," he told a crowd at the Warfield in San Francisco a few months earlier. "It pisses me off."[4] Years later, he got to face down the forty-third president at a Kennedy Center Honors ceremony for the living members of The Who, where he screamed his heart out over that band's call to revolution, "Won't Get Fooled Again."

Vicky departed to Mykonos shortly thereafter, but the phone calls between them continued. Chris had recently written a song that he was eager to sing to her over the phone. It was a touching, acoustic ballad in which he declared that he "Got every kind of love that you will ever need / Dying here on bended knees." As he later told Cameron Crowe, "Her first indication that I was going to ask her to marry me was that song." He added, "She didn't respond enough in a way that I could…draw any conclusions from her reaction. Now she says, 'God, I couldn't believe when you were singing that to me that you didn't show up the next day with a ring.""⁵ While he used the name "Vicky" in the original version that he sang to her, he ultimately changed the name to "Josephine" as an homage to Napoleon Bonaparte's wife and a subtle tip of the cap to their courtship in Paris.

When she visited LA ahead of her own birthday in August, Chris surprised her with a room full of flowers, balloons, and wrapped gifts of all shapes and sizes. And when Lollapalooza finally finished with a performance in St. Helens, Oregon, he practically moved into the Beverly Hills Hotel just to be with her. One morning, while they were still waking up in bed, Chris asked Vicky for the necklace he had given her with a ring on it. She was reluctant but handed it over anyway. He proceeded to cut the chain and said, "I woke up and I had the strangest vision of doing this. I'm not prepared with the real ring, but I want to marry you." She was taken aback, but quickly said yes, and he slid the ring on her finger. Several months later, the couple received the news that Vicky was pregnant.

Chris and Vicky were married in a civil proceeding in Los Angeles not long after. They followed that up with a more opulent ceremony a couple months later inside a Greek Orthodox church in front of all of their friends and family. Jeff Kwatinetz stood as Chris's best man. At the reception at the Plaza Athénée afterwards, while everyone feasted on the six-foot-tall, multi-tiered wedding cake, Chris sang a song he'd recently written for his new bride. "Finally Forever," recounts the way she caught his eye, and the patience it took to win her heart. "There's no hill I would not climb for you," he promised. "No bridge I wouldn't cross."

On September 18, 2004, Chris became a father again when Vicky gave birth to their daughter, Toni, named after Vicky's mother. Then, just a shade over a year later on December 5, 2005, the pair welcomed their second child, a boy named Christopher Nicholas.

With his family growing, Chris bought an apartment in Paris and began splitting time between France and Los Angeles. Walking up and down the posh city's ancient streets, taking in the culture while surrounded by centuries-old, finely crafted art and architecture had a tremendous impact on him. The "City of Lights" made the "Emerald City" of his youth look like a frontier town.

He immersed himself in Parisian culture, learning a little bit of French while dining out at the city's finest bistros. He eventually made a more concrete mark on his adoptive city by opening a restaurant with Vicky's brother Nick Karayiannis. It was a posh spot located in the Eighth Arrondissement across the street from the Four Seasons Hotel George V, and was designed by Victoria's Secret fashion show producer Alexandre de Betak. It was the Christian Dior designer John Galliano, however, who suggested that the interior should be all black, hence the eatery's name: Black Calavados. The caramel quail was reportedly to die-for.

Chris also dipped his toes into the world of fashion, appearing as the face of designer John Varvatos' spring campaign in 2006. For the spread, Chris was photographed by Danny Clinch wearing a variety of trendy coats and semi-formal wear. The shots caused a stir among the self-proclaimed, grunge-loving authenticity police who clutched their pearls wondering whither their flannel-clad God had gone. Chris himself didn't give much thought to their gnashing. "I remember getting a little bit of shit for that," he said. "Then the next person who did it after me was Iggy Pop and that it made it seem like proof. He can kind of legitimize anything because credibility-wise he is untouchable."[6]

While his new wife and young children were rightfully taking up a majority of Chris's time and attention, he didn't lose focus on the demands from his band. The singer continued to write and demo new material for the next Audioslave album. He also reached back into his own personal archives to a song called "Ferry Boat #3" that he'd written in 1991 for *Singles.* The song hadn't yet been commercially released, and he thought Commerford, Wilk, and Morello might help him bring it to life in the explosive way that only they could. His instincts proved right, and the sparse, melancholic demo was transformed into a full-fledged rock and roll anthem. They ultimately tucked the song at the end of their second record, retitling it "The Curse."

After sharing so many stages, hotels, planes, and green rooms around the world over the preceding months, the members of Audioslave had gained a far better collective understanding of what their individual talents and weaknesses were. They'd also forged a stronger bond of trust which made for an exceedingly more efficient communication system. Unlike their first album, where they wrote in a rehearsal space and then headed into the studio, this time around they decided to do things differently.

Rick Rubin was at the helm again, but before they entered Cello Recording Studio, the band spent about two weeks in pre-production. Under the watchful eye of their Zen master, Audioslave finely honed the shapes of the different songs they hoped would make up the bulk of their next record. After that process was finished, Rubin took off and the band spent another two weeks together playing and getting even more familiar with the material.

Just as they had on *Audioslave*, the songs on *Out Of Exile* came together at an astonishing clip. "Doesn't Remind Me," which opens as a relatively sparse ballad before detonating into a fury of guitar and drums, coalesced in a matter of minutes. "I was out of town, and these guys recorded that and a bunch of other stuff on a tape, and [when I returned,] we were working on different things on the tape and then started playing that one and I thought, 'Wow, I'm surprised we're working on this, like somebody wanted to do such a simple chord progression in a song," Chris told MTV. "Personally, I would not have chosen that, which is part of the reason I love being in a band and collaborating with other people."[7]

The general vibe across the album was far sunnier than anything Chris had been a part of before. Songs like "Dandelion," in which he rhapsodizes about hummingbirds and yellow flowers, or "Yesterday To Tomorrow" where he evokes images of a world of "diamond and gold," were nearly inconceivable to Soundgarden fans.

Chris wrote most of his contributions while Vicky was pregnant with Toni and across many of the album's dozen tracks, he sounds like a man with a new lease on life. The title track offers the clearest window into his state of mind at that moment. Crooning over Morello's twitchy guitar, Chris gives the listener a small peek into his redemption as a man isolated on an island with its own fortress, until he found Vicky, "And inside her shone a young light / From her labor I was saved."

"I was already trying to dig myself out, and then that relationship challenged me on every level that way; and all in positive ways," he told Yahoo Music. "I've heard about living in the moment…and I've lived a lot of my life not really knowing what the fuck that's supposed to mean. But having a baby kind of pointed that out to me. When I'm with her I'm not thinking about anything else. It's just a huge, positive thing."[8]

That didn't mean *Out Of Exile* was entirely upbeat. He also shed some light on the darkest depths he'd sunk to in the preceding years. In "Heaven's Dead," he laments the dismal fate of the great beyond when you fall into a depression. In "Drown Me Slowly," he alludes to a sickness, "I can't fix it, not all at once." And in "The Worm," he goes even further, back to his early adolescence "when I hated everything," and "took advice from the wrong shoulder." In "Your Time Has Come," Chris reflects on the tragic, too-early deaths of a number of friends. "It's a bunch of references to people that I knew that…were younger than me who've been dead for years and years, up to a couple of years ago," Chris told MTV in 2005.

Chris didn't limit his grief in "Your Time Has Come," to people he personally knew. A recent visit to the Vietnam Veterans Memorial Wall in Washington D.C. resonated deeply with him. As he gazed at the black granite, he looked past the fifty thousand tiny names engraved so tightly next to one another and considered the real and full lives behind them. In the song he spares a moment for "All of them left brothers and sisters and mothers behind," he sang. "And most of their family and friends alive, doing time."

While he imparted little bits of hard-earned wisdom and insight across the many songs on *Out Of Exile*, Chris managed to distill the greatest lesson he'd learned over the past several years down into a single song that Audioslave chose to release as the album's first single. Over a simple, clean guitar melody and tom-kick drum beat, he soberly pontificates about the many highs and lows encountered along the journey of life—a bouquet of flowers tossed joyously into the air at a wedding countered in the next stanza by a clutch of white roses solemnly laid at the foot of a grave—and the manner in which people handle the challenges thrown their way: "Someone finds salvation in everyone, another only pain / Someone tries to hide himself, down inside himself he prays." In the end, he discovered, there's only one thing to do: "Be Yourself."

"Be Yourself" was a near-spontaneous creation. Tom Morello walked into their rehearsal studio and heard Tim Commerford messing around with a four-note bassline. The guitarist jumped in with a little melody he conceived while thinking back to The Cure's expansive 1989 masterpiece *Disintegration*. "And Chris, over that, just sang that melody in the first half-hour or so," Morello recalled. "He sits there, smoking a cigarette, listening to the groove, and steps to the microphone and sings the damn song."[9]

Three months before *Out Of Exile* went on sale, the band released "Be Yourself." The song was another winner on FM radio and before long hit number one on both Billboard's Mainstream Rock and Alternative Song charts. It was later used as the theme song to *Wrestlemania XXVI* and the sixth season premiere of the popular NBC sitcom *Scrubs*.

For the video, which features numerous opaque close-ups of Chris and the band performing the song in a high-ceilinged apartment, the singer looked back to his biggest artistic inspiration, the Beatles, for guidance. "If you watch *Let It Be*, the look of the film makes the band look like it's an important happening," he said. "I just wanted to look important, like things looked when I was a child."[10]

Critics were far more kind to *Out Of Exile* when the album finally dropped on May 23, 2005 than they had been to Audioslave's debut. David Fricke in *Rolling Stone* praised the way Chris arcs and plunges through notes "with the growling imprecision of a cornered animal," while *Pitchfork* gave the album a score of 6.8. [11] Not a glowing endorsement, but a massive upgrade over the abysmal 1.7 they awarded to *Audioslave*.

Once again, however, Audioslave proved themselves beyond critical reproach with their burgeoning fanbase. In its first week, *Out Of Exile* sold 263,000 copies in the US, enough to bump their friends System of a Down and their album *Mezmerize* from the top spot on the charts, giving the band their first number one album. It was also the first time that Chris had scored a number one record since *Superunknown* over a decade ago.

Shortly before *Out Of Exile* dropped, the band embarked on a small-scale theater tour of North America, hitting places like the Aragon Ballroom in Chicago, Roseland Ballroom in New York, the Agora in Cleveland, and the Wiltern in Los Angeles. In the midst of this, they also took off for their groundbreaking free concert in Cuba, followed shortly thereafter by a twenty-thousand-seat arena gig in Mexico City. It was during this run that they decided to throw aside their rule of not playing songs from their earlier bands, and the setlists regularly featured appearances of Soundgarden songs like "Spoonman," "Outshined," and "Black Hole Sun." Sometimes they even busted out the Temple Of The Dog fan favorite "Call Me A Dog."

Along the way Audioslave taped an appearance on *Jimmy Kimmel Live!* An entire stretch of bustling Hollywood Boulevard was shut down for the performance, but entrance was free to those willing to wait to get in. The LAPD riot squad was called in after the crowd got carried away and started breaking down the metal barricades meant to contain them when the band launched into the Rage Against The Machine cut "Killing In the Name." As the show's host later joked, "Only two times in the almost seventeen years we've been on the air has the LAPD riot police had to be called in; one was for Lionel Richie, obviously, the other was for this band and their fans."

Audioslave stuck around Southern California for another few days to play the KROQ Weenie Roast at the Irvine Meadows Amphitheater, performing ahead of Foo Fighters and the recently reunited Mötley Crüe. After that, they took off on an extensive festival circuit swing through Europe. While the shows at the Roskilde Festival in Denmark and the Montreux Jazz Festival in Switzerland were well-received, the most prominent booking on the calendar was a scheduled appearance in Berlin for the Live 8 mega-concerts.

Live 8 was the brainchild of Bob Geldof, who shook the world twenty years earlier by staging one of the grandest single-day concerts of all-time, Live Aid, that was broadcast from Philadelphia and London simultaneously. During that seminal show in 1985, Led Zeppelin reunited, Queen put on a spectacle the likes of which may never be seen again, and Phil Collins hopped a private jet so that he could perform at both locales. This time around, Geldof upped the ante and staged ten concerts around the globe, from Rome to Paris, Moscow to South Africa, Ontario to Japan, and, of course, London to Philadelphia.

The list of acts the producers managed to book for their event reads like a who's who of the biggest names in the music industry over the last five decades. Neil Young, Snoop Dogg, Stevie Wonder, Simon & Garfunkel, Jay-Z, Destiny's Child, the Eagles, Kanye West, U2, the Who, R.E.M., Linkin Park, Elton John, and Paul McCartney to name just a few. Geldof and the event's organizers even managed to pull off the seemingly impossible and got Pink Floyd to reunite for one last performance. The magnitude of the event cannot be overstated.

At the Berlin show, Audioslave was joined on the bill by fellow American acts like Green Day and Beach Boys mastermind Brian Wilson. The band kicked off their truncated set in front 150,000 people or so spread out in a long line in front of them and at least another billion watching at home with their latest single "Doesn't Remind Me" before lighting into an abbrieviated, solo acoustic rendition of "Black Hole Sun" that segued immediately into their monster hit, "Like A Stone," then finishing with "Killing in the Name." By the end, Chris had leapt off the stage and was passing around the mic to those in front, imploring them to scream "Fuck you, I won't do what you tell me!"

The size of the crowd, the general strangeness of the setup in Tiergarten Park, and most importantly of all, the feeling that he was actually helping to affect positive change in the world impacted Chris profoundly. "There was a really good feeling in the little tent city that was backstage during the two or three hours that we were there that something was happening that had never happened before, and it was a good thing and an important thing, and we were a part of it," he told journalist John W. Ennis. "For us to make any kind of a difference, to show up somewhere and play five songs, it's great! It'd be like a plumber fixing somebody's sink to help stamp out world poverty or some of these problems these countries have with devastating starvation."[12]

After finishing their latest European jaunt, the band returned to America and read through treatments for a video for "Doesn't Remind Me." After that, they largely stayed out of the public eye for the bulk of August and September to begin the pre-production process for their next album. Then it was time to hit the road again for their first-ever US head-lining arena tour.

One of the most exhilarating moments of their newly designed arena show came early on, when a large banner displaying the *Badmotorfinger* cover dropped from the ceiling and the band launched into bracing Soundgarden favorites like "Rusty Cage," "Loud Love," and "Spoonman." During the Pacific Northwest portion of the tour, like the gig in Vancouver, British Columbia, Chris even invited his old friend Artis out, to the delight of the many Soundgarden fans dotting the crowd. To spice things up, they tossed a variety of covers into the set, such as Bruce Springsteen's "Atlantic City" at the Borgata Event Center in Atlantic City.

By October, they had landed in New York City for a pair of perfor-mances at the crown jewel of concert arenas: Madison Square Garden. During the first show, Chris electrified the Big Apple crowd by revealing that the band had finished writing most of their next album. Then he gave the cue and Audioslave debuted a new song, eventually titled "Sound Of A Gun." Chris had only penned the lyrics the week before and had to read off a piece of paper to make sure he didn't mess them up. Along the tour, they also debuted another song, a funky rager titled "One And The Same."

The tour ended with a performance at the Long Beach Arena on November 18, 2005. Nearly as soon as Audioslave came off the road, but not before Chris grabbed some time off to be with his family after Vicky gave birth to their son Christopher in December, the band began work on their next album. It was a quick turnaround from *Out Of Exile*, but Chris liked it that way. "In Soundgarden, it felt like the industry put too much importance into each new release. It had to be the second coming and some epic thing every time. It created tension and pressure on the band," he told the *Pioneer Press* in 2005. "I liked the days when a band like the Rolling Stones could put out a record that I didn't like, but it didn't matter. Hüsker Dü could put out a record I didn't like, but I'd still buy the next one. When you're waiting two or three years for a follow-up, though, chances are you're not going to be so patient."[13]

Like their previous albums, the band studiously prepared by writing a wealth of new material ahead of time and had about twenty tracks in which they were confident. Four or five of them were holdovers from *Out Of Exile*, including the song "Revelations," which ended up becoming the title of their latest work. Despite its affiliation to the apocalypse as described in the Old Testament, the song is more about hypocrites living messed up lives being too willing to tell others how they should live. "You know what to do, you know what I did / Since you know everything, just clue me in," Chris sarcastically sings in the intro.

"When it came time to work on the next record, it sort of felt like, 'Well, it was super fun and easy to work with Brendan, let's do that again,'" Audioslave's manager said. The band wanted to put out music at a faster pace, and with memories of how long it had taken Rick Rubin to pull useable vocals out of Chris on *Out Of Exile*, a process that stretched out to six months, they decided to make a change. The choice of producer was obvious; it had to be Brendan O'Brien.

Audioslave could've hardly picked a better musical partner to help them put together their latest collection of lacerating rock tracks. The band loved the job he had done mixing *Out Of Exile*. He had also worked extensively with Rage Against The Machine, producing both *Evil Empire* and *Battle of Los Angeles*. And, of course, he had helped save *Superunknown* when the mixing process began to go off the rails.

Immediately, the move paid dividends. "He did all the vocals for the *Revelations* in like five or six days," Field said. "Chris was in love with Brendan. He was like, 'That was amazing! He got the best vocals out of me so fast. I love working with him.'"

For the first time since the earliest recording sessions for *Superunknown*, Chris allowed himself to be produced while recording his vocals instead of secluding himself in a separate studio to do them by himself. It was a jarring shift after a decade of doing things his own way, but Chris went along with it because he respected O'Brien's ear and musical ability. He was one of the only people on the planet capable of chiming in with an idea, question, or request for another take with which Chris felt comfortable.

In many ways, Audioslave's third album stands as the band's most cohesive-sounding and consistent work. It doesn't contain the searing "Cochise"-reminiscent highs of their debut, but the flow from song to song represents a fulfilling artistic culmination of their three years together. It's also their funkiest, most pointed release.

One of the biggest sticking points for Chris prior to joining Audioslave was that he didn't want to write political songs. While he'd touched on societal ills while in Soundgarden, especially environmentalism, he didn't care to step into the large arena that Rage Against The Machine had occupied. Along the way, he'd made statements onstage from time to time and encouraged Tom Morello in his own political endeavors. Playing in Cuba was a political act, but he still wasn't comfortable merging his artistic life with his political beliefs.

Some of those concerns fell by the wayside during the writing and recording of *Revelations*. The song "Wide Awake" was a direct shot at the Bush administration's lackluster response to Hurricane Katrina, which resulted in the deaths of more than 1,200 people in and around New Orleans. "Follow the leaders, we're in an eye for an eye, we'll all be blind / Death for murder, this I'm sure in this uncertain time." As a father, he worried more about the world that was being left to his children and channeled his concerns into his music.

Like the rest of the country, Chris was shocked by the vastness of the tragedy. Watching the footage of the Crescent City left him aghast. *How could something so terrible happen in America? How could our leaders seem to care so very little to do anything about it?* Audioslave had the music for "Wide Awake" complete before hitting the road, but Chris wrote the words while travelling to a show. "You don't think of [America] as provinces where one part of the country can be ignored over another part of the country because it's a depressed area," he said. "I felt like it was something I wanted to say and could be done in a way that was poetic and could fit inside the song and not draw undue attention to the topic that kind of detracts from the song but coexists with the music in a powerful way."[14]

Chris had always written with certain motifs in mind. Dogs and the sun pervaded the music of Soundgarden, and the open highway dominated the first Audioslave album. Among the major themes he tackled across *Revelations* were war, violence, and urban decay. The song "Broken City" for instance, was written about Detroit and the struggles the city has endured in the years since industry fled for cheaper labor in China and Mexico. Chris wrote the lyrics while on the road after rolling into Motown and gazing at all the abandoned buildings that once served as the beating heart of America's superpower-crowning manufacturing apparatus. "No one cares about climbing stairs / Nothing at the top no more."

The third track on the record, "Sound Of A Gun," centers around the experience of growing up in a city transformed from a playground to a battleground "Between the wrong and the right." He could easily have namechecked Baghdad, Fallujah, or Mosul. "Sound Of A Gun" was another holdover from *Out Of Exile* that got re-worked and re-written under O'Brien's watch. Chris had always loved the way the song was arranged, but Rubin started tinkering with it, offering different notes and directions, to Chris's chagrin. He hadn't even bothered with singing on it during those sessions, electing to leave it on the cutting room floor. Just before the *Revelations* sessions began, he returned to it, inspired enough to pen some new lyrics before debuting it to a receptive audience at Madison Square Garden.

By March 2006, the band's third album was mostly finished. They'd notched eleven tracks, but O'Brien asked if they had one more in them. He felt the record could benefit from another up-tempo rock song; a last smack across the face to leave the listeners feeling a sting when silence signaled the record's end. The next day, their last in the studio, the band came together and wrote and recorded the entirety of "Moth." Chris went home that night, wrote lyrics, came back the next day, laid down the vocals, and they were done.

"Moth" is a dynamic piece of music that alternates between quiet, contemplative verse sections and cranked-to-eleven choruses. Over the top, Chris swears in a searing voice that he doesn't "fly around your fire anymore." It was the last word on Chris's creative partnership with Audioslave.

CHAPTER XIV

YOU KNOW MY NAME

N ovember 14, 2006. Thousands of people lining the streets behind the barricades in Leicester Square crane their necks as the silver Mercedes slowly rolls to a stop. This is the very heart of London's posh West End, a mere mile down the road from Buckingham Palace and less than a ten-minute walk from the Beatles' one-time Apple Music headquarters on Carnaby Street.

Flashbulbs explode as Chris and Vicky Cornell exit the rear of the vehicle. He looks fantastically sharp in his expensive black suit, with his impeccably manicured hair and mustache. Instead of a bowtie, he's left his collar flared out and wrapped a scarf around his neck. A rock star among royalty. Photographers and fans scream his name, hoping for a nod of recognition. He smiles and waves before slowly strolling toward the red carpet.

Chris is no stranger to star-studded events. He's attended more than his fair share of galas and award shows over the years, but this particular event is different. It is the world premiere of the new James Bond film, *Casino Royale*: one of the most hotly anticipated movies of the decade. The list of luminaries on hand to catch actor Daniel Craig's initial spin as the immortal British spy is too numerous to count. Elton John, Richard Attenborough, Paris Hilton, Richard Branson—even the Queen, Elizabeth II, is in attendance to lend her special weight of gravitas to the occasion.

Chris and Vicky make their way up the stairs leading to the entrance of the Leicester Square Odeon Theatre, eager to see the film for the first time. Along the way they're intercepted by interviewers eager to hear Chris's thoughts on the film and the effort he put into crafting "You Know My Name," the theme song he contributed. "I had the big Paul McCartney anchor around my neck," he admits to one microphone-wielding presenter, referencing the latter's explosive title track to the 1973 entry in the series *Live and Let Die*. "I'm a huge fan, a huge Beatles fan, a huge fan of British music really, and so I did feel that."

After chatting with the press, the pair enters the Theatre and are escorted into a line to meet the Queen herself. Just beforehand, a person hands out mints to everyone so as not to offend the Royal nostrils with any unpleasant breath. Chris stands between one of the film's screenwriters, Neal Pervis, and his musical collaborator, David Arnold, who helped him create the song. When his moment arrives, he uncrosses his arms, gently takes the Queen's gloved hand into his own, flashes her a slight smile and subtly nods his head.

They exchange brief pleasantries, just as she has with everyone else in the receiving line. Her charming demeanor catches him off guard. *She's the Queen of England*, he thinks. "She doesn't have to say anything, but to work that hard at her age and just to be that polite to everybody I thought was amazing. It was the first time it kind of made sense to me; the monarchy in England still existing," he said later to the *Examiner*.[1]

He and Vicky leave to find their seats. As the lights go down, the screen fills with the cold, dark visage of an office building somewhere in Prague. A man in a fur hat enters a darkened office, and is greeted by James Bond, on the cusp of earning his 00 designation to kill on behalf of God and country. Bond dispatches the bad guy, and, then, after a bathroom brawl, the sound of horns blasts out of the theater's speakers and Chris's voice fills the room.

"If you take a life, do you know what you'll get?" he asks the luminaries pinned to the backs of their seats. A kaleidoscope of animated playing card-themed graphics filters across the screen as the song rattles the walls. The opening credits are vintage Bond, with different handguns shooting clubs and hearts. A rifle scope sight morphs into a spinning roulette wheel, and as Chris roars the chorus for the final time his name flashes across the screen.

"You Know My Name"
Performed by Chris Cornell
Written and Produced by Chris Cornell and David Arnold

Chris had worked on songs for films before, but nothing quite to the magnitude and importance of this particular track. As soon as he saw the rough, twenty-minute snippet of *Casino Royale* months earlier and watched Craig's unrelenting, realistic portrayal, he knew he wanted to be a part of the project. It was a huge risk, but the rewards if it worked out were immeasurable.

As he worked on the song with Arnold, he thought about previous Bond themes that he liked. McCartney's for sure, but also Tom Jones's take on "Thunderball." He appreciated the way that Jones crooned his way around the song before ending on a bombastic high note and sought to emulate that in his own work. The producers wanted a strong, male singer that could match Craig's steely-eyed performance in song. Chris was determined to give them what they were looking for.

"You Know My Name" was almost universally applauded in the press after the film debuted. *Billboard* called it the best Bond theme since Duran Duran's "A View to a Kill" in 1985. The song earned him a Grammy nomination but was snubbed from the Oscars; shut out by three different cuts from the Beyoncé-led *Dreamgirls*, a Randy Newman original called "Our Town" for Pixar's *Cars*, and, the eventual winner, "I Need to Wake Up" by Melissa Etheridge for Al Gore's climate crisis documentary, *An Inconvenient Truth*.

"You Know My Name" gave Chris a crucial jumpstart to the solo career the he was just about to renew. I say, "almost universally applauded," because there were of course the inevitable cries online from rock purists wondering aloud what in the hell the Soundgarden/Audioslave frontman was doing surrounding himself in lush orchestral arrangements.

Chris refused to give his detractors the time of day. "I was referred to as the quintessential angry young man," he said. "As far as I'm concerned, I can do anything musically. The perception outside of that is none of my business."[2]

* * *

Revelations wasn't even out yet in the summer of 2006, but word had already leaked that Chris Cornell was preparing his second solo album. Speculation ran rampant that Audioslave was on the cusp of disintegration. Near the end of July, Chris talked to MTV to try and tamp down the rumors, while also admitting that he was plotting his next steps as a solo artist. "You would hope that by now, putting out our third record, people wouldn't be thinking that way or be worried about it, but it comes up," Chris said. "I always just ignore it."[3] The rumors, however, combined with reports that Rage Against The Machine was entertaining seven-figure offers to reunite, were all pointing towards the end of Audioslave.

Revelations was released a few months later on September 4, 2006. Despite the growing chatter about the band's potential split, the record performed well in its first week, selling 150,000 copies and debuting at number two on Billboard's Top 200. *Revelations* was blocked from repeating *Out Of Exile*'s impressive number-one showing, however, thanks to the release of Beyonce's second studio album *B'Day*, which sold half a million copies that same week.

Audioslave decided not to tour in support of the album. The band did the necessary press to satisfy their label, but without a big push and the promise of live shows to entice fans to buy into the songs, the album quickly faded from the Top 200. And yet the lead single, "Original Fire," still managed to break out, hitting numbers three and four on Billboard's Alternative and Mainstream Rock charts respectively. Even as a fading concern, Audioslave remained a commercial success.

Before Chris could dig into his own project, he still had to figure out what to do about *Casino Royale*. It had been nearly two decades since the last time a male singer had recorded a Bond theme. Now, with Daniel Craig taking over from Pierce Brosnan and bringing a decidedly more·

brutal and masculine take on the iconic British spy, Sony Pictures president of music, Lia Vollack, brought Chris in to see if he could create something that mirrored this aesthetic.

After talking things over with Vollack, Chris flew to Prague to get a sense of what the film was about and came away impressed. While in Eastern Europe, he met David Arnold, *Casino Royale*'s composer, and they discussed the different approaches they had in mind. The pair worked on musical ideas and lyrics separately before coming back together and comparing notes. "I went up to his apartment in Paris, and he played me his idea and I played him my ideas," Arnold said. "We'd kind of written parts of the same song simultaneously, and it all came together amazingly well."[4]

One thing they agreed on from the jump was that they didn't want to write a song using the name of the movie. Chris couldn't see a way into the music using *Casino Royale* without sounding corny. Instead, he focused on Bond's journey, and the grueling toll saving the world takes on a human being. There was a bit of himself in the song too. "It is partially inspired by the story, as acted by him, and partially from personal feelings and experience."[5]

After marrying music to words, Arnold and Cornell made a quick demo to show to the film's producers and got their approval to proceed. They rented time at the legendary Beatles producer George Martin's AIR Studios in London and recorded the basic guitar/vocal/bass tracks themselves while bringing in a studio drummer to lay down the beat. By November, he was walking red carpets and chatting with the Queen.

At the same time, Chris was writing songs for his second foray as a solo artist. Of all the records that Chris made in his life, *Carry On* is far and away the most sentimental. The vibe across its fourteen tracks hovers somewhere between adult-contemporary and modern pop. The project reflected his desire to turn away from the searing sounds of Audioslave into a more "mature" direction. The heaviest song on the record, "No Such Thing," was written late in the process after the suits at Interscope worried that there was a dearth of guitar-slathered rock songs for longtime fans to latch onto.

After years of lacerating his vocal cords, Chris craved a more tender sound. *Carry On* is a record about love, written by a guy deep in the throes of it. In "Disappearing Act," he rhapsodizes about "a beautiful girl / Covered cinnamon" while preaching patience in the quest for love on "Finally Forever."

"Arms Around Your Love," is about a woman who leaves her man for another man because he's such a loser. "That song should really be called 'You're an Idiot,'" he joked.[6] "She'll Never Be Your Man," is about a woman who leaves her man for another woman. "Safe and Sound" is about an innate desire to live in a world that's…safe and sound: "A place where you walk safely no matter your color or age."

To produce *Carry On*, Chris tapped celebrated producer Steve Lillywhite. Lillywhite was an esteemed pop-rock music veteran by 2006, who cut his teeth early in the eighties working with the likes of Peter Gabriel, The Rolling Stones, and Rush. He's best known for his work with U2: a partnership that dates back to the Irish band's beginnings when he produced their debut album *Boy*. Since then, he'd helped oversee some portions of eight of the group's subsequent records, including *The Joshua Tree*, *Achtung Baby*, and *How to Dismantle an Atomic Bomb*.

"I heard the demos, but it was more about hearing the voice," Lillywhite said. "He had a great falsetto and a great tenor. Not all singers can tick all the boxes and sing all the octaves, but he really could. Bono has that, but Chris has it even better."

The pair entered NRG Recording Studios in North Hollywood in October. The first thing that struck Lillywhite after meeting Chris was how blissfully unpretentious he was. The producer had logged countless hours with some major prima donnas in his time, but Chris was free of the trappings of being a rock star. He carried his own equipment, didn't have a personal assistant, and kept things low-key.

"I would sometimes walk through the green room and he was constantly on his Blackberry," Lillywhite said. "I was thinking he's running this whole empire from just his Blackberry. He's doing it all himself! Then one time I walked past him, and I happened to look over his shoulder and he was playing the brick breaker video game."

The recording process for *Carry On* went smoothly, maybe too much so. Outside of their request to add a few guitar-heavy songs, the label largely stayed out of their way. To help with guitar, Chris tapped Gary Lucas, who had worked with his old friend Jeff Buckley on the singer's lone studio album *Grace*, while a collection of studio musicians filled out the rest of the music. The most notable hiccup came while Chris was riding to the studio one day on his motorcycle, a $50,000 Exile chopper. He was smashed from behind by a large truck and sent flying twenty feet into the air. As the pavement loomed closer to his face, "I was sort of thinking, 'This is an actual accident. I hope it's not as bad as it feels like it's going to be.'"[7]

Fortunately, he was wearing his helmet and came away scratched up, bruised, and with a potentially broken finger, but no lasting, major physical damage. Instead of heading home or to a hospital, he simply made his way to the studio and got down to the business at hand. "He wasn't the sort of guy to make a big thing out of something," Lillywhite said.

Of all the songs on *Carry On*, the most unexpected entry was Chris's cover of Michael Jackson's "Billie Jean." Most people wouldn't expect a grunge-rocking icon to tackle the "King of Pop," but that is exactly what made the proposition so appealing. It started as a joke. During Audioslave's last tour, Chris regularly took over a portion of the set to play a few songs by himself on acoustic guitar. After a while, he decided to mix things up to make the other three guys in the band laugh. "I figured they had to stand there and watch me every night, I thought I'd do some songs they'd never expect," he said.

Now in the studio with one of those tracks, he couldn't get the bassline to work quite right. "So, I switched it to kind of a 6/8 gospel time signature. Suddenly it wasn't funny, but it was a great song. It's a lament, really." Slowing the music down gave him more space to croon over the verses while accentuating the gripping narrative of the song itself. Whereas on the original Jackson sounds alternately defiant and aggrieved, Chris howls his way through "Billie Jean" like a wounded animal. "We cut that quite late, ten o'clock one night," Lillywhite remembered. "Turned all the lights down. That was a live vocal. He never re-cut the vocal."

At the dawn of 2007, *Carry On* was largely complete. In addition to the twelve original tracks he composed, and the Michael Jackson cover, Chris had worked out a deal with Sony to keep "You Know My Name" off the official *Casino Royale* soundtrack. He included it as the final track on this album. It was a canny bit of marketing on his part that enhanced the album's commercial prospects. Everything was rolling toward a Spring release, but there was one thing he had to do. He had to announce the end of Audioslave.

On January 22, 2007, Coachella revealed their yearly lineup of artists and, even judged against their typical eyebrow-raising standards, it was a doozy. Over the past several years, the Southern California-based music festival had drawn loads of attention for helping reunite a breathtaking array of seemingly un-reuniteable bands like The Stooges, the Pixies, and Bauhaus. That year they topped themselves by nabbing Rage Against The Machine.

Audioslave's end seemed like a mere formality. Chris made it official just a few weeks later, releasing a curt statement. "Due to irresolvable personality conflicts as well as musical differences, I am permanently leaving the band Audioslave," he wrote. "I wish the other three members nothing but the best in all of their future endeavors." The band read about his decision in the press. He hadn't spoken to them directly in months.

Shortly after Audioslave dissolved, Tom Morello suggested that people looking for a definitive answer would be best served watching the satirical mockumentary film *Spinal Tap*. "Bands are either able to get over those hurdles because of friendship or belief in the music or avarice or whatever it is that makes bands stay together, or they're not," the guitarist told JamBase. "We were unable to kind of get past some of the disagreements that we had."[8]

Chris pulled the curtain back on his own motivations while speaking to *Rolling Stone* shortly after sharing his statement. "Getting along as people is one thing, getting along as a group of people that can work together in a band situation...we weren't particularly getting along well, no," he said.[9] "I was tired of what ended up seeming like political negotiations toward how we were gonna do Audioslave business and getting nowhere with it," he added. "We had back-and-forths about that, and we also as a band sat in a room with other people trying to work this out on numerous occasions, and it wasn't really happening."

Even with a new solo album on the horizon and the memory of "You Know My Name" freshly seared into the brains of the millions of fans who bought tickets to see *Casino Royale*, interviewers couldn't help but ask him the same question over and over again in the wake of Audioslave's demise. *Do you think you'll reunite with Soundgarden?*

The fact that Rage Against The Machine seemingly beat the odds and found a way back to one another suddenly made the prospect that Chris would call up Kim Thayil, Matt Cameron, and Ben Shepherd plausible once again. Chris was kind whenever he spoke about his first band and their shared history, but he was also emphatic when the word "reunion" got brought up. Absolutely not.

"My heart was telling me that I shouldn't be in a band for a while," he said in 2007. "When I quit drinking and doing drugs, I kind of had an anxiety attack. I felt like I'd lost time and should be making up for it. I'm in my early forties, and I still feel like there's so much more music to make and experiment with before I die. Which I hope is a long time from now. I have so much to say, and there's so much more I want from music; more access to touring, writing, keeping my own pace that I just realized that I had to do the solo thing. It's where my heart is, and I'm really enjoying it. I couldn't afford to let someone else's opinion or vacation time get in the way of it."[10]

Carry On dropped on May 28, 2007. The album hit number seventeen on the charts in its first week, selling thirty-seven thousand copies. It was Chris's lowest-charting debut since *Louder Than Love*. Reviewers were divided. Some praised the father of three for taking his music in a mellower direction. Others openly pined for the maniacal screamer they knew and loved. Despite the mixed reaction and sluggish sales, Chris was determined to forge ahead alone. Just before the album's release, he hit the road for his first solo tour in nearly a decade backed by a band of hired guns, including Yogi Lonich and Peter Thorn on guitar, Corey McCormick on bass, and Jason Sutter on drums.

"He was looking for a band that could interpret all the eras of his music and do it justice and I think we did a really good job of that," Chris's guitarist Peter Thorn said. Usually opening with "Spoonman," and ending with "Jesus Christ Pose," the shows were crowd-pleasing retrospectives of his entire career up to that point, with everything from Temple Of The Dog, Audioslave, *Euphoria Mourning*, and *Carry On* packed into a sprawling two-hour window.

"He really liked to take chances and live on the edge musically," Thorn said. "At one point he sent us about ten or twelve songs to learn, many from the *Euphoria Mourning* album. Basically, he wanted us to be able to play the whole album. He maybe gave us a week's notice to try them, and we worked hard on the material but for whatever reason maybe I kind of let it go that week and we came to rehearsal at the Ventura Theater in California before a show that night and I remember scrambling trying to get all the material down by soundcheck."

Soundcheck didn't go well. It wasn't a disaster, but it was obvious that they still had work to do to nail the material. "I went up to his dressing room maybe an hour before the gig and I said, 'Hey man, I just wanna say I'm sorry we weren't a little more together in the rehearsal today, but we'll get it. I'll make sure by tomorrow.' He just looked and me and goes, 'No problem man, we're cool.' I got down the dressing room and about twenty minutes before the gig and the setlist shows up and it's all those new tunes. Starting from the beginning of the set, boom, boom, boom, boom; twelve songs. I just put my head in my hands, but then of course we got up there and we did it. That's a little bit of his humor there. In that moment he was being a little bit serious, but also taking the piss out a little bit."

Chris seemed to relish messing around with his new band. During a gig at Webster Hall in New York City much later down the line, the singer brought out a pair of electric clippers and went to town, shearing Yogi Lonich's long hair down to a buzz cut, onstage in front of a shocked crowd. The guitarist shredded as best he could for nearly three minutes of "Reach Down," busting out every trick at his disposal while Chris played barber.

After completing their quick American run, Chris and his band hopped over to Europe for a quick swing through the continent, highlighted by a massive outdoor gig at Hyde Park in London, where he opened for Aerosmith. He must have made a positive impression on the Boston rockers because years later, when Steven Tyler was plotting his own solo career and the other members of the band considered going on without him, one of the first calls they made was to Chris. He declined the opportunity and advised them to get their singer back. He passed on fronting Queen as well when they reached out to inquire about his services. Shortly thereafter, they discovered Adam Lambert and became a touring bonanza once again.

The next year of Chris's life was largely dominated by an unceasing string of live shows. He continued his headlining tour of America through the winter, then the following year he hooked up with Linkin Park for their annual Projekt Revolution Tour, which kicked off in Mansfield, Massachusetts, on July 16, 2008. It wasn't quite Lollapalooza '92, but the camaraderie was real. "That was a great summer," Peter Thorn said. "It was like going to summer camp. We'd all hang out between the bands."

Chris and Linkin Park had met the year before when Chris supported the band during a quick-hitting tour of Australia. Chris hit it off immediately with Chester Bennington, who forever earned his respect after the Linkin Park singer broke his wrist three songs into one of their shows down under. Instead of seeking medical attention, Bennington just kept on singing.

Each night during the Projekt Revolution Tour, Bennington made his way out during Chris's set to duet with him on "Hunger Strike." Chris returned the favor later on in the evening, guesting on Linkin Park's mournful ballad "Crawling." The regular meetings between two of the most celebrated voices in rock shook the arenas to their foundations and sent the crowds into hysterics. After the tour ended, the two singers remained close—so close, in fact, that Chris named Bennington godfather of his son Christopher.

"You have inspired me in many ways you could never have known," Bennington wrote about Chris years later. "Your talent was pure and unrivaled. Your voice was joy and pain, anger and forgiveness, love and heartache all wrapped up into one. I suppose that's what we all are. You helped me understand that."[11]

After *Carry On* faded from the charts, Chris was hanging out with his brother-in-law, a Parisian night club owner, who presented him with the idea to remix some of the album's songs for re-release. Chris's management team got in touch with Timbaland to see if he might be interested in collaborating and making that happen. By 2009, Timbaland was widely regarded as one of the most reliable hit-makers in hip-hop, having worked with the Aaliyah, Jay-Z, Missy Elliott, and Ludacris, to name a few. Several years earlier he crossed over into the pop world thanks to his wildly successful collaboration with Justin Timberlake on the star's debut solo album *Justified* and was as in-demand as any producer on the planet.

Timbaland wasn't sold on the idea of remixing songs Chris had already released but thought it might be cool to work on some new material together instead. It was such an unexpected idea that Chris agreed to get into a studio to see what happened. He knew heading into a project as left field as this one carried tremendous risks. The potential to alienate a dedicated audience he'd worked for over twenty years to cultivate was high.

"I don't think it's going to be like, 'It's not bad,'" he predicted of the reception to the collaboration to *Entertainment Weekly*. "I think it's gonna be 'This is absolute garbage,' or 'This is genius.'"[12] Though the press and larger cultural zeitgeist always pegged him as the savage rock screamer, his tastes had always been far more eclectic. He liked trying new things and surprising people with his music. To his mind, working with Timbaland seemed like another unexpected shift on a long creative arc.

Chris flew down to Miami and over the next five weeks cooked up twenty songs with Timbaland and the hip-hop producer's host of collaborators at both the Hit Factory and the studio inside the Setai Hotel. "I was clearly the odd man out in the group in that room the whole time, but there's also an aspect of that that was the whole reason I wanted to do it and made it exciting," he told the *Stranger's* Sean Nelson. "There were some anxious moments, and some of what we came up with creatively came out pretty special because of the strange combination."[13]

One of his main collaborators was a producer from Philadelphia named Jim Beanz, who worked closely with Chris throughout the writing and recording process and saw just how willingly the Rock God threw himself into the pop world. "He loved the process, and he loved being around other talented musicians. A lot of artists are more about themselves, more close-minded about trying other things and other ideas. Granted, Chris knew what he wanted and knew what he liked, but he respected other artistry and other ideas."

The recording sessions typically began late, some time around ten or eleven o'clock at night, and ended at seven or eight o'clock the next morning. While they were working on different ideas, Chris would strum his guitar or play different parts on piano until it was time for him to lay down vocals. "He would go into the booth with his pad and his ink pen and shut off to the world," Beanz recalled. "He put his headphones on and shut off the lights. We always had candles, these white candles with a pineapple kind of smell." With the ambience just right, Chris would scream or croon his way over the myriad of tracks, working out different ideas and different deliveries, while also tweaking lyrics on the fly.

In addition to Timbaland, Beanz, and another producer named J-Roc, Chris was assisted on the project by two of the biggest hitmakers in pop music: Ryan Tedder of OneRepublic and Justin Timberlake. Tedder wasn't really around during the recording sessions and Chris only interacted with him briefly, but his fingerprints are all over the shiny, heavily-processed, EDM-flavored tracks like "Never Far Away," "Long Gone," "Enemy," "Other Side of Town," and "Climbing Up the Walls." Timberlake's contributions were limited to just a single song; a Middle Eastern-flavored cut called "Take Me Alive." His voice can only be heard faintly over Chris's vocals, the layers of percussion, and the buzzy keyboard melodies, but the former NYSNCer shows up midway through to double-track the song's chorus.

In almost every respect, the music on *Scream* was a dramatic departure from any and everything Chris Cornell had ever worked on. In the opening track, "Part Of Me," for example, he adopts the pose of a nightclub prowling lothario looking for some action over a glitchy, sparsely arranged pop instrumental that seems tailor-made for someone like Christina Aguilera. The chorus is jarring: "That bitch ain't a part of me," he protests, "No, that bitch ain't a part of me." The cover featured a picture of him high in the air just about to smash his guitar into kindling. You don't have to be a rocket scientist to pick up on the subtext.

When *Scream* dropped on March 10, 2009, Chris's prediction that it would either be received as a genre-altering masterpiece or a dumpster fire turned out to be 100 percent accurate. Unfortunately for him, critics and longtime fans took the latter view. Of all people, Nine Inch Nails mastermind Trent Reznor took a characteristically sharp jab, tweeting, "You know that feeling you get when somebody embarrasses themselves so badly YOU feel uncomfortable? Heard Chris Cornell's record? Jesus."[14]

The shot from one alt-rock icon to another spread like wildfire, with numerous blogs piling on to shit all over the album. In the face of intense public ridicule from his peers and critics alike, Chris held his head high. He didn't flail and launch acerbic counterattacks on his detractors. His response to Reznor was dripping with vintage Seattle sarcasm. "What do you think Jesus would Twitter?" Chris asked his social media followers. "Let he who is without sin cast the first stone" or "Has anyone seen Judas? He was here a minute ago."[15]

Scream debuted at number ten on the charts, but quickly dropped. Undeterred by the negative response, Chris hit the road for another round of extensive touring, playing in twenty-one countries along the way, including his first ever stops in Israel and Chile. In a not-so-subtle act of defiance, most of the shows from this run kicked off with "Part Of Me," before segueing into more familiar material.

Off the road, Chris established an unlikely friendship with a fan in Texas. Rory de la Rosa was reeling in 2008. His six-year-old daughter Ainslee had recently died of cancer. Not long after, he was diagnosed with the same cancer and ended up in hospice care. The pair connected over the phone. It was a courtesy call, but after hanging up Chris didn't feel right about how it unfolded and phoned Rory back. The two had an even deeper conversation.

Over the next several weeks, they maintained contact by phone and by email. Eventually de la Rosa sent him a poem he'd written titled "I Promise It's Not Goodbye." Chris was so moved by de la Rosa's words that he set them to music. "What I read gave me such a sense of relief that Rory had an insight, a strength and hope that was inspiring beyond measure," he said. "It was a pleasure to put it to music and an honor that he asked if I would ever consider it."[16]

Opening with a honky harmonica melody, the song quickly morphs into a tender, tear-inducing ballad about life, love, loss, and what awaits us beyond this mortal plane. "Now Daddy, please don't cry," Chris asks on Ainslee de la Rosa's behalf. "I'm still here every day." With Rory de la Rosa's consent, Chris released the song in April 2009 on his website as a free download, while encouraging those who listened to it to contribute to the family's enormous medical expenses. Sadly, Rory de la Rosa passed away just a few months after "I Promise It's Not Goodbye" was released.

While Chris continued to promote *Scream*, he also started looking back on his life and considered all that he had accomplished. That included Soundgarden. One day while he was driving around listening to the radio, "Pretty Noose" started blasting out of his speakers. "Frankly, it just crushed the newer songs before it and after it and had more of a timelessness to it," he thought. For whatever reason, the moment became an epiphany. "I realized Soundgarden had become a 'classic' kind of band, the kind that wasn't going to go away."[17]

As he considered Soundgarden's role as a crucial force along the long arc of rock and roll history, he thought about how neglected their legacy had become. One day he walked into a store hoping to buy a shirt with his old band on the front for his son, only to discover they didn't have a single Soundgarden item in stock. There was a myriad of Nirvana, Pearl Jam, and Guns N' Roses merch ready to scoop up, but that familiar *Badmotorfinger* logo was nowhere to be found.

While his contemporaries were bringing in whole generations of new fans by re-issuing their catalogs, chock-full of unheard gems, Soundgarden's back catalog gathered dust. The band didn't even have an official website. It rubbed him the wrong way, so he reached out to Matt,

Kim, and Ben to see if they'd be down to have a meeting to figure out how to maintain their legacy.

A lot had happened to his former bandmates since that fateful day in 1997 when Chris visited each of their houses to tell them it was over. Cameron had remained the busiest of the three, touring the world several times over and recording three albums as the full-time drummer in Pearl Jam. He wasn't just a hired hand either. Cameron regularly wrote and contributed material to their records—"You Are" on *Riot Act* is stealthily one of the best deep cuts in Pearl Jam's discography—and the band welcomed his intrinsic understanding of music's more difficult-to-comprehend technical aspects. "Matt Cameron writes songs and we run to find step stools in order to reach his level," Eddie Vedder wrote in the liner notes to the compilation album *Lost Dogs*. "What comes naturally to him leaves us with our heads cocked like the confused dogs that we are.... Did we mention he's the greatest drummer on the planet?"[18]

Though a stream of different musical opportunities had been presented to him after Soundgarden broke up, Thayil largely remained out of the spotlight. He participated in collaborations when his interest was piqued, like the song "Blood Swamp" on the Boris/Sunn O))) album *Altar*. He also played in two, short-lived bands with two surviving members of Nirvana: a punk group called the No WTO Combo with Krist Novoselic and Jello Biafra that formed to protest the WTO Ministerial Conference in Seattle in 1999, and a heavy metal side project cooked up by Dave Grohl called Probot five years later. Outside of that, he remained persona non grata in the world of rock.

Shepherd had had perhaps the hardest time of any of them in the intervening years. The end of Soundgarden was a crushing blow. "My whole life seemed over," he told *Spin*. "Soundgarden broke up; my other band, Hater, broke up; my fiancée broke up with me; and then I broke three ribs. I got addicted to pain pills, drank a ton, and wound up *OD*-ing on morphine. I was laid out in my house for five days, and no one knew it."[19]

He still made music, collaborating with the likes of Josh Homme, Mark Lanegan, and Black Sabbath's riff maestro Tony Iommi. But then Soundgarden sold the building where they housed their stuff, and all of his gear was stolen, including the '72 Fender Jazz bass he bought from Andrew Wood and his brother Kevin that he had used on every Soundgarden record. The thieves also took two different solo records that he'd spent massive amounts of time working on. He was devestated. "For a few years I thought, 'Alright, the world's telling me nobody cares—fuck it, I won't play.'"[20] Shepherd took up carpentry and figured that his time as a professional musician was over.

The initial Soundgarden conclave took take place on September 10, 2008. The four members of the band, along with Pearl Jam's manager Kelly Curtis, got together, strolled down memory lane, and started hashing things out. The meeting went well, and for the first time in well over a decade there was a sense among them that Soundgarden might not only be a historical concern. "It felt really great," Chris recalled. "That led to a discussion, 'Maybe we should get back into a room and play songs?'"[21]

As Chris continued with his solo career, back in Seattle his three former bandmates hit the stage together for the first time in a dozen years during a show headlined by another one of his former bandmates. Tom Morello was on the road under the guise of his solo project the Nightwatchman, and had a gig lined up at the Crocodile Café on March 24, 2009. After inviting Kim out to play the MC5 favorite "Kick Out the Jams," along with Mark Arm and Wayne Kramer, Morello announced to the crowd, "I haven't been this fucking excited about something in a long time. It's like I won some type of contest or something!" Then, he introduced Matt Cameron, Ben Shepherd, and Tad Doyle, who ripped into a three-song mini-set of "Nothing To Say," "Spoonman," and "Hunted Down" that left jaws on the floor.

It wasn't Soundgarden—the press took to referring to the quasi-reunion as TADGarden—but it was the clearest indication yet that the tensions had thawed between three-quarters of the band at the very least. "I just really thought it was a cool thing for them to do," the singer said when asked about the show by the *Washington Post*. "The only thing I didn't like is that I wasn't there to see it. If I was there, I probably would've gotten up on stage."[22]

Over the next several months, the chatter about a potential full-blown Soundgarden reunion intensified. It hit a new crescendo in April when Chris and his solo band hit Seattle to play the Showbox SoDo, just down the street from Safeco Field. Though none of his old bandmates joined him onstage, Kim showed up to watch. Afterwards, Chris posed for a photo with his arm slung around the guitarist and social media blew up with fevered speculation.

In the meantime, Chris made a different splashy Seattle reconciliation of his own when he joined Pearl Jam onstage during their encore at the Gibson Amphitheater on October 6, 2009, for an electrifying duet of "Hunger Strike" that sent the LA crowd into a frenzy. "One person's presence can really turn something into a special occasion," Eddie Vedder said. "That's the case and that's what we have for you tonight." Emerging from the shadows in an oversized green coat, Chris hugged or high-fived every member of Temple Of The Dog and then proceeded to sing and scream his lungs out in unison with Vedder for the first time in well over a decade.

Then, on New Year's Eve, a bombshell. After a long spell of careful planning, Chris sent out a tweet ostensibly to give Soundgarden's fans a heads-up that their official website was about to go online. But to the fans who read it, the ones who'd long held out hope for the resurgence of their grunge-metal gods, the message presented a glimmer of hope that their prayers were about to be answered.

"The 12 year break is over & school is back in session," Chris wrote. "Knights of the Soundtable ride again!"

CHAPTER XV

BEEN AWAY TOO LONG

T hirteen years, two months, and seven days.
That's eight years longer than the time it took to construct the tallest building on the planet, the Burj Khalifa in Dubai, nearly four years longer than the time it took for the New Horizons space probe to fly the 4.67 billion miles between the Earth and the former planet Pluto near the outside edge of the Solar System, nearly three years longer than the entire duration of World War I and World War II combined.

Thirteen years, two months, and seven days.

That's how long it took for Soundgarden to play together again after that disastrous evening in Hawaii when it all fell apart. The long-awaited reunion took place at the Showbox; a dark, open-floored venue across the street from Pike's Place Market on 1st Avenue in Seattle. Soundgarden had played there just after *Badmotorfinger* dropped in 1992. One of the city's greatest artistic entities reborn like a phoenix smack dab in the middle of its own beating heart. It *had* to happen here.

To enhance the mystique surrounding their return, the band performed under a pseudonym, scrambling the letters in Soundgarden to become the more evocatively named Nude Dragons. The moniker emblazoned on the Showbox's marquee was a nod back to a similar "secret" gig the band performed at the Central Tavern near the dawn of the nineties. The subtext behind the moniker was blaringly obvious to those in the know. This was a show for the real Soundgarden heads; those who had been there from the beginning, those who had waited so patiently for this exact night, worrying with each passing month that it might never come to pass. The outside world would get their chance to fawn over Soundgarden and celebrate their return in the coming months, but this show was for their truest believers.

From the ferocious opening notes of "Spoonman," it was loudly obvious to the eleven hundred people packed into the Showbox that this wasn't a band content to coast along on reputation alone. They had something to prove, not only to their fans, but to themselves.

Matt Cameron was still the powerhouse polyrhythmic guru driving everything with the force and roar of a V-8 engine. Ben Shepherd brought the menace-inducing low end, stomping around onstage like a pissed-off Frankenstein. Kim Thayil still ripped into solos like no one else, deploying his wah-wah pedal with psychedelic mayhem. And Chris was still screaming with the vigor of a man half his age while swinging the microphone stand over his head as the band blasted into an atomic take on "Outshined."

As incredible and cathartic as the performance was for the four figures onstage, it meant even more for the faces beyond the stage. Scattered among the crowd were some of their oldest friends; those that had helped them take their first steps toward superstardom. Members of Pearl Jam and Mother Love Bone, Sub Pop's Jonathan Poneman, Mark Arm from Mudhoney, and Tad Doyle to name a few. "That was a beautiful show," their onetime sound guy Stuart Hallerman said. "One of the best shows I ever saw them play. Calm, happy; Chris was smiling. Flawless-ish."

The main set ended like so many Soundgarden concerts before and after, with a seismic "Slaves & Bulldozers." The volume swelled and the ceiling shook as Chris repeatedly asked, "What's in it for me?" before being consumed by a massive wall of wailing feedback. "Thanks, everyone out there that's made all the positive comments and been so supportive about us playing music together again," Chris told the crowd. "It's not lost on us."

* * *

That first meeting between Chris Cornell, Ben Shepherd, Matt Cameron and Kim Thayil after so many years apart began with an awkward reticence, but it passed quickly. "After five minutes, we're remembering when the roadie was lighting his farts, and when someone was in a blackout and swinging from a chandelier," Chris told *Revolver*. "That went on for, like, an hour and a half. And once that was going on, it felt like…you just become a band again."[1]

The vibe was good and the four agreed to proceed with plans to negotiate new licensing deals, look into merchandising, and set up a website, among other things. They also decided to dig through their archives with an eye toward re-issuing albums with unheard material.

The first item in the chute was a greatest hits package called *Telephantasm*. The album went platinum right out of the box when it was released on September 23, 2010, thanks to a packaging deal with the makers of *Guitar Hero: Warriors of Rock*, who bundled a million copies with their latest release. *Telephantasm* also fulfilled their original contract with A&M Records, making them free agents should they desire to pick up their instruments again.

To entice diehards and non-gamers who might scan the tracklist and see they had all of these songs, Soundgarden included "Black Rain," a song that hadn't made it onto *Badmotorfinger*. "Black Rain" still needed some work, so Chris rewrote it and re-recorded some of the vocals. After Kim overdubbed guitar, they salvaged it from the scrap heap of history. The song blossomed into a heavy, despair-riddled behemoth that instantly reminded lapsed listeners why they loved Soundgarden in the first place. As an added bonus, the band allowed Brendon Small, the showrunner behind *Metalocalypse*, to direct a video for "Black Rain" featuring incredibly vivid, animated scenes of gigantic monsters battling an army of the future. Ultramega indeed.

With *Telephantasm* complete, the band moved on to digging through Adam Kasper's dormant recordings of their 1996 West Coast tour for a collection dubbed *Live On I-5*. Chris flew in to Seattle and spent a week poring over the mixes inside Bad Animals Studio, now called Studio X, the site of his greatest artistic triumphs during the *Superunknown* sessions. It was the Friday of his second week in town that he confronted the other three guys in Soundgarden with the idea to jam.

The experience was cathartic for Chris, who was delighted to realize that his old band was maybe even better than he remembered. "It was nothing but fun trying to figure out what is the best way to remember some of these songs," he told *Consequence of Sound*. "I was really happy and surprised at how great those arrangements were and how smart we were as record producers and songwriters."[2]

What began casually quickly turned into something more serious. Yet, one member remained reluctant. "I saw them at Studio X the next day and Chris was like, 'That was fun last night! I'm gonna fly home, but when I come back, wanna jam again?'" Stuart Hallerman recalled. "Kim was like, 'No, man! The band is not my girlfriend! That was fun, but I don't want this to keep happening. Then we'll do this all the time!' But then they did. I think by the end of the week the Lollapalooza offer was coming, and they talked about it for a while."

Lollapalooza wasn't the only entity interested in securing a Soundgarden reunion set. Ever since Chris sent out his "Knights of the Soundtable" tweet, a deluge of offers from festivals and promoters poured in hoping to cash in on a big-name return to the spotlight. The eye-popping number of zeros attached to those offers was enticing. Though Lollapalooza had changed a lot—it was no longer a touring festival, existing instead as a three-day musical extravaganza in Chicago's Grant Park and accommodating around a hundred thousand fans per day—there was something about Soundgarden's shared history with the event that made sense.

They accepted the offer and started rehearsing, first at Pearl Jam's space, and then at Hallerman's Avast! "They hadn't played together in thirteen years, but it was their second rehearsal and they could obviously play," the producer said. "Matt's like, 'Yeah, I could play this set tomorrow.'"

Just shy of two years after meeting to deal with their legacy, and four months after the Showbox gig, Chris Cornell strode out onto the Grant Park stage, Gibson ES-335 in hand, ready to remind the tens of thousands bellowing out in the summer darkness what he and his band could do. His hair, nearly back to its '92-era length, cascaded down his white Grand Canyon t-shirt as he screamed the phrase "to the sky!" over and over again throughout the first song, "Searching With My Good Eye Closed."

The dour-looking dudes once derided by some as "Frowngarden" were in great spirits. "This is our millionth time playing Lollapalooza," Chris joked. "It's good to be back!" Before the start of "Outshined," he waded into the sea of fans up front, shrieking the song's opening verse among a roiling churn of humanity.

In the immediate aftermath of Lollapalooza, the future of Soundgarden remained murky to outside observers. It wasn't until several months later that the band gave their fans a measure of clarity via a message on their website. "Over the past few months, we've been busy jamming, writing and hanging out together—exploring the creative aspect of being Soundgarden," they wrote. "It feels great. We have some cool new songs that we are going to record very soon."

In the meantime, Chris worked to maintain a measure of musical independence. In the spring, he embarked on an extensive run of his own, hitting twenty-five intimate theaters on what he called the Songbook Tour. Each night, for two hours, he regaled rapt fans with the power of his voice accompanied by acoustic guitar, pulling out tracks from each era of his career, along with a wide range of covers like the Beatles' "A Day in the Life," Elvis Costello's "(What's So Funny 'Bout) Peace, Love, and Understanding," and Bob Marley's "Redemption Song." Each night was different as he largely eschewed writing setlists, preferring to play whatever came to him in the moment.

The stage was sparce, reflecting the stripped-down vibe of the music. There were two props that had emotional significance to him. The first was Jeff Buckley's red telephone perched on a stool right next to him. As he was packing to hit the road, he had impulsively grabbed it and decided to make it part of the set, drawing comfort from the simple reminder of his departed friend. The second was a record player that he used to play a vinyl pressing of Natasha Shneider's piano on "When I'm Down" that he sang along to. "I had to convince her to play this style of music,"

Chris told the crowd at the Strand Theater in 2015. "She was Russian and didn't think she could do it. She basically said, 'Fuck you, I can't play that shit!' And then she did it unlike anyone ever, so this is the only way I like to sing it."

The solo shows took him outside of his comfort zone. He'd always been more comfortable in a band setting, even as a solo artist. The pressure to entertain on his own was intense, so he committed to rehearsing and nailing the performances. More often than not, that meant playing in the bathroom; the one place a father of young children can find solitude. "Nobody would bother me. People don't want to run in to the bathroom," he said. There was something about the tight walls and echo that appealed to him. It eventually got to the point where once he finished writing a piece of music, he'd have to run it through the washroom to see how it sounded. "Once it's a written song with words, I think 'Well, let's see if this works.' I go in the bathroom and play it."[3]

Months after the solo run ended, Chris collected some of the recordings from the tour and released them as part of a live album dubbed *Songbook* that hit stores on November 21, 2011. Along with unplugged versions of fan favorites and deep cuts was a new song called "The Keeper," that he had recorded for the film *Machine Gun Preacher*.

Chris initially struggled to relate to the film's story of Sam Childers, a biker-turned-activist who founded an African orphanage. Inspiration struck when he considered the aesthetic of one of America's foremost troubadours, Woody Guthrie. "The feeling was that if Sam Childress... if he were Woody Guthrie and he were writing a song, what would that song be?" he said. "Because Woody Guthrie's songs were very simple and very direct like Sam is, and very matter-of-fact."[4] "The Keeper" is one of the more tender and evocative compositions of Chris's latter-day career. It also netted him his first and only Golden Globe nomination for Best Original Song.

Even though his plate was becoming increasingly full, Chris also did a bit of extracurricular recording. He wailed for Carlos Santana's take on the Led Zeppelin classic "Whole Lotta Love" for the legend's *Guitar Heaven*. He also sang on a track called "Lies" by Italian pop group Gabin on their album *Third and Double*. Most sensational of all, he connected with Slash for a song called "Promise" on his eponymous solo project. "'Promise' was probably the most unorthodox piece of music that I'd written, it was very different," Slash told MusicRadar. "I sent it to him, and within forty-eight hours he sent me this great lyric and we were off and running. It was as simple as that."[5]

Meanwhile, behind the scenes, Soundgarden was still rolling forward. They booked festival appearances in Ottawa and New Orleans, before announcing a summer tour while Chris was wrapping up his Songbook Tour. It would keep them on the road through most of July 2011, hitting familiar venues like the Molson Amphitheater in Ontario, which they'd headlined with Nine Inch Nails back in '94, and the magnificent Gorge Amphitheater in central Washington, where they had opened for Metallica in '96.

With every new gig, Chris's confidence and comfort grew. "I don't think it was like riding a bike. I think our body of work is too big, our songs are complicated. There's that 'all eyes on you' kind of thing," he told the *Toronto Sun*. "It wasn't until we actually got out and played a few shows that I started to feel like we were the Soundgarden that I remember."[6]

Things had been looking up within the band since Matt Cameron had sent a message to the guys letting them know he'd been working on new music that he was ready to share with them. This was shortly after Lollapalooza. After checking everyone's schedules, Cameron booked time in the studio in November 2010 and the four of them convened to mess around with the drummer's creations. One song Cameron brought to the group was "Eyelid's Mouth." Cameron had the guitars and drums arranged and wanted to hear what the other guys could add—whether they could Soundgardenize his ideas. If his goal was to inspire his bandmates, it was mission accomplished. "We were trying to get it to be a David Bowie *Diamond Dogs*—sounding era," Shepherd recalled.[7]

Time had done little to dull the chemistry between the four fingers of grunge rock's most vicious clenched fist. They could still punch with frenzied rage. Musical ideas sprung to life in the room and there was no longer any question about making a new album. The only impediment was finding a window in their busy schedules. Fortunately, because they were working without a record deal in place, they could write, rehearse, and record at their own pace, free from external pressure. Soundgarden's musical return would happen on their own terms.

The technological leaps in email since the last time Soundgarden had worked on music in the late '90s certainly helped keep things moving at a good clip. Chris often sang at home over stereo mixes. He edited on his computer and then sent files back to everyone else to critique. An early boon from the band's digital dialogue was a track called "Rowing." Shepherd had cooked up the swirling, mechanical-sounding bass riff during one of their jam sessions. Because they recorded everything, Chris managed to isolate a loop of it on his computer and turned it into a full-fledged song. "That was before we'd even written or jammed out a lot of songs," the bassist recalled. Hearing "Rowing" for the first time was a crystallizing moment for Shepherd who felt that the gloves were truly off. "Chris was motivated and already took the next step so, we had a full, concrete song for once."[8]

By February, they reconvened at Studio X. Adam Kasper was brought in again to produce and was pleasantly surprised to find the band in a prolific mood. "It didn't seem like we missed much of a beat at all," he said. "We had the songs—the demos—and we'd all been listening to them, and we just got to work."

Chris commuted to Seattle from his residence in Miami, but most of the vocals that ended up on the album were actually recorded by Chris at his home studio. Nevertheless, the vibe at Studio X was good. "[Chris] had, like, a buddy with him: this guy Paul who was like a sponsor-type guy," Kasper remembered. "Really nice dude. He would kinda come in with him. It was a good team: family, friends, local guys. Very comfortable atmosphere."

Soundgarden titled their return album *King Animal*. The name was pitched by Thayil after the macabre, bone-strewn image created by sculptor Josh Graham was chosen. It was the first time they had picked a cover before they had landed on a name. "I was badgering Kim to come up with something brilliant, like he's done before," Chris said. "He's the one who blurted out 'Badmotorfinger!' and 'Ultramega OK!'"[9]

Of the thirteen songs that made the final tracklist, four were credited solely to Chris. Three of them were stacked together on the latter half of the album, beginning with a miasmic, acoustic-based track called "Black Saturday." After that was the more pop-flavored "Halfway There," followed by "Worse Dreams," which opens with a frenetic-but-controlled riff that brings to mind AC/DC's "Thunderstuck" mixed with a dull moaning guitar drone that sounds like the guttural death rattle of an ailing mastodon.

His other song is the truly despondent sounding "Bones of Birds." Lyrically, it was inspired by his innate fear of his children losing their innocence when the world inevitably reveals its harsher nature. "It's never a good thing," he said. "It's always because of loss or something bad happened, or something they weren't expecting. I guess it's the stress I feel about it. Not wanting them to have to go through those things, but obviously knowing it's gonna happen."[10]

Just as he had on *Superunknown* and *Down On The Upside*, Chris locked in creatively with Ben Shepherd. They shared credits for "Rowing," which was positioned as the closer, while also hammering together a ferocious rock track that screamed *single*. It didn't have a name while they were working on it, as Chris remained stuck trying to find a thematic throughway to the music. They referred to it as "EBE," after the song's tuning structure, EEBBBB. It was the same tuning that Ben Shepherd had used decades earlier on the *Badmotorfinger* cut "Somewhere."

"I had a hard time writing lyrics to it because it seemed whole," Chris recalled. "One night I couldn't sleep, and I had some uptempo, punk rock-y song in my head, with that line, 'I've been away for too long.' I thought, 'Well, that might be a cool new Soundgarden song.'"[11] "Been Away Too Long" might be a little too on-the-nose for a lead single on a reunion album, but in the face of that exhilarating guitar fade-in, Cornell's blistering vocals, Cameron's thunder of drums, and Shepherd's reliable bottom end, who could complain?

Shepherd had ideas of his own that he'd been honing from years earlier, including a simmering, bluesy track called "Taree" that he originally intended to put out as part of a solo record. He'd never recorded vocals for it, however, and privately hoped to get Chris to sing it one day. The bassist's instincts were dead-on. "When he cut that vocal, I was just like, 'Shit!'" Adam Kasper said. "That was kind of [the] thing with those guys, Chris, Cobain, and Vedder. When they stepped off to deliver it, man, it was like, 'Woo! It's so good.'"

Two of the most compelling songs on the album, however, were written by Thayil. Both of them sounded the like vintage, metal Soundgarden. "A Thousand Days Before" might be the high-water mark of *King Animal*. Prior to naming it, the band referred to it as "Country Eastern." It was a not-so-subtle nod to the Indian flavor Thayil brought to the track, from the raga-sounding opening and an open slide tuning, to the electric tambura added by producer Adam Kasper. The chicken-picking elements account for the countrified portion of the temporary name.

The guitarist's other major contribution was "Blood On The Valley Floor." Just like "Never the Machine Forever" on *Down On The Upside*, the song barely made it onto the finished record. It was presented to the rest of the band late in the process and became the last song they finished. After honing the music together, Chris took the track home and ruminated on a few different ideas before filling Thayil's composition with vivid allusions to things like dried blood and "eleven million clowns" wielding razors.

While recording *King Animal*, another opportunity fell into the band's lap. The producers of *The Avengers* asked Soundgarden to provide them with an original song for the soundtrack. The scale and scope of the Marvel film was beyond any film project to which they had contributed. It especially appealed to Thayil, who was a massive comic book fan. Initially, they considered giving a work-in-progress from *King Animal* before opting to write something new. Chris was cognizant that the song should sound a little more conventional than typical Soundgarden fare. In other words, check the 11/8 time signature at the door. Yet, there's a lot of complexity at work on "Live to Rise": the alternating acoustic verses, the stratospheric choruses, the meandering bridge that leads to a frenzied guitar solo.

Given that Soundgarden's main priority remained finishing *King Animal*, they had to rush to complete the *Avengers* song. "I think we got Matt okayed on a Friday or something," Kasper said. "[Chris] was working with Gary Gersh to get a song approved, he'd written a new song, and all of a sudden we had to get it done by Monday." Fortunately, they managed to get "Live To Rise" in the can in the nick of time, and the song became the public's first taste of new Soundgarden material in over a decade, as part of the highest-grossing film of the year. "Live To Rise" eventually hit number one on Billboard's Mainstream Rock singles chart.

Though they originally expected to finish working on *King Animal* sometime in 2011 and release it that year, the process stretched out much longer. By the spring of 2012, they sewed everything up and eyed an October release, which got pushed back to November 13, 2012. They inked an agreement with Tom Whalley, the former CEO of Warner Bros. Records, on his new imprint Loma Vista Recordings. It was a one-record deal, with an option for a second.

In its first week of release, *King Animal* sold well by contemporary rock standards, moving eighty-three thousand copies. It was good enough to land them a top-five debut on the Billboard album chart, but a long way off from the sales behemoth that was One Direction's *Take Me Home*. The press was largely kind. *Rolling Stone* gave the album three and a half stars, with Jon Dolan noting Chris's ability to roll "around his multi-octave vocal range like some kind of backwoods metal-Mariah."[12] In praising the music, rock critic Steven Hyden wrote for *Grantland* that *King Animal* is "about showing that the sound of Soundgarden slowly inhaling and exhaling as a working musical unit can still be intoxicating like dreamy, smoky sludge sucked out of a honey bear bong."[13]

"Been Away Too Long" hit the airwaves a month and a half ahead of the album and did well enough to secure a number-one showing on Billboard's Mainstream Rock singles chart. The second single off the album, "By Crooked Steps," also hit number one, thanks in no small part to a hilarious music video directed by Dave Grohl featuring the band riding on Segways. If Kim Thayil can't look menacing on a Segway, no one can.

Chris maintained a punishing schedule throughout 2012. It started out in January with a Soundgarden run through Australia and New Zealand. In February, he found himself in San Francisco, the star attraction at a campaign event put together at the Masonic Temple for President Barack Obama's re-election.

Whitney Houston had only passed away a few days earlier, and Chris decided to honor her memory in front of the commander in chief by performing the iconic vocalist's signature song "I Will Always Love You." He taught himself the song while waiting to go onstage in the green room. It must have gone over well, because less than a year later, after coming out on top over Mitt Romney, Chris was invited to perform at the Commander-in-Chief Ball on the night of the inauguration.

He played three songs for military members and their families, none of which he authored. Elvis Costello's "(What's So Funny 'Bout) Peace, Love, and Understanding," made the cut, as did Creedence Clearwater Revival's searing hymnal "Long as I Can See the Light." His set ended with an ode written by his hero: "Imagine" by John Lennon. After the Commander-in-Chief Ball, Chris joined Soundgarden for the official, invitation-only public Inaugural Ball.

Soundgarden was the final act on the bill, and let's just say that some of the DC elite, garbed in their finest attire, weren't exactly thrilled to have their ribcages rattled while Chris screamed about breaking out of his "Rusty Cage." As Kim Thayil told *Pulse of the Radio* a week later, "There were definitely many people making for the exits when we started playing, because we are loud and aggressive and people in their high heels and their ball gowns probably went to some other function and realized that their evening was over."[14]

The rest of Chris's 2012 was an alternating mix of solo performances and Soundgarden shows. Along the way he managed to hit nearly every corner of the world. From Florida to France, Toronto to Tel Aviv, and everywhere in between. 2013 was equally busy. Soundgarden did a dead-of-winter swing through the biggest markets in North America, typically playing back-to-back shows in ornate theaters, twenty dates in places like the Hammerstein Ballroom in New York, the Riviera in Chicago, and the Paramount in Seattle. The last show of the run at the Wiltern in Los Angeles, an epic, two-and-a-half hour, twenty-eight-song barnburner of a set, was filmed by PBS as part of their *Live from the Artists Den* series. It was released on DVD and Blu-Ray several years later.

Soundgarden hit the road again for another nineteen dates a few months later. Then in October, Chris kicked off another thirty-date iteration of his solo tour. He'd finally reached a point in his career where he felt free to do anything, so he did. He expressed a kinship with the wily Canadian artist he'd spent two weeks opening up for while still a young man. "I kind of get Neil Young," he told *Rolling Stone*'s David Fricke. "He goes on tour with Crazy Horse, then he's out with Booker T. & the MGs. Then he's on tour by himself with seven guitars. It makes sense to me now. He's not trying to find who he is."[15]

His Elder Statesman of Rock bonafides were enhanced that April when he was asked by Ann and Nancy Wilson to induct Heart into the Rock & Roll Hall of Fame. He gave a stirring speech that night in Los Angeles, paying tribute to the Wilson sisters and their valiant assault on rock's long-entrenched patriarchy, while also tipping his hat to them for paving the way for Soundgarden and their peers. "Heart was important to us, not just as musicians, but also as proof of the fact that Seattle could produce something beautiful and rocking that the rest of the world might actually care about," he said.[16] Later that night, he checked off a childhood dream when he sang the classic blues track "Crossroads," backed by an all-star coterie of musicians that included the members of one of his all-time favorite bands, Rush.

2014 was all about Soundgarden and looking back. Chris had turned fifty, and milestones like that have a way of causing people to reflect. Coincidentally, 2014 was also the twentieth anniversary of the release of their seminal album *Superunknown*, and Soundgarden intended to celebrate in style. With the record company's backing, they cleaned up their breakout record, remastered it, plucked an array of demos, rehearsal clips, and B-sides out of obscurity, and placed them all in a massive, deluxe package. Later that year, they emptied out the rest of the archives via the three-disc box set *Echo of Miles*.

Superunknown's anniversary remained the big event, however. The band went so far as to play the entire album front-to-back at the SXSW Festival in Austin, Texas, that March. They repeated the feat at Webster Hall in New York City a few months later. In between, they played a few shows in South America before performing "Spoonman" and "My Wave" on the *Tonight Show with Jimmy Fallon*.

Nine Inch Nails' *The Downward Spiral* was also celebrating its twentieth anniversary. Coincidentally, both albums had been released on the same day. A joint tour between the alt-rock legends had originally been penciled for autumn of 1994, but Chris was having issues with his voice and had resolved to rest it. Now, there were plans in the works to finally make it happen. There was just one problem.

Chris hadn't forgotten Trent Reznor's caustic remarks about *Scream*. Reznor wrote Chris a letter of apology, which the singer accepted. Reznor was also effusive in his praise of Chris in public. "I've always been in awe of what Cornell's capable of doing with his voice," Reznor told UK publication the *Skinny* in 2014. "When I was coming up in the seventies, listening to rock music, every singer could somehow sing high as shit, and I thought 'Well, I can't be a singer because my range isn't that high.' When Soundgarden appeared it felt reminiscent of that same kind of great rock singer, like '*Goddammit!*' I was pissed off that he could sing that well. I don't have the skill to sing like that!"[17]

The tour was a go, but then another issue arose. While a July-through-August arena run worked for Chris's schedule, it didn't for Matt Cameron's. Pearl Jam had just put out *Lightning Bolt*, and Cameron's commitments to the band overlapped with the Soundgarden/Nine Inch Nails dates. Rather than call the whole thing off, the band brought in a familiar face, one-time Pearl Jam drummer Matt Chamberlain, to fill in for Cameron. It was an elegant solution and marked the first time since Scott Sundquist left in the eighties that Matt Cameron wouldn't be onstage with Soundgarden.

The tour was a huge hit. Sold-out audiences greeted both bands nearly everywhere they went as middle-aged Gen-Xers and young millenials turned out to see the best of nineties rock in all its savage glory. "When we started as a band almost thirty years ago, and we started writ-

ing songs that were a little bit moody and depressing to a lot of people—
that somehow caught on and there was a whole generation of people that
understood how we felt," Chris told the kickoff crowd in Las Vegas. "Right
now, dance music is really popular, and people like to have fun when they
listen to music and have a positive outlook. That's great, but it doesn't
seem like the world is *better*. We all have our own way of dealing with it."[18]

The tour ended at White River Amphitheatre, just south of Seattle.
With his commitments to Pearl Jam concluded for the time being, Matt
Cameron rejoined his brothers onstage, and the show turned into a triumphant homecoming for the conquering legends. Just a few days later,
they were in an even more celebratory mood when they performed a
tight, six-song set outside of Century Link Stadium in honor of the Super
Bowl champion Seahawks' NFL season debut.

The last remaining Soundgarden items left on Chris's docket that
year were a pair of performances at Neil Young's annual Bridge School
Benefit concert in Northern California on October 25 and 26. Of all
the major grunge bands, Soundgarden was the only one that had never
filmed an episode of *MTV Unplugged*. As an acoustic-only showcase, the
Bridge School Benefit gave them a chance to make up for lost time. For
Chris, who had been alternating between Soundgarden's visceral wall
of sound and his contemplative solo shows, it was the perfect way to
close out the year.

Soundgarden went on in the latter portion of the afternoon on
both days, performing in front of a wall of young children in motorized
wheelchairs, afflicted with varying physical and verbal impairments.
Soundgarden opened with "Fell On Black Days" before slipping into
"Blow Up the Outside World," "Black Hole Sun," "Zero Chance," and ending the set with "Dusty." The only difference in the setlist between the two
shows was the addition of "Burden In My Hand" in the second show at
the expense of "Zero Chance."

Chris and the band had done quite a bit of charitable and philan-
thropic work over the years, but it was clear that the opportunity to help
these particular children in need really resonated. "Make some noise
for the real stars of this event, which are the students behind me back

here," Chris implored the crowd. "We've gotten to meet a few of them and they're amazing." Backstage, he and Matt Cameron even sat down and were interviewed on-camera by one of the school's students.

Cameron pulled double duty that weekend in Northern California, with Pearl Jam on the bill as well. Speculation ran rampant among those in attendance that a Temple Of The Dog reunion was inevitable. Eddie Vedder did little to squelch the chatter when he strode out that first night wearing a black NUDEDRAGONS t-shirt. And then, just after jamming out to "Fuckin' Up" with Neil Young, Vedder summoned Chris from the wings to help him sing "Hunger Strike."

The next night, they repeated the cameo, this time with Vedder decked out in a Mickey Mouse T-shirt. "There's a lot of singers back there," he said. "How about a Chris Cornell-type singer?" At the mention of his name, the man who sparked Temple Of The Dog's inception jogged out. "This right here is the best Chris Cornell-type singer you'll ever hear," Vedder promised as Chris plopped himself down on a stool next him. They smiled, clasped hands and intertwined their voices one more time for the grateful audience.

No one could have known that this would be the last time Eddie and Chris ever sang together.

CHAPTER XVI

NO ONE SINGS
LIKE YOU ANYMORE

5:00 p.m., Wednesday, May 17, 2017.

C hris Cornell is standing outside of the Fox Theatre in Detroit, Michigan. It is unseasonably warm with temperatures hovering around eighty degrees. He flew into town earlier that day from New York, joining the rest of his band after a three-day break between shows. Lingering outside on Woodward Avenue, he pulls his iPhone out of his pocket to snap a picture of the eighty-nine-year old building's large marquee. *Live Nation Presents SOUNDGARDEN. Tonight 8 PM, SOLD OUT.* Satisfied with the image, Chris shares the picture with his nearly two-million followers on Twitter.

"#Detroit, finally back to rock city!!!!" he writes. "#Nomorebullshit."

Detroit has long been a favorite city of Chris and Soundgarden's going all the way back to the days when they hoofed it around the country in their red Chevy Beauville. "Detroit…was always just an amazing experience, because the crowds there just love to go crazy, love to rock," Matt Cameron noted. "Maybe it's just the weather or we just hit the right notes."[1]

Soundgarden is two-thirds of the way through a month-long swing through southern and Midwestern America. Along the way they alternate between ornate, old theaters like the Fox in Detroit and massive outdoor festivals like Rock on the Range scheduled two nights later in Columbus,

Ohio. Though they don't have anything new to promote outside of a re-is-sue of Ultramega OK, they have been steadily working on material for a new album. The tour is a prime opportunity to reconnect with their fans after a nearly two-year hiatus.

Chris appears to be in good spirits. According to his manager Ron Laffitte, "He was as optimistic and happy as I can ever recall him…He was so excited about all these things and a new record we were going to put out in the fall."[2]

At 8:00 p.m. the opening act, the Pretty Reckless, hit the stage. The group is led by onetime actress Taylor Momsen, known primarily for her role as Jenny Humphrey on Gossip Girl. Momsen is a rock and roller at heart and a huge fan of Soundgarden. A few days earlier, her year was made in Indianapolis when, sitting outside of her dressing room, Chris swung by to say hello.

"I'd met him a couple times before in passing, but here he was, actu-ally talking to me," she wrote on Instagram. "We hung out for a while chatting about things like singing and their record King Animal and how much I loved it." [3] Later that night, Chris dedicated the song "By Crooked Steps" to their opening act.

The Pretty Reckless depart. The low hum of guitar amps cuts through the air. Just beyond the stage, five thousand people pulsate with the intox-icating anticipation of an evening full of music, memory, and, for the love of God, volume. Soundgarden is primed to give it to them.

The moment arrives, the one they've been waiting for. The lights go dark, and Chris Cornell strides through the blue-tinged darkness out onto the stage with the adoring screams of the rock and metal-loving horde pinging in his ears. Gripping his black Gretsch guitar, he chucks a few chords while Matt Cameron beats out the beginning to "Ugly Truth."

He's been here before. He knows what to do.

* * *

Chris Cornell was far from finished singing Temple Of The Dog tunes at the dawn of 2015. That January, Mike McCready booked a star-stud-ded show at Benaroya Hall in Seattle in part to honor the memory of his short-lived grunge supergroup Mad Season. Mad Season had only released one album during their existence, *Above* in 1995. John Baker Saunders and Layne Staley's tragic deaths from heroin overdoses in 1999 and 2002 respectively had put an end to any possibility that Mad Season could endure. For this one night, McCready was determined to pay tribute to his departed friends.

Seemingly half of the best and most notable rock musicians that Seattle ever produced in the nineties were on hand to participate. Duff McKagan played bass. Matt Cameron and Sean Kinney from Alice In Chains played drums, along with Barrett Martin from Screaming Trees. Stone Gossard and Jeff Ament were there. And so was Chris. "We rehearsed with the Seattle Symphony, and then Chris came in," McKagan recalled. "That guy can sing! He didn't even have to warm up. He just walked in from his car, got in front of the mic and this huge voice comes out."[4]

After beginning the evening playing a few pieces with the orchestra, McCready invited Chris out for a three-song run of some of Mad Season's best tunes. They began with "Long Gone Day," before shifting into "River of Deceit," and ending with "I Don't Know Anything." After another three-song Mad Season block with Kim Virant and Jeff Angell on lead vocals, Chris returned to sing a pair of Temple Of The Dog cuts—perhaps not coincidentally, the two that highlight McCready's playing the best, the languid "Call Me a Dog" and the expansive "Reach Down." The onstage chemistry between Chris and the Pearl Jam guys was palpable.

A month after the Mad Season gig, Chris and Soundgarden took off for a quick, seven-date swing through Australia and New Zealand. The band's only other show in 2015 was a headlining appearance at Canada's Big Music Fest outside of Toronto in July. The majority of Chris's year was spent writing, recording, and promoting his latest solo album, *Higher Truth*.

Higher Truth was the product of the many different Songbook concerts he'd performed over the last several years. The album sprung from a desire to strip his music back to its barest elements; lush acoustic guitar and his era-defining voice. There was only one edict that he abided by while writing the songs that would comprise the final tracklist to his fourth solo album. "They were all written in the same bathroom," he told Cameron Crowe. "The only rule was that they have to work there first. They have to work in that context first as just a guy playing an acoustic guitar and singing."[5]

After working for months demoing different arrangements and lyrical ideas at his home in Miami, he compiled the best and sent them to Brendan O'Brien, who liked what he heard. O'Brien was on board with the idea of making a largely acoustic album. What he didn't want to do was confine the music to two elements just for the sake of it. Chris remembered O'Brien saying, "'I love the idea of making an acoustic record, but I'm scared of the idea of it just being singing and one acoustic guitar. But if you're open to adding different textures and different things here and there to just kind of keep the songs going, then I think we can make a great record.'" There was a caveat, however. "He also said, 'I don't think anybody but you or I should play on it.'"[6]

For the most part, as the two men recorded *Higher Truth*, that remained the case. Matt Chamberlain was brought in to play drums, while Ann Marie Simpson played strings and Patrick Warren added a bit of piano. Chris showed off his chops on mandolin, harmonica, bass, and percussion while O'Brien added bits of keyboards, bass, percussion, and one of the strangest instruments in the western canon, the hurdy-gurdy.

"I'd run down a couple song takes on acoustic guitar then Brendan would play bass over that, and I would sing to those two instruments," Chris said. "He has a Paul McCartney approach to the bass, which works well with my songs because as a songwriter and arranger, the Beatles are by far my biggest influence. We went for a Beatles [production] approach on *Higher Truth*. It's a little epic but not overdone."[7]

To that end, the duo incorporated sonic flairs that surely would have drawn an approving smile from John Lennon, such as the fuzzy psychedelic guitar solo on "Nearly Forgot My Broken Heart." Then there is the avalanche of chaotic noise that drowns out the end of "Higher Truth," à la The Fab Four's "A Day in the Life," and the frenetic, Eastern-string arrangement on "Our Time In The Universe." You can practically hear

Chris mining the deepest parts of that appropriated Beatles collection from his youth for sparks of inspiration.

One of the characteristics that marked Chris's approach to song creation was the way in which he fleshed out of characters in an attempt to tell stories from a detached point of view. "Only These Words," for example, tells the tale of a young princess who suddenly finds herself stripped of all her luxurious trappings. "Circling" is told from the perspective of a junkie "nodding in the stairwell." "Let Your Eyes Wander" is the story of a heartbroken lover, desperately hoping the object of their affection will see the error of their ways.

Though none of these people are Chris, they bear his DNA. "I think it's easier to allow yourself to share personal experiences, thoughts, feelings and emotions when you're doing it through some character that you've created," he told *Songwriting* magazine. "And at the end of it I can read the lyrics and realize that 'Okay, even though this is a character in a story that I've created, there's a whole lot of me in it.'"[8]

And while there is plenty of dark imagery interspersed throughout *Higher Truth*, its central message is hopeful. The throughway that connects many of these songs is the idea that you have a finite amount of time on this planet, and you have to try to make the most of it. That idea hits hardest on the soaring ballad "Before We Disappear." As he told a crowd in Bogotá, Colombia, in December 2016, it's a song "About letting the people that you love know that you love them because we're all gonna die pretty soon."[9] The song serves as a poignant reminder to appreciate the good things in life. It might be the best song on the record.

Higher Truth dropped on September 18, 2015. The night before its release, Chris was in New York performing the lead single "Nearly Forgot My Broken Heart" on *The Tonight Show* while backed by a four-piece band. Shortly after that, he hopped a flight to San Diego where he kicked off the first show of a thirty-date solo tour across North America accompanied by cellist Bryan Gibson, followed almost immediately by a swing through Australia and New Zealand that was capped by a pair of bravura performances at the famed Sydney Opera House. The next day, on December 13, he flew back to America where he played the Forum in Los

Angeles as part of KROQ's Almost Acoustic Christmas before ending the year a little over a week later with a gig in Aspen, Colorado.

Gibson had gotten the job through a friend. Chris was looking for a multi-instrumentalist who could add distinct textures to the show. After hearing a cello part that Gibson had worked up over a live recording of "Fell On Black Days," Chris knew he had found his man. From the jump, the cellist was struck by just how much Chris simply loved music. "During our first rehearsal, we played 'Like Suicide,' which is one of my favorite Soundgarden songs, and suddenly he stopped playing and was just quiet for a moment as I continued playing," the cellist told Playbuzz. "I wasn't sure what was going on, and then eventually stopped and asked him if something was wrong, and he said no, that he was listening to what I was playing and it was just so good that he lost his place."

Higher Truth wasn't a blockbuster, but the critical response was much warmer than it had been for anything he'd put out under his own name since *Euphoria Mourning*. "This is hardly an exercise in folky restraint: O'Brien's backing tracks and Cornell's nuanced growl, all the more burnished with age, infuse roots music with alt-rock dynamics," Jon Dolan wrote in his *Rolling Stone* review. "For the most part, this is the balance of power and intimacy Cornell has always wanted his solo music to have."[10]

Chris spent much of the next year touring solo, but there was another project taking up an inordinate amount of his time and attention. 2016 marked the twenty-fifth anniversary of *Temple Of The Dog*. Chris hoped to celebrate that milestone in some way, but there was a problem. Rick Parashar, the album's producer and owner of London Bridge Studio, had died in 2014. His brother Raj Parashar came into possession of the master tapes and refused to give them up. As a result, A&M Records sued him.

Chris was furious that someone thought they had the right to hold onto his music, especially after the record company had a signed agreement with Rick Parashar dating back to 1993 where the producer agreed to turn over the tapes in exchange for $35,000. "To pretend he has a right to keep the recordings makes no more sense than the owner of a laundromat claiming he owns the clothes you washed in his washing machine," Chris said in a statement shared with the *Associated Press*.[11]

By the spring of 2016 the lawsuit was settled out of court and the *Temple Of The Dog* master tapes were returned to their rightful owner. The resolution had come just in the nick of time. A couple of months later, Chris announced that Temple Of The Dog planned on hitting the road on their first nationwide tour. He'd be joined by Matt Cameron, Mike McCready, Jeff Ament, and Stone Gossard. Eddie Vedder would be sitting this one out.

The run was limited to eight shows in five cities: two opening performances at the Tower Theater in Philadelphia, an arena show at Madison Square Garden, another two theater gigs in San Francisco, a date at the Forum in LA, and finally, two gigs at the Paramount Theatre in Seattle, the same place where they had come together to celebrate Andy Wood after his untimely death. Tickets sold out almost as soon as they went on sale. Prices on the secondary market soared. The seats closest to the stage were going for thousands of dollars.

By October, the band congregated at Pearl Jam Headquarters in Seattle and started trying to remember how to play the songs. *Temple Of The Dog* spans just ten tracks and adds up to about an hour's worth of music. Considering that Chris regularly performed for upwards of two and a half hours at a time, and Pearl Jam was known to cross the three-hour threshold, the band wanted to add tracks that made sense historically and musically. Pearl Jam cuts were off-limits. So were Soundgarden songs. Instead, they sprinkled the setlist with a collection of their favorite, dynamic classic rock songs like "Achilles Last Stand" by Led Zeppelin, "War Pigs" by Black Sabbath, and "Fascination Street" by The Cure. Mother Love Bone tracks like "Stargazer," "Heartshine," and Temple Of The Dog's namesake "Man Of Golden Words" were cool too. Chris even threw a few of his old Poncier Tape-era compositions like "Seasons" and "Missing" into the mix. The whole set was designed to pay homage to a time and a place when they were all young men, trying to make sense of the senseless loss of a friend.

The night before the first show in Philadelphia, the band was still working to nail down every element of the twenty-three-song setlist. After running through a preliminary take of "Pushin' Forward Back," something didn't sound right. They convened around Matt Cameron's drum kit and listened to the original version through an iPhone while trying to figure out where they went wrong during the breakdown.

The hard work paid off. The performance the next night was a triumph. So was the night after that. So was the gig in New York City, the one at the Forum, both shows in LA, and the tour-enders in Seattle. Though the run was short, the entire experience was more cathartic than Chris could have anticipated, especially the act of performing Andy's songs for so many people. "[*Apple* by Mother Love Bone] is another album like *Temple Of The Dog* that is among the best rock records of its period that did not have a band to go out and support it. Therefore, not so many people heard about it and it's never been toured before," Chris told *Whiplash*. "That was the thing that maybe hit me personally the hardest when this guy died at twenty-four. We all thought of him as among the most talented of anyone in the scene. And for him to go away and no one to ever discover that, that almost seemed harder than anything else. So, to be able to play all of Temple and all these Mother Love Bone songs in the Forum…and seeing that many people out there listening to it, that's super fulfilling to me."[12]

Despite his hectic schedule, Chris managed to carve out time to write and record new music when the right opportunity came along. There was the atmospheric ballad "Til The Sun Comes Back Around" written for Michael Bay's military thriller *13 Hours: The Secret Soldiers Of Benghazi*, released in January 2016. An acoustic track titled "The Promise" he put together for a film by the same name that hit theaters in April 2017. He also recorded covers of the Beatles' "Drive My Car" for the Australian animated television series *Beat Bugs*, as well as a take on Terry Reid's "Stay with Me Baby" for Mick Jagger and Martin Scorsese's HBO drama *Vinyl*.

The most rewarding project that came his way during this time was the chance to work with John Carter Cash on a tribute album to his father, Johnny Cash. Chris had long said that no one really complimented his lyrics until the Man in Black deigned to record a version of "Rusty Cage."

Now, John Carter came to him with a piece of Cash's own writing that had never been set to music. He hoped that Chris could turn it into a song.

The poem was called "You Never Really Knew My Mind." Cash had written it in 1967 about his first wife Vivian, not long after she filed for divorce. Chris instinctually found a powerful, heartbreaking way to turn Cash's no-hold-barred assessment of his relationship—"You did not see me well enough to recognize the signs"—into a mournful ballad, devoid of bitterness, graced with an aching slide guitar and breathless vocal melodies.

"'The first time I heard the song, it was a demo; he recorded it in a hotel room closet," John Carter Cash said. "[Chris] sent me a picture of that closet and the microphone setup, his wife Vicky and his clothes on the hangers around, his guitar leaning on a chair."[13] Though the subsequent album *Forever Words* was packed with incredible interpretations of Cash's words from legendary artists like Kris Kristofferson, Willie Nelson, Alison Krauss, and John Mellencamp, few, if any, managed to match the emotion that Chris imbued into his composition.

All the while, Chris worked on new material for Soundgarden. He could hardly get through a single interview without someone asking him how the follow-up to *King Animal* was coming. "Soundgarden is in the middle of writing songs," he told the *Hartford Courant* in 2016 while promoting *Higher Truth*. "After this tour the songs will become real and we'll put an album out. There's much more to Soundgarden."[14]

"We've had blocks of time where we get together and write, then disperse again for a while, then get blocks of time, like days at a time," Ben Shepherd explained to the *Kansas City Star* on May 10, 2017. "We've done that like four times, maybe five. So, we have an amalgam of songs, kind of. They're not really worked out. And I'm sure we'll do it a couple more times before we hit the studio."[15]

Intermittently, the band shared tantalizing updates on social media, showcasing photos of themselves in rehearsal and studio spaces, ostensibly working on new material. Though they hadn't collected enough material for a full album, they were on their way, with songs bearing titles like "Road Less Travelled," "Orphans," "At Ophians Door," "Cancer,"

"Stone Age Mind," "Ahead of the Dog," and "Merrmas" in various stages of completion.

The band booked several multi-day recording sessions at Strange Earth Studio in the Fremont neighborhood of Seattle throughout August and September 2016, and again at the beginning of 2017 to try to get as much accomplished as they could, but the wait for Soundgarden's latest album would continue after the band announced plans for their first tour in two years. It was a relatively short run; just eighteen dates mostly in the South and Midwest. The itinerary was a mix of large outdoor festivals and intimate, headlining theater dates, set to kick off on April 28, 2017 in Tampa, Florida.

Before the tour began, however, Chris had one more reunion up his sleeve. The election of Donald Trump as President was a dismaying turn of events to millions of Americans, Chris Cornell among them. On January 20, 2017, the night of Trump's inauguration, Tom Morello, Brad Wilk, and Timothy Commerford were performing as part of a super-group named Prophets of Rage along with Chuck D from Public Enemy and B-Real from Cypress Hill, as part of a special Anti-Inaugural Ball concert at the Teragram Ballroom in Los Angeles.

Chris had joined Tom Morello onstage a few years earlier in 2014 for a fifteen-dollar minimum wage increase benefit concert at El Corazon in Seattle, formerly known as the Off Ramp, so it made all the sense in the world that he'd reunite once again with his Audioslave bandmates to voice their displeasure in the loudest terms possible with the incoming commander in chief. The band didn't even bother introducing Chris to the crowd before Morello kicked into the jittery, opening notes of "Cochise." When he emerged to scream his lungs ragged on the opening verse, it was like a bomb had been set off in the small venue.

"Thank you very much," he said after the song ended. "Twelve years is a long time coming!" The next song, their most popular song, "Like A Stone," got the people singing, but Audioslave was out to level them with their final selection, "Show Me How to Live." After the second chorus, Chris did a swan dive into the front row and surfed over the heads of the grateful fans before they returned him to his rightful place onstage.

Chris couldn't have been happier with the way things went that night. "It was interesting because the dynamic for that band was really just there," he told MusicRadar. "We just counted the songs in and they were totally where we left them ten years ago when we'd just got off the road."[16] According to Tom Morello, the singer had been so stoked about the gig that he was all-in on the idea of trying to do some more performances down the line. "The last thing Chris said to me was, 'I had a great time, let's do this again, just let me know when.'"[17]

On April 28, 2017, Chris joined the full Soundgarden road crew in Tampa, Florida, for the first date of their spring tour. They were scheduled to headline a regional festival called Rockfest in front of 6,600 people, playing ahead of local heroes A Day to Remember, who recently received the key to the city of Ocala a short while earlier. The next night they were in Jacksonville, headlining the Welcome to Rockville festival, before heading further south to close down the Fort Rock festival in Fort Myers, Florida, the night after that.

The band got a few days off after their three-day Florida blitz, then hit the ornate Fox Theatre in Atlanta on May 3. They finished off their southern swing at the Beale Street Music Festival in Memphis, then shot north, hitting Indianapolis, Iowa, Wisconsin, and finally the Starlight Theater in Kansas City, Missouri, on May 14, putting on a well-received performance.

"The crisp sound reproduction—vastly superior to Soundgarden's 2013 appearance in Kansas City—allowed fans to appreciate every nuance of the deep groove bassist Ben Shepherd and drummer Matt Cameron created during a faithful version of the 1994 hit 'Spoonman,'" *Kansas City Star* reviewer Bill Brownlee wrote, saving special recognition for the man on the microphone. "His three band mates are excellent musicians, but front man Chris Cornell is a bona fide rock star."[18]

With Kansas City in their rear-view mirror, Soundgarden received a few days off before reconvening for the next show three days later. Chris had missed Mother's Day while out on the road and was eager to spend some time with his family, so he jetted back to New York. Soundgarden's tour was scheduled to end in the middle of Memorial Day weekend, so he talked to his family about maybe taking a vacation somewhere afterwards to decompress. The upcoming run of shows was going to be especially packed. Seven gigs over ten days. First up was Detroit.

Chris flew into the Motor City from JFK in New York the afternoon of May 17, 2017. After snapping a picture of the marquee outside of the Fox Theatre and waiting for the Pretty Reckless to finish their set, he hit the stage around nine o'clock and launched into "Ugly Truth." He seemed like his typical charismatic self.

* * *

"Detroit rock city, hey!" he exclaims after the song ends. "I love you guys up there on the top shelf, but you gotta stand up and show me something. I have bragged about Detroit crowds for thirty years, so stand the fuck up and make some noise!" An explosion of cheers erupts from the balcony. "Now make some noise down here to congratulate them," Chris says pointing to the front row. "That's the spirit!" The band then reaches into the earliest moment of their history to play their first single, "Hunted Down."

"I remember Chris had just gotten in [to town] and was a little tired and his voice was a little rough, but by about the fourth or fifth song it kicked in and then it was just, like, super amazing—beautiful, clear and strong and, I thought, particularly emotive," Kim Thayil later told *Billboard*. [19] At one point, Chris's guitar goes out of tune and he has to leave the stage to grab another, but other than that hiccup it was a largely straightforward Soundgarden performance. Chris smiles between songs, tells stories about the genesis of tracks like "Mailman," and applauds the crowd for their boisterous energy. "I feel bad for the next city," he jokes.

The main set ends with "Jesus Christ Pose." After a few moments of pregnant darkness, Soundgarden re-emerges to rapturous applause and launches into the frenetic "Rusty Cage." And then, just like every other night of the tour, just like he's done hundreds of times in rooms like this one, Matt Cameron begins pounding out the plodding rhythms of "Slaves & Bulldozers." Moments later Chris is screaming his lungs to shreds while a sunburst Gibson Les Paul swings around his hips. Kim Thayil rips into the song's psychedelic solo with furious gusto while Ben Shepherd hammers the central riff home.

Near the end, Chris interpolates some of the lyrics to Led Zeppelin's "In My Time Of Dying" over the jam. "And I promise," he proclaims. "In my time of dying, I ain't gonna cry and I ain't gonna moan / All I need for you to do is drag my body home." Green and then white strobe lights dance around the heads of the audience as the band brings the song to a stultifying close. "Detroit! Thank you! We'll see you soon!" Chris promises over Soundgarden's dense cacophony. Then, he unstraps his Les Paul, walks over to his amplifier, crouches down and begins pulling wailing walls of feedback from the speakers. He stays there, crouched down, while the noise whooshes past his curly mane for just under a minute, before walking out of view.

The crowd's ears are still ringing when, at around eleven o'clock, Chris piles into a car with his bodyguard Martin Kirsten and, along with a police escort, drives less than a mile down the road to the MGM Grand hotel. The rest of the band hops on a bus and starts toward the next town. Once Chris arrives at his hotel, he signs a few autographs and before heading up to Room 1136.

Kirsten followed Chris into his room and worked to fix his computer. After that, he gave him a couple of sleeping pills to help him relax and left for his own room two doors down the hall. Shortly after midnight, Kirsten got a call from Vicky Cornell. "She sounded angry because he wasn't answering his phone," the bodyguard told police. "She told me to go to the room and check on Chris."

According to Vicky, who spoke with *People* magazine weeks later, Chris woke her up by turning their lights on and off in their home remotely. She became alarmed and called him. "He was on a rant," she says. "I said, 'You need to tell me what you took,' and he just got mean."[20] The situation was dire.

After getting in touch with Kirsten, the bodyguard raced down the hall. He had a key to Chris's room, but the door was locked from the inside by an interior latch. He raced back to his room and called security, asking them to open the door, but they refused because it wasn't his room.

Kirsten updated Vicky, and she told him to kick the door down, which he promptly did.

When he entered the room, Chris was nowhere to be found and the bedroom door was locked. Again, Kirsten called hotel officials, asking for security's help in opening the door. Again, they refused.

Kirsten told them he was about to damage their property and asked that the operator call for an ambulance. After about six or seven solid kicks, Kirsten managed to access the bedroom. He walked in and noticed that the bathroom door was ajar. He could only see a pair of feet. Peering deeper into the room, Kirsten saw that Chris had tied a red exercise band around his neck. The other end was latched to the top of the bathroom door, secured with a carabiner clip.

Kirsten untied the band. Chris wasn't breathing. Immediately the bodyguard began performing CPR. At around one in the morning, paramedics finally arrived and began life-saving protocols. For half an hour they tried to revive Chris, but he wouldn't come to. At 1:30 a.m. the doctor on the scene pronounced him dead.

Chris Cornell was gone. He was fifty-two years old.

An autopsy was eventually completed by the Wayne County Medical Examiner's Office, who found several substances in Chris's system, including butalbital, a mild pain medication, a decongestant called pseudoephedrine as well as its metabolite norpseudoephedrine, caffeine, and naloxone, an anti-opioid that is used by medical professionals in overdose situations. They also found the presence of 41 ng/mL of lorazepam, an anti-anxiety medication. Ultimately, the medical examiner ruled that the drugs "did not contribute to the cause of death."

Vicky Cornell called the report "completely misleading," telling the *Detroit News* that, "I lost my husband. My children lost their father. We're in a lot of pain, and we have to deal with these people coming after us. If the autopsy report was thorough, I believe some of this could have been avoided."[21]

"My brother gave freely of his gifts and it was never a struggle," Peter Cornell wrote on Facebook. "He kept himself from the saturation of celebrity in such a humble way. The power and anger and passion of my brother's music was always genuine, original and legitimate. He was the powerful, sensitive, fragile, angry, mystical creature that will exist forever in his body of work. And he did it for ALL of us. Giving it away. Leaving all on the stage or in the recordings that will keep him immortal."[22]

Tom Morello expressed his appreciation and love for Chris on Instagram. "I am devastated and deeply saddened that you are gone dear friend but your unbridled rock power, delicate haunting melodies and the memory of your smile are with us forever," the guitarist wrote. [23] He later penned a poem that he shared with *Rolling Stone* in which he called him "a revealer of visions, you're the passenger, you're a never fading scar / You're twilight and star burn and shade."[24]

Elton John paid his respects online. As did Courtney Love, Perry Farrell, Slash, Joe Perry, Robbie Robertson, Lin-Manuel Miranda, Paul Stanley, Sheryl Crow, Daniel Craig, Alice Cooper, St. Vincent, Chuck D, and Jimmy Page, who summed up the feelings of most in the simplest terms, "Incredibly Talented, Incredibly Young, Incredibly Missed."[25] In his hometown of Seattle, the local radio station KEXP played Chris's music throughout the day.

Chris Cornell's remains were cremated at a private ceremony on May 23 in Los Angeles. His wife Vicky was there. So was his brother Peter, the singer J.D. King, and Linda Ramone, the widow of Johnny Ramone. Hollywood Forever Cemetery was chosen as his final resting place. It was only a half a mile down Gordon Street from Cello Studio where he recorded the first Audioslave album. His plot was located just a few feet from Johnny Ramone in a tranquil spot overlooking the cemetery's swan-strewn pond.

The funeral took place on a Friday afternoon. The typically sun-filled Los Angeles sky was drowned out by gray clouds as Chris's friends and family members gathered to say goodbye. Somewhere nearby, a person had modified a sign on the grounds that typically read "Garden of Legends" to read "SOUND Garden of Legends."

Eulogies were given by movie producer Eric Esrailian, actor Josh Brolin, Tom Morello, Jeff Ament, Kim Thayil, and Matt Cameron, who called Chris his brother and artistic soulmate. Perhaps the most touching moment of the service came when Chester Bennington, accompanied by his bandmate Brad Delson, sang a gut-wrenching rendition of the song Chris's friend Jeff Buckley had made famous: "Hallelujah." Bennington took his own life just a couple of months later on July 20. It would have been Chris's fifty-third birthday.

As mourners filed out of the funeral, the strains of "All Night Thing," the sparse final track of *Temple Of The Dog*, filled the air. Around three o'clock, the public was allowed to pay their respects. One by one they filed by the shiny black headstone emblazoned with Chris's name. One by one, they reached out to touch the letters scrawled into the permanent slab.

VOICE OF OUR GENERATION
AND AN ARTIST FOR ALL TIME
CHRIS CORNELL
1964–2017
BELOVED HUSBAND AND FATHER

A long time ago, practically a lifetime before this somber day, long before Audioslave, Temple Of The Dog, and Soundgarden; long before he became the Rock God and the Sex Idol; long before the Grammy awards, the magazine covers, and the sold-out concerts; long before he rubbed shoulders with presidents and royalty, Chris Cornell was a tall, baby-faced nineteen-year-old kid driving home from work in his crappy green Ford Galaxie. Just another Joe Nobody from a part of the country people hardly paid attention to; a high school dropout for whom a life of food service or manual labor seemed pre-ordained.

It had been an unremarkable evening at Ray's Boathouse, another night of dirty dishes and fish guts, but as Chris piloted his sedan home a moment of clarity washed over him like a soft, Seattle rain. "It occurred to me that there was no guarantee that as a musician I would ever have any kind of financial success, but I was fine with that," he remembered thinking. That night, as he navigated his way through the inky black Pacific Northwestern night, he made a promise to himself. "No matter what happened in terms of success, I was going to be one of those guys playing music until he drops dead."[26]

Because of the tragic way that Chris Cornell's life ended, there's a propensity to view his story as a tragedy. That would be a mistake. Chris Cornell lived his life to the fullest. He overcame seemingly insurmountable challenges time and time again in the pursuit of a dream too enormous to fathom. He used the tools at his disposal—his one-of-a-kind voice, his guitar, and his imagination—to craft era-defining music that many turned to time and again in moments of sadness, anger, joy, anguish, fear, doubt, and love. He lifted the hearts and minds of countless people from all walks of life on nearly every continent on the planet with his unique and unparalleled artistry. He did what he loved, and along the way created a musical legacy that will endure for generations.

Chris Cornell kept his promise.

EPILOGUE

January 16, 2019. Los Angeles, California.

I t's nearly four years to the day since the last time I witnessed Chris Cornell singing onstage. It was the triumphant Mad Season gig at Benaroya Hall in Seattle when he reunited with his friends in Temple Of The Dog. He seemed invincible that night; tall, powerful, and, of course, loud as hell. I get goosebumps whenever I think about how he crooned and screamed his way through "Call Me A Dog."

Now here I am, one person among seventeen thousand packed into the Forum in Inglewood steeling myself for the emotional night of musical transcendence to come. The stars are too numerous to count. Jimmy Kimmel is on hand to serve as the evening's MC. Leonardo DiCaprio is drifting around backstage. Brad Pitt is in the building. So are Courteney Cox, Josh Brolin, Jack Black, Tom Hanks, and so many others. I'm sitting directly behind Michael Kelly, the guy who plays Doug Stamper in the Netflix series *House of Cards*.

We're all here for the same reason: to honor the musical legacy of Christopher John Cornell. For five continuous hours, some of the biggest, most talented, and impactful musical artists of the last half century flood the stage to play a collection of Chris's finest compositions, forty-two songs total.

Before the show begins, the three surviving members of Soundgarden make their way out to an enormous standing ovation. Matt Cameron does most of the talking, expressing how he had mixed emotions about the idea of putting on a tribute show. "I heard his voice and I found my strength," the drummer said. "There's so much I miss about Chris, but what I miss most is him walking into a room. Chris is with us tonight. He's got the best seat in the house." You could only hope.

The Melvins kick the show off moments later, ripping into their set like they were all the way back at the Paramount Theatre in '92 opening for Soundgarden on a sweaty Friday night. After that, Alain Johannes comes out to honor Chris's *Euphoria Mourning* period by performing "Disappearing One" with Nikka Costa. Foo Fighters play three of Soundgarden's deepest cuts before the band departs, leaving Dave Grohl alone to perform a tender, melancholic take on his song "Everlong." Then Josh Homme ambles out and plays a solo, Johnny Cash-ified version of "Rusty Cage" on his tobacco burst Telecaster.

Before Audioslave hits the stage, Jimmy Kimmel recalls the time the band forced the LA Riot squad to flood Hollywood Boulevard during a performance on his show. Then, along with Black Sabbath's Geezer Butler on bass, they tear into a collection of their greatest hits with an assist from Perry Farrell, Juliette Lewis, Brandi Carlile, and, once again, Dave Grohl, who shreds the remnants of his vocal cords on "Show Me How to Live."

Another emotional moment follows when Chris's daughter Toni appears to sing "Redemption Song" with Ziggy Marley on guitar. This is only her third live performance ever, but she is prepared. Only a few years earlier, she had performed the song onstage with her dad at the Beacon Theater in New York City.

Chris's eldest daughter Lily appears onstage and delivers a sage piece of wisdom her dad had imparted to her. "The most influential advice he gave me was that his success did not come from a desire for [success], it was more from a passion and an absolute love for what he did," she said. "He reminded me often it was an added benefit, but that can never be the driving factor. My dad had a beautiful gift but the most important part of it was that he loved what he did, and he did it because he loved it."

Metallica play next, mixing two of their own songs with two of Soundgarden's earliest: "Head Injury" and "All Your Lies." And then there is Temple Of The Dog. Though Eddie Vedder isn't in attendance, my mind is blown away by Miley Cyrus's pained and beautiful take on "Say Hello 2 Heaven." And then, somehow, Brandi Carlile and Chris Stapleton manage to kick things up to an even higher gear during their hair-raising duet of "Hunger Strike."

Not long after that, the three remaining members of Soundgarden emerge from the shadows once again, take their places onstage, and honor their brother with a scorching eight-song set of their most beloved material. Taylor Momsen of the Pretty Reckless sings "Rusty Cage," "Drawing Flies," and "Loud Love." Marcus Durant, Kim Thayil's MC5 bandmate, wails over "Outshined" and "Flower." Foo Fighters drummer Taylor Hawkins has the unenviable task of subbing for Faith No More's Mike Patton, who fell ill before the show, pouring everything he has into "I Awake" and "The Day I Tried to Live."

And then finally, Peter Frampton picks out the haunting, familiar chorus-pedal-painted notes of "Black Hole Sun." A weight falls over the Forum with the painful recognition that this is the end. Brandi Carlile, a native of the Puget Sound area, steps to the microphone, summons all the power of her own show-stopping voice and delivers a performance stricken with raw, gut-twisting emotion. I'm not the only one left with tears streaming down my cheeks.

At song's end, the members of Soundgarden let their instruments feed back for nearly ten minutes. The last sound many hear as they file up the aisles is Chris's guitar that had been set up at the center of the stage; a solemn totem in the center of the sonic maelstrom crying out one last time.

As I walk out into the cool LA evening, the ground around my feet puddled with the remnants of a torrential downpour of rain that snarled traffic to a near-standstill earlier this afternoon, I feel a deep sadness well up in my chest. The entire performance was an amazing tribute to a generational artist. It was the kind of concert you know you're going to remember ten, twenty, fifty years from now. The one you tell people about and watch as their eyes grow wide with awe and wonder as you rattle off name after name after name of the myriad artists who gathered together in salute of someone they admired and respected.

The sheer amount of love, compassion, and effort that went into every second of the show and from every person who took part in it was palpable. It meant something to them. Chris Cornell meant something to them. It meant something to all of us, too, out in the crowd. It was our chance to grieve, but also our chance to collectively remember all the times this singular artist and his music was there for us in times of sadness, anger, and joy. It was our chance to say thank you.

And yet, when it was all over, after every superstar had their turn behind the microphone, you couldn't shake the impossible desire for the man himself to amble out of the wings one more time to show us all how it's really done, in the dynamic, stultifying way that only he could. Call it cliché, but it remains undoubtably true and probably will until the end of time itself:

No one sings like him anymore.

If you or someone you know is suicidal or in emotional distress, please contact the National Suicide Prevention Hotline. Trained crisis workers are available to talk 24 hours a day, 7 days a week. Your confidential and toll-free call goes to the nearest crisis center in the Lifeline national network. These centers provide crisis counseling and mental health referrals.

1-800-273-8255

For more information, please visit the official Suicide Prevention Resource Center at http://www.hspc.org

ACKNOWLEDGMENTS

F irst and foremost, this book wouldn't be possible if not for the love and support from my wife Jenna. Your wisdom, strength, and intelligence are beyond compare, and your talents helped elevate this project to heights I never could've envisioned. Thank you for everything. I love you.

While writing this book, my longtime agent Jim Fitzgerald sadly passed away. I know for a fact that I wouldn't have any kind of career as a writer if he hadn't taken a chance on me so many years ago, and I will always, always appreciate him for that. Thank you, Jim. I hope wherever you are the whisky is strong and plentiful.

To my editor Jacob Hoye, thank you for continuing to believe in me and for helping me realize my grandest dreams. I also appreciate all the times you had to play therapist whenever I hit a wall, and boy, there were many, many walls. You are the literal best.

I'd also like to thank the following folks for helping me along this incredible journey: Michael Croland, Mark Yarm, David De Sola, Lea Marić, Jeff Ansari, Steven Hyden, Greg Prato, Mark Arm, Bruce Pavitt, Stuart Hallerman, Michael Bienhorn, Aaron Jacoves, Chris Hanzsek, Xana La Fuente, Charles Peterson, Eric Johnson, Dawn Anderson, Jack Endino, Steven Messina, Christopher Thorn, Doug Pinnick, Clay Tarver, Matt Mahurin, Mark Pickerel, Drew Canulette, Howard Greenhalgh, Daniel Peterson, Ken Deans, Dave Hillis, Adam Kasper, Jim Tillman, Kevin Wood, Andrew Scheps, Larry Reid, Dave Schiffman, Steve Lillywhite, Alain Johannes, Kurt Danielson, Paul Rachman, Peter Thorn, Artis the Spoonman, Daniel House, Mark Dancey, Perry Farrell, Jim Rose, Dino Galasso, Michael Azerrad, Kevin Kerslake, Geoffrey Weiss, Gianluca

Sirri, Denis "Snake" Bélanger, Jesse Frohman, Ric Markmann, Daniel Field, Clayton Ferrell, Chris Cuffaro, Scott Granlund, The Seattle Public Library, the Museum Of Popular Culture, and Brian Eno's album *Ambient 1: Music For Airports*, which kept me focused during the editing process.

And last but not least, Chris Cornell. Thank you for the music. Thank you for the inspiration. Thank you for everything.

ENDNOTES

Introduction

[1] "Kim Thayil on New Chris Cornell Box: 'The Main Thing Is to Represent His Versatility,'" interview by Corbin Reiff, *Rolling Stone*, November 1, 2018, https://www.rollingstone.com/music/music-features/soundgardens-kim-thayil-talks-new-chris-cornell-box-set-749656/.

Chapter I

[1] "Chris Cornell Episode 502," interview by Marc Maron, *WTF with Marc Maron* Podcast, Earwolf, June 2014.

[2] "Soundgarden Superunknown 25th Anniversary—Chris Cornell," interview by Redbeard, *In the Studio with Redbeard*, March 18, 2019, https://www.inthestudio.net/online-on-demand/soundgarden-superunknown-chris-cornell/.

[3] Peter Makowski-Wordsmith (@PeterMakowskiWordsmith), "Chris Cornell: An Interview," Facebook post, October 1, 2016, https://www.facebook.com/Peter MakowskiWordsmith/posts/110590296611 3795?__tn__=-R.

[4] Ali Lorraine, "Soundgarden's Chris Cornell Steps Out On His Own With An Album Filled With Mystery And Self-Reflection," *Harper's Bazaar*, October 1999.

[5] "Chris Cornell Episode 502," interview by Marc Maron, *WTF with Marc Maron* Podcast, Earwolf, June 2014.

[6] "Interview: Chris Cornell," interview by Howard Stern, *The Howard Stern Show*, SiriusXM, November 16, 2011.

7   Peter Cornell (@petercornellmusic), Facebook post, January 27, 2020, https://www.facebook.com/petercornellmusic/posts/27189758 84851280?__tn__=-R.

8   Peter Cornell (@petercornellmusic), Facebook post, October 14, 2017, https://www.facebook.com/petercornellmusic/posts/1513128865435994?__tn__=-R.

9   "Chris Cornell Interview: Searching For The Real Chris Cornell," interview by Paul Brannigan, *Louder*, February 6, 2018, https://www.loudersound.com/features/archive-the-real-chris-cornell.

10 "Chris Cornell Interview," interview by Opie & Anthony, SiriusXM, October 11, 2005.

11 Rod Yates, "The Life & Times Of Chris Cornell," *Rolling Stone Australia*, September 17, 2015, http://rollingstoneaus.com/music/post/the-life-and-times-of-chris-cornell/ 2273.

12 "Interview: Chris Cornell On Making Music And Movies," Interview by Indiewire Team, IndieWire, September 29, 2011 https://www.indiewire.com/2011/09/interview-chris-cornell-on-making-music-and-movies-51897/.

13 "Chris Cornell," interview by Jeff Ho, *Juice*, January 1, 2008, https://juicemagazine.com/home/chris-cornell/.

14 "Chris Cornell Episode 502," interview by Marc Maron, *WTF with Marc Maron* Podcast, Earwolf, June 2014.

15 "New Day Rising," interview by Morat, *Kerrang!*, December 18, 1999.

16 Jennifer Clay, "Soungarden: Painting Beautiful Pictures," *RIP*, June 1996.

17 J. Chancellor, "Slave To The Sound," *Tribune Business News*, November 27, 2007.

18 "Chris Cornell Interview," interview by Howard Stern, *The Howard Stern Show*, SiriusXM, June 12, 2007.

19 "The End Of Innocence: The Rolling Stone Interview With Chris Cornell," interview by Alec Foege, *Rolling Stone*, January 12, 1995.

20 "Chris Cornell Interview," interview by Jon Wiederhorn, *All Music Zine*, September 1999.

21   Kory Grow, "Chris Cornell on David Bowie's Evolution: 'He Was an Inspiration,'" *Rolling Stone*, Jan 12, 2016.

22   "Chris Cornell Episode 502," interview by Marc Maron, *WTF with Marc Maron* Podcast, Earwolf, June 2014.

23   "Cornell Moody? Not A Chance," *The Province*, November 28, 1996.

24   "Chris Cornell," interview by Jeff Ho, *Juice*, January 1, 2008, https://juicemagazine.com/home/chris-cornell/.

25   "Chris Cornell Episode 502," interview by Marc Maron, *WTF with Marc Maron* Podcast, Earwolf, June 2014.

26   "Chris Cornell Episode 502," interview by Marc Maron, *WTF with Marc Maron* Podcast, Earwolf, June 2014.

27   "Chris Cornell Interview, Part 4," Interview by John Fisher, YouTube, Fish5000, August 28, 2009 https://www.youtube.com/watch?v=sIuV1J3VSrk&feature=youtu.be.

28   "Mike Jones Interview with Chris Cornell," interview by Mike Jones, DC 101, December 17, 2015.

29   "Remembering Chris Cornell: The Quiet Cook at Ray's Boathouse Who Became a Rock God," interview by Michael Rietmulder, *The Seattle Times*, May 18, 2018, https://www.seattletimes.com/entertainment/music/remembering-chris-cornell-the-quiet-cook-at-rays-boathouse-who-became-a-rock-god/.

30   Rod Yates, "The Life & Times Of Chris Cornell," *Rolling Stone Australia*, September 17, 2015, http://rollingstoneaus.com/music/post/the-life-and-times-of-chris-cornell/2273.

31   "Chris Cornell Interview," interview by Howard Stern, *The Howard Stern Show*, SiriusXM, June 12, 2007.

32   "Chris Cornell," interview by Matt Pinfield, *Sound Off with Matt Pinfield*, AXS TV, August 12, 2007.

33   Mark Yarm, *Everybody Loves Our Town: An Oral History of Grunge* (New York: Crown Archetype, 2011).

34   "Chris Cornell Episode 502," interview by Marc Maron, *WTF with Marc Maron* Podcast, Earwolf, June 2014.

35   Jeff Gilbert, "My First Gig," *Guitar World*, March 1991.

36 "Soundgarden: The Veteran Band from Seattle Proves There's Life After Nirvana," interview by Kim Neely, *Rolling Stone*, July 9, 1992.

Chapter II

1   Mark Yarm, *Everybody Loves Our Town: An Oral History of Grunge* (New York: Crown Archetype, 2011).

2   Katherine Turman, "Life Rules," *RIP*, October 1991.

3   Donald Fagen, *Eminent Hipsters* (New York: Viking, 2013).

4   "Chris Cornell Interview: Searching For The Real Chris Cornell," interview by Paul Brannigan, *Louder*, February 6, 2018, https://www.loudersound.com/features/archive-the-real-chris-cornell.

5   "Q&A: Soundgarden Frontman Chris Cornell," interview by Craig Marks, *Details*, April 2012, http://www.details.com/celebrities-entertainment/music-and-books/201204/chris- cornell-soundgarden.

6   "In Town: A Higher Truth with Chris Cornell," interview by Matt Pittman, *The Florida Times-Union*, June 14, 2016, https://www.jacksonville.com/jack/2016-06-14/story/town-higher-truth-chris-cornell.

7   "Chris Cornell Episode 502," interview by Marc Maron, *WTF with Marc Maron* Podcast, Earwolf, June 2014.

8   "Soundgarden's Chris Cornell And Kim Thayil Talk Guitar," interview by Rob Laing, *MusicRadar*, March, 2012, https://www.musicradar.com/news/classic-interview- soundgardens-chris-cornell-and-kim-thayil-talk-guitar.

9   "Chris Cornell's Full 'Ultramega OK' Hall Of Fame Interview," interview by Adem Tepedelen, *Decibel*, May 18, 2017, https://www.decibelmagazine.com/2017/05/18/chris-cornell-s-full-ultramega-ok-hall-of-fame-interview/.

10 "Soundgarden's Kim Thayil: 'I'm not on a first-name basis with my gear,'" interview by Michael Astley-Brown, *MusicRadar*, July 23, 2019.

11 "Kim Thayil on New Chris Cornell Box: 'The Main Thing Is to Represent His Versatility,'" interview by Corbin Reiff, *Rolling Stone*, November 1, 2018.

[12] "Sirius XM Townhall With Soundgarden," *SiriusXM Townhall*, Pearl Jam Radio, November 16, 2012.

[13] "Soundgarden, Incessant Mace, Live 2017," Youtube, EspoProductions, May 18, 2017, https://www.youtube.com/watch?v=9oonh4H df4M.

[14] "MoPop Oral Histories, Kim Thayil Interview," Museum of Popular Culture, Seattle, WA, December 18, 1999.

[15] Daniel House, "Remembering Old Histories And Saying Goodbye," DanielHouse.com, May 24, 2017, http://danielhouse.com/soundgarden-skin_yard.html.

[16] Charles R. Cross, "Soundgarden: The Home Team Wins the World Series," *The Rocket*, December 21, 1994.

[17] Greg Prato, *Grunge Is Dead: The Oral History of Seattle Rock Music* (Toronto: ECW Press, 2009).

[18] Everett True, "Soundgarden: The Mutate Gallery," *Melody Maker*, June 10, 1989.

[19] Christine Natanael, "Blowing Eardrums and Blowing Minds," *Reflex*, December 1991.

[20] "Chris Cornell Extended Interview," interview by Sean Nelson, *The Stranger*, September 23, 2015, https://www.thestranger.com/music/feature/2015/09/23/22901720/chris-cornell-interview-extended-version.

[21] "Kim Thayil Has Revealed His Favorite Chris Cornell Vocal Performance," *Kerrang*, November 20, 2018, https://www.kerrang.com/the-news/chris-cornell-kim-thayil- soundgarden-exclusive-interview/.

[22] Clark Humphrey, *Loser: The Real Seattle Music Story* (Seattle: Miscmedia, 2016).

[23] "Chris Cornell, Kim Thayil Discuss Soundgarden's Future," interview by Chris Gill, *Guitar World*, March 30, 2011, https://www.guitarworld.com/features/chris- cornell-kim-thayil-discuss-soundgardens-future.

[24] "Chris Cornell Episode 502," interview by Marc Maron, *WTF with Marc Maron* Podcast, Earwolf, June 2014.

[25] "Soundgarden's Kim Thayil Talks 'Echo Of Miles' A New Collection Of Originals, Covers And Oddities," Interview by Richard Bienstock, Guitar World, November 24, 2014 https://www.guitarworld.com/

features/soundgardens-kim-thayil-talks-echo- miles-new-collection-originals-covers.

26 "Interview: Chris Cornell On Making Music And Movies," Interview by Indiewire Team, *IndieWire*, September 29, 2011 https://www.indiewire.com/2011/09/interview-chris-cornell-on-making-music-and-movies-51897/.

27 "The Vulture Transcript: Chris Cornell Talks About Soundgarden's Reunion," interview by Rebecca Milzoff, *Vulture*, July 8, 2011, https://www.vulture.com/2011/07/the_vulture_transcript_chris_c.html.

28 Susan Silver, "Silver's Golden Touch," *Rip*, January 1996.

29 Christina Kelly, "Soundgarden: The Unsung Pioneers of Seattle Rock Take the Slow and Steady Route to Stardom," *US*, July 1996.

30 "Chris Cornell Interview," interview by Howard Stern, *The Howard Stern Show*, SiriusXM, June 12, 2007.

31 "Q&A with Chris Cornell," interview by Chris Heath, *Rolling Stone*, October 14, 1999.

32 Dawn Anderson, "Deep Six Review," *The Rocket*, March 1986.

33 Bruce Pavitt, "Sub Pop Column," *The Rocket*, April 1986.

Chapter III

1 "Interview With Chris Cornell Part I," YouTube, HardDrive Radio, June 4, 2014, https://www.youtube.com/watch?v=oYejbFOKz5U.

2 Pearl Jam, *Pearl Jam Twenty* (New York: Simon & Schuster, 2011).

3 Director Scot Barbour, *Malfunkshun: The Andrew Wood Story* (Los Angeles: Dos Ojos Productions, 2005).

4 "Chris Cornell Interview," interview by Pierre Robert, 93.3 WMMR, October 15, 2015.

5 Katherine Turman, "Chris Cornell Talks Missing Andrew Wood, Writing Songs In the Bathroom: Unpublished 2015 Interview Excerpts," *Billboard*, May 19, 2017, https://www.billboard.com/articles/columns/rock/7801053/chris-cornell-2015- interview-higher-truth.

6 "Super Soundman: As Singer-Songwriter Chris Cornell's Career Soars, He Keeps His Outlook Well-Grounded," interview by Gene Stout, *Seattle Post-Intelligencer*, May 24, 1994.

7   Director Scot Barbour, *Malfunkshun: The Andrew Wood Story* (Los Angeles: Dos Ojos Productions, 2005).

8   "The TMN Wellwater Conspiracy Interview with Matt Cameron and John McBain," interview by Jessica Letkemann, Tickle My Nausea, March 1, 2001, https:// nowinvisibly.com/wwc/2001/03/the-tmn-wellwater-conspiracy-interview-with-matt-cameron-and-john-mcbain/.

9   "Soundgarden's Matt Cameron On The Reunion And Singing On Attack Of The Killer Tomatoes," interview by Tom Murphy, *Westword*, July 18, 2011, https://www.westword.com/music/soundgardens-matt-cameron-on-the-reunion-and-singing-on-attack-of-the-killer-tomatoes-5705597.

10 Matt Cameron (@themattcameron), Instagram post, May 18, 2018, https://www.instagram.com/p/Bi7ZzjQhY7R/.

11 "How Does Your Garden Grow?" interview by Annie Leighton, *Livewire*, November 1992.

12 "Soundgarden Interview, Superunknown25," interview by Grant Random, *Lithium*, SiriusXM, March 8, 2014.

13 Michael Azerrad, *Our Band Could Be Your Life* (New York: Little, Brown, 2002).

14 "Soundgarden, Behold the Grunge Messiahs," interview by Mike Gitter, *RIP*, January 1992.

15 "Chris Cornell's Full 'Ultramega OK' Hall of Fame Interview," interview by Adem Tepedelen, *Decibel*, May 18, 2017, https:// www.decibelmagazine.com/2017/05/18/chris-cornell-s-full-ultramega-ok-hall-of-fame-interview/.

16 "Chris Cornell: The Rolling Stone Interview," interview by Alec Foege, *Rolling Stone*, December 29, 1994, https://www.rollingstone.com/music/music-features/chris-cornell-the-rolling-stone-interview-79108/.

17 "Soundgarden: The Unsung Pioneers of Seattle Rock Take the Slow and Steady Route to Stardom," interview by Christina Kelly, *US*, July 1996.

[18] "Prime Cuts: Kim Thayil," interview by Jeff Gilbert, *Guitar School*, May 1994.

[19] Simon Reynolds, "Various Artists: Sub Pop 200," *NME*, January 1989.

Chapter IV

[1] "An Interview with Kurt Cobain," interview by Carlos "Cake" Nunez, *Flipside*, March 1992.

[2] "Chris Cornell Interview," interview by Howard Stern, *The Howard Stern Show*, SiriusXM, June 12, 2007.

[3] "Chris Cornell Interview, Extended Version," interview by Sean Nelson, *The Stranger*, September 23, 2015, https://www.thestranger. com/music/feature/2015/09/23/22901720/chris-cornell-interview-extended-version.

[4] "Digging the Garden," interview by Jonathan Poneman, *Spin*, September 1992.

[5] "Northwest of Hell," interview by Michael Corcoran, *Spin*, December 1989.

[6] "Soundgarden: The Mutate Gallery," interview by Everett True, *Melody Maker*, June 10, 1989.

[7] "The age of innocents: on the 20th anniversary of three of rock's most significant releases-Nirvana's Nevermind, Pearl Jam's Ten and Soundgarden's Badmotorfinger--Billboard talks to architects of the Seattle scene about what they saw, how they won--and what they lost," interview by Mitchell Peters, *Billboard*, September 17, 2011.

[8] "Chris Cornell Interview," interview by Simon Coffey, *Student Radio Network*, 95bFM New Zealand, January 16, 1997.

[9] "Soundgarden to Audioslave: Chris Cornell Weighs In on Select Albums from Career," interview by Dan Epstein, *Revolver*, November 19, 2006, https://www.revolvermag.com/music/soundgarden-audioslave-chris-cornell-weighs-select-albums-career#soundgarden-—-ultramega-ok-sst-1988.

[10] Kim Thayil, *Ultramega OK* liner notes, Soundgarden (Seattle: SST Records, 1989).

11 Kim Thayil, *Ultramega OK* liner notes, Soundgarden (Seattle: SST Records, 1989).

12 "Chris Cornell's Full 'Ultramega OK' Hall Of Fame Interview," interview by Adem Tepedelen, *Decibel*, May 18, 2017, https://www.dccibelmagazine.com/2017/05/18/chris-cornell-s-full-ultramega-ok-hall-of-fame-interview/.

13 "Kashmir," *Sounds*, May 13, 1989.

14 "Chris Cornell's Full 'Ultramega OK' Hall Of Fame Interview," interview by Adem Tepedelen, *Decibel*, May 18, 2017, https://www.decibelmagazine.com/2017/05/18/chris-cornell-s-full-ultramega-ok-hall-of-fame-interview/.

15 "Chris Cornell Rant Before Last Song 29 April 2017," YouTube, posted by Bobby Middleton, May 19, 2017, https://www.youtube.com/watch?v=buRu18YpeSc&list=RDbuRu18YpeSc&start_radio=1&t=19.

16 "Chris Cornell Interview," interview by Simon Coffey, *Student Radio Network*, 95bFM New Zealand, January 16, 1997.

17 "Chris Cornell's Full 'Ultramega OK' Hall Of Fame Interview," interview by Adem Tepedelen, *Decibel*, May 18, 2017, https://www.decibelmagazine.com/2017/05/18/chris-cornell-s-full-ultramega-ok-hall-of-fame-interview/.

18 *Headbangers Ball*, interview by Riki Rachtman, MTV, January 27, 1990.

19 "Chris Cornell's Full 'Ultramega OK' Hall Of Fame Interview," interview by Adem Tepedelen, *Decibel*, May 18, 2017, https://www.decibelmagazine.com/2017/05/18/chris-cornell-s-full-ultramega-ok-hall-of-fame-interview/.

20 "MoPop Oral Histories, Matt Cameron Interview," Museum of Popular Culture, Seattle, WA, December 18, 1999.

21 "Chris Cornell Of Soundgarden Interviewed," interview by Graham Reid, *Pressure Drop*, June 30, 2009, https://www.elsewhere.co.nz/absoluteelsewhere/2334/chris-cornell-of-soundgarden-interviewed-1992-pressure-drop/.

22 "MoPop Oral Histories, Kim Thayil Interview," Museum of Popular Culture, Seattle, WA, December 18, 1999.

23 "Rocketman: Soundgarden's Chris Cornell Comes Clean About His Addiction to Speed," interview by Gavin Edwards, *Details*, June 1996.

24 "Hammer of The Gods," interview by Jonathan Gold, *Spin*, April 1994.

25 Director Scot Barbour, *Malfunkshun: The Andrew Wood Story* (Los Angeles: Dos Ojos Productions, 2005).

Chapter V

1 Mark Yarm, *Everybody Loves Our Town: An Oral History of Grunge* (New York: Crown Archetype, 2011).

2 "An Oral History of Soundgarden's 'Rusty Cage,'" interview by Wiliam Goodman, *Spin*, November 22, 2011, https://www.spin.com/2011/11/soundgarden-rusty-cage- interview/.

3 "Terry Date: Avoiding A Signature Sound," interview by Jake Brown, *Tape Op*, January/February 2018, https://tapeop.com/interviews/123/terry-date/.

4 "Digging the Garden," interview by Jonathan Poneman, *Spin*, September 1992.

5 "Chris Cornell Interview," interview by Simon Coffey, *Student Radio Network*, 95bFM New Zealand, January 16, 1997.

6 "Chris Cornell – 66 Second Interview," interview by NME, YouTube, August 1, 2012, https://www.youtube.com/watch?v=QbYA-VGwCLk.

7 "Kashmir," *Sounds*, May 13, 1989.

8 J.D. Considine, "Louder Than Love," *Rolling Stone*, June 17, 1997, https://www.rollingstone.com/music/music-album-reviews/louder-than-love-191026/.

9 "Axl Rose: The Rolling Stone Interview," interview by Del James, *Rolling Stone*, August 1989, https://www.rollingstone.com/music/music-news/axl-rose-the-rolling-stone- interview-3-184068/.

10 Chris Cornell Episode 502," interview by Marc Maron, *WTF with Marc Maron* Podcast, Earwolf, June 2014.

11 "Kirk Hammett Interview," interview by Toucher & Rich, *The Sports Hub*, WBZ-FM, September 13, 2017.

12 Push, "Mudhoney, Soundgarden: School of African and Oriental Studies," *Melody Maker*, May 20, 1989.

[13] Keith Cameron, *Mudhoney: The Sound and the Fury From Seattle* (Beverly, MA: Voyageur Press, 2014).

[14] Everett True, "Soundgarden: The Mutate Gallery," *Melody Maker*, June 10, 1989.

[15] Greg Prato, *Grunge Is Dead: The Oral History of Seattle Rock Music* (Toronto: ECW Press, 2009).

[16] Clay Tarver, "The Rock 'n' Roll Casualty Who Became a War Hero," *The New York Times*, 2013, https://www.nytimes.com/2013/07/02/ magazine/evermans-war.html? pagewanted=all&_r=1&.

[17] "Soundgarden – Steve Jones Mishap," Concret Planet, March 31, 2009, https://www.youtube.com/watch?v=CGBU3Jxz58w&feature=youtu. be.

[18] Richard Milne, "Remembering Soundgarden's Jawdropping 1989 Cabaret Metro Concert," 93XRT, February 22, 2018, https://wxrt. radio.com/soundgarden-first- chicago-concert-metro.

[19] "MoPop Oral Histories, Kim Thayil Interview," Museum of Popular Culture, Seattle, WA, December 18, 1999.

[20] Chris Cornell, blog post, ChrisCornell.com, December 5, 2008, http:// www.chriscornell. com/blog/.

[21] Parry Gettelman, "Voivod, Soundgarden Shakeup Beacham Theater," *Orlando Sentinel*, February 9, 1990, https://www.orlandosentinel. com/news/os-xpm-1990-02-09-9002083062-story.html.

Chapter VI

[1] "Temple Of The Dog: Oral History," interview by Andy Greene, *Rolling Stone*, September 30, 2016, https://www.rollingstone.com/ music/music-features/temple- of-the-dog-an-oral-history-120453/.

[2] Director Scot Barbour, *Malfunkshun: The Andrew Wood Story* (Los Angeles: Dos Ojos Productions, 2005).

[3] "Temple Of The Dog: Chris Cornell On The Return Of The '90s Grunge Supergroup," interview by Jim Farber, *The Guardian*, November 16, 2016, https://www.theguardian.com/music/2016/ nov/16/temple-of-the-dog-chris-cornell-eddie-vedder-90s-grunge.

4   Chris Cornell, blog post, ChrisCornell.com, August 13, 2008, http://www.chriscornell.com/blog/.

5   "Chris Cornell, blog post," ChrisCornell.com, August 13, 2008, http://www.chriscornell.com/blog/.

6   "Chris Cornell Interview," interview by Damon Stewart, *The New Music Hour*, KISW, April 14, 1991.

7   "Soundgarden," interview by The Technicolor Twins, *Metal Hammer*, May 1990.

8   "Soundgarden, Behold the Grunge Messiahs," interview by Mike Gitter, *RIP*, January 1992.

9   "Blowing Eardrums and Blowing Minds," interview by Christine Natanael, *Reflex*, December 1991.

10   "Ben Shepherd: Soundgarden Take The Grunge Full Circle," interview by Éanna Ó Caollaí, *Irish Times*, September 6, 2013.

11   Michael Azerrad, *Come as You Are: The Story of Nirvana* (New York: Three Rivers Press, 1993).

12   "Interview: Gary Lee Conner," interview by Leonardo Tissot, February 18, 2018, http://www.leonardotissot.com/2019/02/interview-gary-lee-conner.html.

13   "Chris Cornell, Kim Thayil Discuss Soundgarden's Future," interview by Chris Gill, *Guitar World*, March 30, 2011, https://www.guitarworld.com/features/chris- cornell-kim-thayil-discuss-soundgardens-future.

14   Lollapalooza Tour Program, 2003

15   "Chris Cornell Interview," interview by Damon Stewart, *The New Music Hour*, KISW, April 14, 1991.

16   "Life Rules," interview by Katherine Turman, *RIP*, October 1991.

17   "Chris Cornell Interview," interview by Damon Stewart, *The New Music Hour*, KISW, April 14, 1991.

18   Pearl Jam, *Pearl Jam Twenty* (New York: Simon & Schuster, 2011).

19   Greg Prato, *Grunge Is Dead: The Oral History of Seattle Rock Music* (Toronto: ECW Press, 2009).

20   "Temple Of The Dog: Oral History," interview by Andy Greene, *Rolling Stone*, September 30, 2016, https://www.rollingstone.com/music/music-features/temple- of-the-dog-an-oral-history-120453/.

21 "1990: The Making of Pearl Jam," interview by Jessica Letkemann, *TwoFeetThick*, October 18, 2010, http://www.twofeetthick. com/2010/10/18/1990-the-making-of- pearl-jam-a-tft-mini-book/.

Chapter VII

1 "Chris Cornell: Pruning His Future," interview by Tom Lanham, *Illinois Entertainer*, November 1999.
2 "Chris Cornell," interview by Rob Laing, *Total Guitar*, (published) June 9, 2017.
3 "Chris Cornell Interview," interview by James Rotondi, *Guitar Player*, October 1993.
4 "Side-By-Side with Soundgarden," interview on Amazon Music, 2016.
5 "1991," interview on *'90s Backspin*, VIVA2, October 30, 1999.
6 "Defining and Defying the Times: How Soundgarden Made 'Badmotorfinger,'" interview by Mischa Pearlman, *Noisey*, December 15, 2016.
7 "Chris Cornell Looks Back On 20 Years of Soundgarden's 'Rusty Cage,'" interview by William Goldman, *Spin*, November 22, 2011.
8 "Soundgarden: Behold the Ugly Groove," interview by Steve Blush, *Seconds* #17, 1991.
9 "Side-By-Side with Soundgarden," interview on Amazon Music, 2016.
10 "Chris Cornell talks Johnny Cash, Audioslave reunion and Higher Truth," interview by Michael Astley-Brown, *MusicRadar*, November 2, 2015.
11 "Chris Cornell's Enjoying Solo Performances and Rocking with Soundgarden," interview by Ed Condran, *The Courant*, May 18, 2017.
12 "Chris Cornell – Outshined – A Tribute To His Great Sense Of Humor," YouTube, posted by Jonathan Messika, May 21, 2017, https://www.youtube.com/watch?v= sMnCxE1y_5c.
13 "Side-By-Side with Soundgarden," interview on Amazon Music, 2016.
14 "Hereos…And Heroin," interview by Lonn M. Friend, *RIP*, July 1992.
15 "Dear Superstar: Chris Cornell," interview by Steve Kandell, *Blender*, July 2005.

16 "'Singles' at 25: Cameron Crowe on Making the Definitive Grunge Movie," interview by Alexis Sottile, *Rolling Stone*, September 18, 2017.

17 Director Cameron Crowe, *Singles* (Burbank, CA: Warner Bros., 1992) DVD interview.

18 Singles Original Motion Picture Soundtrack (25th Anniversary Edition), Sony Legacy, 2017.

19 "Chris Cornell Flashback Q&A: 'We Have to Be Aware That Life Is So Short,'" interview by Chuck Arnold, Yahoo Music, May 18, 2017, https://www.yahoo.com/entertainment/chris-cornell-flashback-qa-aware-life-short-023857577.html.

20 "Songwriters On The Secrets Of Their Work," interview by Tim Appelo, *The Hollywood Reporter*, December 9, 2011.

21 "Soundgarden Rail Against The 'Jesus Christ Pose' In New and Gripping Video," interview by Levine Schneider, *Public Relations*, October 30, 1991.

22 "Dear Superstar: Chris Cornell," interview by Steve Kandell, *Blender*, June 2005.

23 Lauren Spencer, "Badmotorfinger," *Spin*, October 1991.

24 Craig Tomashoff, "Badmotorfinger," *People*, November 26, 1991.

25 Gina Arnold, "Badmotorfinger," *Entertainment Weekly*, September 27, 1991.

26 "Soundgarden: Booze, Burning Crosses and Badmotorfinger," interview by Greg Prato, *Classic Rock Magazine*, October 8, 2016.

Chapter VIII

1 "How Soundgarden's Fearlessness was Inspired by the Beatles: Exclusive Chris Cornell Interview," interview by Jed Gottlieb, *Ultimate Classic Rock*, July 13, 2011, https://ultimateclassicrock.com/soundgarden-chris-cornell-interview/?utm_source=tsmclip&utm_medium=referral.

2 Slash with Anthony Bozza, *Slash* (New York: It Books, 2007).

3 "Chris Cornell on Soundgarden's New Album, the Queen of England, and Axl Rose," interview by Nisha Gopalan, *Vulture*, November 13, 2012.

4   "Dear Superstar: Chris Cornell," interview by Steve Kandell, *Blender*, June 2005.

5   "Dear Superstar: Chris Cornell," interview by Steve Kandell, *Blender*, June 2005.

6   "Building the Perfect Beast," interview by Chuck Klosterman, *Spin*, February 2003.

7   Slash with Anthony Bozza, *Slash* (New York: It Books, 2007).

8   "Sebastian Bach Remembers Soundgarden Opening for Skid Row and Chris Cornell Spoofing His Moves," interview with Sebastian Bach, *Billboard*, May 24, 2017.

9   "The J.P. Generation: He's Not Gone, And He's Not Forgotten," interview by Jack Broom, *The Seattle Times*, April 4, 1993.

10 "The J.P. Generation: He's Not Gone, And He's Not Forgotten," interview by Jack Broom, *The Seattle Times*, April 4, 1993.

11 "The Real Thing," interview by Mike Rubin, *Spin*, July 1996.

12 "Chris Cornell tells a story about terrorizing a European reporter," YouTube, posted by Elizabeth Daulton, December 8, 2011, https://www.youtube.com/watch? v=1HFgIKVf4Bc.

13 "Chris Cornell Q&A," interview by Austin Scaggs, *Rolling Stone*, July 14, 2005.

14 "Singers, Nirvana & The Seattle Sound," interview by Jeff Gilbert, *Guitar World Magazine*, 1993.

15 Paul Henderson, "Guns N' Roses at Wembley," *Kerrang!*, Issue 398.

16 Pearl Jam, *Pearl Jam Twenty* (New York: Simon & Schuster, 2011).

17 "Ten Past Ten," interview by Eric Weisbard, *Spin*, August 2001.

18 Jim Rose, *Freak Like Me (Real, Raw & Dangerous): Inside the Jim Rose Circus Sideshow* (New York: Dell Publishing, 1995).

19 "Soundgarden – Cop Killer (Miami 1992)," YouTube, posted by All Things Soundgarden, May 9, 2018, https://www.youtube.com/watch?v=ATJPzcspkp0.

Chapter XI

1   "Chris Cornell on Being a Rock Star, Shedding 'Angry Young Man' Persona," interview by Kory Grow, *Revolver*, December 22, 2011.

2 "Chris Cornell, Searching for Solitude," interview by Jonathan Gold, *Details*, December 1996.

3 "Interview: Soundgarden's Chris Cornell Looks Back on 'Superunknown,' Ahead to Nine Inch Nails Tour," interview by Brian Ives, Radio.com, May 12, 2014, http://radio.com/2014/05/12/interview-soundgarden-chris-cornell-superunknown-nine-inch-nails-tour/.

4 "Soundgarden Superunknown 25th Anniversary—Chris Cornell," interview by Redbeard, *In the Studio with Redbeard*, March 18, 2019, https://www.inthestudio.net/online-on-demand/soundgarden-superunknown-chris-cornell/.

5 "Get Yourself Control: The Oral History Of Soundgarden's 'Superunknown,'" interview by Stacey Anderson, *Spin*, June 5, 2014, https://www.spin.com/2014/06/oral-history-soundgarden-superunknown-anniversary-reissue/.

6 "Chris Cornell and Soundgarden remember 'Black Hole Sun': 'I understand it even less now,'" interview by Peter Watts, *Uncut*, May 19, 2017.

7 "Chris Cornell tells stories behind classic 'Superunknown' songs," interview by Kyle Anderson, *Entertainment Weekly*, June 3, 2014.

8 "Journey into The Superunknown," interview by Everett True, *Melody Maker*, March 19, 1994.

9 "What Chris Cornell Told Me About His Depression Years Before His Suicide," interview by Mike Zimmerman, *Men's Health*, May 19, 2017.

10 "Interview: Chris Cornell," interview by Howard Stern, *The Howard Stern Show*, SiriusXM, June 18, 2014.

11 "Soundgarden – Mailman – Webster Hall (June 2, 2014)," YouTube, posted by mfc172, June 2, 2014, https://www.youtube.com/watch?v=GlG497HGvy4.

12 "Soundgarden's Chris Cornell on 'Superunknown,' Depression and Kurt Cobain," interview by Kory Grow, *Rolling Stone*, May 19, 2017.

13 "Gardener's Question Time," *Kerrang*, March 1, 1997.

14 "Chris Cornell and Soundgarden remember 'Black Hole Sun': 'I understand it even less now,'" interview by Peter Watts, *Uncut*, May 19, 2017.

15 "Soundgarden's Chris Cornell Steps Out On His Own With An Album Filled With Mystery And Self-Reflection," interview by Ali Lorraine, *Harper's Bazaar*, October 1999.

16 "The Dark Knight Returns," interview by Chris Smith, *Raw*, May 11, 1994.

17 "Hammer of the Gods," interview by Jonathan Gold, *Spin*, April 1994.

18 "Journey into The Superunknown," interview by Everett True, *Melody Maker*, March 19, 1994.

19 J.D. Considine, "Superunknown," *Rolling Stone*, January 31, 1997.

20 Jon Pareles, "Lightening Up on the Gloom in Grunge," *The New York Times*, March 6, 1994.

21 Ann Powers, "Superunknown," *Blender*, May 1994.

22 "Soundgarden's Chris Cornell Talks 'Superunknown' + More," interview by Full Metal Jackie, *Loudwire*, April 23, 2017, https://loudwire.com/soundgarden-chris-cornell-superunknown-20th-anniversary-summer-tour/?utm_source=tsmclip&utm_medium=referral.

Chapter X

1 "Chris Cornell Interview," interview by Howard Stern, *The Howard Stern Show*, SiriusXM, June 12, 2007.

2 *Request*, October 1994.

3 "Chris Cornell Interview," interview on MTV News, MTV, June 3, 1994.

4 "Chris Cornell Talks Kurt Cobain, Jeff Buckley and Battle with Drink and Drugs," *Irish Independent*, May 19, 2017, https://www.independent.ie/entertainment/music/from-the-archive-chris-cornell-talks-kurt-cobain-jeff-buckley-and-battle-with-drink-and-drugs-in-2009-interview-35732801.html.

5 "Bands Won't Play For Those That Don't Obey," interview by Peter Howell, Toronto Sun, August 4, 1994.

6 "The Pop Life," interview by Neil Strauss, *The New York Times*, June 15, 1994.

7 Tom Phalen, "Soundgarden Closes Tour with Crash-and-Burn Home Performance Many Will Recall for Years," *Seattle Times*, August 15, 1994.

8 Chris Cornell, blog post, ChrisCornell.com, April 1, 2009, http://www.chriscornell.com/blog/.

9 "Soundgarden: Seattle's Sonic Boom," interview by Katherine Turman, *Metal Edge*, July 1996.

10 "Soundgarden: The Home Team Wins the World Series," interview by Charles R. Cross, *The Rocket*, December 21, 1994.

11 "Interview: Soundgarden's Chris Cornell Looks Back on 'Superunknown,' Ahead to Nine Inch Nails Tour," interview by Brian Ives, Radio.com, May 12, 2014, http://radio.com/2014/05/12/interview-soundgarden-chris-cornell-superunknown-nine-inch-nails-tour/.

12 "The Last Temptation of Chris Cornell," interview by Ian Winwood, *Classic Rock*, October 2, 2015.

13 "Kim Thayil of Soundgarden: Down on the Upbeat," interview by Rich Maloof, *Guitar Magazine*, July 1996.

14 "Soundgarden: Seattle's Sonic Boom," interview by Katherine Turman, *Metal Edge*, July 1996.

15 "Gardener's Question Time," *Kerrang*, March 1, 1997.

16 "Soundgarden Returns," interview by MTV News, MTV, April 12, 1996.

17 "Chris Cornell of Soundgarden Looks Back on 'Burden In My Hand,'" interview by Rick Florino, *Artist Direct*, September 13, 2011.

18 "Back In The Sun," interview by Ken Milcallef, *Electronic Musician*, December 2012.

19 "Chris Cornell AP Interview," interview by AltPress, *Alternative Press*, May 18, 2017, https://www.altpress.com/features/chris_cornell_ap_interview/.

Chapter XI

[1] Ivan Kreillkamp, "Soundgarden, Down On The Upside," *Spin*, June 1996.

[2] Rob O'Connor, "Soundgarden, Down On The Upside," *Rolling Stone*, June 1996.

[3] David Browne, "Soundgarden, Down On The Upside," *Entertainment Weekly*, June 1996.

[4] "Soundgarden to Audioslave: Chris Cornell Weighs in on Select Albums from Career," interview by Dan Epstein, *Revolver*, November 19, 2006, https://www.revolvermag.com/music/soundgarden-audio slave-chris-cornell-weighs-select-albums-career#chris-cornell-—-euphoria-morning-interscope-1999.

[5] "Soundgarden," interview by Everett True, *Melody Maker*, May 15, 1996.

[6] "Soundgarden: Interview with Kim Thayil," *Hard Music*, June 1996.

[7] "Perry Ferrell Talks New Mystery Project, Kurt Cobain," interview by Kory Grow, *Rolling Stone*, May 21, 2015.

[8] "Soundgarden: Like Falling Off A Hog," interview by Max Bell, *Blah, Blah, Blah*, June 1996.

[9] Interview on MaxTV New Zealand, January 17, 1997.

[10] "Talking About Sabbath, The Ramones And Nirvana? It Must Be Soundgarden," interview by Murray Engleheart, *Massive*, January 1997.

[11] "Songwriter Interviews: Devo," interview by Carl Weisner, *Songfacts*, https://www.songfacts.com/blog/interviews/devo.

[12] "Sound of Silence," interview by Jeff Gilbert, *Guitar World*, February 1998.

[13] Jerry Ewing, "Peerless in Seattle," *Vox*, December 1997.

[14] "Over the Garden Wall," interview by Tobias Hoi, *Guitar*, November 1999.

[15] "Over the Garden Wall," interview by Tobias Hoi, *Guitar*, November 1999.

16 "An Interview With Chris Cornell," interview by Tim Den, *Lollipop*, September 9, 2007. https://www.lollipop.com/article.php3?content= 2007/09sept/f-chriscornell.html.

17 "The Life and Times of Chris Cornell," interview by Rod Yates, *Rolling Stone*, September 17, 2015.

18 "New Beginnings," *Guitar One*, October 1999.

19 "Audioslave: Not Built to Last," interview by Rachel Clark, *Louder Sound*, May 2, 2007.

20 "Chris Cornell on Timbaland-Produced 'Scream': 'I Think Fans Will Come Around to the Concept,'" interview by Hardeep Phull, *Rolling Stone*, March 5, 2009, https://www.rollingstone.com/music/music-news/chris-cornell-on-timbaland-produced-scream-i-think-fans-will-come-around-to-the-concept-104027/.

21 "Armed Audio Warfare," interview by Tom Lanham, *CMJ New Music Monthly*, January/February 2003.

Chapter XII

1 "Morello Says Audioslave Have Songs for a Second LP Already," interview by Jon Weiderhorn, MTV, October 21, 2002.

2 "Interview with Chris Cornell," interview by David Fricke, *Artist Confidential*, Lithium, Sirius XM, September 18, 2015.

3 "Tim Commerford, Rage Against The Machine," interview by Dan Le Batard, *The Dan Le Batard Show*, ESPN Radio, February 10, 2015.

4 "Chris Cornell," interview by Tom Morello, *UME*, November 16, 2018.

5 "Soundgarden: Alive in the Superunknown," interview by Randy Peisner, *Spin*, August 17, 2010, https://www.spin.com/2010/08/soundgarden-alive-superunknown/.

6 "Q&A: Soundgarden Frontman Chris Cornell," interview by Craig Marks, *Details*, April 2012, http://www.details.com/celebrities-entertainment/music-and-books/201204/chris-cornell-soundgarden.

7 "Audioslave's Brad Wilk Reborn," interview by Michael Parillo, *Modern Drummer*, August 2003.

8 "Chris Cornell = Rock God," interview by Madeline Rayas, *The Stranger*, March 20, 2003.

[9] "Audioslave Interview," interview by Bob Coburn, *Rockline*, Premiere Radio Networks, July 28, 2003.

[10] "Armed Audio Warfare," interview by Tom Lanham, *CMJ New Music Monthly*, January/February 2003.

[11] "Up Close & Personal With Soundgarden," interview on 102.1 The Edge, YouTube, November 15, 2012, https://www.youtube.com/watch?v=D63NEB5o5Yg&t=254s.

[12] "Rock's Mega-Merger," interview by Gavin Edwards, *Rolling Stone*, November 2002.

[13] "Audioslave: The Ex Factor," interview by Kevin Murphy, *Classic Rock*, May 17, 2005.

[14] "Morello Says Audioslave Have Songs for a Second LP Already," interview by Jon Weiderhorn, MTV, October 21, 2002.

[15] "Interview: Chris Cornell," interview by Howard Stern, *The Howard Stern Show*, SiriusXM, November 16, 2011.

[16] "Chris Cornell's 2006 Interview on Audioslave, Addiction, and Reinventing Rock," interview by Dorian Lynskey, *Spin*, May 17, 2017.

[17] "Chris Cornell 'Doesn't Remind Me' (talking about rehab in Malibu) Knight , Charlotte 12.2.13," YouTube, posted by DCRANGERFAN, December 3, 2013, https://www.youtube.com/watch?v=LQ1_A0YkAp8.

[18] Lollapalooza Tour Program, 2003.

[19] "To Hell and Back: Soundgarden's Chris Cornell On Rehab and 'Long Slow Recovery,'" interview by Gavin Martin, *Mirror*, May 18, 2017, https://www.mirror.co.uk/lifestyle/going-out/music/soundgarden-chris-cornell-on-rehab-and-king-1423211.

[20] Pat Blashill, "Audioslave," *Rolling Stone*, November 28, 2002.

[21] Chris Dahlen and Ryan Shreiber, "Audioslave," *Pitchfork*, November 25, 2002.

Chapter XIII

[1] Director Lawrence Jordan, *Audioslave: Live in Cuba* (Los Angeles: Epic, 2005).

[2] Ibid.

3 "Chris Cornell Recalls Audioslave's 2005 Cuba Concert, Gives Advice to Rolling Stones," interview by Associated Press, *Billboard*, March 13, 2016.

4 Neva Chonin, "Audioslave gets political at Warfield/Cornell goes after Bush, Rage-style," *SF Gate*, March 21, 2003.

5 "Chris Cornell with Cameron Crowe: Josephine," YouTube, posted by Chris Cornell, November 8, 2015, https://youtu.be/D_c-wEEz0Yw.

6 "Exclusive: Chris Cornell Talks Writing Music for 'Machine Gun Preacher,' His Career, Soundgarden, Touring, Johnny Cash, Video Games and Much More," interview by Steve 'Frosty' Weintraub, *Collider*, September 30, 2011, https://collider.com/chris-cornell-machine-gun-preacher-interview/.

7 "Chris Cornell Salutes Lost Loved Ones on New Audioslave Single," interview by Corey Moss, MTV, June 1, 2005, http://www.mtv.com/news/1503321/chris-cornell-salutes-lost-loved-ones-on-new-audioslave-single/.

8 "The Straight Talk and Philosophical Musings of Chris Cornell," interview by Jon Wiederhorn, Yahoo Music, May 19, 2017, https://www.yahoo.com/entertainment/straight-talk-philosophical-musings-chris-cornell-052120473.html.

9 "Audioslave Guitarist Tom Morello: 'I'm a Great Believer in a Good Riff,'" *Ultimate Guitar*, January 6, 2006, https://www.ultimate-guitar.com/news/interviews/audioslave_guitarist_tom_morello_im_a_great_believer_in_a_good_riff.html.

10 "Audioslave Frontman Explains Lyrical Inspiration for 'Be Yourself,'" *Blabbermouth*, April 8, 2005, https://www.blabbermouth.net/news/audioslave-frontman-explains- lyrical-inspiration-for-be-yourself/.

11 David Fricke, "Out Of Exile: Audioslave," *Rolling Stone*, June 16, 2005.

12 "Chris Cornell in 2005," interview by John W. Ennis, Facebook, May 16, 2017, https://www.facebook.com/watch/?v=1754576054833325.

13 "We're Just Four Sweaty Guys Making Music," interview by Ross Raihala, *Pioneer Press*, April 22, 2005.

14 "Band Members Discuss Tracks from Revelations [Video]," *Revelations*, 2007.

Chapter XIV

1   "Cornell Relishes New James Bond Role," interview by Examiner staff, *San Francisco Examiner*, December 13, 2006, https://www.sfexaminer.com/entertainment/cornell- relishes-new-james-bond-role/.

2   "Chris Cornell Former Grunge God Goes Secret Agent With 007 Theme," interview by Danica Lo, *New York Post*, November 19, 2006, https://nypost.com/2006/11/19/cornell-chris-cornell-former-grunge-god-goes-secret-agent-with-007-theme-song/.

3   "Chris Cornell Working On Solo LP – But Dismisses Rumors of Audioslave Split," interview by Chris Harris, MTV, July 26, 2006, http://www.mtv.com/news/1537179/chris-cornell-working-on-solo-lp-but-dismisses-rumors-of-audioslave-split/.

4   "In Conversation: David Arnold," MI6 The Home Of James Bond, April 30, 2007, https://www.mi6-hq.com/sections/articles/interview_david_arnold_cr3_ykmn.php3.

5   "Talking Shop: Chris Cornell," interview by Victoria Lindrea, BBC, November 20, 2006, http://news.bbc.co.uk/2/hi/entertainment/6152190.stm.

6   "Chris Cornell Tackles Gospel and Michael Jackson On Solo LP," interview by Chris Harris, MTV, November 1, 2006.

7   "Cornell, Chris Cornell: Former Grunge God Goes Secret Agent With 007 Theme Song," *NY Post*, November 19, 2006, https://nypost.com/2006/11/19/cornell-chris- cornell-former-grunge-god-goes-secret-agent-with-007-theme-song/.

8   "Tom Morello: Walking The Walk," interview by Team Jambase, Jambase, August 21, 2007, https://www.jambase.com/article/tom-morello-walking-the-walk.

9   "Chris Cornell Speaks about His Split with Audioslave," *Rolling Stone*, February 16, 2007, https://www.rollingstone.com/music/music-news/chris-cornell-speaks-about- his-split-with-audioslave-103043/.

10 "An Interview with Chris Cornell," interview by Tim Den, *Lollipop*, September 9, 2007, https://www.lollipop.com/article.php3?content=2007/09sept/f-chriscornell.html.

11 Chester Bennington (@ChesterBe), "With all of my love @chriscornell," Twitter post, May 18, 2017, https://twitter.com/ChesterBe/status/865227703091208192.

12 "Chris Cornell Calls Timbaland Collaboration 'a Leap of Faith,'" interview by Whitney Pastorek, *Entertainment Weekly*, May 18, 2017, https://ew.com/music/2017/05/18/chris-cornell-timbaland-scream-archives/.

13 "Chris Cornell Interview, Extended Version," interview by Sean Nelson, *The Stranger*, September 23, 2015, https://www.thestranger.com/music/feature/2015/09/23/22901720/chris-cornell-interview-extended-version.

14 Trent Reznor (@trent_reznor), Twitter post, March 11, 2009, https://twitter.com/trent_reznor/status/1313265641.

15 Chris Cornell (@ChrisCornell), Twitter post, March 13, 2009, http://twitter.com/chriscornell/status/1321875727.

16 "Chris Cornell Co-Writes Song With Fan," interview by Joe Bosso, MusicRadar, April 16, 2009, https://www.musicradar.com/news/guitars/chris-cornell-co-writes-song-with-fan-203543.

17 "Chris Cornell Talks Soundgarden Reunion," interview by Chris Riemschneider, *Star-Tribune*, January 23, 2013, http://www.startribune.com/chris-cornell-talks-soundgarden-reunion/188382601/.

18 Eddie Vedder, *Lost Dogs* liner notes, Pearl Jam (Los Angeles: Epic Records, 2003).

19 "Soundgarden: Alive in the Superunknown," interview by Randy Peisner, *Spin*, August 17, 2010, https://www.spin.com/2010/08/soundgarden-alive-superunknown/.

20 "A Different Animal: Soundgarden's Ben Shepherd Reveals In Deep Owl," intervewi by Dave Kerr, *The Skinny*, October 2, 2013, https://www.theskinny.co.uk/music/interviews/a-different-animal-soundgardens-ben-shepherd-reveals-in-deep-owl.

21 "Soundgarden Reunion Was Inspired By Fans," ContactMusic, WENN, April 1, 2011, http://www.contactmusic.net/soundgarden/news/soundgarden-reunion-was-inspired-by-fans_1210662.

[22] "Chris Cornell on 'Scream' Criticism, Soundgarden Reunion, Trent Reznor's Twitter Slam and More," interview by J. Freedom du Lac, *The Washington Post*, April 3, 2009, http://voices.washingtonpost.com/postrock/2009/04/chris_cornell_on_scream_critic.html.

Chapter XV

[1] "Soundgarden On Breakup And First New Album In 15 Years," interview by Dan Epstein, *Revolver*, November 1, 2012, https://www.revolvermag.com/music/soundgarden-breakup-reunion-and-first-new-album-15-years.

[2] "Interview: Chris Cornell," interview by Karina Halle, *Consequence of Sound*, September 27, 2011, https://consequenceofsound.net/2011/09/interview-chris-cornell/.

[3] "Chris Cornell Talks Missing Andrew Wood, Writing Songs in the Bathroom: Unpublished 2015 Interview Excerpts," interview by Katherine Turnman, *Billboard*, May 19, 2017. https://www.billboard.com/articles/columns/rock/7801053/chris-cornell-2015-interview-higher-truth

[4] "Chris Cornell on Making Music and Movies," interview by IndieWire Team, *Indiewire*, September 29, 2011, https://www.indiewire.com/2011/09/interview-chris-cornell-on-making-music-and-movies-51897/.

[5] "Slash Solo Album Interview: The Track-By-Track Guide," interview by Chris Vinnicombe, MusicRadar, March 4, 2010, https://www.musicradar.com/news/guitars/slash-solo-album-interview-the-track-by-track-guide-238767.

[6] "Soundgarden Frontman Chris Cornell 'Excited' About New Album," interview by Jane Stevenson, *Toronto Sun*, November 9, 2012, https://torontosun.com/2012/11/09/soundgarden-frontman-chris-cornell-excited-about-new-album/wcm/58a801d8-4601-443e-bc7e-4409d2796b58.

[7] Ben Shepherd and Kim Thayil, "Eyelid's Mouth Commentary," Soundgarden, Soundgarden Recordings LLC, exclusively licensed to

Seven Four Entertainment LLC, and Universal Republic Records, a Division of UMG Recordings Inc, 2012.

[8] "Chris Cornell & Ben Shepherd 'What We Get to Do Is Fun, Exciting… Why Not Keep Doing It?'" YouTube, NikkiBlack, October 9, 2013, https://www.youtube.com/watch?v=aPs_ONr5YWA.

[9] "This Indescribable Chaotic Element: A (Mostly) Unpublished Interview with Chris Cornell," interview by Dan Epstein, *Big Hair and Plastic Grass*, May 16, 2017.

[10] Ben Shepherd and Kim Thayil, "Bones of Birds Commentary," Soundgarden, Soundgarden Recordings LLC, exclusively licensed to Seven Four Entertainment LLC, and Universal Republic Records, a Division of UMG Recordings Inc, 2012.

[11] "Q&A: Soundgarden on Their Reunion Album and Musical Legacy," interview by Gavin Edwards, *Rolling Stone*, November 12, 2012, https://www.rollingstone.com/music/music-news/qa-soundgarden-on-their-reunion-album-and-musical-legacy-180733/.

[12] Jon Dolan, "King Animal," *Rolling Stone*, November 13, 2012, https://www.rollingstone.com/music/music-album-reviews/king-animal-122563/.

[13] Steven Hyden, "Soundgarden, Again," *Grantland*, November 13, 2012, http://grantland.com/features/looking-soundgarden-career-their-new-reunion-album-king-animal/.

[14] "Soundgarden Guitarist Recalls Performing at Inauguration," Blabbermouth, January 31, 2013, https://www.blabbermouth.net/news/soundgarden-guitarist-recalls- performing-at-inauguration/.

[15] "Chris Cornell on Secret Folk Influences, Why He Feels like Neil Young," interview by David Fricke, *Rolling Stone*, September 15, 2015, https://www.rollingstone. com/music/music-news/chris-cornell-on-secret-folk-influences-why-he-feels-like-neil- young-35522/.

[16] "Chris Cornell Inducts Heart at 2013 Induction Ceremony," YouTube, Rock & Roll Hall of Fame, May 19, 2017, https://www.youtube.com/watch?v=8dNrh-8tn9A.

[17] "Came Back Vaunted: An Interview with Nine Inch Nails' Trent Reznor," interview by Dave Kerr, *The Skinny*, May 6, 2014, https://

www.theskinny.co.uk/music/interviews/came-back-vaunted-an-interview-with-nine-inch-nails-trent-reznor.

[18] Steve Appleford, "Nine Inch Nails and Soundgarden Launch Thunderous Joint Tour in Vegas," *Rolling Stone*, July 20, 2014, https://www.rollingstone.com/music/music-live-reviews/nine-inch-nails-and-soundgarden-launch-thunderous-joint-tour-in-vegas-233244/.

Chapter XVI

[1] "MoPop Oral Histories, Matt Cameron Interview," Museum Of Popular Culture, Seattle, WA, December 18, 1999.

[2] "Chris Cornell's Close Friends Remember His Final Days," interview by Chloe Melas, CNN, May 26, 2017, https://www.cnn.com/2017/05/26/celebrities/chris-cornell-final- days-death/index.html.

[3] Taylor Momsen (@taylormomsen), Instagram post, May 10, 2018, https://www.instagram.com/taylormomsen/p/BinAj0mlgpF/?hl=en.

[4] "Interview: Duff McKagan Was Almost a Financial Advisor on Fox News," interview by Brian Ives, Radio.Com, June 16, 2015, https://www.radio.com/2015/06/16/duff-mckagan-interview-watch-gnr-how-to-be-a-man.

[5] Chris Cornell and Cameron Crowe, "Intro to Higher Truth," *Higher Truth* (Santa Monica: Universal Music Enterprises, 2015).

[6] "Former Soundgarden and Audioslave musician will perform in York," *FlipsidePA*, September 23, 2005, http://www.flipsidepa.com/story/entertainment/events/york-hanover/2015/09/23/singer-chris-cornell-talks-solo-career-higher-truth/73565790/.

[7] "Five Questions: Chris Cornell," interview by Ken Micallef, *Electronic Musician*, October 25, 2015, https://www.emusician.com/artists/five-questions-chris-cornell.

[8] "Interview: Chris Cornell," interview by Damien Girling, *Songwriting UK*, September 24, 2015, https://www.songwritingmagazine.co.uk/interviews/interview-chris-cornell/ 26629.

[9] "Chris Cornell [Full Concert] @ Bogotá 4 Dec 2016," YouTube, posted by Concert Geek, December 5, 2016, https://www.youtube.com/watch?v=NqxeT13NDds&t=2546s.

10 Jon Dolan, "Higher Truth," *Rolling Stone*, September 14, 2015, https://www.rollingstone.com/music/music-album-reviews/higher-truth-123545/.

11 "Grunge Star Says Studio Owner Has No Rights to Master Tapes," interview by Gene Johnson, *Associated Press*, April 15, 2015, http://web.archive.org/web/20161226204233/http://bigstory.ap.org/article/a569394faf064ce1b0fe43f41830a4c4/chris-cornell-studio-owner-has-no-right-master-tapes/.

12 "Chris Cornell On Whiplash," interview by Full Metal Jackie, *Whiplash*, KLOS, December 5, 2016.

13 John Carter Cash, "Johnny Cash Forever Words," 2018, https://www.johnnycashforever words.com/chris-cornell/.

14 "Chris Cornell Enjoying Solo Performances And Rockin' With Soundgarden," interview by Ed Condran, Hartford Courant, May 18, 2017, https://www.courant.com/ctnow/music/hc-chris-cornell-at-palace-theater-in-waterbury-20160622-story.html.

15 "Soundgarden's Ben Shepherd on the Bass's Role: Be Like A Mako Shark Under Water," interview by Timothy Finn, *The Kansas City Star*, May 10, 2017, https://www.kansascity.com/entertainment/ent-columns-blogs/back-to-rockville/article 149878027.html.

16 "Chris Cornell on Ultramega OK's essential reissue, new Soundgarden album and Audioslave reunion," interview by Michael Astley-Brown, MusicRadar, February 6, 2017, https://www.musicradar.com/news/chris-cornell-on-ultramega-oks-essential-reissue-new-soundgarden-album-and-audioslave-reunion.

17 "Tom Morello on Unreleased Audioslave Tunes, The 'Trump Idiocy' & Why Prophets of Rage Are Only Just Beginning," interview by Emmy Mack, *Music Feeds*, September 21, 2017, https://musicfeeds.com.au/features/tom-morello-on-unreleased-audioslave-tunes-the-trump-idiocy-why-prophets-of-rage-are-only-just-beginning/.

18 Bill Brownlee, "Soundgarden Relies on Oldies but (Extremely Loud) Goodies at KC's Starlight," *Kansas City Star*, May 15, 2017, https://www.kansascity.com/entertainment/ent-columns-blogs/back-to-rockville/article150560102.html.

19 "Soundgarden's Kim Thayil Says MC5 Anniversary Tour Helped Him 'Come Out of the Fetal Position,'" interview by Gary Graff, *Billboard*, September 5, 2018, https://www.billboard.com/articles/columns/rock/8473679/kim-thayil-mc5-tour-interview.

20 "Chris Cornell's Widow Vicky Opens Up about His Addiction Battle and Final Night: 'He Didn't Want to Die,'" interview by Janine Rubenstein, *People*, June 28, 2017, https://people.com/music/chris-cornell-widow-speaks-he-didnt-want-to-die/.

21 "Chris Cornell Widow Rips Probe Year After Detroit Death," interview by George Hunter, *Detroit News*, May 15, 2018, https://www.detroitnews.com/story/entertainment/people/2018/05/15/chris-cornell-widow-rips-probe-detroit-death/34918321/.

22 Peter Cornell (@petercornellmusic), Facebook post, May 27, 2017, https://www.facebook.com/petercornellmusic/posts/13821234985 36532?__tn__=-R.

23 Tom Morello (@tommorello), Instagram post, May 18, 2017, https://www.instagram.com/p/BUPLwb2jdHH/?utm_source=ig_embed.

24 Tom Morello, "Read Tom Morello's Poem For Chris Cornell," *Rolling Stone*, May 19, 2017, https://www.rollingstone.com/music/music-features/read-tom-morellos- poem-for-chris-cornell-193491/.

25 Jimmy Page (@JimmyPage), Twitter post, May 18, 2017, https://twitter.com/JimmyPage/ status/865129669590384642.

26 "The Life & Times Of Chris Cornell," interview by Rod Yates, *Rolling Stone Australia*, September 17, 2015, http://rollingstoneaus.com/music/post/the-life-and- times-of-chris-cornell/2273.

ABOUT THE AUTHOR

Photo by Jenna Reiff

Corbin Reiff is the author of *Lighters in the Sky: The All-Time Greatest Concerts 1960–2016*. His writing has appeared in *Rolling Stone, Billboard, Pitchfork, Complex, Spin*, Uproxx, *The Washington Post, The Seattle Weekly*, and *The Seattle Times*. He lives in Seattle with his wife, Jenna.